The South East to AD 1000

A Regional History of England

General Editors: Barry Cunliffe and David Hey
For full details of the series, see pp. xiv–xv

The South East to AD 1000

Peter Drewett, David Rudling and
Mark Gardiner

Longman
London and New York

Longman Group UK Limited,
Longman House, Burnt Mill, Harlow,
Essex CM20 2JE, England
and Associated Companies throughout the world

Published in the United States of America
by Longman Inc., New York

First published 1988

British Library Cataloguing in Publication Data
Drewett, Peter
    The South East to AD 1000. – (A Regional
    history of England).
    1. South East (England) – History
    I. Title   II. Rudling, David   III. Gardiner,
    Mark   IV. Series
    942.201   DA670.S63
    ISBN 0-582-49271-8   CSD
    ISBN 0-582-49272-6   PPR

Library of Congress Cataloging-in-Publication Data
Drewett, Peter.
    The South East to AD 1000.

    (A Regional history of England)
    Bibliography: p.
    Includes index
    1. Great Britain – History – To 1066.   2. England –
Antiquities.   3. Anglo-Saxons.   4. Land settlement –
I. Rudling, David, 1956–   . II. Gardiner, Mark.
III. Title.   IV. Series.
DA135.D74   1988   942.201   87–17144
ISBN 0-582-49271-8
ISBN 0-582-49272-6 (pbk.)

Set in Linotron 202 10/12 Sabon Roman
Produced by Longman Singapore Publishers (Pte) Ltd.
Printed in Singapore.

Contents

List of plates

List of figures

General preface

England cannot be divided satisfactorily into recognizable regions based on former kingdoms or principalities in the manner of France, Germany or Italy. Few of the Anglo-Saxon tribal divisions had much meaning in later times and from the eleventh century onwards England was a united country. English regional identities are imprecise and no firm boundaries can be drawn. In planning this series we have recognized that any attempt to define a region must be somewhat arbitrary, particularly in the Midlands, and that boundaries must be flexible. Even the South-West, which is surrounded on three sides by the sea, has no agreed border on the remaining side and in many ways, historically and culturally, the River Tamar divides the area into two. Likewise, the Pennines present a formidable barrier between the eastern and western counties on the Northern Borders; contrasts as much as similarities need to be emphasized here.

The concept of a region does not imply that the inhabitants had a similar experience of life, nor that they were all inward-looking. A Hull merchant might have more in common with his Dutch trading partner than with his fellow Yorkshireman who farmed a Pennine smallholding: a Roman soldier stationed for years on Hadrian's Wall probably had very different ethnic origins from a native farmer living on the Durham boulder clay. To differing degrees, everyone moved in an international climate of belief and opinion with common working practices and standards of living.

Yet regional differences were nonetheless real; even today a Yorkshireman may be readily distinguished from someone from the South East. Life in Lancashire and Cheshire has always been different from life in the Thames Valley. Even the East Midlands has a character that is subtly different from that of the West Midlands. People still feel that they belong to a particular region within England as a whole.

In writing these histories we have become aware how much regional identities may vary over time; moreover how a farming region, say, may not coincide with a region defined by its building styles or its dialect. We have dwelt upon the diversity that can be found within a region as well as upon common characteristics in order to illustrate the local peculiarities of provincial life. Yet, despite all these problems of definition, we feel that the time is ripe to attempt an ambitious scheme outlining the history of England's regions in 21 volumes. London has not been included – except for demonstrating the many ways in which it has influenced the provinces – for its history has been very different from that of the towns and rural parishes that are our principal concern.

In recent years an enormous amount of local research both historical and archaeological has deepened our understanding of the former concerns of ordinary men and women and has altered our perception of everyday life in the past in many significant ways, yet the results of this work are not widely known even within the regions themselves.

This series offers a synthesis of this new work from authors who have themselves been actively involved in local research and who are present or former residents of the regions they describe.

Each region will be covered in two linked but independent volumes, the first covering the period up to AD 1000 and necessarily relying heavily on archaeological data, and the second bringing the story up to the present day. Only by taking a wide time-span and by studying continuity and change over many centuries do distinctive regional characteristics become clear.

This series portrays life as it was experienced by the great majority of the people of South Britain or England as it was to become. The 21 volumes will – it is hoped – substantially enrich our understanding of English history.

Barry Cunliffe
David Hey

A Regional History of England

General Editors: Barry Cunliffe (to AD 1000) and David Hey (from AD 1000)

The regionalization used in this series is illustrated on the map opposite.

*already published

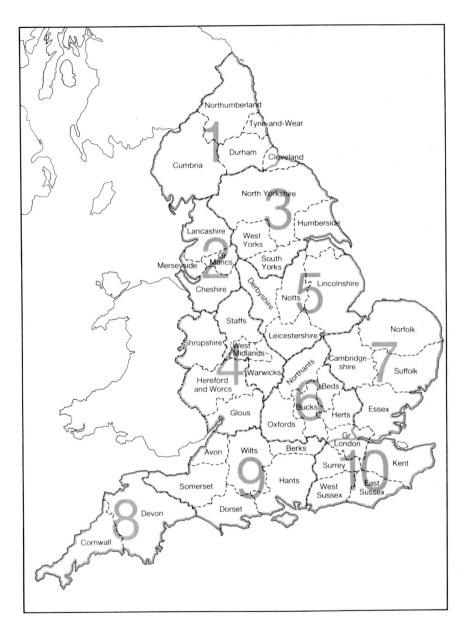

1. The Northern Counties
2. The Lancashire/Cheshire Region
3. Yorkshire
4. The Severn Valley and
   West Midlands
5. The East Midlands
6. The South Midlands and
   the Upper Thames
7. The Eastern Counties
8. The South West
9. Wessex
10. The South East

Acknowledgements

Naturally much of the research on which this work is based is derived from the work of amateur and professional archaeologists who have worked in South-East England before us. Their names, too many to list, appear in the bibliography. To all of them we offer our thanks.

We are particularly grateful to the following for their permission to reproduce plates which appear in the text: M. B. Roberts (Plates 1.1, 1.2 and 1.3); R. Holgate (Plates 2.4, 2.7 and 2.8); Sussex Archaeological Society (Plates 5.1, 5.7(3), 6.2, 6.4, 6.7, 6.8 and 8.4); British Museum (Plate 5.2); Cambridge University Collection: Copyright reserved (Plates 5.3, 5.4 and 7.1); Ministry of Defence: Crown Copyright Reserved (Plate 5.5); Ashmolean Museum (Plate 5.7: 1–2, 4, 6); Chichester Excavations Committee (Plates 5.8, 6.10, 6.11, 7.2); Royal Commission on the Historical Monuments of England: Crown copyright reserved (Plates 6.1 and 6.6) University of Oxford (Plate 6.3); Canterbury Museums (Plate 6.7); Chichester District Museum (Plate 6.9); Canterbury Archaeological Trust (Plate 8.2). All other plates were taken by the authors and are the copyright of the Field Archaeology Unit, Institute of Archaeology, University College London.

All three authors are indebted to Lysbeth Drewett for preparing the line drawings of objects. All other drawings were prepared by the authors. Finally we should particularly like to thank Christine Crickmore, Secretary to the Unit, for the massive task of typing the text and correcting it numerous times and Caroline Cartwright for preparing the index.

David Rudling wishes to thank the following for permission to reproduce figures which appear in the text: Dr M. G. Bell (Figure 5.11); Mr F. G. Aldsworth (Figures 6.6, 6.7 and 6.8); Surrey Archaeological Society and Mr R. and Mrs L. Adkins (Figure 6.9). He is also grateful to Ernest Black, David Bird and Rosamond Hanworth for supplying draft copies of their forthcoming publications, and for advice and information from Ernest Black.

Mark Gardiner is grateful to Dr Martin Welch for his comments on a draft of Chapters 7 and 8, though without suggesting that the latter would agree with the views expressed. He also wishes to acknowledge those who allowed him to cite their work in advance of publication, particularly Dr John Blair and Fred Aldsworth.

Chapter 1

The Formation of the Landscape and its Peopling by Hunters

Geographically the counties of Surrey, Sussex and Kent consist of the Weald, an eroded chalk anticline. Infacing escarpments of the North and South Downs overlook a variety of sediments deposited in a Cretaceous sea. To the south of the South Downs the chalk is exposed as cliffs in the centre of Sussex, while to the west of the county the Downs overlook a broad coastal plain of brickearths and other sediments deposited in the Eocene. To the north of the Weald the North Downs overlook the Eocene deposits now filling the Thames basin. The erosion of the Wealden anticline has resulted in the linear outcropping of a variety of sedimentary rocks, each with its own distinct characteristics. Each of these zones provided a range of geological resources. Although all these resources would have been covered to a varying extent by a variety of soils and vegetation, marine and river erosion would have revealed them to man. All these geological resources were used to a varying degree by man throughout prehistory.

The landscape of the region is dominated by the North and South Downs, a zone of chalk rising to over 290 m above sea-level. The chalk is a soft, permeable, sedimentary rock currently supporting no rivers and little surface water. Within the chalk may be found one of prehistoric man's most widely used geological resources, flint. This occurs both in nodular and tabular form and also as an erosion product in later deposits. Above the chalk are large spreads of clay-with-flints and other Tertiary relict deposits. To the north of the South Downs and south of the North Downs is a narrow linear outcrop of Upper Greensand which consists of sands and marls. Between this and the sands and sandstones of the Lower Greensand is a narrow deposit of heavy blue Gault Clay. The remainder of the Low Weald consists of a broad, flat range of light-grey Wealden Clay.

Rising up from the Wealden Clay are the remaining, heavily faulted, beds of the Lower Cretaceous. These consist of the Tunbridge Wells and Ashdown Sands interspersed with Wadhurst Clays and shales and Ashdown Sands and sandrock. Finally, towards the centre of the High Weald are the Upper Jurassic calcareous shales and limestones of the Purbeck Beds.

The linear geological deposits described are all cut through by large rivers, the Arun, Adur, Ouse, Cuckmere and Rother in Sussex; the Stour, Medway and Darent in Kent and the Mole and Wey in Surrey. These valleys are filled with rich alluvium supporting gley soils. Relic patches of valley gravels survive on the edge of the alluvium.

Geographically the areas of Surrey and Kent to the north of the North Downs lie outside the Weald and consist of the southern part of the Thames basin. Here the Thames river valley cuts through the stiff, bluish-grey London Clay deposited in the Eocene. Localized folding of the underlying chalk has resulted in the erosion of areas of London Clay, revealing the gravels of the earlier Eocene Woolwich and Reading and Blackheath Beds. The Woolwich Beds consist of a series of pebble beds within deposits of clays, loams and sands. Locally these have cemented to form sandstones or conglomerates. The Reading Beds are similar, but the bands of pebbles are much thinner and the sands lighter in colour (Gallois 1965).

Until recently it was considered unlikely that any of the Pleistocene glaciations resulted in ice sheets covering South-East England. The area was thought to be essentially periglacial throughout, with the major southern movements of ice ceasing at the Thames valley. Work by Kellaway *et al.* (1975) however, suggests the probability of glacial activity in the English Channel, perhaps even resulting in some of the clay-with-flints on the South Downs. Seismic profiling of the English Channel has shown a flat bedrock surface bounded by underwater cliffs near Beachy Head and elsewhere to the west. The land forms detected in the Channel are remarkably similar to terrestrial areas known to have been glaciated. A Channel glacier may well explain the large erratics, like the Pagham erratics, known from the South Coast.

The First Hunters

It is possible that man first arrived in South-East England during the warm Cromerian Interglacial period. At this stage Britain was still part of the Northern European land mass (Simmons and Tooley 1981: 55) so intermittent wandering bands may well have moved north into South-East England during warmer stages, or even warmer times of year. Only two sites in the area have any claim to be as early as Cromerian and neither of these is entirely satisfactorily dated. These are the high-level gravel sites of Fordwich, Kent and Farnham, Surrey (Roe 1975).

The Fordwich site probably represents an intermittently used camp site utilizing the readily available gravel flint of the terrace 45 m above the present River Stour. The industry consists of crude, stone-struck handaxes, together

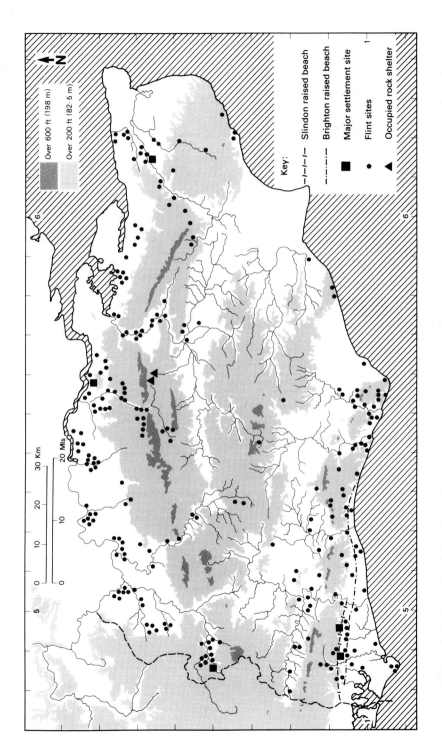

Figure 1.1 Palaeolithic sites in South-East England.

with their manufacturing waste consisting of cores and flakes. A similar industry has been located in the Farnham river terraces (Oakley, Rankine and Lowther 1934). Both industries, containing crude pointed handaxes, are best considered an early phase within the Acheulian tradition, a tradition which, however, lasted over a million years (Wymer 1980).

There is even less evidence for man in South-East England during the ensuing cold Anglian stage. The Anglian ice sheets reached at least as far south as the Thames, inflicting harsh, periglacial conditions on the South-East. However, human occupation may have been possible during warmer phases within the Anglian particularly during summer months. If so, the Clactonian material from the basal levels at Swanscombe, Kent, may well be Anglian rather than of the ensuing warm Hoxnian interglacial (Waechter 1969). However, the occupation clearly extended at least intermittently, through the Hoxnian.

The riverine occupation site at Swanscombe is perhaps the most extensively studied Palaeolithic site in the country. Particularly important are the environmental studies showing the gradually changing environmental context of the site occupied over many thousands of years. The Lower Loams and Lower Gravels suggest occupation on grass-covered mud flats cut by small streams. The mud flats were edged by hazel scrub which merged into mixed oak forest (Hubbard 1980). The site itself was probably on a river estuary opening out onto the Thames. Such a site would be rich in resources utilized by a hunting and gathering community. Bone evidence shows the presence of elephant, rhinoceros, horse and deer which may have been hunted and eaten (Wymer 1980). The estuary would have provided a wide range of marsh resources like birds and fish. The gravel terraces were a ready source of flint for the manufacture of tools to exploit this environment. Within the Lower Gravels large quantities of cores and flakes have been found but no handaxes (Wymer 1980). The industry therefore appears to be a chopper-core industry of Clactonian type.

Towards the end of the warm Hoxnian phase, the Clactonian industry at Swanscombe is replaced by an extensive Acheulian industry, with its many fine handaxes. It is from the Upper Middle Gravels, perhaps laid down in Later Hoxnian times about 250000 BC (Morrison 1980: 45) that the earliest human remains found in this country come. In 1935 Mr A. T. Marston found a human occiput and left parietal. These were followed by the right parietal found by John Wymer in 1955. These skull fragments belonged to a young man, perhaps in his early twenties. The skull appears to be more human than *Homo erectus* and is generally thought of as an early variety of *Homo sapiens*. (Wymer 1980).

Associated with the human remains at Swanscombe was extensive evidence for the manufacture of flint tools including 133 handaxes from Wymer's excavation alone. The site appears to be a riverside living area where over 8,000 waste flakes were discarded, together with the remains of 26 species of animals. Some, or all of these, may have been hunted and eaten by man,

Plate 1.1 Raised beach preserved beneath a chalk cliff collapse at Boxgrove, West Sussex. (Photograph: M. B. Roberts.)

particularly the horse, deer, ox and hare (Wymer 1968). The mammalian fossils suggest a closed forest environment at, or close by, the site but the sparse pollen assemblages are insufficient to confirm this (Hubbard 1980).

Extensive evidence of early hunting communities has also been found on the raised beaches of Sussex. Readily available flint and sea resources no doubt attracted man to these areas. The oldest of the beaches is the Slindon raised beach which reaches some 40 m OD (Woodcock 1978). It runs along the foot of the South Downs from north of Funtington in the west to Arundel in the east. This marks a maximum marine transgression which took place during an interglacial within the Hoxnian. Recent excavations by M. B. Roberts at Boxgrove located both the beach and the denuded chalk cliff line. To the south of the cliff line a wave-cut platform was found overlain by an interglacial marine sand (Plate 1.1). An *in situ* flaking floor was located in this sand. This was sealed by a thin layer of brickearth and 13 m of soliflucted gravel (Roberts, pers. comm.).

A sample area 7 m × 7 m excavated in 1983, located over 900 struck flints, all of which appeared to be unrolled and *in situ* with many conjoinable (Plate 1.2). The waste was derived from the manufacture of small, ovate

Plate 1.2   In-situ Acheulian waste flakes and chips resulting from the manufacture of bifaces at Boxgrove, West Sussex. (Photograph: M. B. Roberts.)

handaxes, two of which were located *in situ* (Fig. 1.2). Earlier work by A. G. Woodcock at Boxgrove located over 400 implements, including 40 handaxes, some in the process of manufacture. Much of this material was, however, abraded with some worn tools bearing retouch carried out at a later date. This perhaps indicates intermittent exploitation over a long period (Woodcock 1978).

More extensive excavations at Boxgrove during 1984–86 produced several *in situ* debitage scatters derived from the manufacture of bifacial tools. Associated pollen analysis by Dr R. Scaife indicates an environment dominated by pine, spruce and fir. In this woodland and in adjacent grassland a variety of small mammals lived and died including shrews, rabbits, lemmings, bank and water voles. Particularly important was the recovery of bones from the rare large shrew *Sorex savini*. Large mammals recovered from the excavation include wolf, beaver (Plate 1.3), mustelid, horse, deer, bovid and bear (Roberts *et al.*, 1986). Future work at this site, and particularly the analysis of the material recovered, is likely to revolutionize our knowledge of Palaeolithic man and his environment in South-East England.

A similar *in situ* worked floor was located earlier this century to the east

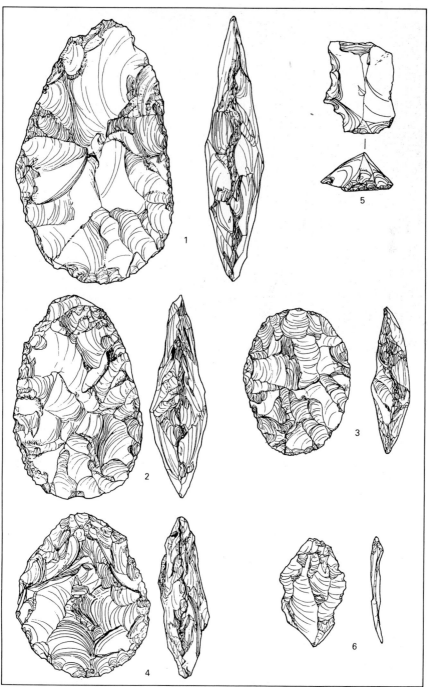

Figure 1.2 Bifacial tools (1–4), scraper (5) and retouched flake (6) from the Lower Palaeolithic site at Boxgrove, West Sussex (scale ½).

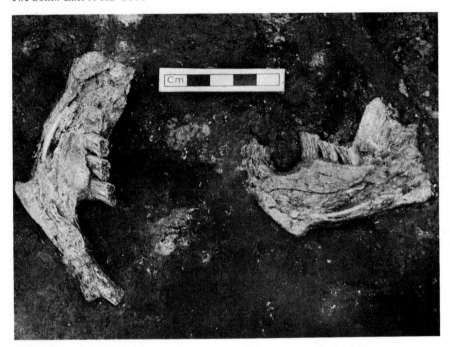

Plate 1.3 Beaver jaws *in situ* at the Palaeolithic site excavated at Boxgrove, West Sussex. (Photograph: M. B. Roberts.)

of Boxgrove in the north-west corner of Slindon Park. Although casual finds of handaxes were made by Curwen (1925) and Fowler (1929) the first serious study of the site was undertaken in 1934 by Mr J. Bernard Calkin (1934). He located a beach deposit which, as at Boxgrove, was covered by soliflucted gravel. On the beach lay 27 handaxes, together with waste material and cores. A further 18 handaxes, casual finds made in previous years, have been located in museums across Southern Britain (Woodcock 1978). A. G. Woodcock's recent excavations at Slindon produced a further four handaxes and over 200 pieces of waste flint. The material from the Boxgrove and Slindon excavations, together with over 50 casual handaxe finds from the Lavant area of the raised beach (Woodcock 1978) all indicate a similar industry. The axes are ovate in form and following Wymer (1968), are typologically Late Middle Acheulian.

Although the best-known evidence for Acheulian activity comes from the river valleys of north Kent and the raised beaches of Sussex, there is extensive evidence, in the form of handaxes, for the utilization of most geological zones in South-East England. Concentrations of handaxes on the North Downs, for example at Ash, and at Folkington on the South Downs (Roe 1968) indicate extensive use of inland resources. Such Downland axes are, however, never found *in situ* as no original surfaces could have survived the later glacial solifluxion, sub-aerial and chemical erosion of the Downs. The existence of many thousands of axes on the Downs and high up the Wealden river valleys does, however, indicate that the Acheulian sites often thought of as 'typical' like Swanscombe and Boxgrove are only part of a much more extensive economic system involving all the South-Eastern ecosystems. Visits to the beaches or river terraces may have been largely orientated to the utilization of readily available flint with other activities concentrated elsewhere, for example hunting in the Wealden forests.

Towards the end of the cold Wolstonian a significant change in the method of heavy tool manufacture appears in South-East England. Instead of flaking cores into handaxes, cores were carefully prepared so that large flakes of predetermined shape could be struck off for use as multifunctional tools. This 'Levallois' technique dominates the industries on sites of the later Wolstonian and the ensuing warmer Ipswichian interglacial.

One of the most extensive flint assemblages from South-East England which uses the Levallois technique was found in 1911 at Northfleet in Kent (R. A. Smith 1911). The site, known locally as Baker's Hole, is within a valley which cuts through deposits containing Acheulian material. The solifluxion material associated with this site suggests a date towards the end of the cold Wolstonian. The large numbers of oval Levallois cores and waste material indicates that Baker's Hole was an extensive manufacturing area, probably utilizing surface flint clearly visible in a periglacial chalkland landscape. Mammoth remains underline man's increasing ability to utilize most inhospitable environments (Wymer 1980).

Although there is little evidence to suggest that Baker's Hole was much more than a quarry site, good evidence for hunting comes from the slightly later site at Crayford in the Thames Valley (Wymer 1968). The Crayford deposits, buried under 15 metres of brickearths, are generally regarded as Ipswichian but could be slightly earlier (Sutcliffe and Kowalski 1976). Directly associated with a Levallois industry were bones of woolly rhinoceros, suggesting hunting during a colder phase. The site was discovered by F. C. J. Spurrell in 1880 and excavated with great care. He was able to reconstruct a flint nodule from a pile of over 60 flakes, indicating a primary flint knapping floor.

Less well investigated open sites with a Levallois industry include those at Ebbsfleet, New Hythe and Bapchild in Kent (Roe 1968). Only casual finds of isolated Levallois implements are known from elsewhere in the South-East, as at Beachy Head, Peacehaven, Selsey and Friston in Sussex (Woodcock 1978).

Towards the end of the Ipswichian and on into the Devensian a distinctive industry appears to derive from the continental Mousterian using the Levallois flake technique and manufacturing small handaxes in the Acheulian tradition. Diagnostic of the industry is a flat-butted type of cordate handaxe (Wymer 1980). This industry is now known as the British Mousterian of Acheulian tradition.

This industry is associated with the movement of an ice sheet as far south as Norfolk so that the area of South-East England must have been subjected to intensely cold tundra conditions. This might partly explain why from this period we get the first occupation of the Wealden rock shelters, some of the few natural places of shelter in a largely treeless tundra environment. So far the only evidence comes from Oldbury Hill, near Ightham, in Kent (Collins and Collins 1970). Two shelters in the Folkestone and Hastings beds on the east side of the hill have indirect evidence for use at this period. Excavations in 1890 and again in 1968–69 by D. and A. Collins revealed a sustantial assemblage of British Mousterian of Acheulian Tradition. However, the material is not in a primary position but appears to have been incorporated in the talus as the rock shelter slowly eroded back into the hill slope (Collins and Collins 1970). Although it may be assumed that many other Wealden rock shelters were used during this period, recent excavations elsewhere in the South-East have produced nothing earlier than Post-Glacial Flandrian dates, with their typical microlithic assemblages.

During the Devensian the last glaciation was a complex period of very cold phases interspersed with warmer phases. The large amounts of water locked up in the ice sheets lowered the water table, thus enabling free access for man and animals across the Channel into Europe. This is the period of extensive occupation of the highland zone cave sites but, somewhat surprisingly very few sites of this date are known from South-East England. The only excavated site was located by Martin Bell under a Romano-British site at Newhaven, Sussex (Bell 1976). The artifacts were found in ice-wedge features formed in Combe Rock deposited in the Ouse Valley. Although only 157 pieces of struck flint were found, the importance of the site lies in the fact that none of the material shows any sign of crushing or rolling. Most of the material came from six concentrations, several of which contained conjoining flakes, indicating *in situ* flaking areas. Only one bifacially worked, but typologically indeterminate, implement was found, suggesting short-term occupation, perhaps only as a flint-knapping site. Geological evidence, however, clearly puts the site into a date range of *c.* 28000 to 14000 BC (Bell 1976).

Few other late glacial sites are known from South-East England and such as there are remain poorly documented. From Kent, the site of Oare, near Faversham, has produced two shouldered points, a saw, a blade and one flake (Wymer 1980). A similar shouldered point came from Old Faygate, Sussex, while a tanged point from High Hurstwood, Sussex may be contemporary (Woodcock 1978). One early discovery from Sussex may, however, originally have been associated with a now destroyed rock shelter. This is an assemblage of some 2,300 struck flints from Nutbourne, near Pulborough, Sussex. The assemblage consists of a number of bifacially worked leaf-points together with long flakes, blades, scrapers and burins (Curwen 1949). It was found in the last century when a drive was cut though a slope formed by a Lower Greensand outcrop.

Post-Glacial Hunters and Gatherers

About 8000 BC significant environmental changes in South-East England coincided with, if not actually caused, many changes in surviving material culture. Particularly important is the massive increase in number of humanly occupied sites, possibly suggesting a substantial rise in population. Food procurement remained, as in the glacial phases, based on hunting wild animals and gathering wild plants but methods and emphasis clearly changed rapidly.

During the period *c.* 8500 – 4500 BC sea-levels changed drastically. Considerable quantities of water locked up in the glaciers and ice sheets of Northern Europe and North America poured back into the seas. In some areas of Britain the rise in sea-level was as much as 10 m (Simmons and Tooley 1981: 86). However, the rise in sea-level was neither continuous nor consistent in the British Isles. It appears to have been an oscillating rise with many small recessions between higher sea-levels (Tooley 1978). In addition to sea-levels simply rising, the removal of a great weight of ice from the land mass resulted in the rise of land as part of its isostatic recovery. Land masses do not, however, rise consistently, confusing relative sea-level rises further.

It is now generally accepted that Britain was separated from the Continent during some glacial phases. As early as 1913 Reid demonstrated that melt water of the ice during the last two glaciations, together with waters of the Thames and the Rhine, must have drained through the Straits of Dover. With a substantial drop in sea-level during the last glaciation, a land bridge would have existed only to be flooded again in early Post-Glacial times. Exactly when this reflooding took place is uncertain, but lithic evidence suggests a date prior to 6000 BC. This shows the absence of several Danish implement types after *c.* 6000 BC confirming a probable separation of Britain from the Continent (Clark, 1932). It is therefore convenient to consider Post-Glacial hunters and gatherers in two phases, one being part of the Northern European tradition and the second phase being a developing insular tradition. The actual hunting strategies of the two phases are, however, essentially similar. Before we can consider hunting strategies and the technology required for such strategies, the environment in which the hunters operated must be considered, for this will have a major influence on the material culture utilized.

Late glacial conditions left South-East England swept bare of many superficial deposits (Sheldon 1978) supporting a sparse tundra vegetation. However, with rising temperatures a natural plant succession rapidly developed, so that by about 6000 BC most of South-East England was forested with oak, elm, alder and lime having replaced the colonizing birch and pine. Hazel persisted and holly, ash and ivy appear increasingly common in the pollen record (Simmons and Tooley 1981). This forest is found on all geological zones in South-East England, including the Greensands, Chalk Downs and the Wealden beds. There is, unfortunately, no bone evidence from South-East

11

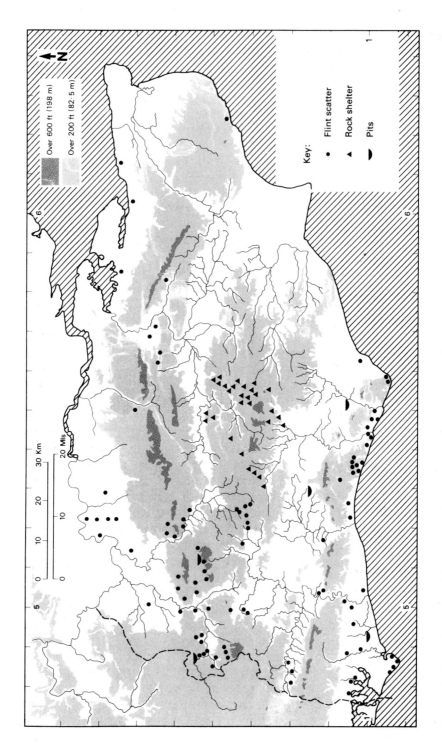

Figure 1.3 Main sites occupied by postglacial hunters and gatherers in South-East England.

England to indicate what animals were hunted in this forest, but it may be assumed that the same species were exploited here as elsewhere in lowland Britain. Wild ox were certainly a dominant species hunted (Carter 1976), while deer, both red and roe, together with pig, all appear in the bone record. These fleet-footed forest animals clearly require a very different technology of exploitation to that required for the lumbering glacial animals of the open tundra.

The surviving material culture belonging to these early Post-Glacial hunters is almost entirely of flint with a little bone and antler. However, this must be only the surviving element, and extensive use must have been made of wood, bark, animal skins, grasses and other organic materials which simply do not survive.

The flint assemblage is characterized by a discrete range of microlithic points including trapezoidal, obliquely backed, bitruncated rhombic, isosceles triangles and convex-backed lanceolate shapes (Fig. 1.4). These were all presumably incorporated into composite wood or bone throwing, thrusting, shooting and sawing implements. The microlithic assemblage is associated with less characteristic types like core adzes, scrapers, burins and serrated flakes (Jacobi 1980). The contemporary debitage indicates the deliberate striking of flakes much broader than characteristic of the final hunter-gathering communities. Associated with the composite microlithic tools are a few surviving barbed bone points like those from Wandsworth and Battersea, two plain points from Mortlake and Battersea and several antler mattock heads from elsewhere in the Middle Thames Valley (Jessup 1970).

Surprisingly, the distribution of early Post-Glacial sites appears largely restricted to Surrey and Sussex with a small flint assemblage from Ditton (Clark 1932) possibly being the only *in situ* assemblage from Kent. A few residual implements, particularly from around Sevenoaks, Swanscombe, Addington and Harrietsham, however, suggest a wider distribution into Kent (Jacobi 1980).

The most extensively investigated site of this period is that excavated on Iping Common in West Sussex. The site is situated on the undulating Greensand ridge near a permanent spring. It consisted of a roughly circular area of stained sand stratified between white sands. The extensive flint industry was all in a fresh condition, none of it appearing to be rolled. This suggests an *in situ* flint knapping site, but the method of excavation precludes certainty on this point. The cortex on the flint, where it survives, is chalky suggesting flint collected from the South Downs and brought to the site. The assemblage consists mainly of waste material including 55 cores, indicating flint knapping was at least one of the site's activities. Tools included 10 scrapers, 108 microliths, gravers, microburins, axe-sharpening flakes, punches and a fabricator. The only implement not of flint was a pick-like tool made out of a white, cherty sandstone and possibly used for digging (Keef, Wymer and Dimbleby 1965).

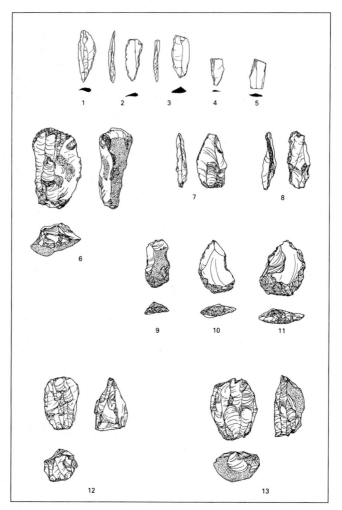

Figure 1.4   A Mesolithic flint assemblage from Halt near Horsham. 1–5: microliths (scale ¹⁄₁); 6–11: scraping and cutting tools; 12–13: micro-cores (scale ½).

The pollen evidence from Iping suggests the primary occupation of the site was in dense hazel woodland but, perhaps during the period of occupation, the area was cleared and the vegetation changed to that associated with heather-covered heathland. It is possible that this site represents a primary-hunting camp with deliberate forest clearance taking place as part of an animal-management strategy. Certainly the site represents a microlith-dominated assemblage (Mellars 1976) with a specialized function.

A broadly contemporary site at Rackham, to the west of Iping but on the same Greensand ridge, was excavated in 1979 (Garton 1981). By plotting the exact position of each struck flake, two or probably three episodes of flint knapping were identified, each perhaps only lasting a few minutes. A scatter of fire-cracked flints, however, probably represented a small camp fire. In all, the Rackham site represents little more than a one-night stop in a woodland environment during a hunting trip.

The density of early sites in Surrey and Sussex remains low and tends to be concentrated on the western side of the Weald and its fringes. These sites are mainly recognized from early excavations or surface collections. In Surrey the flint assemblage from Heath Brow, near Farnham is clearly early (Rankine, in Oakley *et al.* 1939: 115). It was discovered by F. O'Farrell in 1920 on the western side of a heathland plateau. The site is well served by a series of streams which flow out of the junction between the gravels and Eocene beds some 130 m away. The site appears to represent a series of flint-knapping floors where local gravel flint was extensively used. Together with a substantial amount of waste material were discovered 18 complete obliquely blunted microliths, saws, end scrapers and a transverse axe.

Sussex sites tend to be clustered on the Lower Greensand from Hassocks in the east through Storrington, and Iping to West Heath in the west (Jacobi 1978). There appears to be little extensive movement into the central Weald. However, overlapping with the early and later sites, perhaps between 7000 BC and 6000 BC are a large number of sites in the west Weald with their own distinctive flint types associated with types characteristic of later hunters elsewhere in Britain. These assemblages are characterized by numbers of obliquely blunted and basally retouched points, often referred to as 'Horsham' points. In addition, these Wealden assemblages have far more rod-like microliths than the scalene triangles characteristic of later assemblages elsewhere. It would, however, be unwise to consider these assemblages as representing more than local variation within a much more widespread later technology.

Over 80 sites within the Weald, together with a scattering over the Sussex Coastal Plain, represent the later hunter-gatherer phase, a phase ending with the introduction of the earliest farming techniques around 4300 BC. Characteristic of this later period are narrow scalene microtriangles and rod-like backed bladelets (Fig. 1.4). Sites of this period can be divided into occupied rock shelters, sites with pits, flint-knapping sites and specialized activity areas represented by low densities of flints. Several of these classes of site overlap, but they are sufficiently distinct to suggest short-stay activity areas, perhaps part of migratory systems, around longer-stay home bases.

At least seventeen of the High Weald rock overhangs have evidence for hunter-gatherer activity. Only three of these sites have been investigated adequately in recent years, High Rocks (Money 1960), Hermitage Rocks (Jacobi and Tebbutt 1981) and The Rocks, Uckfield (Hemingway, in progress).

High Rocks lies about 1 km south-west of Tunbridge Wells. The site consists of an extensive rock outcrop of Tunbridge Wells sandstone, partly undermined by erosion to provide natural shelters. Pollen work by Professor

G. W. Dimbleby indicated continuous woodland conditions throughout the period of occupation and indeed, up to the present day (Dimbleby, in Money 1960). Pollen from Site E indicated a hazel scrub environment with beech, oak, birch and yew also present. Site F produced less hazel pollen but a similar range of other trees.

Figure 1.5   Plan of a Mesolithic occupation floor within a rock shelter at Hermitage Rocks, East Sussex (after Jacobi and Tebbutt 1981).

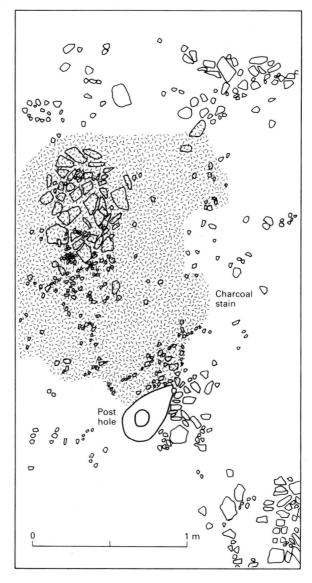

The flint evidence from the High Rocks shelters indicates intermittent occupation, by perhaps only small hunting parties. Microliths were certainly made on the site as the several cores and blades show. A variety of microlithic types was found including scalene triangles, crescents, obliquely blunted points, hollow based points and rods. In all, 54 microliths were found. This hunting equipment was associated with patches of charcoal and burnt flint, suggesting hearths. Carbon 14 dates from the charcoal of 3780 ± 150 bc and 3700 ± 150 bc if calibrated, suggest a date of about 4500 BC (Money 1962). The occupation of High Rocks therefore only marginally pre-dates the arrival of the earliest farming communities.

A more recent excavation under a similar rock shelter at Hermitage Rocks, High Hurstwood, Sussex, revealed a hearth constructed of sandstone blocks (Jacobi and Tebbutt 1981). A total of 4,329 pieces of worked flint was found at the shelter (Fig. 1.5). The tool kit, with its large number of microliths, indicates the importance of hunting. The many notched flints may well have been used in the preparation of arrow shafts. Several burins suggest antler working, but the very few scrapers found indicate little in the way of animal produce preparation. A simple hunting camp extracting woodland resources for use elsewhere is suggested by the excavators. It is probably that the site was periodically occupied with the three carbon-14 dates, 4,850 ± 100 bc, 4,970 ± 110 bc and 5,155 ± 70 bc suggesting a date in the mid sixth millennium bc.

If the Wealden rock shelters were only seasonally occupied by hunting parties, then it is possible that the extensive sites on the Greensand and the adjacent valleys may have been longer-stay home bases. From these sites come more scrapers and axes, suggesting skin preparation and forest clearance. Sites at Selmeston and Hassocks on the Sussex Greensand, Farnham and Abinger in Surrey and at North Bersted on the Sussex Coastal Plain have all produced pits indicating more than casual occupation (Fig. 1.3). It is uncertain what these pits actually represent, particularly as most of the material found in them is probably secondary rubbish. It is possible that they may have acted as shelters of some sort or as working hollows. Some, as at Farnham, may have been dug to extract gravel flint, while others could have been used for storage.

The site at Abinger, Surrey, revealed a single pit some 4.5 m by 3 m, dug almost 1 m into the underlying Greensand (Leakey 1951). In and around the pit, L. S. B. Leakey located 6,561 pieces of struck flint of which 563 were implements, cores and utilized flakes. The actual pit contained 1,056 struck flints, suggesting that most of the flint working probably took place around it. At one end of the pit were two post-holes which may or may not relate to its function (Fig. 1.6). Although there was some charcoal inside, two more probable hearth areas were found outside.

The flint assemblage associated with the pit included 60 microliths but in addition there were scrapers, axe-sharpening flakes and one tranchet axe. The pit group at Farnham produced far more axes and scrapers than Abinger, but in many other ways is a similar site.

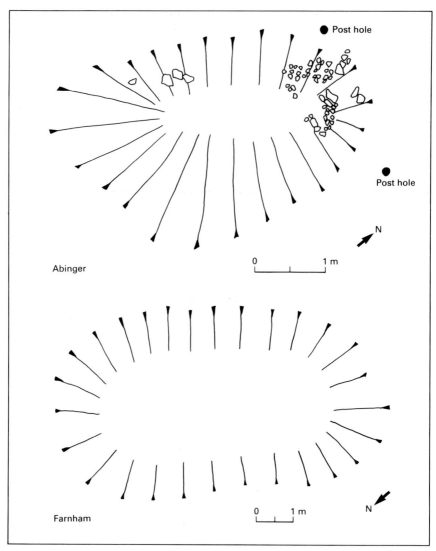

Figure 1.6 Mesolithic pits at Abinger and Farnham, Surrey (after Leakey 1951; Clark and Rankine 1939).

The site at Farnham is situated on a spread of river-gravel near a small spring to the north-east of the town (Fig. 1.7). Four irregular pits were excavated in 1937–38. Pit 2 had an associated post-hole, while Pits 1 and 3 contained patches of fire-cracked flints and charcoal interpreted by the excavators as hearths. A very large flint assemblage, consisting of 39,675 pieces of struck flint, was associated with the pits. This assemblage included 690 microliths, 403 scrapers and 15 axes with the cutting edge formed by a transversely

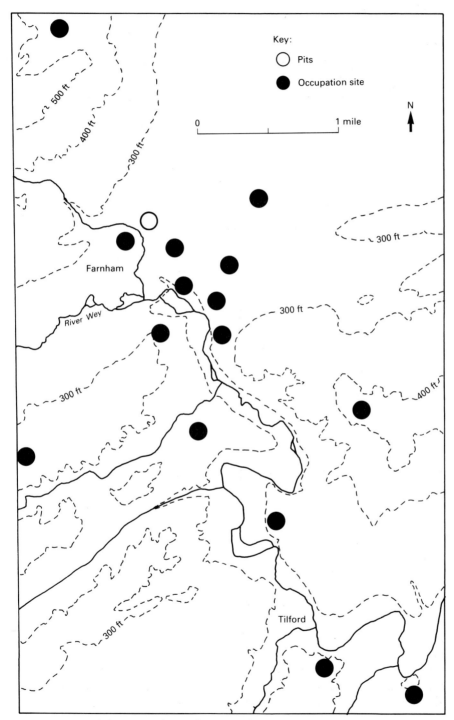

Figure 1.7 Mesolithic sites in the Farnham area of Surrey.

struck blow. The microliths exhibited a wide range of types with obliquely blunted forms dominating, followed by triangular forms. A few hollow-based types were also present (Clark and Rankine 1939).

The flint used for the manufacture of the Farnham flint assemblage was probably local gravel flint, so the possibility remains that the pits were dug to extract flint and subsequently used as working hollows. The irregular nature of the pits, in particular Pit 1, might support such an idea.

From Pit 2 at Farnham came three elongated pebbles, clearly of non-local origin. These are particularly interesting as they came from the south-west peninsula of England, so perhaps foreshadow a redistribution network in third-millennium stone axes. One of the pebbles closely matched a sandy bed in the Gramscatho Beds which outcrop near Helford, Cornwall. Two other siltstone pebbles probably derived from Devonian deposits in South Cornwall or Devon (Rankine 1956). It is possible, however, that they were picked up on south coast beaches having been moved eastwards by long-shore drift. Either way, these stones may represent the first evidence for redistribution networks or at least long-distance collection of specialized resources.

The cluster of three pits excavated at Selmeston, Sussex, in 1933 by Professor J. G. D. Clark were, like Pit 4 at Farnham, irregular ovals in shape. These pits were dug into Lower Greensand at a point near its junction with the Gault Clay. The site is therefore encircled by springs and overlooks the valley of the River Cuckmere. Pits 1 and 3 were dug over 1 m into the sand, while Pit 2 was even deeper. Associated with the pits was an extensive flint industry, including 136 microliths: burins, scrapers, tranchet axes and waste material (Clark 1934).

Excavations at North Bersted in 1975 revealed the only contemporary pit to be found on the Sussex Coastal Plain. It was dug into orange-brown brickearth and appears to be oval in plan, although it was not totally excavated. The pit was some 70 cm deep (Pitts 1980). A small flint assemblage associated with the pit consisted mainly of waste material. A similar low density of flints was associated with a small charcoal-filled pit found under Barrow 1 at West Heath on the Sussex-Hampshire border (Plate 1.4). The importance of this pit is that it provided a carbon-14 date of 6150 ± 70 bc (Drewett 1976).

The bulk of evidence for final hunter-gathering communities comes from the many concentrations of worked flint, particularly from the Greensand ridges. Flint concentrations may be broadly divided into those with extensive evidence of flint knapping and the very low-density flint scatters suggesting specialized activity areas.

Among the most studied groups of flint scatters are those from the Farnham area of Surrey (Fig. 1.7). Here twenty-one sites were studied in detail in the 1920s and 1930s (Oakley *et al.* 1939). The sites concentrate on the sands and gravels along the Wey Valley. Ten of the concentrations were on river bluff sites, eight in the river valley and only three on hill-top sites. Although hill-top

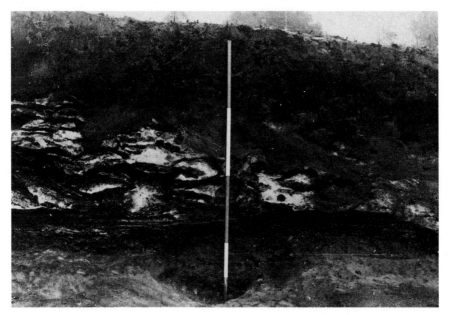

Plate 1.4   Small Mesolithic fire-pit or hearth (at base of ranging pole) protected beneath a Bronze Age land surface and turf barrow at West Heath, West Sussex. The pit contained charcoal dated to 6150 ± 70 bc.

sites may deliberately have been not chosen, it is possible that the apparent bias against this situation may be the result of later erosion.

Sites on all three locations produced evidence for flint working with narrow-blade waste material on all sites, and cores on all sites except two. The main differences are between the river bluff sites and the valley sites, with the hill-top sites more closely related to the river bluff sites. The microburins and microliths concentrate on the river bluff sites, while the tranchet axes concentrate on the river valley sites. This would suggest the manufacture of microliths on the river bluff sites with their use, and loss, in woodland elsewhere. The likelihood of recovering individually lost microliths in a woodland environment is remote. The concentration of axes in the river valley may suggest an attempt to clear riverine forest.

The distinction between microlith-rich sites on sand and gravel ridges and the axe-rich low-lying sites is evident elsewhere in South-East England; the many Greensand ridge sites in Surrey, for example, show evidence for the manufacture of microliths but few axes. The assemblage excavated under the Deerleap Wood barrow consisted of 1,014 struck flints including cores, waste flakes, microliths, microburins and serrated blades, together with only one transverse axe (Corcoran 1963). Similarly the site at Wonham, Surrey, to the east of Deerleap Wood, revealed an assemblage consisting of 31 microliths, 26 microburins, 11 gravers but only one axe. The Wonham site is a classic river

21

bluff situation on the River Mole gravels at its confluence with Shagbrook (Ellaby 1977).

Few low lying sites with heavy axes or adzes have been excavated in South-East England, although high concentrations of casually found axes are well known from the river valleys, particularly the Thames Valley (Lacaille 1966). Two sites at Lower Halstow in the Upchurch Marshes of Kent were, however, excavated in the 1920s (Burchell 1928). The assemblage was recovered from a sticky clay deposit overlain by peat and 2.1 m of alluvium. Heavy tools, particularly adzes, appear to dominate although, as Jacobi has pointed out, sticky clay is not the easiest matrix from which to recover microliths (Jacobi 1980).

Evidence for final hunting and gathering communities on the marshy Sussex Coastal Plain also shows a domination of tranchet axes with few microliths. From Marsh Farm, Binsted, for example, comes a flint assemblage of 353 pieces included eight tranchet axes, a pick and two other core tools, but no microliths (Pitts 1980). Similarly at least six tranchet axes are known from Selsey (Pitts 1980).

In addition to the extensive, microlith-dominated Greensand sites and low-lying axe-dominated flint sites in South-East England, there are also very low-density flint scatters found distributed over many areas of the Weald. These probably represent specialized activity areas like one-night stops for individuals or small groups of hunters.

Practically all the flint scatters of this date on the North and South Downs are very low density. A detailed field survey of the parish of Elsted in West Sussex produced seven sites with small clusters of narrow-blade waste, all indicating short-term activity. Only one of the sites (Site 70) produced any heavy tools, in the form of a tranchet pick (Bell 1975). Similarly a field survey of Bullock Down on the Chalk in East Sussex produced a very light scatter of narrow-blade waste and cores, together with one tranchet axe (Drewett 1982). Earlier casual finds in the same area have, however, produced many more tranchet axes (Wymer and Bonsall 1977) suggesting some extensive clearance of the chalk Downland forest.

Low-density flint concentrations are also characteristic of the Ashdown Forest area of the High Weald. C. F. Tebbutt (1974), for example, records 58 scatters of narrow-bladed flint material, some extremely low in density. Most of the sites produced under 20 pieces of flint. Some, like Site 10 overlooking the Medway at Forest Row, consisted of one core and one microlith. The presence of tranchet axes from Hartfield and Nutley (Tebbutt 1974) perhaps indicates some attempt at forest clearance in the Weald.

Similar low-density scatters of worked flint are known from the poorer bedrocks of Surrey and Kent. The pebble beds on Croham Hurst, Surrey, for example, have produced scatters of narrow blades, microcores together with burins, and a rough tranchet axe (Drewett 1970b).

From the available evidence of Post-Glacial hunters and gatherers in

South-East England it is possible to suggest a range of activities which may perhaps reflect differing social groups. All these activities appear to relate to food procurement. There is no evidence for any ceremonial or ritual sites prior to 4300 BC. This does not, of course, mean that they do not exist. In many hunter-gatherer communities natural features have ceremonial or ritual significance. To the Australian Aborigines, for example, the creation of natural features resulted from the doings and adventures of certain sacred beings at the 'World Dawn' (Radcliffe-Brown 1952). It is possible, but unprovable, that natural features in South-East England, such as rivers or hills, had ceremonial or ritual significance. There is also no evidence for burial practices prior to 4300 BC. This does not, however, necessarily mean that burial was not of great ritual significance but simply that the nature of the burial rite leaves no traces. Exposure or water burial would be two types of burial leaving no archaeological traces. What we are left with are the traces of economic activity.

The large concentrations of flint-working waste, particularly associated with pits and hearths as at Selmeston or Farnham, perhaps indicate home territories. These sites, mainly on the drier Greensand, were perhaps occupied by extended family groups, possibly over the winter months. Microlithic points were manufactured in quantity for use in longer-distance hunting trips. These longer-range hunting and gathering expeditions may possibly be divided into those venturing into the Wealden forest and those onto the coastal marshes. The Wealden forest would provide ample supplies of wild ox, red deer, pig and roe deer, together with nuts and berries. Hazel nuts, for example, were found in the pits at both Farnham and Selmeston. The rock shelters in the Weald were briefly occupied by these hunting bands. Jacobi and Tebbutt (1981) have argued that the social group briefly occupying the Hermitage Rock shelter was a male hunting band, simply extracting food resources from the forest but with food preparation, possibly a female activity, taking place elsewhere, presumably at the home-base territory sites.

Similarly, the evidence from the marshes of Kent and the Coastal Plain of Sussex suggests low-density activity, probably of a seasonal nature. An ample supply of shellfish and marsh birds during the summer months, together with greater mobility in marshland during drier times of year, suggests summer utilization of marsh resources.

Chapter 2

The Earliest Farmers, *c*. 4300–3000 BC

The period *c*. 4400–4200 BC appears to be a phase of major cultural change in South-East England. Within two hundred years appeared the first settled agricultural communities. These earliest farmers introduced new communal monuments and material culture, all reflecting significant changes in the social order (Drewett 1985). The impact of the first farmers on the landscape was considerable (Fig. 2.1).

It is now generally accepted that most of South-East England was wooded prior to 4000 BC (Sheldon, in Drewett 1978; and in Leach 1982). Attempts to suggest otherwise for the Chalk Downs in Southern England (Barker and Webley 1978: 161–85) have been firmly refuted by environmental archaeologists (Evans 1978: 185–6). Irregular hollows found on many archaeological excavations are interpreted as fossil tree holes (Evans 1972: 219). Most are insecurely dated and may be derived from later re-afforestation. The many tree holes within the causewayed enclosure at Offham may derive from trees known to have been cleared this century (Drewett 1977). More securely dated, however, are the tree holes buried under hill wash that has accumulated over the past 6,000 years in dry valleys at Kiln Combe (Bell, in Drewett 1982) and Itford Bottom (Bell 1981). A polished quartz diorite axe or mace-head fragment from a tree hole (Fe 707) at Bishopstone (Bell 1977: 7) and part of a flake axe from an irregular hollow (Fe 14) at Saxonbury (Bedwin 1979*a*: 102) both suggest possible clearance activity prior to 3000 BC.

Molluscan analyses at five enclosures constructed prior to 3000 BC were undertaken by Dr K. Thomas of the Institute of Archaeology. To this may be added a pre-war analysis from Whitehawk, a sixth enclosure constructed prior to 3000 BC. Four of the enclosures, Offham, Combe Hill, Bury Hill and Barkhale appear to have been constructed in woodland, while the Trundle and Whitehawk were constructed in areas that had been fairly recently, but extensively, cleared.

At Offham samples were taken from the buried soil under the outer bank and both the inner and outer ditches. The land snails were extracted by

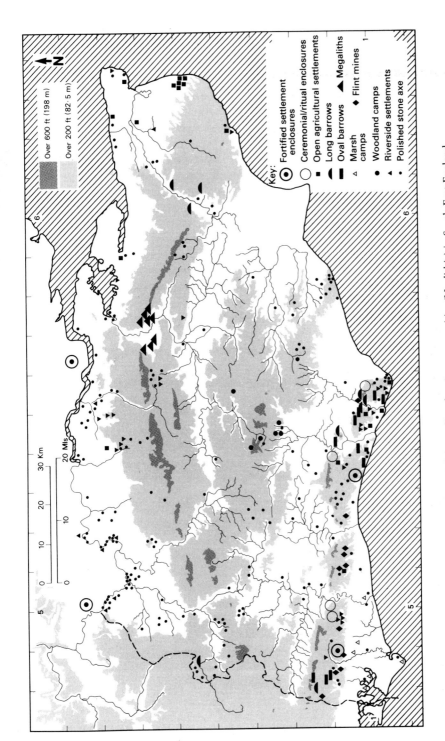

Figure 2.1 Ceremonial, settlement and industrial sites of the earliest farming communities (Neolithic) in South-East England.

Key:

- Fortified settlement enclosures ⊙
- Ceremonial/ritual enclosures ◯
- Open agricultural settlements ■
- Long barrows ◖
- Oval barrows ▮
- Megaliths ◣
- Marsh camps △
- Flint mines ▲
- Woodland camps ●
- Riverside settlements ◀
- Polished stone axe ♦

Over 600 ft (198 m)
Over 200 ft (82·5 m)

wet-sieving and identified by Dr K. Thomas. From this it is possible to suggest the following sequence of events (Thomas, in Drewett 1977: 239):

1. A small clearing was made in the woodland, possibly by the use of fire.
2. A bank and ditch were constructed. Early weathering into the ditch brought in old shells from the lower levels of the woodland soil to form layer 4.
3. The molluscan fauna changed from one indicating woodland conditions to one suggestive of 'clearance' conditions. Such a fauna is found in layer 3 of the ditch and in the soil under the bank associated with a later, outer ditch. A few open-country species succeeded in establishing themselves, but did not reach high abundance.
4. A second bank and ditch was constructed around the first one. The lower layers (3 and 4) of the ditch contained woodland molluscs. This is taken to indicate the closeness of the woodland edge of the ditch.
5. The woodland may have regenerated over the site after abandonment.
6. At some later period much more widespread deforestation was carried out, allowing large numbers of open-country forms to reach the site and establish themselves. These molluscs occur in levels 2 of both ditches. Unfortunately, these levels are mixed and so cannot be interpreted with any certainty.

This picture of woodland locally cleared for the construction of an enclosure is closely paralleled at Bury Hill. Here, out of 333 individuals identified by Dr Thomas from the two lowest layers in the ditch (Thomas, in Bedwin 1981a), only one individual was an open country species. This provides strong evidence that Bury Hill was constructed in a woodland clearing.

The evidence from Barkhale is not entirely satisfactory due to the sparse assemblage recovered. However, of the twenty-five individuals indentified, none is a decidely open country species (Thomas, in Leach 1983), while none is an obligate shade-lover. Although cautious in his interpretation, Dr Thomas suggests that Barkhale was also constructed in a temporary clearance in woodland.

A similar picture is evident at Combe Hill. Several soil samples collected by the excavator of Combe Hill (Musson 1950) were analysed by Dr Thomas who again reported a dominance of shade-loving species. The suggestion that the enclosure on Combe Hill was constructed in a wooded environment is supported by the presence of a few cheek teeth of the bank vole *Clethrionomys glareolus* which has a strong preference for woodland.

The molluscan evidence from the enclosures on the south side of the Downs is somewhat different. At the Trundle a number of distinctly woodland elements were living in the area, including *Aconthinula, Ena, Cochlodina* and *Helicogona*. Within this assemblage, however, were consistent representations of open-country forms (Thomas, in Bedwin, 1981b). The high frequencies of catholic species and *Pomatias elegans* indicates broken-up ground. Dr Thomas, therefore, suggests that the Trundle was constructed in a fairly recently, but extensively, cleared area.

The land snails recovered in a non-systematic way from the 1935 excavations at Whitehawk and identified by A. S. Kennard (Curwen 1936) indicate a somewhat similar pattern with low densities of woodland species like *Acanthinula aculeata* and *Cochlicopa lubrica* together with large numbers of *Pomatias elegans*, indicating broken-up ground.

The evidence from the enclosures is supported by limited molluscan evidence from contemporary flint mines in Sussex. Land snails were collected by hand in a non-systematic way from three flint mines, Blackpatch (Goodman 1924; Pull 1932), Harrow Hill (Curwen and Curwen 1926; Holleyman 1937) and Eartham (Salisbury 1961). The method of collection of this data makes direct comparison with the enclosure data impossible; however, the presence of *Carychium* at Harrow Hill is of interest in that it occurs in faunas of 'woodland' character (Thomas in Drewett 1975a: 150). Also present at Harrow Hill is *Pomatias elegans*, a species often associated with phases of woodland clearance (Thomas, in Drewett, 1975a: 150). The very low numbers of specimens described from Blackpatch or Eartham make any detailed comment particularly unreliable, but in both cases species requiring a more shady habitat than is current on the Downs were present.

The molluscan evidence from the South Downs, therefore, consistently shows a wooded environment prior to 4000 BC (for dating of enclosures see below) with extensive clearance on the south side of the Downs during the early fourth millennium (Whitehawk and Trundle) but little significant clearance on the north side of the Downs.

Molluscan analysis, naturally, does not indicate what woods were actually growing on the Downs during the fourth millennium. Some indication may be provided by the charcoals present on the sites of this period. Naturally, charcoal identifications will only indicate species utilized within the catchment area of the site. Some species may therefore have been collected off the Downs and taken up for use on the Downland site. However, the frequency with which *Crataegus* sp. (hawthorn), *Corylus* sp. (hazel) and *Quercus* sp. (oak) are found suggests that these may well have been growing on the Downs.

More reliable information on the nature of the early fouth-millennium woodland, and its subsequent clearance by man, is available from pollen studies in river valleys, on the Greensand and further into the Weald.

River valleys provide practically the only anaerobic conditions in which pollen is preserved in isolated peat deposits. Such ideal conditions have been found in the Ouse valley near Lewes and these deposits have now been studied by several workers. Ann Thorley produced two pollen diagrams from peat deposits in the Vale of the Brooks south of Lewes, just north of the Upper Rise. She demonstrated that the peat deposits started forming in the seventh millennium BC and continued to the second millennium BC. The pollen deposited down to about 4000 BC confirms that the area was well wooded, for arboreal pollen types consistently occur in higher values than non-arboreal pollen values (Thorley 1971: 47). High value of *Alnus* (alder) pollen occur throughout this phase, suggesting it is derived from a local source. Relatively high percentages of *Pinus* (pine) suggests deeper and more widespread loess deposits than survive in the area today. Such deposits do survive on both the Downs (Thorley 1971: 48) and on the Greensand as at Selmeston (Macphail, in Rudling 1985a). Such deposits may have formed the basis of the Downland soils which supported the woodland cover indicated by both the molluscan and pollen evidence.

The Lewes II diagram (Thorley 1971: 48) shows a dramatic change in the percentage of the arboreal to non-arboreal pollen in the late second millennium BC (associated with a carbon-14 date of 1240 BC. Tree pollen declines and is replaced by a much higher percentage of *Pteridium* (bracken) spores and pollen of weeds of arable and pasture land. Thorley therefore suggests that major deforestation of this area did not take place until the late second millennium BC. (Thorley 1971: 48).

Although this late second-millennium deforestation of the Ouse valley is confirmed by Wing (1980) at Wellingham, north of Lewes, he was able to isolate an earlier clearance phase in the mid fourth millennium BC. This was associated with an increase in frequency of grass and cereal pollen. However, arboreal pollen increased again in the mid third millennium, with an associated decrease in grass and cereal pollen.

Current work by R. Scaife on pollen in the Ouse Valley, associated with sedimentological studies, suggests not only periodic clearance prior to the late second millennium BC, but also that some of the pollen indicating grassland and cultivation may have been derived from higher up in the Weald than suggested by earlier workers (Scaife and Burrin 1983). This fits in extremely well with the archaeological data for the primary settlement of farming communities in the fourth millennium and suggests that Thorley's sequence may indicate an atypical valley sequence, applicable only to a small but very wide area of Ouse flood plain.

For reasons of preservation, the Greensand has been more extensively studied in terms of changing pedological and vegetational conditions than most areas. Classic studies by Dimbleby at Iping Common (Keef, Wymer and Dimbleby 1965; Dimbleby 1962) and at Rackham (Holden and Bradley 1975: Dimbleby and Bradley 1975) have been extended by the study of pollen from barrows at Minsted (Dimbleby in Drewett 1975b) and West Heath (Baigent in Drewett 1976 and Scaife in Drewett 1985).

At Iping Common pollen analysis showed some degree of deforestation in the eighth and ninth millennia, indicating clearance possibly associated with herding well before the introduction of agriculture. *Calluna* (heather) increased at the expense of arboreal pollen and was associated with increased podsolisation of the soil (Keef, Wymer and Dimbleby 1965). This led to a collapse of the soil structure and extensive erosion. Such early deforestation and subsequent destruction of the forest soil which probably originally covered the Greensand, may have been very localized until perhaps the second millennium.

At Rackham, for example, *Quercus* (oak), *Betula* (birch), *Corylus* (hazel) and *Alnus* (alder) dominate in the early fourth millennium but are dominated by *Calluna* (heather) by the second millennium. (Dimbleby in Holden and Bradley 1975). The suggestion that the movement of late second-millennium flint artifacts down the soil profile by worms at Rackham indicates that the heavily leached acid podsol at Rackham was originally a forest brown earth in which earthworms could live. As such, it would be ideal for agricultural communities, unlike the very acid leached podsol of today.

At Minsted mixed woodland pollen with high frequencies of *Alnus* (alder), *Quercus* (oak) and *Corylus* (Hazel), together with *Calluna* (heather) was found on a land surface buried under a turf barrow constructed in the second millennium BC (Dimbleby in Drewett 1975*b*). This suggests the construction of the barrow in a lightly wooded environment. However, this area may well have been regenerated woodland cleared by fire for grazing prior to the seventh millennium BC. This is suggested by a second buried land surface, this time under wind-blown sand, under the barrow. This surface shows a dominance of *Calluna* (heather) and low percentages of arboreal pollen. A very high percentage of *Hedera* (ivy) was, however, present. This Professor Dimbleby (in Drewett 1975*b*) had interpreted in cultural terms, suggesting it represents collection of winter fodder by hunting communities.

The barrows at West Heath also provided pollen evidence for clearance with some light woodland in the second millennium BC. The West Heath barrow group appears to have been built on a cleared sandy ridge, surrounded by open *Calluna* (heather) heathland, but with *Corylus* (hazel) thickets. This heathland may have been surrounded by denser primary woodland in the valleys, providing the lower densities of *Alnus* (alder), *Quercus* (oak) and *Tilia* (lime) in the pollen assemblage (Baigent in Drewett, 1976).

Little environmental work has been undertaken in the High Weald, largely because of a lack of suitably dated contexts. At High Rocks (Money 1960 and 1962) there is clearly considerable intermixing of artifactual material with a late hunter-gatherer flint assemblage dated by Carbon-14 to 3780 ± 150 bc and 3700 ± 150 bc These dates, if calibrated using the Suess calibration, suggest dates of 4400–4500 BC which would be entirely consistent with the microlithic assemblage. The pottery in the same context has, however, been dated to 3324 ± 375 bc by thermoluminescence dating (Green, pers. comm.). This clear artifactual intermixing must cast doubt on the reliability of the associated pollen assemblage. Having said this, the pollen in fact show continuous woodland conditions, dominated by *Quercus* (oak) but with some *Betula* (birch), *Taxus* (yew) and *Corylus* (hazel) together with a little *Fagus* (beech). No evidence of clearance was found at any stage (Dimbleby in Money 1960: 217).

Environmental evidence related to the period of primary farming activity on the North Downs is slight. Professor Godwin's classic pollen diagrams from Frogholt near Folkestone, and Wingham near Canterbury, suggest that forest clearance had taken place by *c.* 1400 BC but possibly much earlier. The basal peat at Frogholt indicates a cleared environment associated with a date of 1030 ± 130 bc, while the base of the peaty deposit at Wingham has a date of 1155 ± 110 bc (Godwin, 1962).

Earlier clearance of the North Downs is indicated by molluscan analysis undertaken by Kerney at Brook. Here, in a combe called the Devil's Kneading Trough, two sections of hillwash deposit were examined. Both sections indicated woodland environments with the earliest clearance not taking place until perhaps the third millennium BC (Kerney *et al.* 1964).

Three pollen diagrams, derived from samples taken by Professor Dimbleby in the Keston area of Kent, all show a predominantly woodland spectrum. The three sites sampled are all on the Blackheath Pebble Beds. The first site, at Keston Camp, showed that the first millennium enclosure was constructed in a forest of *Quercus* with *Corylus*, *Betula* and *Ilex* as subordinate species. On Keston Common a second site sampled showed a similar forest picture, but with less complete dominance of *Quercus*. At the third site at Keston Copse, the pollen was not well preserved and there appeared to be considerable mixing of the soil (Dimbleby 1961). From the environmental evidence currently available from the South-East, it is possible to draw certain general conclusions. Future work will, no doubt, show numerous local variations in this picture.

At present there is no environmental evidence from the Coastal Plain of Sussex or Kent. It is difficult to know, with existing techniques, how to remedy this situation, as snails do not survive on the coastal brickearths and no peat or other deposits suitable for pollen studies are known. It may be argued, on archaeological grounds, that these areas may well have been utilized by the earliest farming communities, if not earlier.

Evidence from the Downs suggests that the more gently sloping, south-facing southern side of the South Downs was being cleared early in the fourth millennium BC with sites like the Trundle and Whitehawk being constructed in extensive clearings. The enclosures at Offham, Combe Hill, Bury Hill and Barkhale, however, appear to have been constructed in woodland with clearance not taking place until the second or even first millennium BC. Similar dates for clearance of the North Downs appear likely. The river valleys, if represented by the Ouse, show temporary clearance in the fouth millennium in some areas, but extensive clearance also took place on the Greensand in the second millennium, this being the clearance of regenerated woodland, perhaps first cleared by hunting-and-gathering communities prior to 4000 BC. Finally, the limited evidence from the High Weald and the Blackheath Pebble Beds suggests no major forest clearance in the prehistoric period.

Material Culture

The material culture surviving from the activities of the earliest farming communities consists of flint and stone tools, pottery, bone, chalk and sandstone objects. It must be assumed that the bulk of the material culture actually used was made of organic materials like wood, skin, bark, grass and hair, which do not survive under normal conditions in South-East England.

Lithic tools may be divided into several functional groups or tool kits, indicating the main areas of activity in a primary agricultural context. Firstly the heavy woodcutting tools, essential for clearing land for agriculture, consist of flaked and polished flint axes, polished stone axes (Plate 2.1) and chopping tools. Agricultural tools include heavy flint picks suitable for breaking up the ground and single-piece sickles or curved knives for cutting crops. Alternatively, grain crops may have been simply pulled out of the ground.

Projectile points, probably used for hunting, were leaf-shaped flint arrowheads, either flaked all over or just along the edges and one tip. The laurel-leaf points may also have been used to kill animals. Trapped or domestic animals may have been killed using the flaked discoidal knives, and the carcases and skins prepared using a variety of flint tools. These included the long- and short-end scrapers, side scrapers, flint choppers, backed and discoidal knives and serrated blades. For making fire, short rods of flint, called 'fabricators', may have been knocked against iron pyrite nodules. Craft tools consisted of hammerstones for making flint tools and a variety of tools suitable for wood and bone working. Such tools include the end, side and hollow scrapers, notched flakes and awls.

The earliest pottery in South-East England consists of round-based bowls and cups. These bowls vary from shallow to deep, with a few being carinated or necked. The potting industry was probably domestic, with each settlement producing its own pottery to a common pattern. An analysis of fabrics in Sussex, for example, shows widespread use of most locally available fillers, including flint, shell, sand, grog and chalk (Drewett 1981). Although most of the pottery was plain, a variety of decorative techniques is known, including incised lines, fluting, finger tip and nail impressions, perforations and impressions, particularly of twisted cord. Lugs are the only attachments on the pottery and although not nearly as common as in the South-West of England, are a recurring feature.

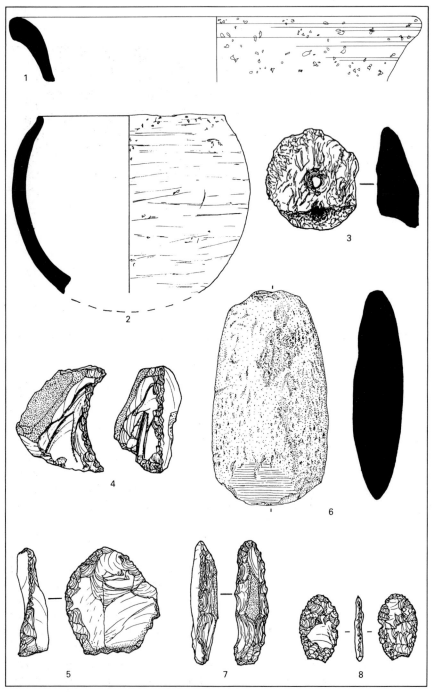

Figure 2.2   Material culture of the earliest farming communities in South-East England. 1–2: round-based bowls; 3: chalk spindle whorl; 4–5: flint scrapers; 6: polished stone axe; 7: flint strike-a-light; 8: leaf-shaped arrowhead (scale ½).

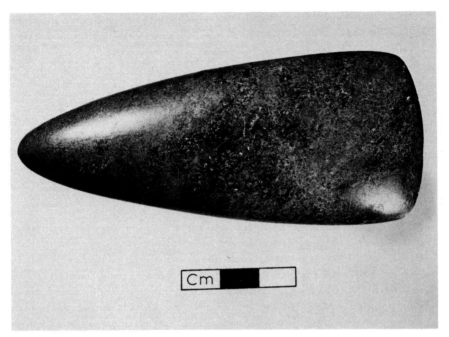

Plate 2.1 A finely polished greenstone axe found on the surface of a ploughed field on Bullock Down, Beachy Head, East Sussex.

Antler was extensively used in the manufacture of tools, including picks, combs, hammers, rakes and chisels. It is therefore surprising that bone was only used to make simple bone points like those from Whitehawk (Williamson 1930: Fig. 14, No. 18).

Sandstone was used in the fourth millennium to make grinding stones. These consist of a dished lower stone and rounded upper stones. Often referred to as 'grain rubbers' (e.g. Curwen 1934a: 131) or 'querns' (I. F. Smith 1965: 121) they may have been used for grinding cereals, but could equally well have been used for grinding a variety of other foodstuffs.

Although large quantities of chalk would have become available during the digging of flint mines and the construction of enclosures, it was not widely used in the fourth millennium. A few distinct types are, however, known. The actual function of all these chalk artifacts is uncertain. The hour-glass perforated chalk pieces clearly fall into two types, based on size and position of hole. Curwen describes one of the smaller type, found at the Trundle in 1930, as a 'small piece of chalk resembling an asymmetrical spindle-whorl but of unknown purpose' (E. C. Curwen 1931: 143). Dr Smith, considering Windmill Hill finds, suggests that the larger examples may have been used as weights and the smaller ones as pendants (I. F. Smith, 1965). Simple practical experiments by the author, however, show that small irregular perforated chalk blocks of

33

40–80 gm function perfectly well as spindle whorls, while 2,000–4,000 gm perforated blocks are ideal as loom weights. Practical experiments of this type do, however, indicate only that a particular artifact could be used in a particular way, not that it was used in such a way. The earliest baked clay spindle-whorl from Southern England does not appear until the end of the third millennium BC, at Durrington Walls (Wainwright and Longworth 1971: 188), so the possibility that the knowledge of weaving was present in the fourth millennium is of some interest in economic terms.

The function of the small, hollowed-out chalk 'cups' is difficult to determine. The larger ones could have functioned as oil lamps, but none show any evidence of burning to suggest that this was the case. Chalk is too soft for them to have been used for grinding small quantities of foodstuffs like herbs. The cut marks and scratches in the base of some cups, often thought to have resulted from their manufacture, may equally well have resulted from the cutting up, rather than pounding of, foodstuffs.

The regularity of occurrence of line motifs on the incised chalk blocks suggests more than Curwen's 'few moments of idleness' (E. C. Curwen 1929: 17). Whether the blocks represent some kind of tally system or other form of written communication, or even mobile art, is difficult to determine. The regularity of occurrence of specific motifs is, however, of great importance in raising these markings above the level of arbitrary doodling. It may be of some significance that all the motifs, except the parallel lines crossing at right angles, also occur on fourth-millennium pottery in Sussex. The parallel lines at right angles motif is, however, present on fourth-millennium pottery elsewhere in Southern England.

The recognizable field monuments associated with the earliest farming communities in South-East England may be divided into eleven types: fortified settlement enclosures, ceremonial/ritual enclosures, open agricultural settlements, marsh camps, woodland camps, riverside settlements, flint mines, surface flint working sites, long barrows, oval barrows and megaliths.

Enclosures

Six enclosures may be dated to the fourth millennium BC by Carbon-14 dating or pottery styles. All are in Sussex, although there may have been a similar enclosure at Chalk in Kent (Holgate 1981: 230). The known examples are the Trundle, Whitehawk, Barkhale, Bury Hill, Offham and Combe Hill. Excavations have been undertaken at all the enclosures and all except Barkhale produced material suitable for Carbon-14 dating. The dates obtained are as follows:

Location	Radiocarbon date(bc)	Calibrated date(BC)	Lab. No.:
Trundle			
1. Primary silt (Ditch 2)	3290 ± 140	4320–4010	I–11615
2. Primary silt (Ditch 2)	3090 ± 170	4190–3900	I–11616
3. Secondary silt (Ditch 2)	2910 ± 100	3690	I–11612
4. Secondary silt (Ditch 1)	2895 ± 95	3690	I–11614
Whitehawk			
1. Primary silt (Ditch 3)	2750 ± 130	3500–3410	I–11846
2. Primary silt (Ditch 4)	2695 ± 95	3500–3410	I–11847
Bury Hill			
1. Primary silt (Ditch)	2730 ± 80	3500–3410	Har 3596
2. Primary silt (Ditch)	2620 ± 80	3450	Har 3595
Offham			
1. Primary silt (Ditch 2)	2975 ± 80	3710	BM 1414
2. Secondary silt (Ditch 2)	2790 ± 60	3650–3540	BM 1415
Combe Hill			
1. Primary silt (Ditch 2)	2640 ± 110	3400	I–11613

These dates would suggest that although the Trundle was almost certainly the first enclosure to be constructed, all enclosures were in use at the same time. Unfortunately, excavations at Barkhale produced no organic material suitable for Carbon-14 dating. There is, however, nothing in the ceramic or lithic industries to suggest that it need be anything other than contemporary with the other five enclosures.

Fourth-millennium enclosures in Sussex may be divided into those situated on the south side of the Downs (Trundle and Whitehawk) and those on the north side of the Downs (Bury Hill, Barkhale, Offham and Combe Hill). All the enclosures are situated on local high points of the Downs, although only the Trundle is actually situated on the top of a hill. Whitehawk and Combe Hill are situated on level tracts of land with adjacent higher land (on three sides in the case of Combe Hill, but only on one side at Whitehawk). Bury Hill, Barkhale and Offham are all situated below the crest of the hill. All enclosures overlook at least one river within 2½ miles (4km).

The location of fourth-millennium enclosures may have depended on numerous factors, social, economic, environmental or religious. The range of factors will depend partly on the function of the enclosures. One important aspect of location is likely to have been visibility both from the enclosures, and of the enclosures from the landscape around. Redistribution or social centres are perhaps more likely to be visible or accessible than cult or burial centres, which may perhaps be taboo to part of the population.

By looking outwards from each enclosure on a fine day and plotting the landscape visible from within the enclosure, it is clear that the enclosures fall into two groups; those that are multi-directional and those that are essentially one-directional. From the Trundle it is possible to look in all directions with visibility covering most of the Downs in West Sussex, all the Coastal Plain and as far as Ashey Down on the Isle of White. The environmental evidence, showing that the Trundle was constructed in an extensively cleared area, would indicate that such a view was possible in the fourth millennium. Conversely it is possible to see the Trundle from virtually the whole of the southern part of West Sussex (Drewett 1985).

Whitehawk offers similar, extensive views of the Down and the Coastal Plain from Selsey in the west to Seaford Head in the east. A localized rise to the north-east, however, blocks visibility in that direction. Whitehawk does, however, provide maximum local visibility. Movement onto higher land to the north-east would have reduced both the extensive western view and the 18 km view to the east. As with the Trundle, environmental evidence suggests that these views would have been possible in the fourth millennium.

The landscape visibility of the four northern enclosures presents a very different picture. Each enclosure is, presumably deliberately, false crested. This prevents multi-directional visibility. Barkhale is located in such a way that it looks south across a small section of the Downs and then across the Coastal Plain to the sea. The other three enclosures, Bury Hill, Offham and Combe Hill, all look north across the Weald to the Ashdown Ridge. Both Bury Hill and Offham overlook practically the whole Wealden section of major rivers. Combe Hill, because of local Downland configurations, also has a narrow view of the sea to the south-east and a view across the Downs to the south-west. The environmental evidence, however, suggests that Barkhale, Bury Hill, Combe Hill and Offham were constructed in woodland clearings. Consideration of visibility may therefore appear at first sight irrelevant. However, at each site, if the woodland clearance extended a minimum of 15m outside the enclosure, these extensive one-directional views would have been possible over the tops of trees on the lower slopes. Tree cover would only have blocked the two southern views from Combe Hill. Examination of landscape visibility, taking into consideration known environmental evidence, therefore suggests that the northern enclosures are orientated in a very different way to the southern enclosures.

The construction technique used at each of the six enclosures, was basically the same, although slightly modified at Bury Hill. At each enclosure the ditches were dug as a series of pits, either left as separate pits with frequent causeways as at the Trundle, very roughly linked as at Offham, or all linked as at Bury Hill. Although continuously ditched, the beaded nature of the Bury Hill ditch, and irregular depth of the base of the ditch indicates it was a pit-dug ditch (Bedwin 1981a). At each enclosure the chalk from the ditches was used to construct largely continuous dump banks inside the ditch. Only at Whitehawk was there any apparent attempt to strengthen the dump bank with the construction of a palisade. To this is linked the only possible gate structure.

Internal features are absent or scarce in all enclosures. This may be partly due to limited excavation. Only the interior of Offham has been extensively excavated, although large transect samples have been excavated across Bury Hill and Whitehawk (Fig. 2.3). A few internal trenches were excavated at Barkhale but little of the interiors of Combe Hill or the Trundle have been excavated. Pits were found internally at Whitehawk and the Trundle, and one was found in the bottom of a ditch at Offham. Post holes were located at

Figure 2.3 A fortified settlement enclosure (causewayed enclosure) at Whitehawk above Brighton, East Sussex. Excavated ditch sections in black. Dots indicate excavated pits and post-holes (after Curwen 1934*a*).

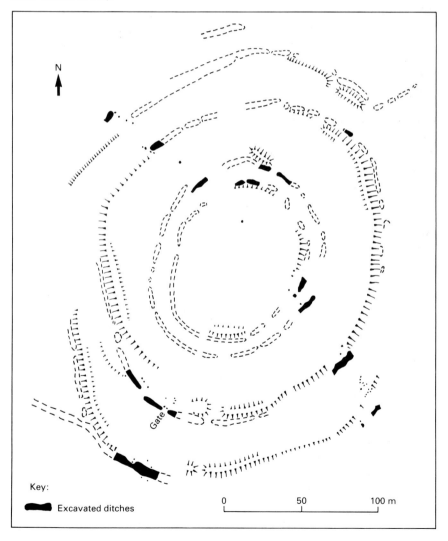

N

Key:

⬛ Excavated ditches

0   50   100 m

Gate

Plate 2.2 The excavation of a small ceremonial/ritual causewayed enclosure on Offham Hill above Lewes, East Sussex. The wide space between the two parallel lines of ditches originally held a low bank.

roughing out of cores for use elsewhere. At Offham, out of the 6,830 pieces of struck flint only 0.3 per cent were implements, while at Bury Hill out of 4,936 struck flints only 1.3 per cent were implements. This contrasts markedly with the percentage at known settlement sites of the fourth millennium elsewhere. At Bishopstone, for example, 7.1 per cent of the assemblage were implements (Bell 1977) while at Hurst Fen 8.8 per cent were implements (Clark *et al.* 1960). Unfortunately, flakes were not consistently kept from the earlier enclosure excavations in Sussex. However, if the collection of flints from Dr V. Seton-Williams's unpublished excavations at Combe Hill, as stored in Lewes Museum, is complete, then only 1.5 per cent of the 737 struck flints are implements. However, if the Trundle collection of 2,197 struck flints from the 1930 excavation is complete, it contained a higher percentage (2.7 per cent) of implements.

Tools for killing animals and food/skin preparation tools were present on all sites, in high numbers at Whitehawk and the Trundle and in low numbers at Barkhale, Bury Hill, Offham and Combe Hill. The only fire-making tool (fabricator) was found at Barkhale. Offham and Combe Hill produced no lithic tool-making tools, wood/bone-working tools or agricultural tools. All these were present at Whitehawk. At the Trundle all were present except the agricultural tools. Wood/bone working tools also came from Barkhale and Bury Hill.

From this we may conclude that the widest range and number of tool types came from Whitehawk and the Trundle. Bury Hill and Barkhale both have a range of tool types, but few examples of each type. Finally, few of the flints from Offham or Combe Hill may relate to the use of the site, as most possibly belong to the construction phase.

Pottery appears to offer little towards the functional interpretation of the enclosures. The range of fabrics suggests proximity to sources rather than functional differences. Likewise pottery forms are widespread. Other artifacts, with the exception of two fragments of grinding stones from Combe Hill, are all restricted to the Trundle and Whitehawk. Bone tools, perforated chalk, chalk cups, incised chalk and sandstone grinding stones are all present. These may indicate both weaving and grinding grain or other foodstuffs.

Food remains are widespread at Whitehawk. Although no seeds have been found at any enclosure, impressions of naked barley (*Hordeum* sp.) were found in pottery from Whitehawk. Also found at Whitehawk was extensive evidence of the utilization of marine resources, including winkle (*Littorina littorea*), cockle (*Cardium edule*), mussel (*Mytilus edulis*) and oyster (*Ostrea edulis*). The only other marine shells found in an enclosure of this period were two cockle shells from Combe Hill, however, these may have been intrusive. Hazel nuts were also found only at Whitehawk.

The full range of cattle, pig, sheep/goat and deer bones were found at the Trundle, Whitehawk, Bury Hill and Offham while only cattle and pig were found at Combe Hill. Dog remains were found at Whitehawk, Bury Hill and Offham, while Offham produced the only remains of beaver. Bone did not survive at Barkhale, so cannot be taken into account, either here or when considering human remains. Human remains, both articulated and disarticulated, were found at Whitehawk and Offham (Plate 2.3). An articulated burial was found at the Trundle and disarticulated fragments at Bury Hill.

From the data presented from these six fourth-millennium enclosures, certain broad conclusions may be drawn. From these conclusions, a working hypothesis relating to function can be suggested. If the hypothesis is correct, one would expect that later use of the site may reflect the differing primary functions.

Although it is clear from the ethnographic literature (e.g. Orme 1981: 218–54) that in pre-literate societies many aspects of ritual and religion are so interwoven with secular life as to make their separation difficult to anthropologists and therefore virtually impossible to archaeologists, it is also clear that in many societies the physical separation of certain ritual and ceremonial activities is extremely well marked off from secular life. One only has to think of Melanesian cult houses or Australian aboriginal Bora (ceremonial earth

Plate 2.3 A crouched burial of a young man aged 20–25 years old, found in the bottom of the causewayed ditch on Offham Hill, East Sussex.

circles surrounded by banks). The problem is, however, how to define these ritual/ceremonial sites in the archaeological context, particularly if ceremonial/ ritual activities also took place in a secular context.

The evidence from Sussex would suggest two distinct types of enclosure:

(a) fortified settlement enclosures;
(b) unfortified ceremonial/ritual enclosures.

This distinction is clearly not between causewayed enclosures (e.g. Barkhale) and continuously ditched enclosures (e.g. Bury Hill) but depends on environmental, locational and structural evidence linked to activity information derived from artifacts and ecofacts.

When considering the total evidence from Whitehawk and the Trundle it is very difficult not to conclude that these enclosures were fortified settlement enclosures. Environmental evidence shows that both were constructed in extensively cleared areas, suggesting the existence of pasture and/or ploughed fields around and/or inside the enclosures. Both are situated in such a way as to give wide-ranging multi-directional views, a valuable asset both when protecting extra-mural fields and herds and also for protection of the settlement. Clear evidence of fortification, in addition to the bank and ditch, was present at

Whitehawk in the form of a palisade and gate structure. Such additions were also possible at the Trundle. A full range of features, artifacts and ecofacts was present as required to indicate mixed farming, seasonal food collection and craft activities. Tools for the clearance of land, the harvesting of crops, killing animals and preparing food and skins were present. Storage pits were also found, suggesting the storage of foodstuffs over the winter.

At both sites a wide range of crafts was practised, including making flint tools, wood and bone working, pottery making and possibly weaving. The only material suggesting any possible ritual or ceremonial activity was human skeletal material but, as Whittle (1977) has pointed out, such material is also found in flint mines (e.g. Cissbury and Blackpatch) and can hardly show the function of the mine as a whole. The bone phallus from the Trundle (E. C. Curwen 1929) could also be considered ritual. However, in a later context, a chalk phallus from Itford Hill is clearly in a settlement context.

In contrast to Whitehawk and the Trundle the other four enclosures (Barkhale, Bury Hill, Offham and Combe Hill) show little evidence of permanent settlement. All are constructed in woodland and are one-directional in terms of visibility. Locations suggests defence was not a major consideration, a point emphasized by the shallow ditches and dumped banks which were not palisaded. Also, none of the excavated causeways contained gate structures. The bulk of the artifacts were those required during the construction of the enclosure or could, like core preparation, be considered a spin-off from the construction process. Food and skin-preparation tools are present only in very low quantities and the total percentage of flint tools to waste was less than 2 per cent. Agricultural tools were absent, with the exception of two grinding stone fragments from Combe Hill which may, however, be intrusive. No bone tools (other than construction phase antler picks) or chalk objects were found, so weaving was certainly not practised. The only evidence of food collection comes from two possibly intrusive cockle shells from Combe Hill. The range of animal bones matched those from Whitehawk and the Trundle, but also included such rarities as beaver. No evidence of food storage was found, the only pit at Offham being better interpreted as ritual or ceremonial in origin. Offham at least was away from, although overlooking at a distance, an area (the Ouse Valley) not only ideal for early agricultural settlement but also an area which had been cleared and where pollen showed an increase in grass and cereal pollen at this time. The evidence against these enclosures being settlement enclosures is therefore strong, and their role as ceremonial/ritual enclosures is proposed.

A final piece of evidence underlining this proposed distinction between fortified settlement enclosures and unfortified ceremonial/ritual enclosures is the post-fourth-millennium use of the sites. Ceremonial/ritual sites with their associated taboos are likely to remain in folk memory long after they go out of use. Deserted settlement sites are unlikely to have such taboos. Although scattered pottery of the third, second and first millennia BC were found in most

43

enclosures, only at Whitehawk is there any evidence of real resettlement in the late third millennium (a Beaker storage pit) and at the Trundle, where the site was re-used for a defended hilltop enclosure in the first millennium BC. The only clear re-use of the area immediately around the ceremonial/ritual enclosures was of a ceremonial/ritual character, that is the construction of round barrows in the second millennium. Barkhale, Bury Hill, Offham and Combe Hill are all surrounded by barrow groups.

There appear to be no enclosures on the North Down that can be dated to the third or fourth millennia BC. This is surprising, given the contemporary long barrows and megaliths in the Kentish valleys. Excavated examples at Orset (Hedges and Buckley 1978) and Staines (Robertson-Mackay 1962) to the north of the river in the Thames valley suggest that enclosures may have existed in Kent and Surrey north of the North Downs.

The evidence available from South-East England would suggest that the fortified settlement enclosures were at the top of a hierarchical arrangement of settlement and economic activity areas. These consisted of open agricultural and riverside settlements, strand and salt marsh resource utilization camps, woodland hunting camps, flint-mining sites and surface/natural exposure flint-working sites.

Open Agricultural Settlements

Open agricultural settlements in South-East England are represented by a number of sites where storage pits have been found. All sites were found by accident or while excavating a site of a later period and preservation of these sites has been uniformly poor. None of the sites has produced any building plans, although traces of shallow gullies at Bishopstone, Sussex, could represent the last traces of structures.

The settlement at Bishopstone is situated on a chalk hilltop overlooking the English Channel in East Sussex. A series of storage pits and shallow gullies was all that survived of an extensive open agricultural settlement (Bell 1977). A detailed analysis of the contents of the pits and gullies enables us to determine a basic range of activities which took place on an open, agricultural settlement. The presence of tree holes, polished and flaked axes and a range of charcoals including oak, hazel, ash, hawthorn and yew indicate initial land clearance of a woodland environment. This clearance is also attested by the molluscan evidence. Having cleared the land, the excavation with antler picks of irregular gullies suggests the construction of huts which have not survived later agricultural denudation.

The contents of the pits indicate both food production and craft activities. Carbonized grain including emmer wheat and six-row barley formed the basic evidence for crop production. The antler picks and flint-chopping tools could, however, have been used for breaking up the surface of fields, slight evidence for which survived in the form of a field boundary ditch under a later lynchet. The serrated blades may have been used to harvest the cereals. Bones of cattle, pig, sheep and/or goats indicate animal husbandry. Such animals would provide milk, hides and skins as well as meat. It must not, however, be assumed that farming was the only, or necessarily the main, form of food procurement by the earliest farming communities. Hunting and collecting wild food continued extensively. At Bishopstone marine mollusca collected included mussels, oysters, cockles and limpets, while at least the roe deer was hunted, perhaps using the several leaf-shaped arrowheads found.

Craft activities at Bishopstone included the manufacture of flint tools as evidenced by the presence of cores, waste flakes and tools broken in the process of manufacture. The pottery from Bishopstone was almost certainly made and bonfire-fired on the site, while flint awls, notched flakes and flint scrapers suggest leather and woodworking.

The excavations at New Barn Down during the 1930s, high on the Downs in West Sussex, involved the somewhat unsystematic excavation of small holes over a series of shallow depressions then visible (E. C. Curwen 1934b). Seven depressions were excavated by Curwen but the description of six of them (shallow, irregular hollows containing no artifacts) suggests tree holes. One hollow, however, turned out to be two adjacent pits containing a substantial fourth-millennium artifact assemblage.

The largest of the two pits was oval in shape 2.6 m × 1.83 m and dug 0.6 m into the chalk. The second pit was almost round with a diameter of 1.22 m but only dug 0.23 m into the chalk. Both pits contained a wide variety of artifacts and ecofacts indicating their secondary use as rubbish pits. As at Bishopstone, the primary use of these pits for food storage is likely. The presence of axes, knives, grinding stones and storage pits, together with animal bones and scrapers, suggests a small mixed farming agricultural settlement, perhaps growing crops and tending herds. Unfortunately, information on the whereabouts of the fields, what was being grown and what animals were being tended, was not forthcoming from New Barn Down.

Similar sites are known from Kent, but in that county most sites are riverine or coastal rather than Downland. The most extensive group of storage pits indicating the presence of an open agricultural settlement was recovered at Gravehurst near Sittingbourne in the last century (Payne 1880: 122). Although inadequately recorded, the presence of quern stones indicated cereal production while horns, skulls and other bones of *Bos* suggest animal husbandry.

Several accidentally found single storage pits from East Kent (Dunning 1966: 1) indicate the presence of many more open agricultural settlements. A pit at Wingham produced a bone pin associated with red deer antler and fragments of plain, round-based bowls. The storage pit at Nethercourt St Lawrence at Ramsgate, which contained marine shells, was later re-used as a burial pit (Dunning 1966: 1).

Strand and Salt Marsh Resource Utilization Camps

The utilization of strand resources, particularly the collection of shell fish, was clearly undertaken from both fortified settlement enclosures (e.g. Whitehawk) and open agricultural settlements (e.g. Bishopstone). Both these sites are, however, very close to marine resources. For sites further away, the establishment of temporary camps for the utilization of strand and salt marsh resources appears probable. Such sites are likely to prove both difficult to locate and particularly difficult to date. They will almost certainly have to be defined from specialized flint assemblages.

One such assemblage was excavated by Owen Bedwin at Chidham where it was being eroded out of a low cliff edge into Chichester Harbour. The flint assemblage is probably fourth millennium in date because of the presence of three incomplete leaf-shaped arrowheads (Bedwin 1980). The most peculiar aspect of the assemblage is the astonishingly high number of implements which could be used as scrapers. These included many hollow scrapers and notched flakes. Clearly this assemblage represents some specialized activity, perhaps the preparation of osiers to be plaited into wicker fish traps or the manufacture of arrowshafts and spears for fishing and fowling. Careful search along the foreshore of North Kent may produce similar flint assemblages, although most may have been submerged through marine transgression as the Neolithic sea level was as much as 7 m lower than the modern sea level. (Evans 1953: 128).

Woodland Hunting Camps

The distribution of polished stone axes high up into the Weald suggests utilization of the Wealden forest resources. Although the concentration of such axes along the river valleys suggests some forest clearance, perhaps for open agricultural settlements, there is no evidence for forest clearance in the High Weald. Pollen analysis from High Rocks, for example, shows continuous forest cover throughout the fourth millennium. The large numbers of casual finds of leaf-shaped arrowheads from the High Weald clearly indicates the use of the Wealden Forest. Curwen, for example, lists 147 leaf-shaped arrowheads from the High Weald (E. Curwen 1936).

Whether the Weald was being used simply for hunting or also for feeding herds of pigs, some temporary woodland hunting or pasturing camps are likely. Only one excavated and independently dated camp site can be dated to the fourth millennium BC. This is the re-use of a rock shelter first occupied by hunter-gatherers in the fifth millennium at High Rocks (Money 1960). A thermoluminescence date of 3324 ± 375 BC was obtained from a Fabric I sherd from an Early Neolithic round-based bowl. The fourth-millennium activity at High Rocks consists only of a few flint implements and pottery sherds, no features being located. The fourth-millennium implements consisted of two leaf-shaped arrowheads and a bifacially worked scraper. The evidence from High Rocks, where the assemblage lacks even evidence of flint working, suggests simply a hunters' camp site, perhaps occupied only for single nights. The presence of pottery is, however, of considerable interest as it does suggest either the transport of food into the woodland environment and possibly its preparation and cooking.

Riverside Settlements

The fact that most of the long barrows and megalithic monuments in South-East England overlook the flood plains of the main river valleys suggests intense utilization of the rich river valley sediments. Later sedimentation has largely masked all traces of any settlements in these river valleys. A few sites have, however, been located in the Middle Thames Valley, both in Surrey and Middlesex. Sherds from round-based bowls have been found in riverine deposits at Kingston and Wisley in Surrey and north of the Thames at Twickenham and Brentford High Street. The most important site is, however, the one discovered during the construction of a new Thames Bridge at Runnymede (Longley 1980). This site produced evidence for a branch platform associated with round-based pottery, flintwork and two polished stone axes. The exceptional preservation of the pottery enabled a detailed study of food residues to be undertaken by Mr J. Evans. He found traces of fish residues, salt and protein suggesting salted meat, pork fat and beeswax. The exact nature of these riverside settlements is unclear. They may have been specialized seasonal camps, occupied only intermittently and linked to open agricultural settlements on adjacent higher land or, with a lower sea level, they may have formed the main mixed farming settlements.

Flint Mines

Mining was clearly an integral part of the activities of the earliest farming communities, both in Britain and North-West Europe. The need for the extensive clearance of forest for agriculture, together with the construction of monumental timber structures in long barrows, required a continuous supply of sound flint axes. As the Sussex flint mines are the earliest in Britain, Church Hill Findon and Blackpatch north of Worthing both having dates prior to 4000 BC, it has long been assumed that the idea of flint mining, if not the miners themselves, crossed the Channel with the first introduction of farming economies.

It is only in areas of dense occupation where the chalk is relatively soft and the all-important floorstone is at a reasonable depth that we find flint being mined. The three areas in Britain that conform to these three criteria are Central Wessex, Norfolk and Sussex. Kent and Surrey do not appear to have any adequately dated flint mines. Possible examples at East Horsley and Farnham in Surrey are unlikely to be prehistoric (Jessup 1970: 74) while the many shafts claimed in Kent appear to be dene-holes dug for marling fields mainly in the post-Medieval period.

The earliest excavations of flint mines were those undertaken by Colonel A. H. Lane-Fox at Cissbury in September 1867 (Lane-Fox 1869). At least 97 shafts were originally dug at Cissbury, although others may be buried under the first-millennium ramparts. Cissbury is therefore the second largest mining complex in Sussex, Harrow Hill having some 160 shafts. Unlike previous excavators at Cissbury who interpreted the hollows left by the mine shafts as cattle pens, Lane-Fox arrived at the right conclusion as to the function of the pits. 'For what use then were they formed?' he asks in his 1869 report. He replied, 'I am inclined to think for the purpose of obtaining flint.'

The next group of mines to be excavated were those on Stoke Down, 3½ miles north-west of Chichester. These mines were discovered by Major A. G. Wade in 1910 and he excavated three shafts during the next three years (Wade 1924). The first shaft excavated, described in the excavation report as 'Wellington boot shaped', was some 4 m in diameter and 5 m deep. The second shaft was smaller, being only 3 m in diameter and depth. This shaft produced a greensand saddle quern. The third shaft excavated was oval in shape and some 4.5 m deep.

In 1919 Mr C. H. Goodman discovered the flint mines at Blackpatch, north-west of Worthing. Excavations began in 1922 under the supervision of Mr J. H. Pull. The excavation of Shaft 1 was fully published (Goodman 1924). Shaft 1 has the layout of a classic mine shaft with radiating side tunnels. It was roughly circular, 6 m in diameter and nearly 4 m deep with vertical sides and seven galleries radiating out from its base. During the 10 years following the excavation of Shaft 1, a further seven shafts were excavated at Blackpatch, together with four flaking floors and twelve later round barrows (Pull 1932).

Perhaps the most important of the Sussex flint mine excavations were those undertaken at Harrow Hill (Fig. 2.5) by the Curwens in 1924–25 (Curwen and Curwen 1926), Mr Holleyman in 1936 (Holleyman, 1937) Gale Sieveking in 1982 and Robin Holgate in 1986. Harrow Hill is in the extreme

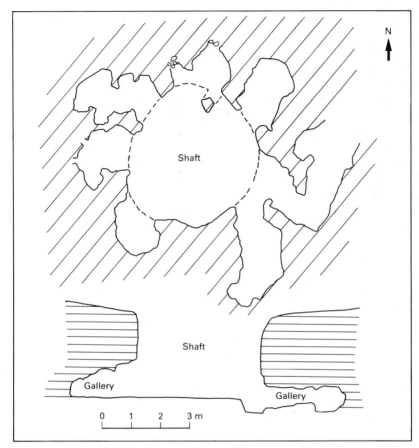

Figure 2.5 Plan of flint-mining shaft and side galleries at Harrow Hill, West Sussex. Section of shaft below.

north of the parish of Angmering, six miles north-west of Worthing and four miles west of the mines at Cissbury. At least 160 mine shafts can be seen on this hill. In 1924, Pit 21 was selected for excavation. The shaft proved to be roughly oval in plan and some 7 m deep. Five side galleries led off the main shaft, linking this pit with adjacent pits. Three further pits were excavated by Mr Holleyman in 1936 and one more by Mr Sieveking in 1982. During excavations in 1986 Mr Holgate located shallow open-cast flint mining and an extensive flint-working floor. (Plate 2.4).

The hollows on Bow Hill in West Sussex look superficially like flint mines, but they are clearly dug into a double-lynchet trackway and so must postdate its use. Excavations in 1933 produced no conclusive evidence as to the nature of these pits. It is most likely that they are quarries either for flint or chalk, but their relation to the double-lynchet trackway suggests a possible post-Roman date (Hamilton 1933).

Plate 2.4 The partly infilled remains of a side gallery at the Neolithic flint mines on Harrow Hill, West Sussex. (Photograph: R. Holgate.)

The only known group of flint mines in East Sussex is that on Windover Hill. Although recognized by E. C. Curwen as mines (E. C. Curwen 1928), no excavation was undertaken until 1971, when Mr E. Holden trenched one shaft in an attempt to collect flint samples for the British Museum's research programme examining trace elements in flint. Although the excavation only sampled the top of the shaft, some 3 ft, it confirmed Curwen's interpretation of the site (Holden 1974).

The discovery of a single mine shaft on Slonk Hill (Hartridge 1978) suggests the possibility that many more single shafts await discovery. It is also possible that open-cast cliff-face mining was practised. It is interesting to note that the only group of mines in East Sussex east of Whitehawk is in the most northerly position on Windover Hill, some six miles from any coastal flint. In addition to deliberate mining or open-cast cliff working, there is strong evidence from several sites that ditches dug for other purposes, for example around barrows or causewayed enclosures, were systematically worked for flint in the same way as flint mines. Likewise there is the problem of how widely surface flint was utilized, a point which we will return to below.

The extensive mining of flint would suggest the production of more implements than required by the individual miner for his own use. The probability therefore exists that some at least of the products from the mines were distributed out of their area of production. For many years stone axes have been thin sectioned and the source of the stone identified by comparison with rocks of known source. Such petrological examination of flint was for long considered fruitless, as it was believed that the stone consists simply of silica and water with a crystalline structure which can vary, even within the same nodule.

Recently published work by the British Museum Research Laboratory has, however, offered a more promising approach by considering the presence of trace elements in flint (Sieveking *et al.* 1970). Up to twenty trace elements have been recognized in flint by emission spectroscopic analysis. The British Museum is in the process of analysing a random sample of 8,000 or so known Neolithic flint axes in museum collections. Only on the completion of this work will it be certain whether flint axes were distributed locally, nationally or, indeed as in the case of some stone axes, internationally. Currently available results do, however, suggest distribution at least as far as Central Wessex with South Downs axes appearing in fourth-millenium contexts at Windmill Hill and Maiden Castle. Work by Ferguson (1980), however, suggests that it may be over-optimistic to expect that trace-element analysis will enable us to identify the products of specific mines on the South Downs.

Surface/natural Exposure Flint-Working Sites

Flint mining was apparently concentrated in small areas on the South Downs, so elsewhere in South-East England surface flint or natural outcrops were no doubt utilized. Coastal flint in Kent and East Sussex would have been a ready source of flint but erosion of the coastline since the fourth millennium BC has, however, removed all traces of such activity.

The use of surface flint is shown by the many concentrations of waste flakes on the chalklands of Kent and Sussex. Only one adequately excavated site of this type has, however, been shown to be fourth millennium in date. The larger flint concentrations that have been studied in detail appear to be third millennium in date (e.g. Bullock Down, see Ch. 3). The main problem appears to be how to date surface concentrations of waste material without the location of pottery excavation.

The excavation of a late third-millennium settlement at Belle Tout by Richard Bradley (1970) produced a specialized fourth-millennium flint assemblage reconsidered by Bradley as representing a 'quarry' or surface flint-working site, perhaps producing a specialist range of flint tools (Bradley in Drewett 1982). Associated with the flint assemblage were sherds from round-based carinated bowls. The flint assemblage is somewhat confused by the late third-millennium assemblage on the same site. The certain element of the assemblage consisted of 24 arrowheads, 18 of which were broken or unfinished, and 3 possibly made as blanks, 5 flint picks, serrated flakes, end scrapers and axe fragments. Associated with these was waste material characterized by a narrow-flake technology and narrow-flake cores.

Long and Oval Barrows

Barrows of pre-3000 BC appear to be of two types, long barrows (defined as mounds longer than twice their width) and oval mounds (defined as mounds shorter than twice their width). Although round barrows are clearly constructed prior to 3000 BC elsewhere (Kinnes 1979) the only possible examples from the South-East are somewhat doubtful. These consist of three possible ring ditches from Kent and Barrow 3 at the Blackpatch flint mines (Pull 1932: 69–70). This mound was not systematically excavated (e.g. see Pull 1932: Plate 15) and from the description may have been a crouched burial in the upcast from a mine shaft rather than a specifically constructed mound. The implements 'surrounding' the skeleton and used to date it (Kinnes 1979) are all of the type made at the flint mines and may or may not have been deliberately buried with it. Poorly excavated and recorded data of this type may well only confuse the picture, so until adequately excavated and dated evidence is forthcoming, the possibility of round barrows prior to 3000 BC in South-East England can be taken no further.

Little systematic excavation work has been undertaken on the long barrows in South-East England. An excavation at Long Burgh in 1767 produced a 'skeleton and an urn' (Horsfield 1824). The description suggests this was a secondary burial, as complete urns are unknown with burials prior to 3000 BC (Ashbee 1970). Unfortunately the urn cannot now be traced. In 1980 a single trench was excavated by the author over the ditch of Bevis's Thumb, Sussex, in an attempt to date the mound without damaging the unploughed mound itself.

The long barrow at Bevis's Thumb, high on the Downs north of Chichester, is one of the longest in South-East England, being 70 m in length. A single trench 1 m wide was excavated across the western end of the southern flanking ditch. The ditch was 1.42 m deep and appears to have silted in naturally. The primary silts of chalk rubble probably accumulated rapidly after the excavation of the ditch. No artifacts were found in these layers. Immediately above the primary silts was a 'rubbish' layer of dark, charcoal-rich soil. The charcoal, consisting of hazel and hawthorn, was dated to 2595 ± 95 bc which may be calibrated to *c.* 3400 BC (Drewett 1981).

More extensive excavations were undertaken on the only known long

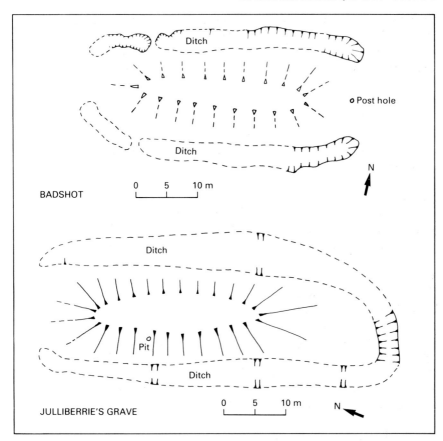

Figure 2.6 Reconstructed plans of Neolithic earthen long barrows at Badshot, Surrey (top) and Julliberrie's Grave, Chilham, Kent (bottom). Both had been partly destroyed by quarrying prior to being recorded.

barrow in Surrey at Badshot, and at Julliberrie's Grave at Chilham in Kent, one of only three known earthen long barrows in Kent (Fig. 2.6).

The Badshot long barrow is situated on the North Downs, some two miles east of Farnham. Unfortunately, most of the site had been quarried away prior to limited excavations by Alexander Keiller and Stuart Piggott in 1936 (Keiller and Piggott 1939). The excavators located two flanking ditches, suggesting a barrow originally over 50 m long. The only other feature located was a single post-hole, centrally placed in the earthen causeway. The ditches produced sherds of round-based bowls and, among the flint assemblage, two leaf-shaped arrowheads and part of a polished stone axe. Without a Carbon-14 date this material suggests a date prior to 3000 BC for the construction of the barrows. However, sherds of Peterborough Ware indicate continued use into the third millennium BC.

Overlooking the Stour Valley in East Kent is a small group of three earthen long barrows. Only one, at Julliberrie's Grave, has been excavated. Unfortunately the northern end of the barrow has been lost into a chalk pit, but originally it must have been some 50 m long. Excavations in 1933–38 located several previous excavations and a small Roman cemetery, all indicating later disturbance of the site. The original mound appears to have had flanking ditches joined around the southern end. As at Bevis's Thumb and Badshot, the ditches silted in naturally, without any attempt being made to keep them clean. A single pit was located under the mound but this contained only a few worked flints. The only dating evidence consisted of a broken, but finely made, polished flint axe from the inner turf core of the barrow and two small sherds, probably from round-based bowls from the primary ditch silts.

Turning now to the excavated oval mounds, the smallest known example, that at Alfriston, Sussex, was totally excavated and the two oval mounds at Stoughton together with one at North Marden were sampled by the author. The false-crested oval mound at Alfriston overlooks the Cuckmere Valley and has extensive views into the High Weald. Unfortunately, ploughing over the last twenty years has largely removed the surviving remains of the mound, so that when excavated in 1974 (Drewett 1975*a*) it consisted largely of a preserved rise in the chalk. The extent of the surviving old land surface, some 14.5 m long and 5.5 m wide, however, gave some indication of the original extent of the mound. From this surface came fragments of sheep bone and antler picks, together with hawthorn and birch charcoal. Both of these species suggest open scrub resulting from forest clearance and agricultural activities. This confirms the molluscan evidence discussed earlier (Fig. 2.7).

The actual mound appears to have been a simple dump of material derived partly from the flanking ditches and partly from a certain amount of scarping on the eastern side of the mound. We do know, however, that prior to recent ploughing the mound was some 2 m high (Grinsell 1934: 220) so originally it is likely to have been a substantial mound. Surrounding the mound were rough pit-dug ditches. These had been left to silt naturally and incorporated considerable evidence for the manufacture of flint cores, presumably for use elsewhere. In addition a group of shattered pot sherds from a round-based bowl were found on the ditch floor, together with an antler pick which gave a Carbon-14 date of 2360 ± 110 bc. If calibrated, this would suggest a date of around 3000 BC, indicating that the Alfriston mound may have been one of the last of its type constructed in South-East England. The mound covered two pits, one containing a crouched burial of a young female. She was facing east wih her head towards the north. No artifacts were associated with this burial, which in many ways foreshadows the single crouched burial rite associated with the later round barrows.

The oval barrow at North Marden, West Sussex, was extensively plough-damaged but the surviving flanking ditches indicated a barrow some 46 m long by 30 m wide (Plate 2.5). No burials were found under the site of the mound,

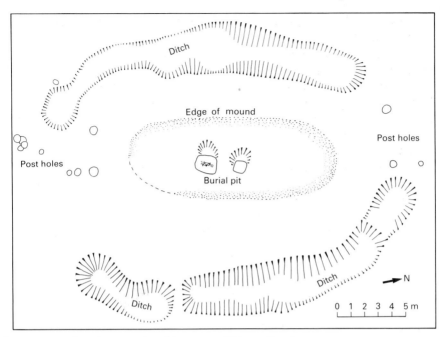

Figure 2.7   Plan of excavated oval barrow at Alfriston, East Sussex.

Plate 2.5   The excavation of a Neolithic oval barrow at North Marden on the West Sussex Downs. The two figures mark each end of the now ploughed-out mound.

Plate 2.6 A vertical section through the fill in the ditch surrounding the Neolithic oval barrow at North Marden, West Sussex.

but disarticulated human skeletal material was found in the ditches. The main flanking ditches appear to have silted in naturally with evidence of Beaker activity in the upper levels. (Plate 2.6). Some evidence of deliberate back-filling, including the burial of carved chalk objects, was found in the ditches at the east end. A Carbon-14 date of 2760 ± 110 bc suggests use of the barrow around 3400 BC (Drewett 1986).

Limited excavations at similar oval mounds at Stoughton I and Stoughton II (Curwen and Curwen 1922) were undertaken in 1980 but although indicating structural similarity, failed to provide any close dating (Drewett 1981).

Megaliths

The distinction between long and oval barrows may well be reflected in the small group of mounds incorporating large stone blocks built in the Medway

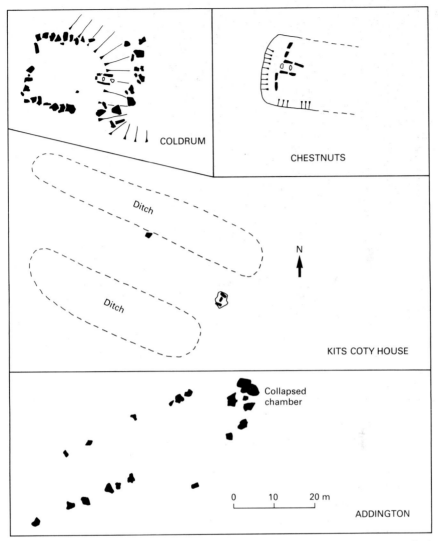

Figure 2.8   Megalithic burial chambers in the Medway Valley of Kent. 1: Coldrum stone circle; 2: Chestnuts; 3: Kits Coty House; 4: Addington (after Holgate 1981).

Valley of Kent. A recent re-analysis of these monuments by Robin Holgate (Holgate 1981) suggests that perhaps eight of the many putative megaliths are in fact deliberately constructed, with others, like those at Cobham and Blue Bell Hill being groups of natural sarsens.

The best-known monument of this group is Kits Coty House. The mound, perhaps originally over 70 m long, was revetted by a sarsen stone kerb and flanked by quarry ditches. At the east end of the mound an H-shaped

Plate 2.7 Remaining portion of the megalithic burial chamber originally buried under an earthen long barrow at Kits Coty, Kent. (Photograph: R. Holgate.)

sarsen stone setting probably represents part of a chamber originally, at least partly, within a chalk rubble mound. A sample excavation in 1956 located the southern ditch but produced no dating evidence (McCrerie 1956). The few artifacts loosely related to the barrow include 'rude pottery found under the monument' recorded by Thomas Wright in 1854 and sherds of Later Neolithic and Beaker pottery found in the surrounding ploughed fields (Cook 1936). This material, however, suggests later use as structurally Kits Coty was almost certainly constructed between 4300 and 3000 BC (Plate 2.7).

South of Kits Coty a jumbled heap of some twenty stones, referred to as the Countless Stones or Lower Kits Coty House, probably represents a sarsen stone chamber. This was possibly set in a small oval or sub-rectangular mound revetted by a stone kerb.

In addition to the two Kits Coty megaliths there are at least three other probable megaliths on the east side of the River Medway forming a tight group north-west of Aylesford. These consist of the Coffin Stone, Smythe's Megalith and the Upper White Horse Stone. All could be natural sarsen stones, perhaps moved for agricultural reasons, but as both the Coffin Stone and Smythe's

Megalith have produced human skeletal material, this is unlikely (Jessup 1970).

The group of three megaliths to the west of the River Medway survive better, and have been more extensively investigated than those to the east of the river. John Alexander's excavations at the Chestnuts Megalith located a rectangular sarsen stone chamber and facade set in the east end of a sand mound. No traces of quarry ditches or a revetment were located. This would suggest the probability of a turf structure, particularly with turf revetting the sand mound. Excavations, both in the forecourt and within the chamber, produced sherds of plain round-based bowls together with Peterborough and Beaker pottery. This again would suggest construction prior to 3000 BC but continued use well into the third millennium BC. The disturbed remains of at least ten individuals were located, including nine adults and possibly two children (Alexander 1961).

The Chestnuts barrow (Plate 2.8) is situated adjacent to the very much larger Addington Long Barrow which may originally have had a mound over 60 m long, revetted by a kerb of large sarsen stones. At the north-east end lie the remains of a sarsen stone chamber. No artifactual dating evidence has been

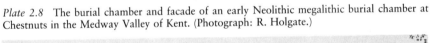

Plate 2.8 The burial chamber and facade of an early Neolithic megalithic burial chamber at Chestnuts in the Medway Valley of Kent. (Photograph: R. Holgate.)

found but in 1845 a local parson, L. B. Larking, recovered pieces of 'rough pottery' from the chamber (Jessup 1970).

To the north of the Addington barrow is the well-preserved megalith at Coldrum. This consisted of a rectangular sarsen-revetted mound with a chamber set in the east end. Excavations in the 1920s cleared the chamber and located the remains of twenty-two individuals, mixed in age and sex. The associated 'rude pottery' has unfortunately not survived (Bennett 1913).

Social Organization

At the top of the hierarchy of sites of the period 4300–3000 BC are the fortified settlement enclosures. These are mixed farming settlements utilizing a wide range of natural resources. Their construction would have involved large numbers of people, many of whom may have then lived in the enclosure, but others may have lived in the second-tier settlements, the open agricultural settlements. If this were so, the fortified settlement enclosures may have fulfilled the function of a 'central place' offering protection, redistribution and meeting facilities to the outlying open settlements.

The utilization of flint resources was probably undertaken on a daily but seasonal basis from both types of settlement, although the large-scale activity of flint mining, involving a greater labour input, is more likely to have been undertaken from the fortified settlement enclosures, with their larger population, than from the open agricultural settlements. The everyday flint needs on the open agricultural settlements are more likely to have been provided by the surface flint working sites which could be utilized with minimum labour.

The utilization of resources away from the settlement sites would have involved the establishment of temporary, and presumably seasonal, marsh and woodland camps. Such camps were probably used during slack periods in the agricultural cycle.

This integrated system, based on a hierarchy of sites, would provide total self-sufficiency in economic terms. The agricultural system was fully supported by a complementary system of wild-food collection and natural-resource use. Contact with an adjacent system appears unnecessary in strictly economic terms. However, the presence of non-local stone axes in South-East England and the movement of flint axes out of Sussex shows that inter-regional exchange, and therefore contact, did take place. The economic evidence suggests, however, that such contact may have been of a social or ceremonial nature rather than economic. Explanations for inter-regional exchange in terms of bride-wealth, gift exchange and the acquisition of status appear more likely than the need to acquire axes to fell trees.

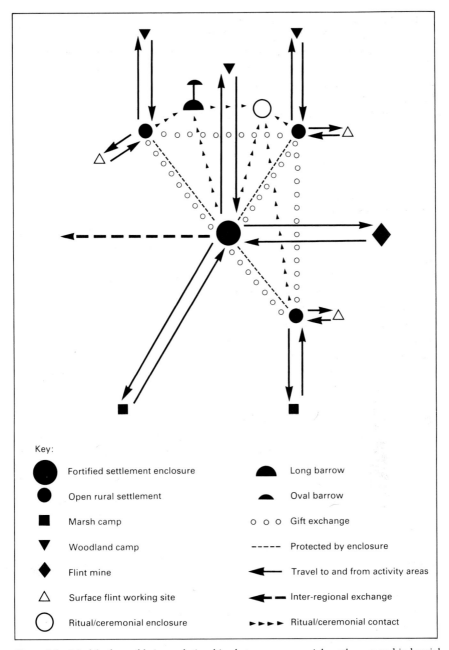

Figure 2.9 Model of possible interrelationships between ceremonial, settlement and industrial sites of the earliest farming communities in South-East England (Neolithic).

Integrated with the economic sites are ritual or ceremonial sites, consisting of enclosures, long and oval barrows, some containing stone settings. Burials are present at all these sites, but burial should perhaps be considered secondary to a more wide-ranging religious use of such sites.

From this hierarchy of sites it is possible to suggest a variety of social roles required for the working of such a system. At the top of the social hierarchy there is likely to be a group or individual responsible for the construction, organization and defence of the fortified settlement enclosure. This suggests a leadership. This may have been an individual or group with hereditary or acquired power or status. Ethnographically, this would be within the range of Elders, Bigmen and Chiefs. It should be borne in mind, however, that complex village construction can be undertaken without any leadership other than ever-changing activity leadership. The Nuer, for example, show a complex but leaderless society (Evans-Pritchard 1940).

The fact that the fortified settlement enclosures could only be efficiently protected if some group was available to protect them would suggest that in order to organize the protection group, some form of permanent leadership was required. Even if the protection group was not permanent, some individual or group would require sufficient power or status to be able to summon a protection group when required. The protection group is likely to be composed of those most suited to the physical demands of such a role. Physical protection usually rests with younger men who may, or may not, form themselves into a discrete 'warrior'class.

The mainstream economic life of most pre-literate societies rests with the food providers and craftsmen. In the context of the period 4300–3000 BC these would have consisted of farmers, herders, fishermen/strandloopers, flint miners, potters, weavers, toolmakers and builders. There is no evidence that any of these activities involved specialists, although individuals no doubt became known as experts in specific area of food production or craftsmanship.

The existence of specialized ceremonial-ritual sites (the enclosures, long and oval mounds) suggests the possibility of ritual specialists. However, once again these may not have been permanent specialists. The role of ceremonial-ritual specialists may well have been combined with the secular leadership suggested earlier, or may have rested with individual farmer-craftsmen with an acquired or hereditary reputation for ceremonial-ritual knowledge and powers.

Chapter 3

Farming Communities, *c.* 3000–1400 BC

The domination of the economic system by the fortified settlement enclosures appears to come to an end around 3000 BC. The following 1,600 years is a period of rapid change in pottery styles, tool types, ceremonial and ritual structures, particularly those associated with burial. The cultural traits, evidence for which survives from the period 3000–1400 BC, show clear signs of indigenous development from the fourth millennium, but with increasing contact with adjacent areas enabling the introduction of new technological processes and tool types (Fig. 3.1).

Material Culture

As with the preceding period, the bulk of surviving material culture consists of flint and stone tools, and pottery. In addition, however, we see the introduction of bronze and rare non-local artifacts of lignite, shale, faience and amber. It is probable that gold was also used in small quantities, but the datable objects from South-East England appear to post-date 1400 BC (Taylor 1980).

The range of lithic tools manufactured increases after 3000 BC although the definable tool kits remain similar to the range present in the previous period. Woodcutting tools consisted of flaked axes, polished flint axes and polished stone axes (Woodcock *et al.* undated). The range of arrowheads for killing small animals increased significantly after 3000 BC. It is uncertain for how long into the period leaf-shaped arrowheads were manufactured. Two types, one flaked all over and one flaked only on the edge and tip, were probably still being manufactured but transverse arrowheads, oblique arrowheads and barbed-and-tanged arrowheads became the characteristic types.

Tools used for food preparation and preparing skins include at least eleven types of scraper and three varieties of knife. Scrapers were manufac-

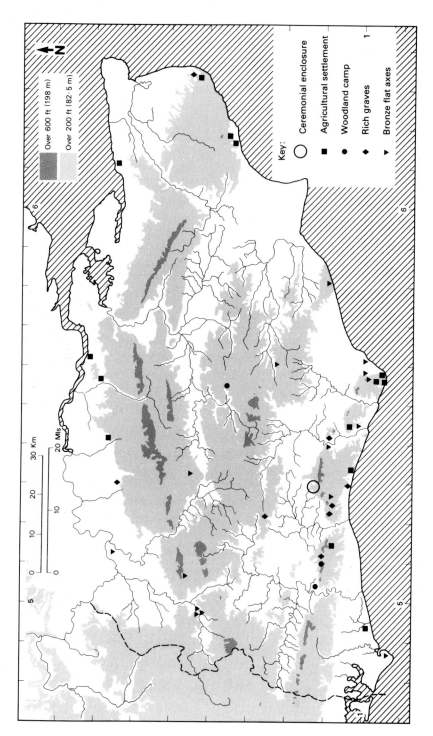

Key:

○	Ceremonial enclosure	
■	Agricultural settlement	
●	Woodland camp	
◆	Rich graves	
▶	Bronze flat axes	

Over 600 ft (198 m)

Over 200 ft (82·5 m)

Figure 3.1   Settlement sites, flat bronze axes and possible ceremonial enclosure (Wolstonbury) of the period 3000–1400 BC in South-East England.

tured in practically every possible form, including end scrapers, side scrapers, disc scrapers, hollow scrapers, end and side scrapers, double-end scrapers and, increasingly, scraper edges chipped on irregular flakes. Cutting tools consisted of flaked discoidal knives, backed knives and plano-convex knives. Some of the discoidal knives have polished cutting edges. Hammerstones and flaked rods of flint or 'fabricators' may have been used for making fire, but equally well could have been used in the manufacture of other lithic tools.

Many of the scraper and knife types could also have been used for working bone and wood. Specialist wood and boneworking tools included notched flakes, awls, burins and serrated flakes. Heavy flint picks were probably used to break up the land prior to agriculture. Less common types include the heavy flint points (laurel leaves), flint daggers and perforated stone tools. The daggers and perforated stone tools, including 'mace heads' and 'battle axes', probably represent prestige rather than functional tools, and so replace the non-functional stone axes of the preceding period for gift and ceremonial exchange.

No settlement sites in South-East England of the period 3000–1400 BC have produced any bronze artifacts. Indeed, only two pieces have any independent dating associations. Both of these come from the very end of the period. The Hove Barrow (E. C. Curwen 1954) produced a bronze dagger associated with a carbon-14 date of 1239 ± 46 bc, suggesting a date about 1500 BC. A simple bronze finger ring was found in a Secondary Series Collared Urn at Oxteddle Bottom, near Lewes (Curwen 1954). Typologically the earliest bronze objects from South-East England are the flat bronze axes (Burgess 1980) but all except one of these have been found as stray finds. A single bronze flat axe was found together with two bronze daggers, associated with two crouched burials at Aylesford, Kent, at the end of the nineteenth century (James 1899). It is uncertain how early bronze flat axes arrive in South-East England. The earliest dated example from Southern England comes from the ditch around the henge monument at Marden in Dorset (Wainwright 1979). This was probably deposited in the century prior to 1500 bc, indicating a calendar date of about 2000–1720 BC.

In addition to the flat axes, flat daggers and simple finger rings, a scatter of bronze awls and pins can also be dated to before 1400 BC. Although the axes, daggers and awls are all tool types, the exceedingly low density of bronze, coupled with the fact that several of the tools are in mint condition, suggesting little or no use, perhaps indicates their use as prestige items rather than everyday tools.

There are, unfortunately, no large, stratigraphically associated assemblages of pottery from South-East England dating to the period 3000–1400 BC. Most of the pottery consists of single pots from barrows, isolated sherds or small, loosely associated groups from settlements. The dating of this material must therefore rely on associations elsewhere in Southern England. All the pottery types current during the period 3000–1400 BC are present throughout

Southern England, suggesting many overlapping pottery distribution centres and redistribution networks.

The earliest group of pottery derives directly from the round-based traditions of the previous period. These are the Peterborough Style pots. The Peterborough tradition has been divided into three distinctive styles, Ebbsfleet, Mortlake and Fengate (Piggott 1962). The Ebbsfleet Style consists of round-based necked bowls, some with a marked carination. The rims are usually simple in form, and the fabric is often fine with well-ground flint grit. The walls of the pots are thin, with decoration concentrated on the upper part of the pot. The decoration is usually finely incised lattice work, twisted or whipped cord impressions. Pits made by impressing the fingertip into the neck of the pot before firing are frequent.

The type assemblage of this style comes from the bed of the Ebbsfleet at Northfleet in Kent, and was found under a peaty alluvium which immediately overlay a grey, sandy silt. The pottery from this silt included necked pots with incised lattice decoration, round impressions, fingernail impressions and diagonal parallel grooves. In addition there were several sherds of plain Ebbsfleet Ware (Burchell and Piggott 1939). Ebbsfleet Ware is found throughout the South-East, although rarely in large quantities. A few sherds were found at Baston Manor, Kent (Smith in Philp 1973), a single pot from Selmeston, Sussex (Drewett 1976) and small groups in secondary contexts at Whitehawk and Combe Hill, both in Sussex.

Overlapping with the Ebbsfleet Style is the Mortlake Style, with its type name derived from the discovery of several bowls from the River Thames. Mortlake bowls continue to be round-based, but their thick walls are tempered with very coarse flint grit. The rim forms became more complex with an often extensively decorated internal bevel. Often the complete outer surface of the pot is decorated. Whipped or twisted cord impressions are characteristically laid out in a herringbone pattern. Coarse finger impressed decorations are common, together with impressions of bird bones. Mortlake Ware is concentrated in the northern half of the region, with sites like Baston Manor producing 23 sherds (Smith in Philp 1973). It is, however, found down to the South Coast, with several sherds coming from Bullock Down above Beachy Head in East Sussex (Drewett 1982).

Associated with Mortlake sherds, both at Baston Manor and Bullock Down, were sherds of the third Peterborough Style, the Fengate Style. This style is characterized by a developed rim, developing into a collar, with a sub-conical body and a flat base. Although earlier decorative styles continue, finger-pinched and fingernail decoration dominated the body, while impressed cord decoration is common on the collar. These overlapping styles dominate the period *c.* 3000–2500 BC (Fig. 3.2).

Overlapping the latter end of the series, a new type of pottery, Grooved Ware, appears in many areas of Britain. This thick-walled, grog-tempered pottery with deeply incised grooves appears hardly to have entered South-East

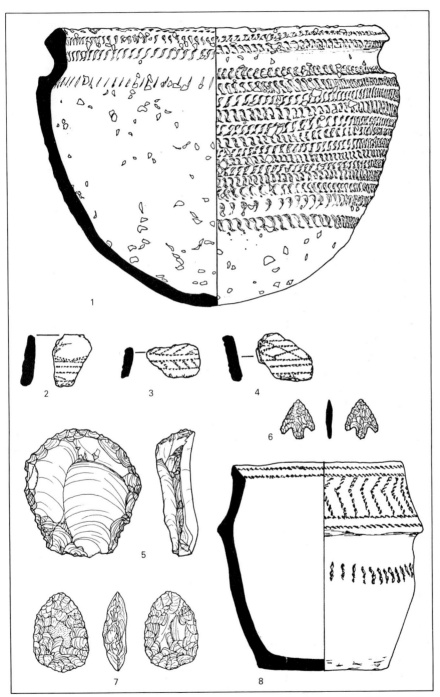

Figure 3.2 Material culture of the period 3000–1400 BC. 1: Ebbsfleet pot from Selmeston, East Sussex; 2–4: Beaker sherds from Black Patch, East Sussex; 5: Flint scraper from Bullock Down, East Sussex; 6: barbed-and-tanged arrowhead from Bullock Down; 7: laurel leaf from Chanctonbury Ring, West Sussex; 8: collared urn from Black Patch, East Sussex (scale ½).

England, with only a few sherds recorded from Snodland, Kent and Findon, West Sussex (Wainwright and Longworth 1971).

Overlapping with the Peterborough Tradition and the Grooved Wares are the initially intrusive Beakers, which in three main phases span most of the period 3000–1400 BC (Case 1977). The Early Phase Beakers are decorated with all-over-cord impressions. Dutch radiocarbon dates suggest very early dates back to 3000 BC. In Britain the earliest dates come from Skendleby in Yorkshire, where two associated dates of 2460 ± 150 bc and 2370 ± 150 bc suggest calendar dates of about 3000 BC. Little of this very early Beaker material is present in South-East England, the only two recorded examples coming from Mortlake in Surrey (Clarke 1970). These Thames valley find spots may suggest the primary introduction of Beakers into the South-East along the Thames valley.

The Middle Phase Beakers are thought to be associated with the arrival of settlers from Northern Europe. New beaker types appear around 2500 BC. These start with the arrival of the finely made and decorated European Bell Beaker, closely followed by rapidly evolving styles, changing both in Britain and Northern Europe. In South-East England, European Bell Beakers are known only from Kent, with examples from Barham, Highstead and Maidstone (Clarke 1970). By about 2000 BC the developed Middle Phase beakers, particularly the Barbed Wire and East Anglian Styles, are common over the whole of South-East England. East Anglian Style Beakers, for example, are known from Kew in Surrey, Cissbury, Shoreham and Kingston Buci in Sussex, and more than eleven sites in Kent, including Barham, Bromley, Dover, Erith and Ightham.

The Late Beaker Phase sees an insular persistence of Beakers well after their manufacture had ceased in Europe. Four developed styles have been suggested for Southern England, with examples known from Brendly and Folkestone in Kent, Kew and Mortlake in Surrey and at least five from Sussex, including Brighton, Sompting and Telscombe (Clarke 1970).

Overlapping with the Middle Phase Beakers and contemporary with the Late Phase Beakers are the Collared Urns which perhaps derive from the Peterborough tradition with Beaker influence. The characteristic features of a Collared Urn are the collar, a simple pointed or flattened rim, and a narrow base. The fabric is generally smooth, with grog being the usual filler. The collar is the main decorative zone with whipped cord, twisted cord and incised motifs most common. The Collared Urns have been divided into two overlapping series, the Primary Series (Longworth 1961) and the Secondary Series (Longworth 1970). Primary Series Collared Urns are thinly scattered over South-East England with examples from Stodmarsh and Sumner Hill in Kent, Coome Warren and Haslemere in Surrey and Lewes, Hassocks and Westbourne in Sussex. Secondary Series Collared Urns are more common, particularly the South-Eastern style with its rows of loops or 'horseshoes' in cord impression on the shoulder of tripartite urns.

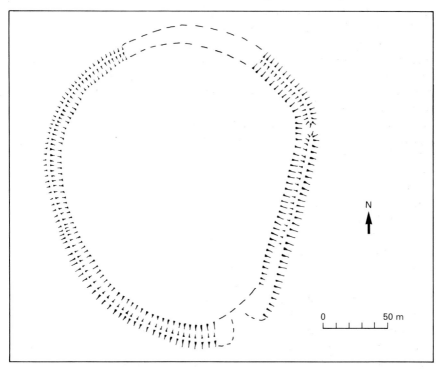

Figure 3.3 The enclosure at Wolstonbury Hill, Sussex has an internal ditch. This, together with the discovery of a sherd of Food Vessel from the bottom of the ditch, indicates it may be a ceremonial enclosure of the 'henge' type (after E. C. Curwen 1930).

Overlapping with the earlier Collared Urns, and probably derived from the Grooved Ware Tradition, are the Wessex Biconical Urns. Although rare in South-East England, five are known from Sussex (South Heighton, Charmondean, Telscombe Tye and two from Alfriston). One of the Alfriston urns has relief horseshoe decoration which is considered a Wiltshire variant (Ellison 1980). Wessex Biconical Urns also appear further west in Kent with examples from Ringwould and Capel-le-Ferne (Ashbee and Dunning 1960).

Often associated with the urns in a burial context in Wessex are miniature vessels. These are extremely rare in South-East England, although examples are known from the South Downs at Clayton, Lancing Down and Firle Beacon (Musson 1954).

A second rare type of pottery in South-East England are the Food Vessels, common in Northern Britain. Food Vessels probably derive from the Peterborough Tradition but are influenced by Beakers and Collared Urns. Odd examples from the South-East include those from Peppering and Belle Tout in Sussex, Deal and Ashford in Kent (Champion in Leach 1982) and Abinger Hammer, Dippenhall and Seale in Surrey (Wood and Thompson 1966).

69

The remaining surviving material culture of the period 3000–1400 BC in South-East England is minimal. Although the lithic industry suggests bone-working, no bone tools from the region can be conclusively dated to this period. Bone pins, like those from Wessex are one type that were no doubt manufactured. A few whetstones are known from this period, notably the fine, siliceous sandstone whetstone from the Hove Barrow (E. C. Curwen 1954) and a mica-schist whetstone from Rackham in West Sussex (Holden and Bradley 1975). A hard, red sandstone grinding stone (probably from the Wealden Series) was also found at Belle Tout (Bradley 1970).

Exotic non-local artifacts include faience beads from Ringwould, Kent and a faience pendant from Oxteddle Bottom, Sussex, lignite and shale beads and the famous amber cup from the Hove Barrow. Although small in quantity, most of this rich imported material comes from a small area in Central Southern Sussex. It shows clearly evidence for extensive redistribution networks stretching to the Baltic and well south into Europe.

Major Enclosures

The existence of fortified settlement enclosures in the South East in the previous millennium, together with the presence of massive earthwork enclosures (henges) in Wessex during the period 3000–1400 BC, suggested that South-East England may have had large enclosures during this period. However, only one known enclosure has any claim to belonging to this period. All others are demonstrably fourth millennium or first millennium in date, with the exception of High Down Hill, Sussex which may be late second millennium in origin.

The enclosure at Wolstonbury, Sussex encloses 2.2 ha and may have had entrances on either the north or south-eastern sides, both areas being destroyed (Fig. 3.3). The surviving bank and ditch is peculiar in that the ditch is inside the bank. It is the only known enclosure of this size in South-East England to exhibit this feature. This is, of course, characteristic of the Wessex 'henge' enclosures. Dr Curwen sectioned the ditch in two places and showed it to be a flat-bottomed ditch some 2.5 m wide and 1.80 m deep. The only sherd from the primary silts was a single rim sherd from a Food Vessel (E. C. Curwen 1930). All other layers contained first-millennium pottery. No flint tools were found during the excavation, although a 'number of small flint flakes' (exact number not recorded) was found. A perforated stone tool was found outside the enclosure. Although few conclusions can be drawn from these very small excavations, the possibility remains that Wolstonbury is of early second-millennium date. The location of the site, together with the absence of flint tools, suggests that it is possibly in the tradition of the fourth-millennium ceremonial or ritual enclosures rather than the fortified settlement enclosures.

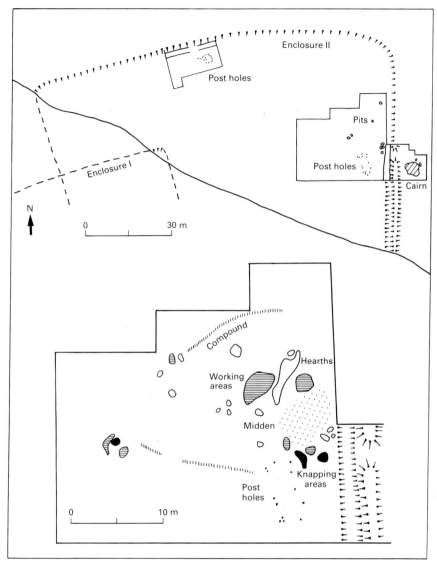

Figure 3.4   A Beaker enclosure at Belle Tout, Beachy Head, East Sussex (top) and detail of area excavated inside eastern entrance (bottom) (after Bradley in Drewett 1978).

Economic and Settlement Sites

The economic activity areas definable from these periods are of four types: small enclosed agricultural settlements; open agricultural settlements; woodland camps; and surface or natural exposure flint-working sites (including reworking flint mine dumps). The only two small enclosed agricultural settlements to have been adequately excavated are the two consecutive enclosures at Belle Tout excavated by Toms (1912) and Bradley (1970). The first enclosure was sampled by Toms in 1909 but has since been lost by coastal erosion. The second enclosure was 120 m by at least 60 m, with an internal ditch and an entrance on the eastern side. Two large areas within this enclosure were excavated by Richard Bradley during 1968–69 (Bradley 1970). Since that report, the site has been extensively reconsidered (Bradley in Drewett 1982).

The most important result of this reconsideration was to invert the major two-phase sequence at Belle Tout (Fig. 3.5). The original analysis of the pottery suggested an early phase, defined by all-over-corded Beakers, followed by a later phase defined by beakers decorated with comb impressions, fingernail impressions and plastic rustication. In fact the Late Beakers were associated with a few sherds of Grooved Ware (Bradley 1970: Figs 13, 38 and 40) originally mistaken for Beaker. This phase overlaps with a second phase characterized by sherds of Food Vessel (Bradley 1970: Figs 11 and 12, nos 2, 3, 13 and 34). There is, however, no stratigraphic distinction between these two phases, so given that Grooved Ware, Late Beakers and Food Vessels can overlap *c.* 2000–1800 BC, then a continuous development of the site is possible.

The certain structural elements belonging to the period *c.* 2000–1800 BC consist of two hut structures, Structures 1 and 5 in the original report, marked by settings of post-holes and a cluster of pits around the entrance in Area II.

From the structural and artifactual evidence at Belle Tout, it is possible to define a range of activities which took place there. The first activities relate to the construction of the site. Soil, clay-with-flints and chalk were excavated to construct the bank and ditch. Post-holes were excavated and probably the flint knives and scapers were used in hut construction. Within and around the enclosure was evidence for food production and craft activities. Evidence for crop growing survived in the form of carbonized emmer wheat and barley found in pot sherds, together with some evidence of lynchet development. As the site is on acid clay-with-flints, animal bones did not survive, but it may be presumed that animals, perhaps sheep, pigs and cattle, were kept. The presence of animals would partly explain the construction of the enclosures. The flint scrapers and knives; the grinding stone and several flint hammerstones may all have been used in food preparation. Both food and water could have been stored, either in pots or the shallow pits excavated.

Evidence for craft activities at Belle Tout is slight. Pottery was probably made on site using local clay-with-flints, while cores, waste flakes and hammerstones all indicate the manufacture of flint tools. Flint scrapers and awls perhaps hint at leather, wood and boneworking, but the acidic nature of the site has left no trace of these materials. The evidence for external exchange at Belle Tout is slight, but the presence of a Wealden Sandstone grinding stone and a shale bead suggests further trade contacts.

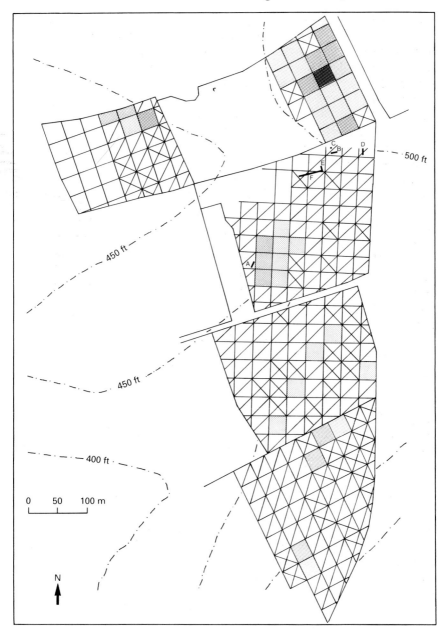

Figure 3.5 Surface scatter of flint flakes over Later Neolithic settlement site on Bullock Down, East Sussex.

From this evidence of activities it is clear that the Belle Tout enclosures could have functioned as largely self-sufficient mixed farming settlements. As such, they continue the tradition of fourth-millennium agricultural settlements. The internal ditch of the second enclosure suggests, however, that it is geared more towards stock control than defence. Such enclosures should therefore not be considered descendants of the Fortified Agricultural Settlements of the fourth millennium.

No large-scale excavations of an undamaged open agricultural settlement have been undertaken in South-East England. An extensive surface survey and trial excavation of one such site was undertaken by the author on Bullock Down (Drewett 1982). Other slightly later sites were located during dry-valley excavations at Kiln Combe (Bell in Drewett 1982) and Ashcombe Bottom (Allen 1984). Fragments of other sites were found during excavation at Itford Hill (Burstow and Holleyman 1957), Whitehawk (E. C. Curwen, 1936) and North Bersted (Bedwin and Pitts 1978) together with an accidental discovery during building work at Findon (Bedwin, 1979c). In Kent two sites, Ebbsfleet and Baston Manor, appear to be similar sites. All these sites were relatively short-lived, but together span the whole period 3000–1400 BC. Bullock Down, with its Mortlake and plain Peterborough pottery, together with Ebbsfleet (Burchell and Piggott 1939) and Baston Manor (Philp 1973) may be dated to pre 2500 BC. Itford Hill, Whitehawk, North Bersted and Kiln Combe are within the range *c.* 2400–1800 BC, while Findon is probably *c.* 1700–1400 BC.

The open agricultural settlement on Bullock Down was studied by the author as part of a multiperiod project (Fig. 3.5). This involved extensive ground and air survey coupled with sample or total excavations (Drewett 1982).

The most extensive area of third-millennium activity is centred on and around the 160 m contour at the top of the scarp slope to the east of Bullock Down Farm. The area has been well known for flint collecting for many years. Between 1976–78 most of the area of this site was walked on a 30 m grid. Limited excavations showed that artifacts, both flintwork and Mortlake Style pottery, survived in the plough soil. Unfortunately, as the site on Bullock Down was situated on acid clay-with-flints, no organic materials survived and because of the limited nature of the excavations, no features were recovered. The function of the site must therefore rest on the definition of the function of the lithic tool kits. The possibility that this site represented a surface/natural exposure flint-working site was ruled out by the many used and broken tools, few tools in the process of manufacture and considerable quantities of pottery (in relation to the very small areas excavated).

Using the lithic tool assemblage it is possible to suggest a range of activities which took place on Bullock Down. These included woodcutting, killing animals, preparing food and skins, making fire, making flint tools, wood and boneworking and possibly agriculture. Unfortunately, the use of

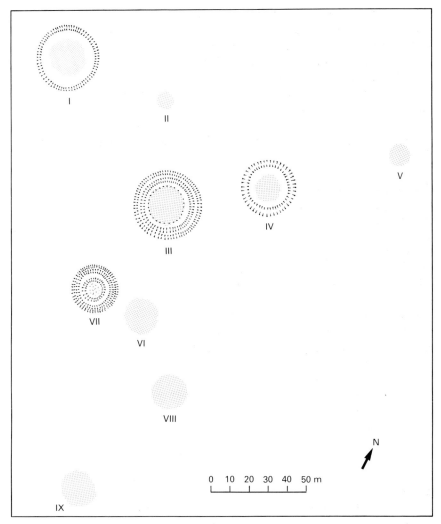

Figure 3.6 Plan of nine excavated round barrows at West Heath, Harting, West Sussex. Stippled circles are ditchless turf stacks.

flint tools in agriculture rests on the uncertain use of picks to break up the soil and the serrated blades for harvesting.

A somewhat similar site was excavated at Baston Manor, Hayes, Kent during 1964–66 (Philp 1973). Again no structural elements were located, although a concentration of burnt flint may indicate a hearth. The pottery was mainly Fengate Style but with some Mortlake, Ebbsfleet and Beaker material. The bullk of the flint assemblage was waste material indicating flint knapping on the site. The tool types consisted mainly of scrapers, knives and blades, with a possibly residual polished axe and leaf-shaped arrowhead. Although Baston Manor may have been an agricultural site the flint assemblage, with its high percentage of scrapers and knives, perhaps indicates a greater emphasis on the treatment of animal products, particularly skins.

The site at Ebbsfleet, Kent, almost certainly represents an open agricultural settlement. It is well situated at the junction of Brook Vale and the Ebbsfleet, an area well provided with water and good agricultural land. Unfortunately the excavations in 1938 were limited, but the substantial amount of Ebbsfleet pottery recovered clearly indicates more than a hunting camp (Burchell and Piggott 1939).

The evidence for open agricultural settlement at Whitehawk and Itford Hill consists of the chance finding of pits of the period *c.* 2400–1800 BC during the excavation of sites of different periods. A single pit was located at Whitehawk during the excavation of the Fortified Settlement Enclosure (Curwen 1934*a*: 106). It was a somewhat irregular pit with a lip diameter of 1.5 m tapering to 75 cm at the base and dug 1.5 m into the chalk. The pit contained Beaker pottery, a flint scraper, burnt flint and a few unidentified bones. This pit may best be interpreted as a storage pit later used for the disposal of rubbish.

A second, broadly contemporary, pit was found during the excavation of the later site at Itford Hill (Burstow and Holleyman 1957: 175). Only the base of this pit survived, the top having been removed during the construction of a later house terrace. The pit was oval (1.1 m x 0.8 m) and dug 0.33 m into the chalk. When originally dug, it would have been well over double this depth. Its secondary use was as a rubbish pit, but as with the Whitehawk pit, it may have originally been for storage. The secondary rubbish contained Beaker pottery, a Greensand grinding stone fragment, a flint hammerstone, a lower milk molar from an ox, a human left and right tibia and fragments of a human child's femur and tibia.

The third occupation site of the period *c.* 2400–1800 BC was found by accident by M. Bell while sectioning a dry valley at Kiln Combe (Bell in Drewett 1982). No features were located, but the presence of unabraded Beaker sherds, forty-three decorated with comb, fingernail, circular impressions or finger pinching, indicates the close proximity of a settlement site. Little more can be said about this site without more extensive excavation, but the significance of its location under some 2 m of hillwash is that many more such sites await detection.

Part of a small occupation site of the period *c.* 2400–1800 BC was located during the excavation of a late-first-millennium site at North Bersted on the Sussex Coastal Brickearths (Bedwin and Pitts 1978: 302–9). An area of dark soil some 6 m x 8 m was found containing Late Beaker pottery and flintwork. A total of 432 struck flints was recovered (including those from later contexts). These included barbed-and-tanged arrowheads, scrapers, notched flakes, fabricators and an awl.

The final site of the period *c.* 3000–1400 BC consists of a single pit found during building operations at Cross Lane, Findon (Bedwin 1979*c*). This pit was 1 m in diameter and dug 1 m into the underlying chalk. The contents of the pit included large quantities of ash (*Fraxinus* sp.) charcoal, charred acorns and fourteen pottery sherds. The pottery consisted of late fingernail decorated Beaker and a rim sherd with a finger-impressed carination, best paralleled in a post-1400 BC context. This pit therefore probably dates towards the end of the period under consideration. The nature of this pit is of considerable interest in that an interpretation other than storage can be offered for it. Acorns are a well-known source of food in times of famine (e.g. among the Californian Indians). Although the raw kernels are very bitter, by chopping and roasting they can be made into a coarse ground meal. The Californian Indians prepare their acorns by burying them in a shallow pit with charcoal and watering them from time to time until they become sweet (Mabey 1975: 34–5). The residue of such an operation would be identical to that found at Findon. Alternatively, the pit was originally a storage pit and the acorn/charcoal mixture the rubbish deposit derived from the treatment of acorns close by. Either way, it shows the importance of wild foods to the second-millennium economy.

Because of the nature of the sites excavated, particularly the poor survival of organic material, little can be said about the agricultural basis of the period 3000–1400 BC. Indirect evidence of crops being grown in the area (although not necessarily on any particular site) comes from the study of carbonized grain and grain impressions in pottery. The greatest range came from pottery from Belle Tout (Bradley 1970: 374–5). Food Vessel sherds produced 1 carbonized grain of emmer wheat, 2 impressions of emmer wheat and 1 of six-rowed barley. Late Beaker sherds produced 1 carbonized grain of emmer wheat, 3 impressions of emmer and 5 of barley (at least 2 being six-rowed, 1 four-rowed and 1 naked).

Helbeck, in his classic study of 'Early crops in Southern England' (Helbeck 1952) located a single impression of hulled barley on a Collared Urn from Telscombe. A study of pottery from sites excavated by the author only produced two further grain impressions. These were on a Secondary Series Collared Urn from Bullock Down. Mrs P. Hinton identified two impressions of hulled barley, together with a blackberry seed impression (Hinton in Drewett 1982).

Woodland Camps

The distribution of bronze flat axes high up into the Weald suggests a continued utilization of the Wealden forest resources. The pollen evidence from

High Rocks however shows no sign of forest clearance throughout this period, while large numbers of barbed-and-tanged arrowheads from the High Weald (Curwen 1936 lists 361) and the Low Weald (E. Curwen 1936 lists 56) confirm extensive use of the Wealden resources. The third millennium, however, also provides evidence for reforestation of areas of the Downs cleared in the fourth millennium. Evidence of woodland resource use and hunting camps are therefore to be expected on the North and South Downs, as well as in the Weald. Extensive later erosion of the Downs as a result of agriculture is likely to have destroyed most traces of these rather ephemeral sites. One such camp may have existed at Chanctonbury Ring, Sussex, where a small flint assemblage associated with a Secondary Series Collared Urn sherd was found during the excavation of the first-millennium enclosure (Drewett in Bedwin 1980*a*).

The rock shelters at High Rocks in the High Weald have produced evidence of brief occupation, possibly little more than a one-night woodland camp. A single sherd of Grooved Ware from Site F and a transverse arrowhead from Site B suggest activity in the late third millennium (Money 1960).

The only extensively excavated woodland camp of this period is that at Rackham on the east side of Amberley Wild Brooks (Holden and Bradley 1975: 85–103). Pollen analysis shows that this site was situated in a minor woodland clearing which returned to woodland after the site was deserted. No pottery or pits were found during the excavation, but the nature of the flint assemblage and the presence of hearths and stake holes suggests the site is more than a surface flint-working site. A Carbon 14 date from the site of 2000 ± 140 bc suggests that the site was occupied about 2500 BC.

The site consisted of stake holes, two certain hearths, together with four other burnt patches, and some 13,062 pieces of struck flint. The stake holes may represent simple wind breaks, or possibly racks relating to the processing of some woodland production. One of the main activities practised on this site was the manufacture of a specialized flint tool kit. Waste products from flint knapping consisted of 11,855 flakes and 170 cores. The very large numbers of scrapers and knives recovered suggests that this was a specialized woodland resource-processing site. Unfortunately, evidence for what was being processed does not survive because of the dry, acid nature of the soil. The severe wear on some of the edges of the flint tools (Holden and Bradley 1975: 102) suggests that bone could have been processed as well as skins. In addition, wood and bark may have been processed for use elsewhere. We may therefore see this site as a specialized woodland processing site situated on the edge of the Wealden forest, serving the open agricultural settlements on the Downs to the south and probably also on the fertile alluvium of the Arun Valley.

It has been suggested that the anomalous site at Playden may have fulfilled a similar function to the site at Rackham (Holden and Bradley 1975: 102) but that site may be more satisfactorily interpreted as a ploughed out round barrow (Cleal 1982).

Surface/natural Exposure Flint-Working Sites (including reworked flint mines)

The latest radiocarbon date from a Sussex flint mine is 2700 ± 150 bc, suggesting a date about 3500–3410 BC. It is possible, although by no means certain, therefore, that flint mining had ceased in Sussex prior to 3000 BC. However, if this is the case, then it is highly probably that the waste dumps at flint mines were used well into the third millennium. A sherd of Grooved Ware was found at the mines at Findon (Smith 1956) and a recent surface find of a Peterborough sherd from the Long Down mines (Drewett 1983) shows a presence at both these sites. The re-use of the site of the Blackpatch mines as a barrow cemetery (Pull 1932), however, suggests that some mines may not have been re-used in the same way. The use of surface flint is shown by the many concentrations of waste flakes on the North and South Downs. It may also be presumed that the readily available cliff exposures of flint in East Sussex and East Kent were utilized, although coastal erosion has removed all traces of such activity.

The evidence for surface/natural exposure flint-working sites during the period 3000–1400 BC does, therefore, appear somewhat slender. The re-use of flint mine waste appears very likely as a presence on these sites is shown by odd sherds. The excavated sites at Rackham and Bullock Down both, however, show extensive use of rough flint nodules, indicating surface collection of flint.

Ceremonial and Ritual Sites

As yet no ceremonial, ritual or burial sites associated with Peterborough or Grooved Ware have been located in South-East England. A single sherd of Peterborough pottery from Mound 11 at Black Patch, East Sussex, must be considered residual as two Collared Urns were found in primary contexts (Drewett 1982). From *c.* 2500–*c.* 1400 BC, however, large numbers of internally variable ceremonial/ritual mounds were constructed in South-East England. Although concentrated on the Chalk and Greensand, groups and individual mounds are also known from the Weald (Tebbutt 1974). In addition considerable air photographic evidence, held by the Royal Commission on Historical Monuments, indicates the ploughed-out remains of mounds on the North Kent Coastal Plain. Grinsell (1934 and 1940) lists 1,059 mounds in Sussex while the total figure for South-East England is probably in excess of 2,000. Very few of these sites have adequate dating evidence, and even fewer have been totally excavated. At least twenty-eight of the excavated Sussex mounds contained

Saxon burials, mostly in primary contexts. The large clusters of small mounds, particularly in East Sussex, are likely to be of Saxon date. Only an extensive excavation programme can unravel this problem.

Mounds in South-East England of the period *c.* 2500–1400 BC are found clustered in six main ways: Nucleated, Dispersed, Nucleated/dispersed, Linear, Dispersed linear and Area. Although there is a clear gradation between these types of clustering, the basic distinction is between mounds that cluster either tightly (Nucleated) or loosely (Dispersed) or both (Nucleated/dispersed) around a given point, and those that are arranged in closely or widely spaced lines. In addition there are areas which have mounds in no apparent groupings (areas). Only one nucleated group of round mounds has been totally excavated in South-East England. All other excavations have been of individual mounds.

The group of nine mounds at West Heath, West Sussex, was excavated by the author between 1973 and 1980 (Fig. 3.6). The entire hill on which they were situated is in the process of being removed by sand quarrying. The area between mounds 1–3 was also systematically excavated, while the areas between the remaining mounds were watched during top-soil stripping by the quarry operators. No features were found between the mounds.

West Heath is situated on the Folkestone Beds of the Greensand, but with

Figure 3.7   Rich graves of the period 2000–1500 BC in central Southern Sussex.

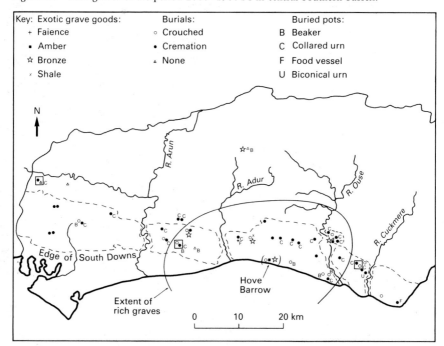

clay-rich bands which impede drainage, so producing the typical gley podzols. Soil studies by Dr R. Macphail indicate that the mounds were constructed on highly degraded soils, differing in no real way to the present podzol cover of the heath. This destruction of the soil is likely to have taken place prior to 4000 BC, perhaps by hunter-gatherer bands as there is little evidence of activity during the period *c.* 4000–*c.* 2200 BC. Such activity as there was during this period is likely to have been non-intensive, enabling the re-establishment of a light, hazel dominant woodland with extensive grass and heather cover (Drewett 1976).

Mound III appears to have been the focal point of the group and was probably the first to be constructed (Plate 3.1). A Carbon 14 date of 1680 ± 100 bc (*c.* 2100 BC) was obtained from a charcoal sample from the top of the buried land surface under the first phase of this mound. Phase I consisted of a large turf mound some 20 m in diameter around the foot of which was a circle of stake holes, indicating the existence of hurdling (Plate 3.2). Some 2 m out from the stake circle a ditch was dug, and the resultant material piled in the triangle created by the slope of the turf mound and the vertical hurdling. The very fine sand soon washed through the hurdling, thus protecting its vertical

Plate 3.1 The excavation of Barrow III at West Heath, West Sussex. This two-phase barrow originally had a wickerwork revetted turf mound surrounded by a single ditch. This first phase was buried and preserved by the upcast of the second-phase outer ditch.

Plate 3.2 A reconstruction of Barrow III at West Heath, West Sussex during its first phase, around 1700 BC.

face, and it must have rotted within a few years of its erection. At some stage after the silting up of the Phase I ditch, a second ditch was dug around the mound. This buried the Phase I ditch and sealed a lens of charcoal in the top of the Phase I ditch. From this was obtained a carbon 14 date of 1270 ± 180 bc (*c.* 1500 BC). No burials or burial pits were found associated with either phase (Plate 3.3).

Six other turf mounds excavated were found to contain no signs of burial. Two of these turf mounds were surrounded by ditches, while four were simply stacks of turf (Nos II, V, VIII and IX). Even phosphate analysis of the buried land surfaces failed to produce any hint of burial. The final two mounds excavated (Nos VII and VI) did, however, produce burial evidence. Mound VII consisted of two concentric ditches encircled by a low bank. In the central area was a low sand mound covering an oval pit some 3 m x 2 m. In the pit was a smashed Secondary Series Collared Urn containing a cremation. Mound VI also covered a pit. The pit was almost circular (1.5 m diameter) and contained five Secondary Series Collared Urns carefully packed in turf. One contained a cremation. In addition, two Secondary Series Collared Urns containing cremations were inserted into the mound during its construction. No other objects were found with any of the burials or under any of the other mounds (except residual flintwork of the period *c.* 6000–4300 BC).

From this excavation it may be concluded that the elaborate wickerwork revetted mound (III) was probably constructed for some purpose other than

Plate 3.3   A section through the turf stack of Barrow III at West Heath, West Sussex. In the centre are the remains of a recent robber trench.

---

burial. This mound held continued significance, being remodelled some 600 years after its primary construction, and around it was constructed a series of other mounds, at least six of which showed no sign of burial. Only two mounds produced any burial evidence (VI and VII).

The total excavation of an outlying mound related to the Iping Common group, also in West Sussex, showed a similar picture to the empty turf stacks at West Heath. This mound was also situated on the Folkestone Beds of the Lower Greensand. The low turf mound was constructed on a natural knoll. It consisted of an oval mound of turf surviving little over 1 m in height. Again no evidence of burial was located (Drewett 1975*b*).

A similar picture comes from the excavation of the much finer mound on the Surrey Greensand at Deerleap Wood, Wotton (Corcoran 1963). This mound survived to a height of almost 2 m. It consisted of a turf mound capped with ironstone blocks. Around the mound was a ditch some 35 m in diameter, with a low mound outside the ditch. Clearly the mound was intact but no trace of a burial was located.

It is clear from these few examples that some of the mounds usually referred to as 'barrows' and thought of as burial mounds contained no burials. Although poor soil conditions or poor excavation are usually quoted as possible reasons for 'empty' barrows, they are found on the same soils as barrows with surviving burials. Empty mounds are well known elsewhere. Empty long mounds include South Street, Horslip and Beckhampton Road (Ashbee, Smith and Evans 1979); empty oval mounds include Thickthorn Down (Drew and Piggott 1936) and empty round mounds include Crig-a-Mennis (Christie 1960), Six Wells 267 and 271 (Fox 1959) and Ashey Down 9 (Drewett 1970a). Mounds without burials, therefore, span the whole period of mound construction and include long, oval and round mounds. There is, therefore, a distinct possibility that some mounds were being constructed for purposes other than burial. All structures conventionally referred to as 'barrows' are here referred to as ceremonial/ritual mounds, so enabling a slightly wider interpretation than simply that of burial. Perhaps all 'barrows' should be considered primarily as ceremonial/ritual constructions, with burial only an element in some cases. A Medieval parallel would be the parish church, a ritual monument surrounded by burials, but *not* a burial monument.

Several mounds excavated in the South-East have, however, produced burials, some with rich grave goods. Two substantial mounds on the Chalk Downs at Ringwould, Kent, were excavated in 1872. One mound contained no burials, but the other covered four pits, each with a cremation in an inverted Biconical Urn. Associated with the burials were also miniature vessels and faience beads. Further miniature vessels of the slotted type, sometimes referred to as 'incense cups', came from Tilmanstone and Luddington Wood, both in Kent. A cluster of Collared Urn burials are known from other East Kent mounds, as at Capel-le-Ferne, Nackington, Westbere and Stodmarsh.

The richest group of burials under mounds in the South-East came from the Hove area of Sussex (Fig. 3.7). The group is centred on the large Hove Barrow, destroyed in 1857. The mound was described by the Rev. J. Skinner in 1821 as being 12 ft high and 180 paces in circumference, but this is possibly an overestimate (Curwen 1954). On the old land surface was an oak coffin containing human bones, probably from an inhumation, an amber cup, a perforated stone battle axe, a bronze dagger and a whetstone. All other exotic grave goods from Sussex come from Central Southern Sussex, within 20 km of the Hove Barrow. Faience is known from two burials, one at Oxteddle Bottom, Glynde (E. C. Curwen 1954) and the other at Upper Beeding (Wilkinson, pers. comm.). The Oxteddle Bottom assemblage also contained amber pendants and beads, together with a bronze spiral finger ring. A crouched inhumation under a mound at Newtimber was found associated with a bronze knife and pin, together with a shale disc bead (Grinsell 1934). Finally, almost 20 km north-west of the Hove mound, a small mound excavated at Washington produced a burial of a young woman with a bronze dagger (Ratcliffe-Densham 1968).

The only adequately excavated round mound within the Weald was the 'Money Mound' excavated on Tunbridge Wells Sandstone in Lower Beeding Parish (Beckensall 1967). This sand mound was revetted with sandstone

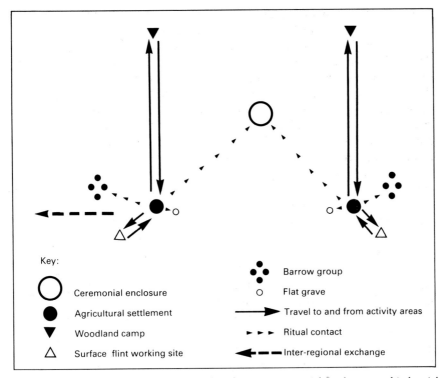

Figure 3.8 Model of possible interrelationships between ceremonial, settlement and industrial sites of the period 3000–1400 BC.

blocks. Although no burial was found, a flint knife, a barbed-and-tanged arrowhead and three bronze rivets, together with Beaker sherds came from the central area.

Although burials are often associated with round mounds, it is likely that flat graves were the norm in this period. However, such graves will only be recognized as of this period if associated with datable grave goods. For example, a series of flat graves was located by accident on Bullock Down, East Sussex (Drewett 1982). Here an empty Collared Urn was set in a shallow pit adjacent to two other shallow pits containing adult cremations. Some 150 m north-east of the Collared Urn were two female crouched burials without any associated grave goods.

A possible parallel of an empty urn, this time a Food Vessel, comes from Abinger Hammer, Surrey (Wood and Thompson 1966). This pot was found in the side of a silage pit which had already destroyed the southern part of the site. Careful excavation failed to produced any sign of a barrow or burials, but these may have been destroyed when the silage pit was dug.

Social Organization

The presence of the rich Hove grave and other graves containing 'exotic' objects suggests the existence of some high-ranking individuals during this period. Rich graves appear to be concentrated in Central South Sussex and in East Kent, possibly suggesting the development of two rich territorial groupings. If Wolstonbury is a ceremonial monument of the 'henge' type, then its construction on top of the scarp slope in Central Southern Sussex may underline the prestige of the Sussex Group.

During the period 3000–1400 BC the mainstream role group of farmer-craftsmen appears to continue from the previous period. However, other role groups may have changed or disappeared. For example, if every farming community constructed its own mounds for ceremonial and burial purposes, as the large number of round mounds suggests, then each agricultural settlement may have had someone with specialized ceremonial or ritual knowledge. Alternatively, there may have been itinerant ceremonial specialists. As no fortified settlement enclosures were constructed during this period, we have no, even indirect, evidence for the existence of a protective (warrior) group during this period. However, such a group may simply have protected individual settlements. Alternatively, the development of rich groupings in South Sussex and East Kent may suggest the existence of a protective group which may have been part of the extensive redistribution networks suggested by the amber, shale, bronze and faience. Such redistribution networks, developing during this period, probably became firmly established soon after 1400 BC with the construction of enclosures on the edges of the trade areas.

Chapter 4

Farmers and Craftsmen, 1400–600 BC

About 1400 BC the archaeological database improves dramatically. This is partly due to a change in building techniques utilizing house terraces, which results in excellent preservation, but it is mainly due to a major change in the economic system. The economically independent units linked by small-scale redistribution, probably based on gift exchange, bride wealth and the acquisition of status, suggested for the previous 1600 years are replaced by highly organized mixed farming and economically specialized units linked over long distances by extensive commercial redistribution networks. Although 1400 BC may be considered a realistic starting date for this phase, it is clearly, in economic terms, a formative phase foreshadowing the centralizing power and control of trade networks current in the first millennium BC. It may therefore also, in economic terms, be considered part of a phase which lasted until the development of urban centres towards the Roman Conquest (Fig. 4.1). As much of the evidence for redistribution is based on surviving mobile material culture, this will be considered first.

Material Culture

It is clear that soon after 1400 BC bronze replaced flint for the bulk of tool types in everyday use. The evidence for this survives not only in the bronze tools themselves, but also in the dramatic decline in flint tool types. Indeed, the only ones to survive in any numbers are those not easily or more efficiently adapted to bronze. As bronze is a recyclable raw material, it is hardly surprising that little direct evidence for bronze use comes from the settlement sites. Certain associations on settlement sites are, however, known from Plumpton Plain (Holleyman and E. C. Curwen 1935: 32–3), New Barn Down (E. C. Curwen 1934*b*: 144) and Black Patch (Drewett 1982) with possible associations at

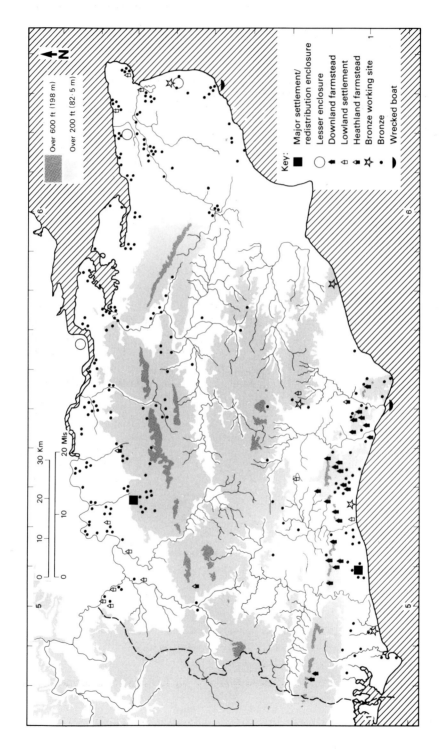

Key:

■	Major settlement/redistribution enclosure
○	Lesser enclosure
⊟	Downland farmstead
◄	Lowland settlement
☆	Heathland farmstead
•	Bronze working site
	Bronze
►	Wrecked boat

Over 600 ft (198 m)

Over 200 ft (82·5 m)

Figure 4.1 Distribution of enclosures, settlement sites, industrial sites and bronze artifacts of the Later Bronze Age (*c.* 1400–600 BC) in South-East England.

West Blatchington (Norris and Burstow 1948: 9) and Kingston Buci (E. C. Curwen 1931: 215). Most bronze comes from either hoards or stray finds with particular concentrations in North Kent and in the river valleys in all three counties. Bronze artifacts may be broadly divided into four main groups: axes, weapons, ornaments and other tools. The axes included flanged axes, palstaves, winged axes and socketed axes. Although overlapping chronologically, these four axe types represent a development throughout the period. The weapons consist of dirks, rapiers and swords, together with a developing series of spearheads. Ornaments reach their greatest variety during this period with bronze penannular armrings, Sussex loops, spiral twisted torcs, coiled plain and single loop finger rings, and plain and quoit-headed pins. Other tool types include chisels, knives, awl-tracers and possibly anvils (Rowlands 1976).

It is clear that some flint tools persisted after 1400 BC and were used in conjunction with bronze tools for specific activities. Scrapers dominate the flint assemblages, with most being roughly made end, side, disc or hollow scrapers. The hollow scrapers merge into a series of notched flakes. Fabricators, awls, hammerstones and other retouched pieces occur.

By combining the bronze tools with the flint tools it is possible to suggest a range of tool-kits used in the performance of a specific set of tasks. The axes and knives were probably woodcutting tools, while other knives and scrapers were almost certainly food and skin preparation tools. The fabricators and hammerstones may have been used in fire-making but could also be used in making flint tools. The bronze anvils were probably used in the manufacture of other bronze tools, while the chisels, knives, awls, scrapers and notched flakes may have been used in a variety of craft activities, particularly wood and boneworking.

Pottery of this period has been studied in detail by Ellison (1975) and Barrett (1979). Styles change rapidly about 1400 BC with further significant changes around 900 BC (Fig. 4.2). These changes, however, appear to take place earlier in the Thames valley than along the South Coast.

All pottery of this period contains flint filler. The heavier wares have extremely coarse filler, but even the finer imported wares use flint, although ground much finer. Ann Ellison has suggested that ten types of pot were current from about 1400 BC:

1. Shapeless, baggy jar, sometimes with turned over simple rim.
2. Ovoid or straight-sided jar with plain, unperforated applied lugs at maximum diameter.
3. Ovoid jar with plain, unperforated lugs and outflared rim.
4. Straight-sided small pot with perforated, applied lugs.
5. Small ovoid pot with perforated lugs.
6. Plain, large urn with slack, biconical profile and slightly emphasized carination.
7. Globular jar with bar handles and incised geometric decoration.

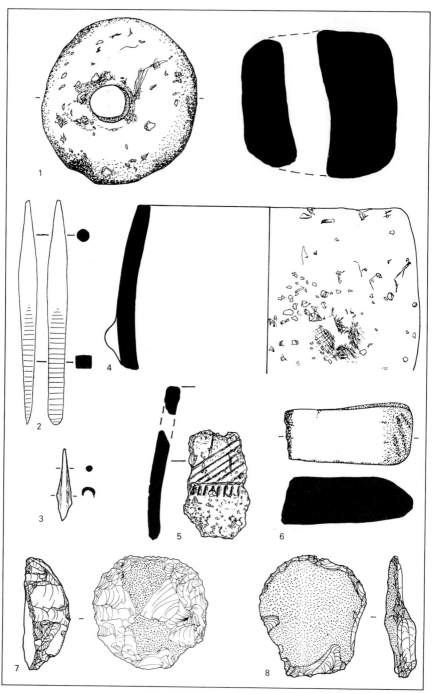

Figure 4.2 Material culture from the Later Bronze Age downland farmstead at Black Patch, Alciston, East Sussex. 1: loom weight; 2: bronze awl/tracer; 3: bone point; 4–5: bucket urns; 6: whetstone; 7–8: flint scrapers (scale ½).

  8. Plain bucket-shaped urn.
  9. Bucket urn with line of fingertipping applied directly onto body.
10. Bucket urn with fingertipped cordon.

About 1000 BC in the Thames valley, but perhaps as late as 900 BC in Sussex, pottery styles change and Ann Ellison has defined nine types which occur together after about 900 BC:

11. Squat, ovoid jar with protruding base and applied fingertipped cordon at maximum diameter.
12. Large-shouldered jar with outflaring rim and applied fingertipped cordon in hollow of neck.
13. Large-shouldered jar with fingertip cordon around carination.
14. Plain, large-shouldered jar with slack profile.
15. Small, rounded pot with incised geometric decoration.
16. Urnfield imports.
17. Plain, ovoid jar with protruding foot.
18. Plain, straight-sided jar with protruding foot.
19. Plain, low bowl with incipient foot ring.

These types survive to about 700 BC when increased decoration becomes apparent. Fingertip decoration becomes more common, with the finer jars having a range of incised motifs. Carinated bowls are similarly decorated, and a few cups appear in assemblages.

In addition to pottery, the ceramic industry in this period also involved the manufacture of weaving equipment. This consisted of loom weights and spindle whorls. The loom weights are characteristically cylindrical early in the period and triangular later, and range from fairly light (435 gm) to quite heavy (1.2 kg). A series of weights from Black Patch, Sussex, could be divided into heavy weights of 1–1.2 kg and lighter weights of 435–770 gm (Drewett 1982). The variations in weight may reflect the weaving of different grade fabrics. The spindle whorls exhibit a variety of shapes, including cylindrical, biconical and oval.

A variety of stones from the Weald, including Wealden sandstones and Greensand, were used to make saddle querns and grinding stones. Whetstones were made from ferruginous and micaceous sandstones. Natural quartzite pebbles functioned as hammerstones at Black Patch, Sussex (Drewett 1982), while iron pyrites nodules may have been used with fabricators to make fire. The excavators of Itford Hill, Sussex suggested that beach pebbles found at that site were sling stones, but there is no direct evidence for this (Burstow and Holleyman 1957: 204).

The only known bone tools from the Downland farmsteads in South-East England are simple bone points, but extensive evidence of bone working has come from the riverine settlements. Evidence from Runnymede Bridge, Surrey, for example, shows on-site antler and boneworking with antler off-cuts and partly worked pieces together with an unfinished antler cheek piece. Other types found include bone points and pins, bone pegs and toggles and more complex pieces like bridle fittings (Needham and Longley 1980). Runnymede Bridge also produced a small wooden cup or ladle bowl, underlining the probable extensive use of wood, evidence for which rarely survives.

Imported materials include objects of shale, amber and particularly gold. Shale armlets and perforated amber beads were found at Runnymede Bridge, while almost eighty pieces of goldwork from South-East England probably date from this period. Poor associations and indeterminate types, however, make the dating of much of this goldwork difficult. Most of the goldwork consists of torcs, bracelets and rings and comes mainly from North and East Kent, and Southern Sussex. Only one small, plain ring comes from Surrey. This was a casual find from Kingston, now in the British Museum (Taylor 1980). Kent has produced several hoards of gold, two from Wansunt near Bexley and two from the River Medway near Aylesford. Likewise Sussex has produced hoards of bracelets from Beachy Head and bracelets and torcs from Mount-field near Battle (Taylor 1980).

The main sites associated with material culture datable to the period 1400–600 BC can be divided into nine types. The largest sites appear to be major settlement and redistribution enclosures. Beneath these are smaller enclosures and then three overlapping types of settlement, Downland farm-steads, lowland settlements and the heathland farmsteads. From limited evidence it is possible to hypothesize bronze-working sites, although bronze working may have taken place on the lowland settlements. Ceremonial or ritual sites can be divided into huts and platforms, with burial being a major element in their definition as ritual. Finally there are off-shore sites in the form of wrecks of traders' boats.

Major Settlement and Redistribution Enclosures

The enclosure on Highdown Hill (Fig. 4.3) stands well apart from all other enclosures on the Sussex Downs in that it encloses one hectare and so is over four times the size of the next largest enclosure in Sussex. Only limited excavations have taken place at Highdown, but enough to show that in its original phase, which may be dated on pottery evidence to *c.* 1400–1200 BC, it consisted of a subrectangular enclosure defined by a single bank and ditch. The ditch was some 4 m wide and 2 m deep, with a flat bottom (Wilson, 1940 and 1950). Within the bank on the north-western side of the enclosure was a round hut marked by roof support posts in a 4.75 m circle. Inside the hut was a hearth area. On the hut floor were pottery sherds of Ellison types 7 and 8 together with a spindle whorl, a loom weight and a saddle quern. Other hollows, containing burnt flint, together with several post-holes, may represent a second phase of hut use, but the limited area excavated makes this uncertain.

Highdown Hill appears to be at the edge of a number of artifact distributions. On the basis of this, Dr Ellison has suggested that Highdown Hill is one of at least five major enclosures in Southern Britain which fulfilled a significant role in redistribution networks during the period *c* 1400– *c*. 600 BC. (Ellison 1981). The accumulation of wealth at Highdown, as shown by casual finds of metalwork, perhaps begins in the period 1400–900 BC with, for example, several now lost palstaves (Grinsell 1931). The bulk of the metalwork, however, is of the period 900–600 BC and includes a tanged chisel and knife (E. C. Curwen 1954), a socketed knife (Grinsell, 1931) and a gold penannular ring (Taylor 1980: 86, Sx 10).

If Ann Ellison's arguments for the location of large redistribution enclosures are correct, then it is possible to predict a second major enclosure in South-East England, perhaps towards the east coast of Kent. Bronze tools, and particularly ornaments, appear to concentrate around these large enclosures,

Figure 4.3 Major redistribution/settlement enclosure at Highdown Hill, West Sussex (after Wilson 1940).

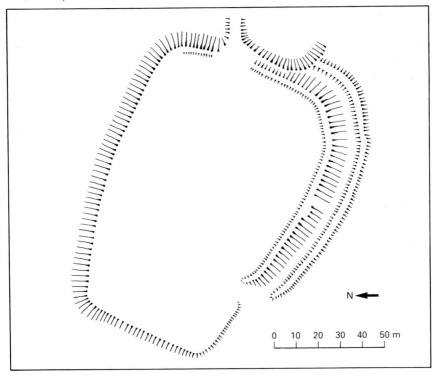

N

0 10 20 30 40 50 m

so concentrations in east Kent make it likely that such an enclosure may be found (Ellison 1980).

Towards the end of this period a second type of major settlement enclosure appears. This is the round or more irregularly shaped enclosure, on the higher land overlooking the Thames valley. In Surrey at least four enclosures may be of this date. These are on St Ann's Hill, St George's Hill, Caesar's Camp near Wimbledon and Queen Mary's Hospital at Carshalton (Needham and Longley 1980). Only the enclosure at Queen Mary's Hospital has any good dating evidence, following excavations in 1905, 1937 and 1939 (Lowther 1946). The excavations revealed an enclosure some 170 m in diameter. None of the interior of the enclosure was excavated, but pottery from the ditches suggests a date in the eighth or seventh century BC. Loosely associated with the pottery were several vertically perforated cylindrical loom weights and a fragment of a bronze axe.

Smaller Enclosures

With more discoveries it is likely that the smaller enclosures may be found to merge into the larger enclosures. However, at present there are a few enclosures which perhaps represent a single farming unit rather than some larger communal group represented by sites like Queen Mary's Hospital, Carshalton. Two sites in Kent, Mill Hill, Deal and Highstead are probably enclosed farmsteads (Fig. 4.4).

The site at Mill Hill lies on a chalk ridge overlooking Deal (Stebbings 1934). The limited excavated evidence, together with air photographic evidence, suggests a circular enclosure some 50 m in diameter (Champion 1980). A single entrance causeway on the southern side of the enclosure was protected by a gate structure represented by six post-holes. About a third of the encircling ditch was excavated by Stebbing, who found it to be almost 2 m deep, with an eroded width of 2.5 m to 4 m. Little of the interior of the enclosure was excavated, but an area of burning was located and interpreted as a hearth. A small pit was also located, together with a shallow depression some 3.5 m in diameter. Although Stebbing interpreted this as a 'hut circle' its description suggests it to be more like the hollows interpreted as ponds, frequently found on Sussex Later Bronze Age sites (e.g. Drewett 1982: Fig. 5). However, these recurring hollows could also be interpreted as threshing floors, or even pig wallows. If the circular depression at Mill Hill is not a 'hut circle', then one could reasonably expect free-standing timber structures to be found elsewhere within the enclosure.

The Mill Hill enclosure is particularly important in the South-East be-

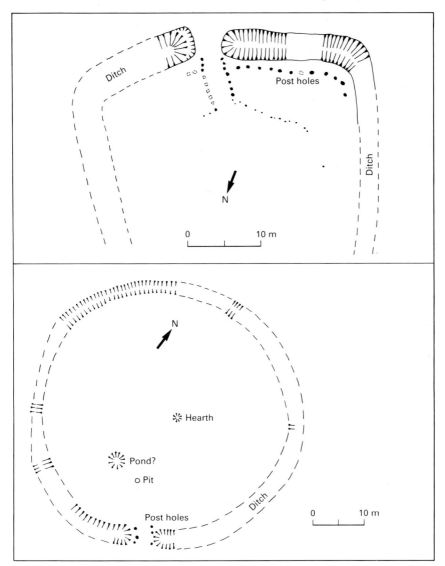

Figure 4.4 Later Bronze Age enclosures in Kent. Highstead (top) and Mill Hill, Deal (bottom) (after Champion 1980*a*).

cause the ditch silts contained evidence of bronze working. Bronze working is clearly a significant activity within the middle-range enclosures overlooking the Thames and on into south Essex, with bronze-working debris also coming from the Highstead enclosures in Kent and from two of the main south Essex enclosures, Mucking (Jones and Bond 1980) and Springfield (Buckley, pers. comm.) Mill Hill produced a clay mould for making small bronze rings, acompanied by a ring which could have been cast in the mould. Other bronze included a nail-headed pin and part of a blade (Champion 1980).

The enclosure at Highstead, Chislet, Kent was partly excavated on a gravel terrace in 1976. It appears to be a subrectangular enclosure. Inside the deep ditch was a stout palisade and the single entrance causeway on the southern side was well protected by a substantial timber passageway. Insufficient of the interior was excavated to locate timber huts, which we may presume were originally inside the enclosure. Bronze working debris was, however, found, particularly moulds for casting pins (Champion 1980).

Highstead has some parallels with the well-preserved enclosure on Harrow Hill in West Sussex. This strategically placed subrectangular enclosure is only a little bigger than Highstead and was protected by a substantial bank and ditch. It has two entrances, and excavation of the western one produced a substantial gate structure. Very limited excavations in the interior of the enclosure did not locate any hut structures. The limited pottery dating evidence would suggest a date towards 600 BC. The discovery of some 13 or 14 ox mandibles together with teeth, but only two limb bones, perhaps indicates that the processing of animal products was at least one activity which took place on this site.

Downland Farmsteads

Known Downland farmsteads are almost entirely restricted to the South Downs, where at least twenty-four probable sites are known. Several of these sites have been extensively excavated over the last fifty years, revealing very detailed evidence for the economic basis of these Downland farmsteads. Itford Hill and Black Patch to the south-east of Lewes in East Sussex were the most extensively excavated sites.

Black Patch is situated on the western slope of a dry valley between the 91 m and 152 m contours on the South Downs, some 3 km west of the River Cuckmere (Fig. 4.5).The site was discovered by George Holleyman in 1949 and first published in E. C. Curwen's *Archaeology of Sussex* (1954). Unfortunately, since then the site has been largely levelled by continuous ploughing. Originally the site consisted of a system of small, rectangular fields marked by lynchets. Set within these fields was a series of hut platforms and enclosures. A hollow way and a double-lynchet trackway enter the fields from the east. A series of eleven round mounds is situated on the ridges surrounding the settlement.

Two hut clusters, 1 and 4, were totally excavated, while other platforms and enclosures were sampled between 1977 and 1979 (Drewett 1982). Prior to

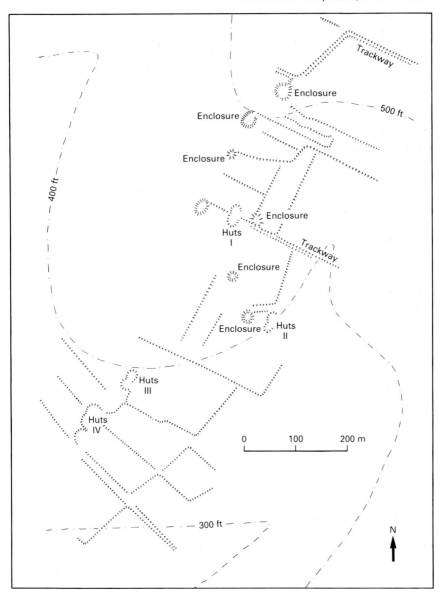

Figure 4.5 The Later Bronze Age farmstead at Black Patch, Alciston, East Sussex. Enclosures and hut platforms set in lynchetted field systems.

excavation, Hut Platform 4 appeared to consist of two large, joined platforms cut into the slope of the hill. A very slight detached platform survives to the north of Hut Platform 4. After total excavation of the platform by hand, it became clear that the individual house terraces had been recently levelled by bulldozing bank material from the west. The greatest depth of this material had been pushed over Hut 1. Having removed this bulldozed material and the post-war plough soil, it became clear that much of the site survived in a remarkable state of preservation.

Five hut terraces were located, running in a line from south-west to north-east. Each terrace contained settings of post-holes indicating a hut structure. In addition six fence lines, two shallow depressions and several single post-holes, paired posts and post clusters were located. Hut 1 was a two-phase structure (Plate 4.2). The first phase consisted of a hut terrace some 7 m in diameter; roof supports were indicated by a circle of post-holes and at least one further post-hole was probably destroyed when a pit was dug just inside the porch. Within this hut was a linear arrangement of post-holes, perhaps indicating a fixed bench. This hut was replaced by levelling up the floor with clean chalk, probably derived from enlarging the hut terrace. The new hut terrace was 8.5 m in diameter. On this was constructed a hut with roof supports set in a circle 6 m in diameter and a porch facing south-east.

Hut 2 was constructed on a very slight terrace. The roof was supported on an oval of posts 5.5 m × 4.5 m. On the south-east side was a large porch

---

Plate 4.1   Hut 3 excavated at the Later Bronze Age farmstead at Black Patch, East Sussex. Note the substantial porch post sockets on the left and grain storage pits on the right. These pits contained the remains of over 56 kg of carbonized barley.

Plate 4.2 Hut 1 excavated at the Later Bronze Age farmstead at Black Patch, East Sussex. This house terrace has clearly been recut.

structure, and cut through the floor of the hut was a widely spaced linear setting of post-holes, perhaps indicating some internal fittings. Hut 3 consisted of a large terrace 8 m in diameter with the roof supported on a circle of post-holes 5.5 m in diameter (Plate 4.1). A porch structure faced south-east, and set against the back edge of the terrace were three oval pits. Within the main circle of posts was a circle of smaller posts. Hut 4 was constructed on a shallow terrace 7 m in diameter with the roof supported on a circle of posts 5 m in diameter. A porch structure consisting of paired post-holes linked by parallel grooves was located facing south-east. Hut 5 comprised an irregular setting of post-holes on a very slight terrace some 6 m in diameter. Within the structure was a short linear setting of post-holes, again suggesting some internal fittings.

The excavators at Itford Hill suggested that all the hut types were free-standing structures, simply using the terrace as a house platform (Burstow and Holleyman 1957). This suggested very small, round huts contrasting sharply with the massive huts known from the later first millennium BC. The idea of little round houses some 5–8 m in diameter survived into the 1960s in reports like that on excavations at Shearplace Hill, Dorset (Rahtz and ApSimon 1962). However, in 1969 Avery and Close-Brooks, and independently in 1970 Musson, suggested re-interpretations which brought the structure more into line with evidence from sites of post 600 BC date. The suggestion was that rather than the outer circle of posts representing the walls of the hut, it in fact represented the roof supports inside the hut. The outer wall was suggested as being a very much lower structure, either in a wall trench (e.g. Features 1 and 21 at Shearplace Hill) or on the outer lip of the house platform itself (Musson 1970: 269). Clear evidence for the second suggestion was thought unlikely to survive because 'traces of shallow set posts or low rubble walls could easily have been removed by subsequent erosion' (Musson 1970: 269).

During the excavations at Black Patch, great care was taken to examine the full extent of the terraces and particularly the upper lip of each terrace. As was expected, this area was badly eroded, but around Hut 4 were the surviving bases of five post-holes, suggesting slanting roof supports. These clearly suggested that the back wall of the terrace was the back wall of the house itself. In order to construct a balanced roof, the front of the roof must have been supported on some form of low wall. As no trace of a wall trench of the Shearplace Hill type was located, it may well have been a low flint wall of the type proposed by Musson in a conjectural reconstruction of House II at Amberley Mount (Musson 1970: 269). All five huts at Black Patch produced substantial areas of large flint nodules which could well have derived from such walls.

Unfortunately, erosion around Huts 1, 2, 3 and 5 was such that no traces of post-holes were located on the outer lips of these hut terraces. However, two further types of evidence make it clear that these huts should be reconstructed in a similar way. Firstly the position of the three storage pits in Hut 3 clearly confirms that the whole terrace was roofed. If the post circle had represented the position of the hut wall, then these pits would not only have filled with water running off the edge of the terrace, but also that running off the roof. Secondly, the spread of artifacts over all hut floors shows activity areas spread over the whole house terrace and not just the area enclosed by the post circles. By bedding the feet of the main rafters securely into the ground around perhaps two-thirds of the circumference of the hut, likelihood of movement due to lateral stress is minimized. The southern side of each hut would, however, present a potential element of weakness. Lateral movement in this direction was no doubt prevented by the construction of large porches bedded in deep double-post-holes. The suggested flint wall around the southern edge of each terrace would therefore be unlikely to support much weight. To help counteract possible differential stress-support provided by earthfast rafters on one side and rafters supported by a porch on the other side, a ring beam may have been introduced to transfer individual rafter stress into circumferential stresses, passing around the ring beam. Alternatively, such outward pressure may have been reduced by the introduction of a centre post. Several huts had clusters of shallow post-holes towards their centres which could represent replaced centre posts. Similar post-holes were, however, dotted over the floors of all the huts and may best be interpreted as relating to hut furnishings (e.g. looms or benches) rather than structural supports.

The details of the structures are naturally purely conjectural. Certainly the tool kit was available for elaborate carpentry (Rowlands 1976), but huts of the Black Patch type could well have been lashed together, as can be seen in ethnographic examples, e.g., the roof of a Tiv (Nigeria) house (Bohannan 1965: 520). Although there is no direct evidence as to the selection of wood for hut construction, the bulk of the charcoal from the site was of oak, with some hazel and hawthorn. Oak would naturally make excellent vertical posts and rafters, while woven withies of hazel and hawthorn could have been used to make a supple ring-beam and a woven framework for thatch. Thatch straw would have been available as a by-product of growing barley and emmer wheat, ample evidence for which was found in the pits of Hut 3. Turf, however, may well have been used instead of thatch.

In an attempt to establish what activities were practised in which huts, all artifacts below the modern plough soil were two-dimensionally plotted. The rubbish on the floor of Hut 1 consisted of pottery, flint flakes, fire-cracked flints, foreign stones, animal bones and carbonized seeds. Two bronze spiral finger rings were also found on the floor of the hut. Given that the two rings were found close together, casual loss appears unlikely. It is possible, therefore, that they were carefully stored in a safe place in the roof of the hut and fell to their position on the floor after its collapse. Either way, this indicates the activity of personal decoration within this hut. High concentrations of pottery suggests food and water storage and food preparation and cooking. The evidence for actual cooking in the form of a hearth is slight. Very few fire-cracked flints were found, but these do tend to concentrate in the south-east corner of the hut which was the best-lit area, just inside the porch. The flint flakes also concentrate in the best-lit, eastern half of the hut, suggesting an activity requiring light. The foreign stones from the hut floor include seven fragments of Wealden sandstone, perhaps broken from the interior of a quern-stone. If so, it may have been used for grinding wheat or barley, carbonized grains of both being found on the floor. The few animal bones found derived from sheep and cattle.

Hut 2 shows a very different range and density of rubbish on its floor. Only nineteen widely scattered pot sherds were found, together with a concentration of fire-cracked flint, against the east wall. As this was an unsuitable area for a fire, the flints may have been stored for later use as flint filler in pottery. The flint flakes appear to cluster around a single-flint core. This may indicate a briefly used primary knapping area. Flotation of the floor soil produced only nine grains of barley and two of wheat.

Hut 3 produced four bronze objects. These consisted of a razor from Pit 3, a knife and two awl/tracers. Pottery was scarce on the hut floor (more coming from secondary redeposited contexts above the floor) but does appear to cluster around the edge of the hut, indicating a completely different picture

101

of pot use to that found in Hut 1. The loom weights found comprised three clusters of three and three odd ones, against the north-east wall, together with three more in the entrance area. Flint flakes were found scattered fairly evenly over the hut floor, so do not suggest any specific activity area within the hut. The distribution of fire-cracked flints shows two general clusters, one in the entrance area and one in the north corner of the hut. The cluster inside the entrance indicates the most likely position for a hearth. The second cluster of burnt flints in the north corner of Hut 3 cannot be interpreted in this way, as a fire in this position would be too close to the junction of roof and floor. This group could be a store of burnt flint awaiting use as a filler in the locally produced pottery. Flotation of the soil on the hut floor produced 5 grains of wheat and 55 of barley. Animal bones consisted of sheep, cattle and pig.

The rubbish on the floor of Hut 4 includes the range of all the types found in Huts 1–3. Two bronze objects were found, a slender bronze blade and a solid, circular tapering point. The pottery clusters in two areas closely match the concentrations of burnt flint, one just inside the porch and the other in the north-west corner of the hut. The fire-cracked flint concentrations may both indicate hearths. Although widely spread, there is also a tendency for the flint flakes to cluster around the hearth areas. Flotation of the soil on the hut floor produced 1 grain of wheat and 12 of barley.

The floor of Hut 5 produced very few artifacts. A small, centrally placed group of fire-cracked flints was found, together with two potsherds. As with Hut 2, the flint flakes were associated with cores.

The broad conclusions we can draw from this evidence is that Hut 1 was probably essentially a food preparation hut, Hut 3 was a living hut where craft activities and storage took place, while Huts 2 and 5 may have been used for some activity leaving little artifactual trace like calf or lambing huts, with flint knapping perhaps practised when not in use for animals. If these suggested functions are correct, then it may be possible to suggest what sort of social group occupied this hut cluster.

The close proximity of the huts would suggest a close relationship between the occupants (Fig. 4.6). This is, of course, the ethnographic norm, although it must be remembered that an age set may be considered as closely related, or even more so, than a family group. The range of activities present at Black Patch does, however, suggest a family group more than an age set, which is more likely to be brought together for a specialized activity like herding. The range of old and young adults together with children in the Itford Hill barrow (Holden 1972) suggests that family groups probably stayed together. The Black Patch hut group therefore suggests a family or extended family group. If it was a simple nucleated family of mother, father and children, the separate fenced yards become difficult to explain. If, however, we consider a small extended family, the proximity of huts demonstrates closeness, but the fences underline independence (Plate 4.3). In a Jie (Uganda) homestead, for example, each wife owns a yard containing a living hut, a hut for calves and an area for

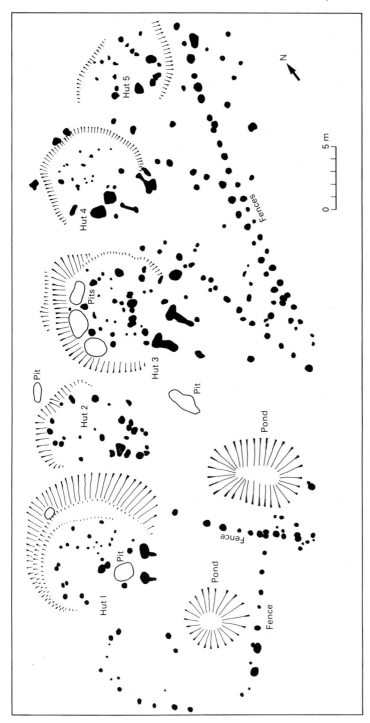

Figure 4.6 Hut Platform 4 at the Later Bronze Age farmstead at Black Patch, Alciston, East Sussex. Black dots indicate post-holes and open shapes pits.

Plate 4.3 A Bronze Age fence line revealed by post sockets cut into the chalk at Black Patch, East Sussex.

granary baskets. Unmarried daughters, at a certain age, may fence off a bit of the mother's yard and construct their own living hut. They remain dependent on the mother for food, so do not have an independent hut for calves or granary baskets. Even the independent wife units may pool resources, for example, sharing a kitchen hut (Gulliver 1965).

This element of independence and sharing is a recurring feature in the extended family compound situation. Among the Hausa (Nigeria) for example, the main hut is the husband's. His wives live in separate huts but as a family unit share granary, goat house and kitchen. Married sons would have a section of the compound fenced-off for them with their own hut and granary, but may still share cooking areas and water supply, and so are still under the head of the compound. Unmarried sons would have their own fenced off-area with sleeping huts, but are otherwise totally dependent on the resources of the compound head (Smith 1965). A Tiv (Nigeria) compound is arranged in hut clusters with the main hut in each cluster belonging to the husband. Around this are arranged the wives' huts in which all aspects of food preparation and child rearing take place (Bohannan 1965).

This concept of a united, sharing compound with independent units is clearly evident at Black Patch. One arrangement could be that Hut 3 is the head person's (man or woman) hut. In this hut the winter's supply of grain was stored and the full range of craft activities practised. To suggest that this was a male preserve, as indicated by the razor and other bronze items, is perhaps pushing the evidence too far. Directly associated with Hut 3 was the subsidiary Hut 2. There is little direct evidence to indicate what function these subsidiary huts had. Their use as sleeping huts has been suggested, but seems unlikely. These huts must have been very damp and cold in the winter. It seems more likely that people would sleep in the larger, heated huts. The likely uses are either storage of fodder or perhaps most likely for young animals like the calf huts in the Jie compounds (Gulliver 1965). The large pond 2 could have supplied water for Hut 3 and any young animals being housed in Hut 2.

The occupant(s) of Hut 1 had some degree of independence from Huts 2/3, as indicated by its fenced yard. The pottery, quernstone and hearth indications suggest that food preparation and cooking was a major activity within the hut. However, it is clearly too big to be a simple cooking hut. The presence of two fine bronze spiral finger rings would suggest some status for the occupant. Is this perhaps the wife's hut where food is prepared and children reared away from the craft activities practised in Hut 3? This division of activities between Huts 1 and 3 does not appear in Hut 4, where a case could be made for both food preparation and craft activities. Hut 4 is clearly to some extent independent, having its own fenced yard, but must have been dependent on the Hut 2/3 unit for water and stored grain. Could the occupants of this hut perhaps no longer be in the mainstream of economic activities on the site? Grandparents perhaps? The fact that Hut 5 is fenced off from Hut 4's yard may suggest that it is not directly linked. The fact that it is not a living hut but does have a yard makes the suggestion that it is for young animals rather than storage more likely.

From this evidence it is possible to suggest that the Black Patch compound was occupied by more than a conjugal family. Huts 1, 2 and 3 probably represent the living unit of a conjugal family. Hut 4, however, suggests an additional element. This could be unmarried siblings but alternatively could represent the parents of the compound head. It is therefore suggested that, at the point of desertion of this hut group, we are looking at a joint family compound. Naturally such an arrangement is probably part of a developing cycle of nuclear, joint and extended families. This picture of small family groups is clearly reflected in the only scientifically analysed contemporary burial site in East Sussex. The relationship between the people represented in the Itford Hill Barrow (Holden 1972) suggests a joint family similar to that postulated at Black Patch.

Food production was clearly a major activity at Black Patch. The four main elements of food procurement were crop growing, animal husbandry, hunting and gathering. Barley is clearly the major crop to survive in the archaeological record. It should be borne in mind, however, that as only carbonized seed survives, it may be that more barley survives simply because barley was treated in such a way that more became carbonized than is the case with other grains. Wheat, mainly emmer but some spelt, was also grown and appears in most samples. Although beans were not recovered from Hut Platform 4, their presence on Hut Platform 1 suggests that their absence may be due to poor preservation rather than non-exploitation. Evidence for the cultivation of green vegetables rarely survives in the archaeological record, so the possibility that some of the *Brassica* seeds recovered represent cultivated cabbage is of particular interest.

Evidence for animal husbandry is surprisingly slight, with only 187 identifiable bones of domestic animals from the entire settlement excavation. This number of bones represents only a minimum number of 13 individuals. The reason for this very low number of bones may be one of several. Firstly it is possible that these Downland settlements were essentially arable, and stock raising was simply a very minor element of the economy. Secondly, it is possible that the bone refuse was discarded away from the settlement. Thirdly, it might be that stock was kept on lowland pasture, slaughtered and jointed there, with only meat being brought up onto the settlement. The cattle may have been present on the Downs essentially for draught, while the immature calves and sheep may have died while being hand-reared away from the main herds and flocks on the lowland pasture. From the slight evidence we have cattle appear to dominate, closely followed by sheep and pigs. In addition to the domestic animals there is slight evidence for hunting, with seven fragments of red deer antler and one bird bone.

Gathering wild food is likely to have been a major, if seasonal, activity of most rural communities throughout prehistory, and indeed history (Drewett 1982). Hut Platform 4 provided ample evidence of the utilization of marine resources in the form of 14 mussel, two periwinkle, one cockle and one limpet shells. Given the distance to the sea (1 hr 35 min. walking time) and the undulating country to be traversed, it is possible that some shell fish may have been removed from their shells prior to transport, thus leaving no archaeological trace.

Wild fruit in the form of sloes, blackberries and hazel nuts were collected. The use of wild plants and 'weeds' associated with cultivated grains is always a problem to determine archaeologically. It is clear that several of the plants associated with the grain could have been used. The brassica, if *oleracea*, could have been collected on the coast and, after a couple of boilings to remove the bitter taste, eaten as a vegetable. If *Brassica nigra*, it may have been used as a mustard for flavouring. Chickweed (*Stellaria*) was used as a green vegetable in the Middle Ages and may well have been used in prehistory. Both spear-leaved orache and common orache can be eaten in a similar way. The roots of *Potentilla* may be eaten either as a vegetable or ground into flour for bread and gruel. Goosegrass (*Galium aparine*) also makes a tolerable green vegetable when boiled, and has the advantage that it is available after frost has killed off most other green plants.

The site of Itford Hill is very similar in many ways to Black Patch (Fig. 4.7). It is again situated on a south-facing Downland slope with rectangular lyncheted fields to the south. When originally excavated, it was interpreted as a single farmstead, all broadly contemporary with a short period of occupation (Burstow and Holleyman 1957). However, the site has recently been re-interpreted by Ann Ellison who has suggested the existence of four successive settlement units (Ellison 1978). The first settlement consisted of a banked terrace cut into the hillside, on which was constructed a porched living hut together with a food preparation and storage hut. As at Black Patch, evidence for food preparation and storage was found in the form of pits, scrapers and querns. This hut cluster was replaced by a second cluster built to the east. This second cluster was again terraced into the hill slope but was much larger, consisting of five huts. The main living hut was porched, with an adjacent food preparation and weaving hut. A second food-preparation hut contained only quern fragments, while two subsidiary huts may be interpreted as a work hut containing scrapers and loom weights, and a small animal hut. This hut cluster was then replaced by a line of three low-banked enclosures containing four huts. None was porched, but two may have been living huts, with querns in both suggesting food preparation. To the west of these living huts were two subsidiary huts, possibly used for young animals or storage. The final phase is represented by a pair of huts constructed to the south-east of the three original clusters. It is possible that this series of hut clusters represented an expanding and then contracting family unit, with maximum hut accommodation being required in the second phase, perhaps representing an extended family unit.

Within the Downland block containing Black Patch and Itford Hill there were originally at least three more contemporary farmsteads. Two, Charleston Brow and Denton Hill, have not been excavated, while a third is merely hinted at by pottery finds located during excavations at Bishopstone. The site at Charleston Brow was discovered during the excavation at Itford Hill. It consisted of two small enclosures, again on a south-facing slope. The site has not been excavated, and since its discovery it has been levelled by ploughing. The site on Denton Hill was located by Dr M. Bell in 1973 during fieldwalking around the important multiperiod site he was excavating at Bishopstone, some 4 km to the south of Charleston Brow. The site survived only as a concentra-

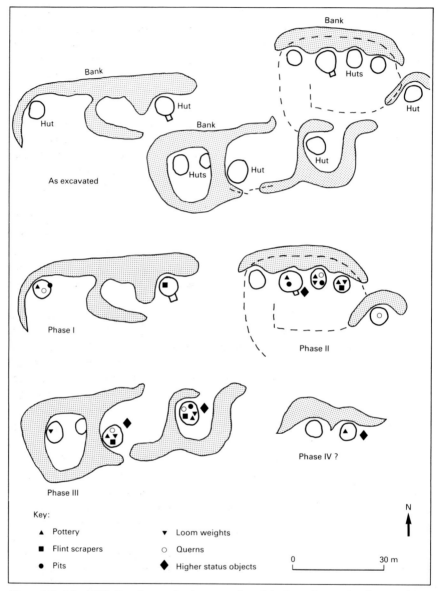

Figure 4.7 Itford Hill, East Sussex. A reinterpretation of the Later Bronze Age farmstead (top) suggesting three or four consecutive phases (after Ellison in Drewett 1978).

tion of pottery, saddle querns and flintwork in a ploughed field, but the location is again very similar to Itford Hill and Black Patch. The final site within the Ouse-Cuckmere block of Downland is at Bishopstone. Here a scatter of Itford Hill-type pottery found in later features strongly suggests a farmstead site, probably destroyed in later prehistory (Bell 1977).

A second cluster of Downland farmsteads which have been sampled by excavation are on the block of Downs to the north of Worthing, between the rivers Arun and Adur in West Sussex. Here the sites of New Barn Down, Amberley Mount, Cock Hill, Blackpatch (not to be confused with Black Patch in East Sussex) and Park Brow all show similar hut clusters to Itford Hill and Black Patch.

The two enclosures at New Barn Down (E. C. Curwen 1934*b*) are set in a system of rectangular lyncheted fields connected by a double lynchet trackway. Within the enclosure bank was a strong wooden palisade. The enclosure protected at least two circular huts. The main hut contained considerable amounts of pottery, together with several fragments of quernstones, a bronze knife, and part of a bronze spearhead. The hut to the north was probably an animal or storage structure, as it produced only six sherds of pottery and the only quernstone had clearly been re-used as a packing stone in a post-hole. Similar enclosures have been located to the north-east of New Barn Down at Cock Hill, and to the east at Blackpatch. Limited excavations at Blackpatch located one round hut (Ratcliffe-Densham and Ratcliffe-Densham 1953) while more extensive excavations at Cock Hill located five huts within the enclosure (Ratcliffe-Densham and Ratcliffe-Densham 1961).

Sample excavations of hut platforms within a system of rectangular lyncheted fields at Amberley Mount, to the east of Cock Hill, located two further circular huts (Ratcliffe-Densham and Ratcliffe-Densham 1961). The huts excavated at Park Brow (Wolseley *et al.* 1927) appear to represent similar, unenclosed huts set in rectangular lyncheted fields. The last of the excavated Downland settlements was discovered towards the northern edge of the Downs in East Sussex at Plumpton Plain (Holleyman and Curwen 1935). Three out of four connected enclosures were partly excavated and all produced evidence for circular huts similar to Black Patch and Itford Hill.

Although practically all the Downland farmsteads excavated in South-East England came from the South Downs, the site at Minnis Bay, Birchington, Kent (Worsfold 1943) may be assumed to be the eroded base of a similar Downland farmstead. The timber structures at Minnis Bay are almost certainly Medieval or later fish-weirs. The settlement site associated with a bronze hoard discovered on the foreshore in 1938 was originally on dry land (Champion 1980). The surviving evidence appears to be the eroded basis of chalk-cut pits and one larger hollow, similar to features excavated on the South Downs sites.

The Downland farmsteads appear to be essentially small mixed farming family units, growing crops, tending livestock and practising a range of craft activities including weaving, potting and possibly wood and leatherworking. The thin Downland soils and lack of surface water suggest, however, that these settlements may have been forced onto peripheral land, as a result of pressure on better land in the river valleys and elsewhere. The nature of the Sussex river valleys, with deep sedimentation (Scaife and Burrin 1983), makes the location of river-valley settlements almost impossible. Extensive evidence for lowland settlements is, however, coming particularly from the Thames Valley.

Lowland Settlements

Of the cluster of sites recently located in the Thames Valley in North-West Surrey, the remarkably well-preserved site at Runnymede Bridge, Egham, is clearly the most important (Needham and Longley 1980; Longley 1980). The site consists of a settlement area situated adjacent to the Thames, the bank of which had been carefully revetted with vertical stakes driven into waterlogged deposits. A linear arrangement of parallel rows of stakes was traced for at least 50 m. The stakes were of young oak trunks, only about 20 cm in diameter. The function of this revetting is probably more than simply to protect the settlement area to the south-west from flooding. It is presumably a timber river frontage, operating as a quay for river traffic. Adjacent to the river frontage, extensive evidence for occupation in the form of post-holes, pits, a cobbled area, artifacts and animal refuse was located. Several Carbon 14 dates (670 ± 70 bc, 800 ± 70 bc, 750 ± 70 bc and 720 ± 70 bc) suggest fairly close dating for the site.

As the result of skilful observation and rescue excavations at Runnymede Bridge, it is possible to suggest a settlement area stretching back over 100 m from the waterfront. A dense spread of post-holes suggests closely set buildings, but whole building plans are difficult to deduce because of the small areas investigated. The range of artifacts recovered indicates something of the importance of the site. Particularly important is evidence of Continental imports like a notch-backed bronze razor and a vase-headed pin, together with non-local materials like amber and shale. Perhaps such materials were imported by river craft which were tied up on the revetted water frontage.

If the site at Runnymede Bridge was an impressive quay, it was also a living site where a wide range of craft activities took place. In addition to weaving, flint working and perhaps potting, all craft activities found on the Downland farmsteads, Runnymede Bridge also produced evidence for metal-working in the form of casting debris, moulds, scrap metal and a pottery crucible. There was also considerable evidence for bone and antler working in the form of cut-offs and semi-worked pieces.

Direct evidence for arable farming at Runnymede Bridge is slight. Evidence for pastoralism is however, considerable, with bone evidence indicating cattle, sheep/goats and pigs. Pastoralism would, of course, be ideally suited to the rich riverine pastures and ready supplies of river water. If pastoralism in the form of meat, and particularly dairy products, was the basis of the settlement economy of the river valley sites, then the large ditch terminal excavated at the nearby site of Petter's Field may have been a stock enclosure.

The site at Petter's Field to the south-west of Runnymede Bridge was trial trenched in the early 1970s in advance of the construction of the M25 (Johnson 1975). This site produced a similar range of animal bones including cattle, sheep and pig, again suggesting a strong pastoral element to the subsistence economy. Post-holes indicating dense settlement were found on both sides of the large ditch terminal in which was deposited a bronze founder's hoard containing Carp's Tongue elements. This provides additional evidence for bronze working on the low-lying settlements in river valleys.

If pastoralism, perhaps particularly the production of dairy products, was the basis of the subsistence economy of the lowland settlements, as opposed to crop production on the Downland farmsteads, then the extensive ditch systems revealed on air photographs of the Thames Valley (e.g. Longley 1976) may well indicate land management of the water meadows. The density of casual finds, particularly of bronze, in the Thames valley probably indicates many, as yet unlocated, pastorally orientated farmsteads in the area.

The density of settlement evidence in the Thames valley is reflected in other river valleys in South-East England, although the evidence comes mainly from casual finds. The actual settlement sites themselves have proved extremely elusive, probably because they are buried under many metres of alluvial and colluvial deposits; the Cuckmere valley having, for example, some 6 m of deposits (Scaife and Burrin 1985). Sites on the coastal plain have been subjected to almost continuous agricultural operations ever since they were deserted. The density of bronze finds of this period on the Sussex Coastal plain shows clearly that this area was extensively utilized. The only certain settlement site was, however, destroyed without proper excavation earlier this century. The destruction of the site at Kingston Buci was fortunately observed by Dr E. Curwen, who collected a wide range of artifacts. The artifacts appear to have been related to a series of storage pits (E. Curwen, 1931: 185) but no details of these, or associated huts, were recorded. The area containing these pits does, however, appear to have been fairly extensive, suggesting a substantial settlement, perhaps more akin to the Thames valley settlements (Bradley *et. al.* 1980) than the small Downland farmsteads. The pottery located consisted of Ellison Types 1 and 10. Probably, although not certainly, associated with this pottery were saddle querns and cylindrical loom weights. Unfortunately it is no longer possible to associate any of the animal bones directly with this material. The large quantities of sheep and ox bones found may be related to the period 1400–900 BC but more probably relate to the late first millennium and Romano-British occupation of the site (E. Curwen 1931: 212).

Other evidence for activity on the Sussex coastal plain includes burnt flint concentrations and mounds. The exact nature of these sites is uncertain, although the extraction of salt from sea water is a possibility on some sites. A recent sample excavation of a burnt flint concentration by David Rudling at

Yapton, Sussex, located shallow pits associated with worked flints, daub and pottery dated to the ninth–eighth centuries BC (Rudling 1987).

Two sites in the Cuckmere valley may be of the period 1400–900 BC but both could be slightly later. At Selmeston, on a slight rise in the Greensand on the western edge of the river valley, Dr Curwen noted a short length of ditch containing part of an Ellison Type 10 pot. The ditch was recorded in section and noticed again on a second visit after it had been cut back some 2.5 m. Unfortunately, no further excavation was undertaken. The ditch was quite substantial, being over 4 m wide at the top and dug almost 2 m under the underlying sand. From the drawn section and Dr Curwen's comments (Curwen and Curwen 1938: 195–8) it may have been two parallel ditches, one possibly recutting the other. The only other casual find of this date from Selmeston is a bronze rapier blade fragment (Lewes Museum).

Further north up the Cuckmere valley the casual find of a cylindrical loom weight at Cross-in-Hand (Holden 1979) strongly suggests a river valley farmstead well up into the Weald. The environmental evidence suggests extensive woodland clearance of the Downs River valleys by c. 1000 BC. Utilization of woodland resources would therefore require movement well into the Wealden Forest. This would suggest the probability of short duration woodland camps. None of these has actually been located, but the widespread, if thin, distribution of bronze palstaves indicates utilization of woodland resources.

The presence of farmsteads on the poor acid heathlands of Kent and Surrey underlines the density of settlement during this period. The small farmstead on Hayes Common, Kent, was constructed on the extremely infertile Blackheath and Woolwich pebble-beds, while the acid Lower Greensand soils of Weston Wood, Surrey are not much better for crop growth. Both sites appear, however, to be small mixed farms.

A series of small trial trenches dug on Hayes Common from 1960 to 1966 located 2 joining ditches, 3 post-holes and 30 small pits, suggesting a settlement area spread over half an acre (Philp 1973). Several of the pits contained domestic rubbish including pottery, loom-weights, fragments of quernstones, flint tools and burnt flints. Unfortunately, the dry acid nature of the bedrock prevented the survival of bone refuse, but the presence of loom weights probably indicates sheep, while pigs and cattle were also possibly kept. Although no grain was recovered, the quern fragments suggest some grain processing, so this site may be interpreted as a small heathland mixed farm.

A similar picture emerges from Weston Wood, where excavations between 1961 and 1963, in advance of sand extraction, located a small farmstead. A small hut some 7 m in diameter was supported by a central post and contained a storage pit. A second, smaller hut contained a quern, suggesting that it may have been a food preparation hut. Between the huts were possible hearth areas, scatters of pottery and two bronze lumps, suggesting some metalworking. A shallow ditch was cut between the two huts. To the north-east of the main living hut were two small rectangular plots with evidence of spade-cut furrows. These plots have, unfortunately, never adequately been proved to be contemporary with the hut structures and are exceedingly small compared with contemporary Downland fields. Cereals were, however, stored and processed on the site if not actually grown there. A pit located to the south-west of the food-preparation hut produced carbonized barley (*Hordeum* sp.) and wheat (*Triticum* sp.).

Bronze-working Sites

None of the Downland farmsteads excavated in South-East England revealed evidence for bronze-working. Bronze-working appears to be restricted to the low-lying areas, particularly in the Thames and other river valleys. Settlement sites with evidence for bronze-working at Petter's Field and Runnymede Bridge in the Thames valley have already been mentioned. Evidence for bronze-working elsewhere is slight. The river valleys, particularly higher up into the Weald, would have a ready supply of wood for charcoal and water. The other raw materials required, either ore or bronze scrap, would initially, at least, have to be imported into the South-East. Once sufficient bronze was present in the region, much of it may have been recycled for long periods. At least twenty-five bronze hoards of the period have been found in Sussex for example. Only four, however, show any evidence of being bronzesmith's hoards and three of these are from off the Downs. The Bognor hoard contained a number of palstaves with remnants of casting flashes and are unsharpened (Rowlands 1976: 263–4). A recent hoard from Yapton, West Sussex, was found close to a cake of remelted bronze (Aldsworth 1983). The St Leonards Marina hoard (Rowlands 1976: 269) contained a bronze anvil and the third, unlocated hoard ('near Brighton') contained three fragments of bronze ingots (Rowlands 1976: 265). The remaining hoards contain both completed objects and some broken items, perhaps being collected as scrap. Such hoards may therefore represent distribution and scrap collection networks rather than bronze-working sites. Several of the smaller 'hoards' may, however, represent grave groups or casually found groups from unlocated settlement sites.

The best evidence for a river valley bronze-working site comes in the form of a bronze-casting header found close to a tributary of the Cuckmere River, high up in the Weald at Framfield (Tebbutt 1979). Unfortunately, this object was a casual find, unassociated with other objects or features.

Ceremonial and Ritual Sites

The problem of isolating ceremonial/ritual buildings from any other type of building is fraught with difficulties in a prehistoric context. The greatest problem is that of the integration of religion into everyday life. Any of the huts at, for example, Itford Hill or Black Patch may have had a ceremonial or ritual, as well as a domestic function. Does the upright chalk phallus in the porch of Hut D at Itford Hill (Burstow and Holleyman 1957: 202) indicate ceremonial/ritual activities within the hut related to, perhaps a fertility cult, or does it simply indicate a brothel?

One is on safer ground when one considers structures which have a significant burial element suggesting ritual activity at the structure. Only one such structure has been located and excavated in South-East England. This is the so-called 'cemetery-barrow' at Itford Hill (Holden 1972). This structure was situated some 160 m north of the Itford Hill settlement (Burstow and Holleyman 1957). It consisted of a circle of post-holes some 5 m in diameter, set in a shallow ditch which may be interpreted as a palisade trench (Fig. 4.8). A gap on the south side (facing the settlement) indicates the probable entrance to the structure. There is little doubt that the structure could have been roofed, although as the excavator points out, it is unlikely to have been an ordinary domestic structure re-used as a ceremonial structure, because of the slope on which it was constructed (Holden 1972: 88). In the centre of the structure lay the cremated remains of an old man (Holden 1972: 114). He was buried under a platform of large flints which may have been the floor of the structure. Outside were the cremated remains of at least eleven men, women and children (Holden 1972: 113–15).

The Itford Hill structure unfortunately has no direct parallels in South-East England, although the elements are present elsewhere. At Cock Hill cremations were found inside what are most likely to be domestic hut structures grouped within an enclosure (Ratcliffe-Densham and Ratcliffe-Densham 1961). At Steyning Round Hill (Burstow 1958) cremations were clustered around a very slight semicircular trench beneath a flint platform. Only 1 cremation was inside the trench, while 2 were in it and the remaining 33 cremations were outside it. This suggests, if not a structure, at least a defined ceremonial area. Although not closely dated, a flint platform was the only structural element under Barrow 4 at Black Patch (Drewett 1982).

The evidence for ceremonial/ritual buildings and platforms is therefore slight and only appears after 1400 BC. It does appear, however, that such structures do replace mounds as focal points for ceremonial/ritual activities of which the only surviving evidence is the ritual burial of human remains.

The isolation of ceremonial/ritual objects presents even greater problems to the archaeologist than the isolation of ceremonial/ritual structures. A domestic pot, for example, used in a ritual ceremony, becomes a ceremonial/

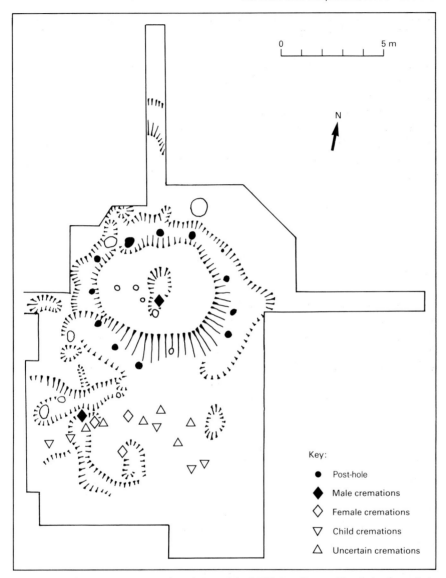

Figure 4.8 The Later Bronze Age burial site at Itford Hill, East Sussex. The circle of post-holes suggests a hut structure around an ancestral burial with all other burials clustered outside the structure (after Holden 1972).

ritual object for the duration of the ceremony or ritual. It may then return to a domestic function and so be undetectable archaeologically. Pots deliberately buried with cremations or inhumations may be considered to be, at least in their final context, mobile ceremonial/ritual objects. Likewise the exotic objects of faience, amber, bronze or shale have a final ceremonial/ritual function

115

when used as burial objects. Objects of a ceremonial/ritual nature not associated with burial can only be suggested when such objects do not have an immediate practical function. Such a simplistic approach does, however, raise the problem that childrens' toys (if such were made) or models made for other purposes may be misinterpreted in many ways. Only two are known from South-East England. A bone phallus came from a pre-3000 BC context at the Trundle (E. C. Curwen 1929: 59) while a chalk phallus came from a post 1400 BC context at Itford Hill (Burstow and Holleyman 1957). On the basis of two such objects it would be unwise to suggest a major fertility cult, although such a cult remains a possibility.

Wrecks

Trade between South-East England and the Continent during later prehistory was almost certainly considerable. Foreign trade goods like the vase-headed pin and notch-backed razor from Runnymede Bridge, have already been mentioned. Such trade goods almost certainly crossed the Channel by boat. Although no actual wrecks have been located, the considerable quantity of bronze axes from the sea bed off Langdon Cliff, just east of Dover Harbour, almost certainly indicates a wreck (Muckelroy 1981). Similarly, bronze objects from the sea bed off Seaford Head may indicate a possible wreck (Dean, pers. comm.) At Langdon Bay most of the bronzes came from within a 50 m radius. No ship remains were found, but the quantity of objects (189) makes it certainly a wreck site. The cargo included 42 median-winged axes, 38 palstaves, 81 rapier/dagger blades, 3 socketed spearheads, 6 socketed chisels, a socketed knife and 4 pins.

Social Organization

The evidence from South-East England for the period 1400–600 BC indicates extensive use of land which must be regarded as peripheral in agricultural terms. The thin chalk Downland soils were intensively utilized, and settlement even pushed onto the Greensand and pebble-beds of Surrey and Kent. This dense population must have been highly organized, but the nature of the sites surviving from this period suggest very different organization from that of earlier periods. The earlier farming communities in South-East England show strong evidence for ceremonial-ritual activity in the construction of long, oval and round barrows together with ceremonial enclosures. Such activities almost certainly assisted social cohesion, particularly if ceremonial-ritual specialists moved between social groups. After 1400 BC the archaeological evidence for ceremonial/ritual activity declines with such activities almost certainly being family-based. The Itford Hill ceremonial hut, for example, looks very like a single family 'shrine'. Social cohesion from 1400–600 BC appears more related to economic and trade development than ceremonial/ritual activities.

At the top of the hierarchy of sites, in terms of labour input at least, are the major settlement and redistribution enclosures (Fig. 4.9). High Down Hill and a possible site in East Kent perhaps represent focal points on the edge of redistribution areas. High Down Hill faces the rich areas of the Hampshire Basin and Wessex, while East Kent may have formed an important trading link with the Continent. Beneath these major enclosures was a series of settlement

Figure 4.9 Model of possible interrelationships between settlement, industrial and ceremonial sites of the period 1400–600 BC.

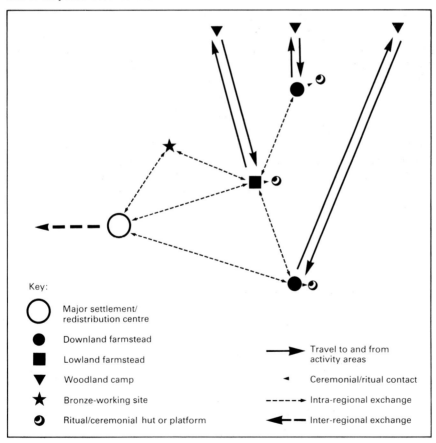

Key:

○ Major settlement/redistribution centre

● Downland farmstead

■ Lowland farmstead

▼ Woodland camp

★ Bronze-working site

☾ Ritual/ceremonial hut or platform

→ Travel to and from activity areas

◄ Ceremonial/ritual contact

-----► Intra-regional exchange

◄— — Inter-regional exchange

sites attempting to utilize all parts of the landscape from the rich river valleys, through the thinner Downland soils and on to the poor sands and pebble beds. Particularly dense population may be postulated in the Thames valley. In addition to the settlement sites excavated and the air photographic evidence of ditched divisions of the landscape, the great density of bronze objects from the Thames (Needham and Burgess 1980) suggests many more settlement sites washed away by the meandering river. Competition between the Thames side settlements may be reflected in the quantity of fine bronze work from the Thames. The weapons and ornaments in particular perhaps reflect the status of individuals or groups. Continued pressure on land in this area may, however, finally have resulted in the need to construct fortified enclosures, like that at Queen Mary's Hospital, Carshalton.

The period 1400–600 BC can therefore be seen as a period of rapid economic and social development, resulting in a significant increase in population causing pressure on the best land in South-East England. Social cohesion was perhaps first underpinned by the demonstration of personal status in terms of rich bronze paraphernalia and by extensive trade networks. Finally, however, military defence in terms of the construction of fortified sites became necessary. The development of fortified centres, the 'hillforts', became an important element of the period 600–100 BC.

Chapter 5

Centralizing Power, 600 BC–AD 43

The seven hundred years prior to the Roman Conquest witnessed very rapid social and economic development in South-East England. Traditionally referred to as the 'Iron Age', this period is characterized by a series of major social, economic and technological changes, one of which was the important introduction of iron technology. Many aspects of Iron Age culture, such as hillforts and pottery, however, have their roots in the first half of the first millennium BC.

The archaeological record (particularly settlement sites, which are more numerous, more varied and frequently larger than those of the Bronze Age) suggests that during the Iron Age there was an expanding population with a resulting pressure on good agricultural land. Such population pressure, causing social unrest, is thought to have been a major factor behind the dramatic increase in fortified enclosures which are characteristic features of the period. Relatively rapid changes in artifact styles probably indicate competition in expanding trade networks. This period also saw the development of specialized industrial sites for producing iron and salt, probably for wide-scale redistribution. The principal social and economic unit, however, remained the small agricultural settlement operating a mixed farming economy. The development of substantial areas of static field systems, particularly on the South Downs, together with the use of large storage pits and (?)granaries, suggests the production of excess, designed for exchange.

During the Iron Age, the area covered by this book did not form a common cultural and geographical region. Professor Cunliffe (1982) has suggested that Kent and Surrey should be considered as part of eastern Britain, and that then the cultural differences between these areas and that of Sussex, which has close links with Central Southern England, become more significant than the previously over-emphasized similarities. For recent 'county' summaries of the Iron Age in the South-East, the reader is referred to articles by Bedwin (1978a, 1984a; Bishop (1971); Hanworth (1987), and Cunliffe (1982).

Approaches to the Study of the Iron Age

The development of Iron Age studies has been dealt with in detail elsewhere (Cunliffe 1978a; Megaw and Simpson 1979), and only a brief outline is necessary here. The idea of an 'Iron Age' was an integral part of antiquarian thought (the 'Three Ages System') throughout most of the nineteenth century, and the period was provided with chronological divisions following the ordering of material from the continental sites of Hallstatt (A–D) and La Tène (I–III). The British finds were compared with those from across the Channel, and similarities explained by the theory of migration from the Continent.

By 1931 there was sufficient Iron Age data from Britain for Christopher Hawkes (1931) to propose a new independent scheme, a threefold division into Iron Age A, B and C. Although based on observed differences of British Iron Age culture, this arrangement was still closely related to the Continental scheme for both chronology and explanation. Thus, Iron Age A (the earliest phase) was ascribed to invaders from Hallstatt Europe: Iron Age B was represented by groups in Yorkshire and the South-West with affinities to Continental Early La Tène, and Iron Age C referred to cultural groups resulting from Late La Tène ('Belgic') invasions into South-Eastern England. Despite various modification (particularly with regard to regional differences), the basic ABC system was to serve as the basis of Iron Age studies in Britian for more than thirty years: the essentials of the invasion theories remaining unchallenged.

Finally, the ABC scheme was challenged by Professor Hodson (1960; 1962; 1964). He argued against the restrictive nature of the geographical and chronological framework, and suggested that instead regional groups should be defined independently by their characteristic types. He attributed much of the British Iron Age to indigenous Bronze Age origins, and in 1964 proposed the idea of an underlying 'Woodbury Culture', upon which were superimposed intrusive La Tène elements representing the 'Arras Culture' of Yorkshire and the 'Aylesford-Swarling Culture' of South-Eastern England. Hodson's approach therefore did not altogether deny the principle of culture change by invasion. Instead, it focused upon the indigenous traditions and required an assessment of the quantity of Continental material involved, and asked how much material was necessary to warrant the suggestion of an invasion. The alternative explanation was that of trade.

Recent approaches to the British Iron Age have used the alternatives of trade (of goods or ideas) or invasion to explain the similarities between the Iron Age in Britain and that on the Continent. Harding (1974) restates the case for Hallstatt, Early La Tène and Late La Tène immigrants as the impetus for changes in the British Iron Age. In contrast, Cunliffe (1978a) incorporates much of Hodson's approach and provides some of the missing regional grouping. This grouping is mainly based on a detailed study of pottery styles and the definition of 'style-zones' – 'areas of contact'. There are, however, various possible explanations for the patterning of these 'style zones'(for example they could represent the market area of a single pottery production centre *or* be an area in which technology and fashion developed in common over an extensive region) and *the zones do not necessarily relate to social identities.*

Nevertheless, a framework based on pottery does have many advantages, especially in the South-East where there was a vigorous ceramic tradition throughout the Iron Age, and where pottery is the most abundant domestic find from Iron Age sites. Thus, by means of stratigraphy, pottery can be used to build up regional sequences, which can then be compared with developments in neighbouring areas. On its own, however, Cunliffe's stylistic approach to Iron Age pottery is not sufficient. It needs to be combined with analytical techniques designed to isolate the places of origin of both the clays and tempers used to make the pottery. Unfortunately, such petrological examination is very much in its infancy in the South-East, the notable pioneer in this field being Sue Hamilton (examples of her valuable work are included in Bell 1977; Hamilton 1984; Bedwin and Holgate 1985). In addition, recent work has shown that there are a number of dating problems with the chronology of Cunliffe's pottery scheme, particularly with regard to the Late Bronze Age/Early Iron Age transition (Barrett 1980; Champion 1980). Future research will hopefully improve Cunliffe's scheme and ultimately provide a more useful framework for the Iron Age in the South-East. In the meanwhile, Cunliffe's ceramic studies (Cunliffe 1978a; 1982) do at least provide a relative chronology for the area, and throw some light on the outside influences to which the region was subjected.

Pottery Styles

After 600 BC it is possible to see diverging ceramic styles in South-East England, with Kent and the Lower Thames Valley increasingly sharing characteristics with Essex, while Sussex and much of Surrey have closer links into Central Southern England.

Cunliffe (1982) has recently suggested three general pottery styles present in Kent from *c.* 600–100 BC. The earliest style (the 'Park Brow-Caesar's Camp Group') probably developed before 600 BC and may have survived into the third century. The main types consist of shouldered jars, often with fingernail or fingertip decoration on the rim tops or shoulders, fine-shouldered bowls with flaring rims and plain bucket-shaped pots. These types clearly derive from forms developing in the previous five hundred years and so are best seen as part of a local indigenous development.

The beginning of the second group of pottery styles is marked by the

Plate 5.1 Pottery urn: a distorted waster with traces of haematite finish and a row of concentric lozenge decorations in black on the shoulder of the vessel. Early Iron Age. Found at Green Street Drove, Eastbourne, East Sussex. (Photograph: Sussex Archaeological Society.)

development during the fifth century BC of large, onion shaped urns with pedestal bases and outcurved rims. The significant group, including wasters (Plate 5.1), found at Eastbourne, Sussex, indicates local production, although the type may have been inspired by contemporary continental forms (Hodson 1962). Pedestal-based pottery, including a wide range of derivative bowls, is well made, usually burnished and sometimes decorated with painted geometric designs. Foot-rings soon became popular throughout Kent, Surrey, Sussex and Southern Essex.

The final pre-wheel ceramic development in Kent took place in the second century BC, when curvilinear decoration becomes popular, particularly on the shoulders of large, everted-rimmed jars. This distinctive form of decoration, which is thought to be the result of local innovation, is Cunliffe's 'Mucking-Crayford' style, and is found on both sides of the Thames Estuary. It lasted only a relatively short period, and disappeared after the arrival of the potter's wheel during the first century BC.

The introduction of the potter's wheel (perhaps by immigrants) was followed by the mass production of exceptionally high-quality pottery (the 'Aylesford-Swarling' or 'Belgic' types) in North Kent and Essex, nearly all of which is wheel-made. The wheel enabled the production of tall, elegantly shaped urns with pedestal bases, conical urns, corrugated pots and many different types of cordoned and grooved bowls. In addition, lesser quantities of butt beakers, platters, tazze and lids were also made. All these types suggest strong Continental influences, and the large quantities produced indicate commercial production by specialist potters. Local types may also have been transformed by the new technology, and the coarser, narrow-mouthed jars with their outer surfaces wiped or scored into crude patterns were probably derived from local forms. The various types of 'Belgic' pottery in South-Eastern Britain have recently been studied by Isobel Thompson (1982).

After the middle of the first century BC, the locally produced pottery was supplemented by imports from the Roman Empire and its northern fringes. The earliest of these imports were the large Italian wine-filled amphorae. These vessels, whilst made and imported as containers of wine, were subsequently used for a variety of purposes. After about 15 BC, other imports included *terra rubra* and *terra nigra* platters, Gallo-Belgic butt beakers, Arretine Ware and finally Samian Ware from Roman Gaul.

In ceramic styles, Sussex and part of Surrey diverge from Kent during the third and second centuries BC. At this time, Sussex and Surrey clearly became part of an extensive style-zone covering much of Southern England. This zone is characterized by vertical-sided 'saucepan pots' and jars with rounded shoulders and beaded rims (Fig. 5.1). Although saucepan pottery has a number of minor local variations, the Sussex pots with their simple, regular and asymmetrical curvilinear designs (the 'Caburn–Cissbury' style) are essentially similar to types found in Surrey (the 'Hawk's Hill–West Clandon' style).

From about 50 BC pottery production in East Sussex diverges markedly from both earlier forms and surrounding areas. Instead of adopting the wheel, hand-made production continues. This ceramic tradition (which forms part of Cunliffe's 'Eastern Atrebatic' style zone) has become known as 'East Sussex Ware' and has a distinctive grog temper (Green 1980). The forms are somewhat limited, including jars and large, globular-bodied storage vessels with narrow necks. Applied cordons and decorative arcs ('eyebrows') are characteristic. This curious pottery type dominated East Sussex production throughout the Roman occupation, but appears never to have spread much further than the existing county of East Sussex. A similar, perhaps related, hand-made grog-tempered pottery tradition also developed at the end of the Iron Age in parts of North-East Surrey and West Kent. Known at 'Patch Grove Ware', this pottery type also continued into the Roman period.

Pottery development on the western side of the Weald after the decline of 'saucepan' pottery is markedly different to that in Kent and East Sussex. It is part of a style zone ('Southern Atrebatic') centred on Hampshire, and involves the use of the potter's wheel. High-shouldered jars with wide mouths and

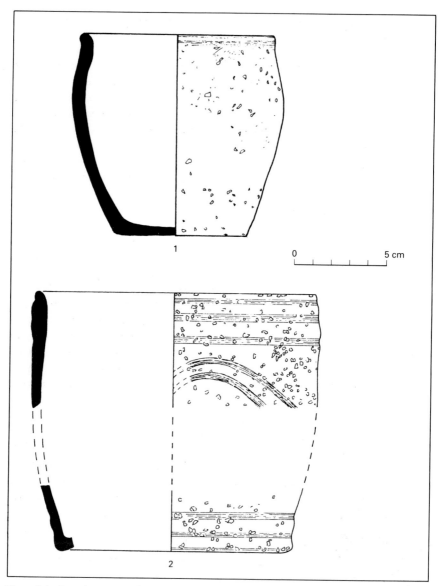

0   5 cm

Figure 5.1 Iron Age pottery from North Bersted, West Sussex. Vessel 1 is a small plain jar, and Vessel 2 is a saucepan pot decorated with bands of grooves and curvilinear patterns.

beaded rims, together with necked jars and high-shouldered bowls with simple, upright rims dominate the assemblages from about 50 BC. Prior to the Roman Conquest, these forms are joined by imports and copies of Gallo-Belgic platters and butt beakers.

Metalwork and Continental Contact

Metalwork provides some of the main evidence for long-distance trade and Continental contacts during the Iron Age. Many of the recovered metal artifacts, however, are actually the products of indigenous smiths who copied and modified Continental prototypes (Stead 1984). Most of the items of Continental manufacture can probably be explained in terms of trade rather than as the results of immigration.

The characteristic weapon of the Hallstatt C period is the long bronze cavalry sword, which came into use during the seventh century BC. The majority of the British finds of such swords have been in the Thames area, especially from the River Thames itself (Cowen 1967). Unfortunately, most of these swords are stray finds (many having been found during dredging). One specimen was also found near the River Mole at Charwood, Surrey. Cowen's study of the various swords shows that they include both Continental and locally produced types, and it is clear that the inventiveness of the local smiths led to the development of a popular and distinctive *Thames Type* sword, which was even exported to the Continent. It also seems that these various Hallstatt type swords must have been used by the British aristocracy rather than by Hallstatt immigrants (Cunliffe 1978*a*). The main reasoning behind this theory is the fact that none of the characteristic Hallstatt burial mounds has been found in Britain (with one possible exception at Ebberston, Yorkshire). Other Hallstatt C type bronze artifacts found in the South-East include razors, phalerae and pins.

One of these phalerae (of hollow, conical form) formed part of a hoard discovered at Sompting, Sussex (E.C. Curwen 1948). The hoard also consisted of seventeen Late Bronze Age type axes, a bronze cauldron of a type (Class B2) which is thought to have been imported from along the Atlantic coasts of Iberia and France during the seventh and sixth centuries BC; pieces from one or more other cauldrons and a boss-shaped object of bronze. One of the bronze axes had some corroded iron adhering to it, and this is thus an extremely interesting association between Bronze Age type metalwork and the use of iron (possibly the earliest example of such use in the South-East).

During and after the sixth century BC, Hallstatt D type objects became fashionable, including short iron swords and daggers and also fibulae. As with the Hallstatt C imports, local craftsmen soon began to copy and modify the Continental versions. Again, the bulk of such artifacts have been found in the Thames area. Evidence during this period for longer-distance contacts includes a sixth-century bronze bucket from Weybridge, Surrey (found near the Brooklands site discussed below). This vessel is a type known to have been produced in the Alpine region north of Venice (Stjernquist 1967).

From the mid-fifth century BC onwards, the archaeological record bears witness to La Tène I contacts. As in the past, the imported goods (especially

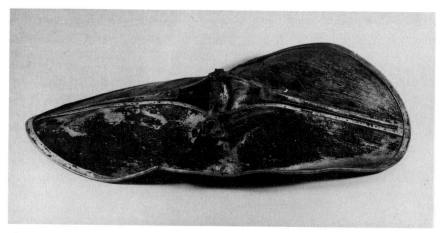

Plate 5.2   The Chertsey shield; made of bronze. Fourth/third century BC. Found in an old river bed at Chertsey, Surrey. Length: 780 mm. (Photograph: British Museum.)

swords, scabbards, daggers, and fibulae) were imitated and modified by local craftsmen. After about 300 BC, and continuing until the first century BC the influence from the Continent on British metalwork seems to have been considerably reduced, and La Tène imports are very rare, although an important example is a third-century silver ring from Park Brow, Sussex. During this period British metalwork appears to have continued and developed largely independently from that on the Continent. From 100 BC the importation by trade and/or migration of La Tène metalwork (La Tène III) significantly increased in importance and again affected the development of local production. It was during the period second century BC to first century AD that most of the well-known pieces of warrior parade gear (shields and helmets) were produced by British craftsmen and some of the more important examples of such metalwork have been recovered from the River Thames. Recently an oval shield (Plate 5.2) was recovered from the gravel of an old river bed at Chertsey, Surrey. This shield has been dated to the fourth/third centuries BC.

Examples of other forms of metalwork which indicate long-distance trade are Greek and Continental Celtic coins. Various examples of Greek coins, dating from the third century BC onwards, have been discovered in the South-East (Curwen 1954; Hanworth 1987). Some of these may have reached Britain as part of Atlantic trade (Cunliffe 1978a). The significance of Celtic coins is discussed in greater detail below, but some of the Continental types found in South-East Britain probably indicate cross-Channel trade.

The Settlement Pattern

The distribution of known Iron Age sites within the region composed of Kent, Surrey and Sussex (Fig. 5.2) is very uneven. Although this pattern can be partly attributed to variable amounts of archaeological research (the Sussex Downs, for instance, having been the scene of relatively intensive fieldwork over a long period), some of the empty zones are probably true gaps. Such areas include the Surrey heathlands where it is thought that earlier human activity had already resulted in the exhaustion of the soils, and large tracts of the Weald, particularly the heavy clays which were probably still forest. Settlement density is therefore hard to estimate, especially since there have been only a few intensive area surveys. Those surveys that have been undertaken were all located in the region between the River Ouse and Eastbourne, Sussex. On Bullock Down, an area of the Chalk Downs, a multiperiod project was undertaken (Drewett 1982). Despite intensive fieldwalking and survey, only a single Iron Age settlement (sixth/fifth century) was found in an area of *c.* 5 km^2. To the west of Bullock Down, a major fieldwalking project in the Cuckmere Valley sampled a variety of geological and environmental zones, but revealed only minimal quantities of Iron Age pottery (Garwood 1984). In addition, only nine settlement sites are recorded for the large block of Downland between the Rivers Cuckmere and Ouse. Thus, settlement density on the Downs in East Sussex does not appear to be as concentrated as that recorded for the chalklands in the Chalton area, Hampshire, where survey has revealed fourteen settlement sites (four Early Iron Age; ten Late Iron Age) in an area of 7 km^2 (Cunliffe 1978*b*).

In contrast to the South Downs, research into the settlement history of the Coastal Plain of West Sussex is still at an early stage, and here there are various problems which make the location of sites very difficult (Bedwin and Pitts 1978). The area, however, is favoured with particularly fertile (though heavy) soils, and gradually a picture is emerging of the colonization of this region during the Bronze and Iron Ages (Bedwin 1983). During the Roman period the Coastal Plain was intensively settled (Pitts 1979), and it is likely that further fieldwork will reveal a high level of activity/settlement for the Late Iron Age, and possibly earlier. The results of rescue archaeology in West Kent also indicate a high density of Late Iron Age sites (Philp 1984), and in the case of Kent generally during the Late Iron Age, we should also note Caesar's comments (in the *Gallic War*) that the 'population is exceedingly large, the ground thickly studded with homesteads'.

Other areas of the South-East are sadly lacking in basic field survey and fieldwalking research, and therefore at present a discussion about settlement density in these areas would be unwarranted. Some general observations are, however, worth making. Firstly, Iron Age sites are much more numerous than those of the Bronze Age. Secondly, there seem to be more known Late than Early Iron Age sites. Thirdly, during the Iron Age (especially in the later period)

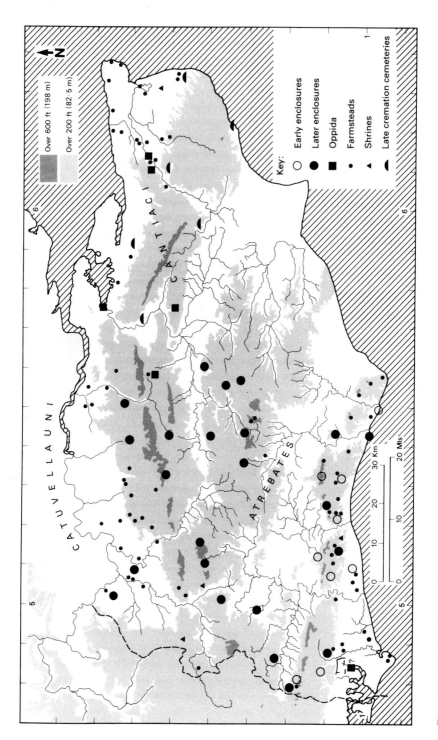

Figure 5.2 The distribution of Iron Age sites in South-East England.

there appears to have been a movement of population into previously marginal areas, such as the Coastal Plain of West Sussex and the Weald. These observations suggest a continuing growth in population.

Even if we were to have a fairly accurate picture of the Iron Age settlement pattern for an area, there would still be various major problems regarding its interpretation and use for indicating levels of population density. These problems would include such factors as the interpretation of site functions, settlement hierarchies, estimating the numbers of people that can be expected to have lived in the various settlement types, and establishing the contemporaneity or otherwise of the individual sites, and length of occupation of sites.

Cunliffe (1978*b*) has examined these various issues for the British Iron Age in general, and concludes that the overall population was probably much greater than has previously been postulated (it possibly exceeded that for the Early Medieval period) and suggests that there was an exponential growth rate. He points out that such an increase in population can only occur so long as the carrying capacity of the environment allows, and that ultimately its rate of growth will be slowed by internal constraints. Should an 'overshoot' situation occur, the results will be 'stress', which will lead to a drastic reduction in the overall population as a result of various checks, either natural, such as malnutrition and disease; or cultural, such as warfare and infanticide. One possible solution to the stress situation however, would be the movement of part of the population into adjacent or marginal situations, hence conserving the resource base of the original territory. Another solution would be technological innovation: either to allow an increase in the carrying capacity of the area under stress *or* to make possible the movement of part of the population into previously marginal areas. A 'stress' situation could also develop, or be increased, as a result of declining soil fertility (with a resulting reduction in the carrying capacity of the land).

Some of the demographic factors outlined above may help to explain changes in, and aspects of, Iron Age settlement patterns and culture. Cunliffe (1978*b*) has attempted to provide a general explanatory framework, particularly with regard to the development of hillforts and *oppida*. In addition, in the South-East, where the evidence suggests a substantial increase in population, the demographic models may help to explain the increased exploitation of the West Sussex Coastal Plain and the Weald. While both cases may partly have involved technological innovations (the construction of extensive systems of drainage ditches on the Coastal Plain; and iron smelting technology for the Weald), the significant development of settlement on the coastal Plain may have resulted from migration from overpopulated areas and/or areas of declining soil fertility on the South Downs.

Farmsteads

There is considerable variation in the form and size of farm settlements, some being 'open' sites, while others are enclosed by an earthwork or palisade. Whether there were significant variations in the functions or status between open sites and enclosed is not clear, and it is possible that some of the open sites may originally have been enclosed by hedges or delimited by the inner boundary of a field system. At Bishopstone, Sussex, there were both types of settlement during the Iron Age, two phases being open sites and the other phase having an enclosure.

Factors affecting the location of settlements vary according to the geology, and are perhaps best understood in the case of the South Downs where sites are often located on south-facing spurs in areas surrounded by, or adjacent to, contemporary field systems. Defensive criteria do not appear to have been important factors affecting the location of such settlements. Despite the large number of known Iron Age farmstead sites in the South-East, few have been systematically investigated on a reasonable scale or according to modern standards. This section will therefore concentrate on a selection of the more extensively excavated and better understood sites.

The site at Bishopstone, Sussex, is of particular interest since it spans the period from the mid-first millennium BC until the Roman Conquest, and was possibly continuously occupied (Bell 1977). Three broad phases have been identified, the first and last being unenclosed, while the other was enclosed by a ditch and possibly a bank. The only definite evidence for the first phase are three pits which are stratigraphically earlier than the enclosure. The pottery contained within these pits was of types present in the later, enclosed settlement and it is likely that the two phases represent a continuous development towards an enclosed form of settlement. Some of the other features (pits and postholes) within, and particularly those outside, the enclosure including two four-post structures and one six-post structure may also belong to the first phase, but stratigraphic proof is absent.

The Early Iron Age ditched enclosure was located just to the south of the brow of the hill, and amongst contemporary fields. Although it was only partially investigated, it would appear that the enclosure was subrectangular in shape, with rounded corners and two simple entrances (breaks in the ditch), one for the northern and one for the southern side. No evidence remained of any bank or entrance structures. The area enclosed was approximately 1 ha (2½ acres). Excavation within the interior of the enclosure revealed two distinct settlement areas. One contained material identical to that from the enclosure ditch, while the other represented a Late Iron Age unenclosed settlement. Features attributed to the Early Iron Age enclosure include storage pits, other pits, four-post, six-post and two-post structures; and a grave dug partly into the fill of the enclosure ditch. Four- and six-post structures are a recurrent feature of Iron Age sites in Britain and they have generally been interpreted as granaries, although ethnographic data suggest that they may have fulfilled a wider range of storage and other functions (Ellison and Drewett 1971). Similarly, two-post structures have often been interpreted as drying frames, although a wide range of other functions is also possible. At Bishopstone there is the possibility that one linear complex of two-post structures may actually represent a single, long building, or two six-post structures on the same alignment.

The Bishopstone enclosure is similar in form (subrectangular with two opposing simple entrances) to many of the other Early Iron Age earthworks on the South Downs, including some of the more substantial earthworks which are usually referred to as hillforts (see below). In particular, the two earthworks on Thundersbarrow Hill (Curwen 1933) are very similar to that at Bishopstone. At Thundersbarrow the first enclosure contained about 0.6 ha, and was subsequently replaced and doubled in size by a new earthwork. During 1985 plough damage assessment excavations were undertaken at Thundersbarrow Hill by the writer (D. Rudling), and these yielded important dating evidence for the earlier enclosure, which can now be attributed on the basis of the pottery finds to the eighth century BC (Sue Hamilton, pers. comm.). Thus this type of enclosure in Sussex clearly goes back to the Later Bronze Age. The purpose of these early enclosures has often been assumed to be primarily concerned with pastoral activities (Bradley 1971*a*) but the Bishopstone example clearly demonstrates that it would be wrong to assume that all the similar earthworks were purely pastoral. It has been pointed out that if at Bishopstone only a small excavation had been made in the enclosure anywhere other than on the southern side, the results would probably have indicated that the site was unoccupied (Bell 1977: 62). This observation is important since very few sites have been excavated on a reasonable scale, and the cumulative results from small-scale investigations may lead to incorrect generalizations. It is possible that most Iron Age enclosures may have had large, open areas used for storage, drying, or cattle and sheep pens, with smaller, very discrete areas reserved for human occupation.

The Late Iron Age unenclosed settlement at Bishopstone duplicated the range of features for the enclosed settlement, and also included an unusual rectangular five-post structure. The relative frequencies of the main types of features are different, however, with the later phase having a greater number of storage pits and fewer post structures than Phase 2. The excavator notes a similar paucity of pits during the Early Iron Age at Muntham Court, Findon, Sussex (where the excavations revealed only one pit, but over 900 post-holes) and offer one possible explanation: that pits and four-post structures may have successively fulfilled the same function of cereal storage. No domestic structures were recognized for any of the three phases at Bishopstone.

The excavations at Bishopstone provide us with various sources of information about the economic activities associated with the site. The basis of the economy was clearly a mixture of arable and pastoral farming. The discovery of carbonized seeds indicates that the cultivars included spelt, six-row barley, oats and peas. Further evidence of arable farming is provided by the storage pits, possible granaries, and saddle and rotary querns. The site also produced possible evidence (fire-cracked flints and what may be fragments of clay ovens) for corn drying. The evidence for the pastoral aspects of the economy is mainly in the form of animal bones, the main species being cattle and sheep/goat, with lesser quantities of horse, pig and domestic fowl. Cattle would have constituted the predominant supply of meat, but there is some evidence to suggest that sheep may have increased in relative importance towards the end of the Iron Age, a tendency which has been noticed elsewhere in Southern England (Cunliffe 1978a).

The diet was supplemented by the results of hunting (red deer, roe deer, fox, gull, swan, seal, whale and fish) and gathering (various types of marine molluscs, crabs and presumably also wild plant foods). Other productive activities included weaving, attested by spindle whorls and loomweights, pottery and possibly cheese making and salt production.

Another Iron Age settlement on the South Downs which was occupied for a long period (sixth to first century BC) was that discovered on Slonk Hill, Shoreham, Sussex (Hartridge 1978). This unenclosed site, situated on the crown of a hill, was partially excavated and, like Bishopstone, had three recognizable phases. Representing the first phase were several pits and gullies, and three square structures: a typical four-post structure, a similar structure but with an extra post hole doubling the length of one side, and a larger six-post structure with an extra post in the centre of the square. The second phase comprised two four-post structures, various pits and post holes, a gully and a hollow containing a mass of burnt flints (such features may have been used for drying corn – see Cunliffe 1978a). Features belonging to the final phase were mainly confined to a small area of the earlier settlement and include a number of pits and two graves. The absence in this phase of 'granary' structures, and a corresponding increase in the number of pits, provides another parallel for this pattern which is discussed above, for the Bishopstone site. Again, none of the phases provided evidence for domestic structures/houses.

Finds reflecting the farming activities of the settlement on Slonk Hill consist of a few seeds (spelt and barley), an iron ard tip, quern fragments, and animal bones (cattle, sheep/goat, pig, horse and domestic fowl). As at Bishopstone, there is again evidence to suggest that the importance of sheep increased during the occupation of the site. There is also evidence to show that some of the stock was kept to full maturity, thus indicating that over-wintering was not a problem, and that before slaughter full economic use could be made of the animals in the form of wool, dairy produce and traction. Although there is very little evidence for hunting (a few red deer bones), the gathering of marine molluscs was obviously important, especially mussels (which were also the predominant type found at Bishopstone).

Other economic activities included weaving and metalworking. The latter is of particular interest and involved both copper-based alloys and iron. The discovery of parts of two crucibles (one containing a drop of tin-bronze) shows that castings were being made. In addition, a lump of copper slag indicates that the smith was not just melting down and recasting scrap bronze, but was actually smelting copper and adding tin to it. In contrast, the evidence for ironworking was forging slag (i.e. secondary ironworking). It would be interesting to know whether the smith (or smiths) formed part of the farming community, or was an itinerant craftsman. Access to the raw materials involved and the skills required, especially for the working of copper alloys, possibly favours the idea of an itinerant smith. Whatever the case, other small rural settlements have also yielded smiths' deposits (Wainwright and Spratling 1973).

Another Downland farmstead, that discovered on Heathy Brow, Beachy Head, Sussex provided unusual evidence for domestic structures (Bedwin 1982*a*). The subsoil on this site is largely a capping of clay-with-flints, but features showed up well against the stony subsoil and included two huts, post-holes and working hollows. There was no evidence for an enclosure ditch, and the settlement was probably an open one.

The two features interpreted as huts consisted of intense, well-defined concentrations of calcined flints, with much pottery, charcoal and sandstone fragments. One hut was rectangular (Fig. 5.3), the other oval/round. If the interpretation of these features is correct, it follows that the construction of the hut walls was such as to leave no trace in the ground (see below). The post-holes were mainly found in two clusters, but there was little indication that they represented structures. The distribution of the features is interesting, each hut site having a nearby working hollow and post-hole cluster. Bedwin has suggested that this arrangement may represent some form of operational unit within the settlement. The dating of the site is based on the pottery finds, which suggest a date centring on the sixth century BC.

Unfortunately, the soil conditions on Heathy Brow were not favourable for the survival of direct evidence for the economy, which was probably based on mixed farming. The site is situated, however, just to the east of an extensive Early Iron Age field system, and the discovery of a spindle whorl suggests at least the keeping of sheep. The discovery of part of a Kimmeridge shale bracelet is evidence for long-distance trade/contacts (a similar shale bracelet was found at Slonk Hill).

The well-known Early Iron Age settlement at Park Brow (Wolseley and Smith 1924; Wolseley *et al.* 1927) which was located (Fig. 5.4) only a short distance from the Bronze Age settlement also provided evidence of possible domestic buildings and site organization. The investigations located 'five large excavated areas about 2 ft. deep and of roughly rectangular plan'. One of these areas was excavated and revealed two parallel rows of post-holes. As in the case of the 12-post-hole structure found at Bishopstone, it is uncertain whether

Figure 5.3 A rectangular hut, Heathy Brow, Bullock Down, East Sussex. The hut is defined by a marked concentration of burnt flints.

Key:

- Burnt flint
- Unburnt flint
- Sandstone
- Pot sherd

N

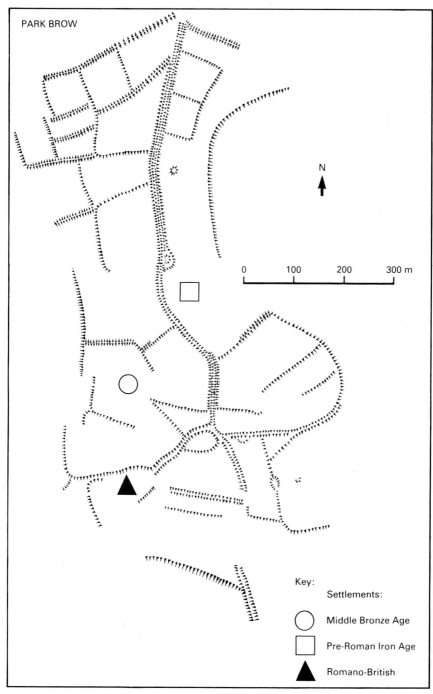

PARK BROW

N

| 0 | 100 | 200 | 300 m |

Key:

Settlements:

○ Middle Bronze Age

□ Pre-Roman Iron Age

▲ Romano-British

Figure 5.4 Prehistoric and Romano-British settlements and lynchetted field systems at Park Brow, West Sussex.

Park Brow structure represents a long hut or two buildings (a four- and a six-post structure) on the same alignment. The discovery, however, of many pieces of daub, some exhibiting wattle marks, encouraged the excavators to interpret their rectangular areas as 'the actual sites of wattle-and-daub huts'.

One of the 'huts' (the one containing the 12-post structure(s)) was associated with a sub-rectangular palisade enclosure or compound. The significance of this (?)special treatment for one of the huts/structures is not known. The investigations also revealed various pits and post-holes, and yielded economic data including querns, animal bones (cattle, sheep, pig and horse), spindle whorls, loomweights, a weaving comb and marine molluscs (mainly mussel and a few oyster).

In contrast to the relatively large number of Iron Age farmstead excavations that have taken place on the South Downs, there have been very few examinations of sites on the West Sussex Coastal Plain. Two sites, North Bersted (near Bognor Regis) and Oving are of particular importance and were both the subject of reasonably large-scale excavations.

The site at North Bersted is located on a brickearth subsoil at approximately 4 m OD (Ordnance Datum). Excavations and watching briefs during construction work revealed that during the Iron Age, an extensive network of drainage ditches had been made in this low-lying area (Bedwin and Pitts 1978). The ditches, which formed the boundaries of rectangular or subrectangular fields, imply the existence of a settled community, which was able to invest a large amount of labour in the initial digging of the ditches. Once constructed, the ditch network would have required regular maintenance (cleaning out) if it were to continue to provide effective drainage of the land. The ditches were traced over an area of 5 ha, but the total area could have been much larger. Surface water would have been carried away down the slope towards Aldingbourne Rife.

One of the enclosures defined by the ditches contained the remains of a circular hut in the form of a well-defined ring gully approximately 6 m in diameter (Fig. 5.5). The gully, which had a single gap for an entrance and one terminal post-hole, is thought to have functioned as a bedding trench for the upright stakes or posts of a small hut. Various finds of daub both within the hut and in its vicinity, may be further traces of the building.

To the north of the hut was a distinct group of stake holes, five post-holes (one pair and a possible group of three), and three pits, one of which was circular and contained a hearth. The excavators suggest that this hearth may possibly have been involved in the production of iron slag, fragments of which were found in many of the Iron Age features.

Unfortunately, the economic basis of this settlement cannot be fully assessed since the flotation of various soil samples failed to yield any plant remains (probably due to poor preservation). In contrast, despite being badly preserved, fairly large numbers of animal bones were recovered. Cattle bones were the most numerous, followed by sheep and pig. Other species included

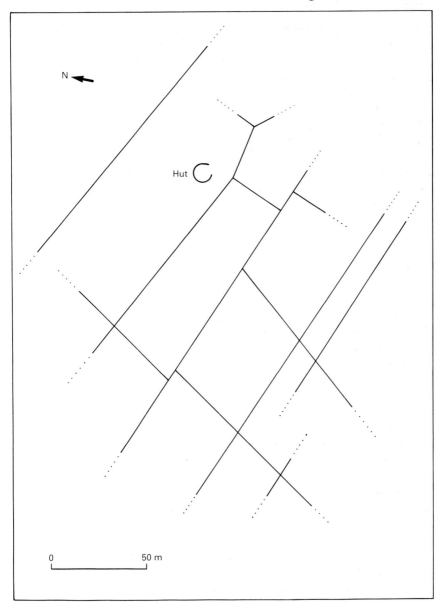

Figure 5.5 A circular hut and ditched field system at North Bersted, West Sussex.

horse, dog, hare and two types of bird. This evidence indicates that at North Bersted cattle were by far the most important source of meat, and that hunting was a very minor activity. There was only one marine mollusc, an oyster, which is very surprising given the proximity of the sea (the absence of other shells is probably a reflection of poor preservation).

The pottery finds (Fig. 5.1) indicate that the settlement was occupied from the third century BC to the late first century BC. It is possible that during the late first century BC, the ditches in the vicinity of the hut were no longer left open, the whole area round the hut may have been cleared and levelled, and some of the features may have been deliberately filled in. This abandonment, however, appears to have been quite localized, and elsewhere the ditched field system apparently continued in the Roman period.

Another Iron Age settlement site on the Coastal Plain, at Copse Farm, Oving, was discovered during the study of crop marks on aerial photographs. The site, which is located on freshwater alluvium and is within the area defined by the Chichester Dykes (see below), forms part of a complex of enclosures linked by field boundaries and double-ditched trackways. A programme of sample excavations was undertaken in order to investigate and date the crop mark features, and Enclosure Complex 1 proved to be of the Late Iron Age (Bedwin and Holgate 1985). The four enclosure ditches differed in form from one another and it appears that the excavated enclosure is merely part of a much more extensive enclosure, which is defined by the larger ditch which forms the south and west sides of the investigated area. The ditches presumably functioned both for demarcating the rectangular plots of land and for drainage purposes. There was a simple entrance on the eastern side. No traces survived of any former banks which might have existed on the inner edge of the ditches. Features within the enclosure include a circular depression which is interpreted as an industrial working area, and various pits and post-holes, many of which are located within the circular depression. One definite four-post structure was identified. All of the pits are fairly shallow, and none is thought to be suitable for grain storage. The discovery of pieces of daub is interpreted as indicating structures such as ovens.

Immediately outside the entrance to the enclosure was a penannular ring gully, approximately 7 m in diameter. This, and associated post-holes, are interpreted as the remains of a round house. Other post-holes in the vicinity of the hut include a group which might be a second four-post structure. The hut and nearby features suggest that a more extensive 'living area' may have existed to the east and north of the investigated enclosure, which was probably part of the working area or 'farmyard'.

Evidence for the farming aspects of the settlement includes an abundance of animal bones (cattle, sheep/goat, horse and pig), but, in spite of extensive flotation, very few carbonized seeds. The seeds that were recovered were all in a very poor state of preservation and included hulled barley, spelt, (?)bread wheat and oats. Cattle supplied the greatest proportion of the site's meat, but the other domesticated animals were clearly also of economic importance and the excavation report suggests that the economic basis of the farm was largely pastoral. The finding of a bronze terret ring (Fig. 5.6) indicates that one of the uses of the horses was for transport.

Other economic activities included hunting/gathering, weaving, metal-

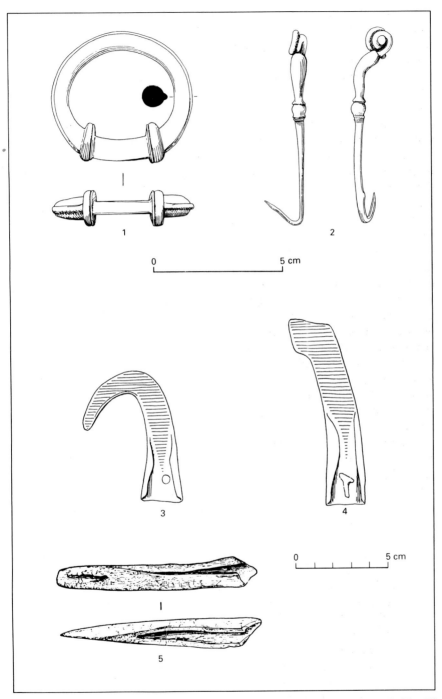

Figure 5.6 Selection of finds from Oving, West Sussex. Copper-alloy: 1: terret ring; 2: La Tene III brooch; Iron: 3: socketed hook; 4: socketed object; Bone: 5: point.

working and possible wood and/or leatherworking. Of these, hunting and gathering were apparently fairly minor activities, wild species being represented only by two bird bones and six oyster shells. The evidence for metalworking consists of iron smithing slag (including the possible remains of shallow hearth bottoms) and a piece of hearth lining. The site has also yielded some circumstantial evidence which may suggest possible bronze working.

The dating of the Oving site is mainly based on the pottery finds, which collectively suggest a span of second to first centuries BC. The pottery assemblage is of particular interest since stylistically it includes both 'saucepan' pottery and 'Aylesford-Swarling' type wheel-thrown pottery (a similar possible overlap of pottery styles/types also occurs at North Bersted). Other ceramic finds include sherds of Mediterranean wine amphorae (Dressel types 1, and 2–4). Further examples of external contacts include fragments of Kimmeridge shale, a mica-schist (?)whetstone from Cornwall and a fragment of Mayen lava quernstone from the Eifel district, Germany.

In comparison with the situation regarding the South Downs, there have been considerably fewer large-scale investigations of Iron Age farmsteads on the North Downs. One of the best-known sites is that at Hawk's Hill, Leatherhead, Surrey. Investigations of this open site during the 1960s revealed twelve storage pits, a large number of post-holes and a drainage gully (Hastings 1965). The only structures recognized from the pattern of the post-holes were a 'drying-rack' and two four-post 'granaries'. The pottery suggested occupation over a long period.

Although there is no direct (seed) evidence for arable farming, this activity is suggested by the discoveries of the storage pits, the possible granaries, and fragments of querns and rubbers. Animal husbandry is attested both directly (bones) and indirectly (spindle whorls and loom weights). The domestic animals included cattle, sheep/goat, pig, horse and dog. Their relative importance in terms of the percentage amount of meat supplied is cattle (53%), sheep (23%), pig (13%) and horse (10%). The faunal report indicates that the majority of the cattle killed for food appear to have been less than three years old, and that sheep and pigs were eaten when mature but not old. It seems that there was a preference for young animals at a prime age, and that there must have been efficient methods of fodder collection and storage in order to allow the over-wintering of the animals. Horses were also eaten when mature, but before they became too old to be palatable.

The faunal assemblage also includes some wild species (deer, fox and birds), but these form less than 1 per cent of the total number of specimens, and thus indicate that hunting was only a very minor source of meat. One other activity undertaken at Hawk's Hill was metallurgy, evidence including iron slag and a possible crucible.

On the Downs in Kent a Late Iron Age farmstead has been totally excavated at Farningham Hill (Philp 1984). This site, which is about 0.2 ha in size, is within a roughly pentagonal ditched enclosure. There were originally four entrances, but later only three. Fifty-six features were located within the enclosure and these were largely confined to the western part of the site. They comprised a probable circular hut about 5 m in diameter (the remains included post-holes and a shallow gully), three groups of pits, and post-holes. Sixteen of the pits were substantial enough to be classed as grain storage pits. The eastern side of the enclosure was largely 'open' and may have been used for such activities as surface storage, drying, or for cattle and sheep pens.

The evidence again suggests a mixed farming economy. Arable farming is mainly indicated by the discovery of the storage pits, some of which contained seeds of wheat and hulled barley. Other indirect evidence for cereal production includes quernstones and large quantities of fire-cracked flints (possibly used for drying grain). The main domesticated animals were cattle, sheep/goats, pigs and horses. Cattle again provided the bulk of the basic meat diet. The cattle and sheep were kept at least until sub-adulthood and mainly until maturity, suggesting that their main purpose was for providing milk and wool. The importance of the pastoral element of the site's economy is further indicated by the finding of spindle whorls and possible loom weight fragments, and may also be reflected in the results of a limited amount of environmental sampling on the site which produced molluscan data containing open country fauna, especially *Vallonia costata*, a species of stable grassland such as pasture. The meat diet was supplemented by the results of hunting: the bones of wild animals including deer and possibly wild boar.

The date range for the Farningham site is provided by the pottery, which spans the period between the mid-first century BC and the mid-first century AD. This dating is consistent with that for two Potin Class II coins found on the site.

The final settlement that I wish to consider is located on the east bank of the River Wey, on Brooklands Farm, Weybridge, Surrey. The site, which is situated on a small promontory of Bagshot Beds Sand, lies around the 50' contour and is not liable to flooding. The settlement possibly dates from the sixth century BC and occupation continued until the Roman Conquest. The excavated area revealed a round house, pits, post-holes, two parallel gullies (of unknown function) and various ironworking structures (Hanworth and Tomalin 1977).

The house was represented by a ring gully (14 m in diameter) which contained post-holes, thus suggesting its use as a bedding trench for a stave-built wall. The hut had a single entrance facing west. Although there were no traces of any external entrance porch, various post-holes inside the hut may have belonged to an internal entrance structure. An interesting discovery in the doorway of the house was an iron latch lifter. Within the hut were discovered a ring of post-holes about 1 m inside the ring gully, an open hearth placed between the circle of post-holes and the ring gully (the excavator points out the serious fire risk caused by such an arrangement), a pit and various post-holes. Immediately outside the entrance to the house was found the start of another ring gully, but lack of time prevented the full investigation of this feature.

The excavations exposed eighty-four pits, but most of these were too small to be regarded as suitable for the storage of grain in bulk (only thirteen had an apparent capacity of over 1.5 m^3). In addition, the majority of the pits contained very few finds and they were therefore not regarded as rubbish pits. Several of the pits may have functioned to store raw clay, lumps of which were found in some of the fills. One pit contained much material associated with ironworking and another has been interpreted as a charcoal burner's clamp. The excavators have made the interesting suggestion that some of the pits may have served as latrines. Possible evidence in support of this theory includes the discovery within several of the pits of bands of podsol (possibly the result of a succession of sand layers being individually deposited in the pits) and the high phosphorus content of material derived from them. Six of the pits were covered by hearths made up of burnt flints, clinker and burnt daub with wattle impressions (the possible remains of a fired clay cover for the hearth). The proximity of these hearths to one of the ironworking areas has led to the suggestion that they had some unexplained purpose connected with iron-working.

There were two main concentrations of ironworking. In the western area features included five small, round furnaces (the most complete of which had a bowl-shaped base), various patches of burnt material, four pits (of uncertain function) and a possible seven-post structure (approximately 5 m x 4 m). If contemporary, one of the furnaces would have been inside this structure. The eastern ironworking area consisted of a main hearth with several attendant features. In the centre of the circular hearth were pieces of slag. Suitable iron ore was available locally from the Bracklesham Beds.

The ironworking features of the Brooklands site are very important and represent the most complete establishment of its kind that has yet been exca-vated from this period. Henry Cleere (in Hanworth and Tomalin 1977) has suggested that the two ironworking areas appear to have been devoted to different processes, the western area being used for smelting iron, and the eastern area for forging artifacts. A similar occurrence of both smelting and forging activities has been noted by Cleere for the site at Purberry Shot, Ewell, Surrey (Lowther 1947). In general the slag debris at Brooklands was very meagre, and the scale of ironworking operations must have been small. In spite of this fact (and the long occupation of the site), Cleere has put forward the hypothesis that ironworking was the main business of the settlement, which was perhaps the homestead of a specialist iron smith and his family. Unfortu-nately, it is now impossible to test this theory since the rest of the site has been destroyed.

The argument, however, that farming 'seems to have played little, if any, part' in the life of the settlement, can partly be explained by the soil conditions, which were not favourable for the survival of bone (the Iron Age areas of the site produced a total of only sixty-six bones, species including cattle and sheep/goat). Possible evidence for agriculture includes a few carbonized seeds (although significantly more might have been recovered if flotation had been used), quernstone fragments and the larger (?)storage pits. We should also note that several of the other settlements described above have yielded signs of metallurgy and Cunliffe, whilst reviewing the general evidence for iron smelting in Iron Age Britain, has concluded that 'iron extraction and forging was a normal home craft and not solely a skill in the hands of specialists' (Cunliffe 1978*a*: 291). Thus the status of the Brooklands site, as either a farmstead or the homestead of a specialist craftsman, remains uncertain. However, the long occupation of the site and the small amount of slag tend to indicate that for most (if not all) of its occupation, it functioned primarily as a farm.

A fairly rare feature of the farming landscape during the Iron Age in South-East England are the banjo-enclosures, which are an earthwork class largely centred on Wessex. These earthworks, which date to the Middle and Late Iron Age, consist of small enclosures, usually about 0.2–0.4 ha in size. The enclosure is approached by a funnel-like entrance formed by approximately parallel ditches, which run away from the enclosure and then swing outwards, sometimes in order to create a larger enclosure containing the smaller one. These earthworks are generally thought to have been designed in order to corral cattle. Other farming functions are also possible however (the banjo enclosure at Micheldever Wood, Hampshire, for example, contained a number of storage pits and carbonized plant remains – Monk and Fasham 1980), and some sites have yielded evidence for domestic occupation or are located near to such occupation (the unexcavated site at Tadworth, Surrey, appears to have houses within it – Clark, 1977).

Examples of banjo enclosures in the South East include Effingham and Tadworth (both in Surrey), Selhurst Park Farm, Denge Bottom and Carne's Seat (all in Sussex), and Fawkham (Kent). At Carne's Seat the banjo enclosure may have been associated with two concentric enclosures dated to the Middle Iron Age (Holgate 1986). These enclosures are interpreted as a defended farmstead, which on pottery evidence appears to have continued into the Late Iron Age.

This section has dealt in some detail with a selection of Iron Age farms in the South East. The amount of space devoted to this aspect of the settlement pattern has been deliberate since the farms were the principal social and economic units during the period, yet have generally received relatively less archaeological attention than the more spectacular hillforts (see below). What conclusions then, can be made about Iron Age farming in the area covered by this book? It appears that most (perhaps all) of the farms depended upon a mixture of crop and animal husbandry, and that these activities were probably combined to form an intensive and integrated system. The arable crops included wheat, barley, oats and peas; while the main domesticated animals were cattle, sheep/goats, horses, pigs, fowl and dogs. Cattle were the main source of the meat diet and may also have been very important for dairy produce, as a source of raw materials (e.g. leather) and for traction. Sheep were another

Plate 5.3 'Celtic' fields on the Downs near Jevington, East Sussex. (Photograph: Cambridge University Collection: copyright reserved.)

major source of meat, but were also kept for their wool. Horses, in addition to their meat value, were also important for traction (and presumably also for riding). The farming system was clearly capable of ensuring the over wintering of animals, thus allowing the farmers to choose the optimal age for killing them. The diet was supplemented by the results of hunting and gathering, but neither activity seems to have been very important.

The farm settlements, which are often located amongst contemporary field systems, varied considerably in form, size and the spatial arrangement of activities. Common features include pits, post-holes, various multi-post structures, hearths, working hollows, houses, industrial features/areas, and graves. The settlements were the scene of both domestic and farming activities, including such crafts as weaving, metallurgy and perhaps potting.

Most of the communities appear to have been involved in trading or exchange networks which enabled them to acquire goods or materials from outside their neighbourhoods. Some of these goods had been transported over considerable distances, such as the Kimmeridge shale bracelets (present at both

144

of the Surrey sites and also at three of those in Sussex) and the Mediterranean amphorae (occurring at both Oving and Carne's Seat).

Iron Age farmsteads and their associated field systems, especially those located in areas off the Downs, are still a high priority for future research. Archaeology is still in the teething stages of expanding its interests from the investigation of individual sites (such as settlement sites) to broader based studies which consider such sites in their wider contexts (farming complexes/landscapes). Very little attention has been paid to Iron Age field systems, and those that still survive on the Downs represent a category of earthworks, 'Celtic' fields (Plate 5.3) which, due to the politics and economics of modern farming, are under increasing threat of destruction. Unfortunately only a few large-scale regional surveys of such field systems have been undertaken, a notable effort being that by George Holleyman (1935). In more recent years there have been various modern, scientific approaches to specific blocks of ancient fields, examples of such work including those by Martin Bell (1977) and Peter Drewett (1982). The cross-ridge dykes are also worthy of study, especially given their possible interpretation as 'ranch boundaries' (Bradley 1971*a*).

Hillforts

Apart from farm settlements, the other major type of Iron Age site in the South-East is the hillfort. The chronology, development and distribution of hillforts, however, varies markedly from area to area within the region, and some areas never had such enclosures. Presumably these areas had different social and economic systems to those present in the hillfort-dominated zone. The term 'hillfort' is used to describe a very heterogeneous group of defended hilltop enclosures. Such enclosures vary considerably in size, type of defences and function. The smallest examples compare in size with farm settlements (and may themselves be simply defended farmsteads – example the Caburn, Sussex), whilst the largest are massive earthworks covering 20 ha or more. It is thus very unlikely that all of the enclosures commonly referred to as 'hillforts' shared a common function or functions.

The origins of hillforts can now be traced back to the first half of the first millennium BC (Chapter 4) and their development has been described elsewhere (e.g. Cunliffe 1978*a*). Most of the hillforts in Southern England are of the so-called contour type, often starting as an earthwork consisting of a single bank and ditch (univallate) encircling the crest of a hill. In other areas, such as the Weald, forts were located in order to take advantage of promontories and other defensive possibilities of the landscape. Some of the hillforts were later increased in size and/or given improved defences, such as additional defensive circuits (multivallate) or new ramparts or gateways. Cunliffe (1976*a*) has identified two successive phases of hillfort construction during the Iron Age in Central Southern England (including the Sussex Downs) and he distinguishes between *Early hillforts* and *Developed hillforts* (those sites which continued to be intensively used after the beginning of the fourth century BC). For Sussex, Bedwin (1978*a*) has added a third category, *Late hillforts*, a term which he used to refer to the various defended hilltop enclosures which appear to have been occupied in the 150 years before the Roman Conquest (in contrast to the developed hillforts). The development of hillforts in the Weald, Surrey and Kent is very different from that outlined above, and there is little evidence for hillfort building in these areas before the middle of the fourth century BC (Cunliffe 1982).

Although many of the hillforts in the South-East have been subjected to sample excavations, in most cases the investigations have concentrated on the rampart defences, with little or no examination of the forts' interiors. Thus, whilst these excavations have provided reasonably good dating evidence for the constructional history of the forts, they have yielded very little information about the activities which went on inside them.

The first phase of hillfort construction is centred on the sixth and fifth centuries BC and in South-East England appears to be restricted to the South Downs. It is possible, however, that some of the earlier Surrey enclosures, like Caesar's Camp, Wimbledon (Ch. 4) remained in use in this phase. The early enclosures differ greatly in size and shape, have relatively simple (sometimes feeble) defences and appear to have minimal occupation within them. Their primary function as stock enclosures has been suggested (e.g. Bedwin 1978*a*) and the term 'hillfort' may be misleading.

Examples in Sussex of defended enclosures dating to the sixth and fifth centuries BC include Hollingbury, Harting Beacon, Chanctonbury Ring, Seaford Head, Ditchling Beacon, possibly Goosehill Camp, and the larger of the two enclosures on Thundersbarrow Hill (Fig. 5.7). The enclosed farming settlement at Bishopstone and a recently sampled enclosure at Binderton, West Sussex (Kenny 1985) also belong to this period and are similar in size to the 'hillforts' on Thundersbarrow Hill and at Chanctonbury. Other enclosures on the South Downs were formerly thought to be of sixth- to fifth-century date, but now appear to be either earlier or later. Thus the sites on Bury Hill and Court Hill have now been dated to the third millennium BC, and similar dating is possible for Halnaker Hill (Bedwin 1981*a*; 1982*b*; 1984*b*). Harrow Hill and Highdown are now thought to date to the early first millennium BC (Ch. 4), as is the small enclosure on Thundersbarrow Hill (see above). In contrast, the very large (in excess of 25 ha) feebly defended enclosure at Belle Tout may be Romano-British or later, since the snail *Helix aspersa*, a species not thought to have been introduced into Britain until the first century AD, was found in quantity in the primary ditch silts during recent excavations (Thomas in Drewett 1982). The odd site of Ranscombe Camp, although probably of sixth-to fifth-century date, is now reinterpreted as a cross dyke, whilst the other unusual earthwork, that at Wolstonbury (where the ditch is *inside* the bank), may be a henge monument (Bedwin 1984*a*). Other possible Early Iron Age enclosures in Sussex include the undated enclosure which formerly existed on Castle Hill, Newhaven and the Devil's Dyke (unexcavated). We are therefore left with a much thinner distribution of 'Early hillforts' than recent models suggest (e.g. Bedwin 1978*a*: Fig. 24).

Harting Beacon is the largest of the Early hillforts and its defences consist of a single bank and ditch on three sides of a sub-rectangular area enclosing some 12 ha. No defences have been detected on the fourth (northern) side, which is at the top of the steep scarp slope of the Downs. There is a single entrance on the west side of the enclosure, and a geophysical survey of the interior revealed little evidence of occupation (Bedwin 1978*b*; 1979*a*). A survey of the region round the site has produced no evidence of prehistoric field systems, but a complex of cross-dykes lies to the east of the fort. Excavations directed by Owen Bedwin during 1976 and 1977 involved the defences, a sample of the interior of the enclosure, and a re-examination of the gateway area (previously excavated during the 1940s, but still unpublished).

A section across the southern defences showed that there had been two phases of rampart construction, at least one of which (the earlier one) had included a timber retaining structure at the front of the rampart. The investigation of the gateway area revealed a pair of large entrance post-holes and two ditch terminals. Excavation of the ditches provided dating and environmental evidence, including mollusc samples which suggest that the local environment during the Iron Age was open, overgrown grassland, with no indication of intensive grazing or cultivation.

The investigations of part of the interior of the enclosure involved the excavation of 1,750 m^2 in the south-eastern corner. Few features were found: 4 four-post structures, 1 six-post structure, several post-holes and 4 shallow pits (one of which contained quantities of bone and pottery). The interpretation of the multi-post structures is uncertain, but there is circumstantial evidence (the absence of adjacent field systems and the molluscan data) against the interpretation of the four-post structures as granaries. Perhaps they are the remains of domestic buildings or structures for storing animal fodder (e.g. hay).

The small quantity of faunal remains includes bones of domesticated animals (cattle, sheep/goat, horse and pig) and wild species (deer and (?)wild boar). Although sheep predominate, they appear to have been of similar importance to cattle in terms of the meat diet. The report on the 1976 excavations draws attention to the relatively large number of immature bones and teeth.

The few small finds from the site (including quern fragments, two spindle whorls, a loom weight and a piece of bloomery slag), together with the pottery and bone finds, are evidence for a limited amount of domestic/craft activity. The role of the enclosure on Harting Beacon remains uncertain, but the most likely function is that of a large stock enclosure with a few possible domestic structures located in the more sheltered south-east corner.

Chanctonbury Ring, high up on the scarp slope between the Arun and Adur rivers is in a similar position to Harting Beacon, but is only a tenth of the size (1.2 ha). This small, oval univallate earthwork had one entrance to the south-west. The enclosure is positioned in the middle of a long plateau with easy access from east and west. On the plateau are two cross dykes, which are situated respectively about 200 m to the east and west of the fort. The site provides extensive views; northwards across the Weald to the North Downs, and to the south, over a long stretch of coastline. Recent excavations of about 10 per cent of the interior (a reasonably good random sample since the three main areas investigated were widely spaced apart) produced virtually no settlement evidence (Bedwin 1980*b*). A section across the defences showed that these consisted of a ditch and simple dump rampart (with no wooden retaining structure). Molluscan analysis of samples from the defences showed a lack of open country species and indicated surroundings free of severe human disturbance. This molluscan data, together with an absence of field systems in the area, again suggests that the enclosure may have been for stock. A section across the cross dyke located to the west of the enclosure produced evidence which indicates that the dyke is Roman or later.

Ditchling Beacon is the third broadly contemporary enclosure situated on the northern scarp slope of the South Downs. It is sub-rectangular in shape, had a simple dump bank and enclosed an area of 5.5 ha. Limited excavations (Crow 1930; Rudling 1985*b*) have revealed virtually no settlement evidence. As the enclosure is on clay-with-flints, molluscs did not survive in the ditch silts, so the contemporary environment is uncertain. A function similar to Harting Beacon and Chanctonbury can, however, be postulated. Two of this group of sites have produced almost no signs of settlement, whilst at Harting Beacon the evidence is fairly minimal and need not indicate permanent occupation. Possibly all three enclosures were used only seasonally as centres for upland grazing, perhaps by settlements at the foot of the Downs which would have been well positioned to exploit the fertile arable land on the Upper Greensand bench (Bedwin 1979*a*).

Four univallate enclosures on the south side of the Downs, Highdown Hill (1 ha), Thundersbarrow Hill (1.2 ha), Hollingbury (2.7 ha) and Seaford Head (in excess of 4.2 ha) were almost certainly used, if not (as in the case of Highdown Hill) actually constructed, in the sixth–fifth centuries BC. Both Highdown and Thundersbarrow (Fig. 5.7) are surrounded by lynchetted fields, but a similar situation is not recorded for either Hollingbury or Seaford Head. Excavations within Highdown (Wilson 1940; 1950), Thundersbarrow (Curwen 1933; and by the writer during 1985) and Seaford Head (Pitt-Rivers 1877; Bedwin 1986) were all too limited to establish the presence of any permanent occupation. At Seaford Head the recent excavations concentrated on the defences, and demonstrated that there had been timber revetting at the front of

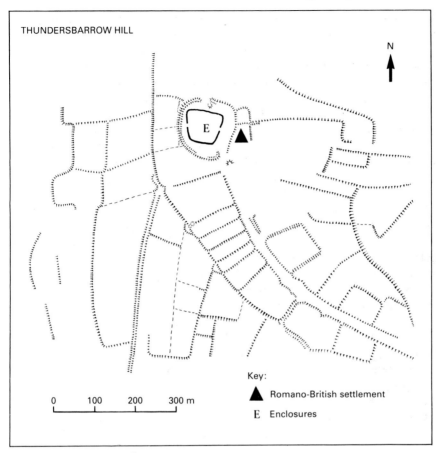

THUNDERSBARROW HILL

N

Key:

▲ Romano-British settlement

E Enclosures

0   100   200   300 m

Figure 5.7 Prehistoric enclosures, lynchetted fields, and Romano-British settlement on Thundersbarrow Hill, West Sussex.

the rampart. The excavations also produced environmental evidence from the buried Iron Age soil beneath the bank. Pollen indicated open country conditions, but it was not possible to determine whether this had been an arable or pastoral environment. An analysis of the buried soil itself, however, showed that tillage had occurred right up to the time of the construction of the enclosure. This information is very interesting, especially since no prehistoric lynchets have been recorded in the vicinity.

Larger-scale excavations have been undertaken at Hollingbury (E. C. Curwen 1932; Holmes 1984). The earlier excavations concentrated on the main defences, the east gate, a palisade trench and a bank and ditch belonging to an earlier earthwork. The perimeter bank was shown to be of box-rampart construction, with a sloping bank behind the inner face of the inner row of timbers. Evidence for the east gate consisted of a post-hole on either side of the

149

inner face of a gap in the box-rampart. The enclosure also had a second entrance on its western side. Although this has not been excavated, it is a more elaborate structure than the east gate and involves a passageway formed by the inturned ends of the rampart wall. The relatively sophisticated nature of the earthworks, together with the discovery of possible sling stones, indicates that defence may have been an important function of this enclosure.

Inside the fort, Curwen's excavations revealed a palisade trench lying parallel to the eastern rampart. Its function and date are unknown, but it included an entrance opposite the east gate. In 1967 John Holmes re-examined the gap in the palisade trench and revealed another pair of post-holes parallel to those flanking the entrance. The group of four post-holes is possibly the remains of an entrance structure.

The 1967–69 excavations also sampled parts of the southern half of the fort, and in the south-west corner exposed traces of five round huts, ranging in size from 5.5 to 13 m in diameter. These huts were recognized by the presence of ring gullies, and also, in some cases, by post-holes. Apparently occupation lasted long enough for one of the huts to become obsolete and to be replaced by another. The excavator, who has identified the smallest building as a weaving hut, is of the opinion that the five huts 'can only be a sample of the whole number ... and there is no doubt that more would be found if it were possible to excavate the whole interior of the earthwork' (Holmes 1984: 37). In addition to the huts, the excavations revealed a few shallow pits, but no larger storage pits or four-post structures. There were very few finds: a total of only 488 pottery sherds from the 1967–69 excavations (a surprisingly small number for a settlement which is thought to have been permanently occupied for a number of years), a loom weight, a quern, and sling stones. Unfortunately, there was no bone (due to the soil conditions). A fabric analysis of the pottery suggests the exploitation of resources from both north and south of the Downs, with the possibility of trade up to 20 km inland (Hamilton 1984).

The interpretation of the enclosure at Hollingbury remains uncertain. The sophistication of the defences, however, is in contrast to the other 'Early hillforts', as is the amount of evidence for domestic buildings. The latter, however, may be concentrated into a relatively small area of the enclosure, the rest of which may be largely empty and thus suitable for keeping animals.

To conclude, the Early hillforts of Sussex appear to be a group of enclosures that were generally either unoccupied or had only limited occupation. The possible exception is Hollingbury, but even there the amount of domestic refuse found was very small. The function of these enclosures is uncertain, but their location and the limited environmental data available would suggest that they were generally not in the centres of grain production (but note the evidence for tillage at Seaford). A factor common to all of the enclosures is the presence of large areas of 'empty' space, a phenomenon which has also been observed at two extensively excavated Early Iron Age enclosures in Hampshire: Balksbury (Wainwright 1970) and Winklebury (Smith 1977).

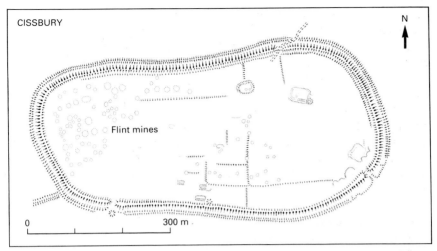

Figure 5.8 Cissbury hillfort. Within the hillfort are traces of Neolithic flint mines and post-hillfort lynchetted fields.

One of a possible range of functions could be for the intermittent rounding up, and perhaps protection, of stock. If this interpretation is correct however, we are faced with the task of explaining what happened when the enclosures went out of use (Bedwin 1986). For instance, did the pastoral side of the economy become less important, or was there a change in the management of animals? The 'Early hillforts' were a major feature of the South Downs during the sixth and fifth centuries BC, but appear to have been abandoned after this period.

Enclosures constructed from the fourth to first centuries BC in South-East England appear to fulfil a very different function from that of those constructed during the sixth and fifth centuries. In particular, they display an increased concern for strong defences and several can best be interpreted as defended settlements, either permanently or irregularly occupied. The usual term 'hillfort' appears appropriate for these enclosures in a way it did not for most of the earlier stock enclosures. Hillforts of this period are spaced widely over the South-East (including the High Weald), and they form part of a large zone of forts stretching from North Wales, through the Welsh borderland and Wessex to Kent (Cunliffe 1976a).

The hillforts of the fourth to first centuries BC in the South-East can perhaps best be considered in three groups, those on the South Downs, those in the Weald and on the Greensand, and those mainly on the North Downs and beyond. As major field monuments, all have been subjected to some excavation, but as with the earlier enclosures, interior investigations were small-scale or non-existent.

On the Downs in Sussex there are three characteristic Developed hillforts: Cissbury (Fig. 5.8), Torberry and the Trundle (Plate 5.4). Although they vary considerably in size (20, 2.5 and 4 hectares respectively), each had strong

Plate 5.4 The Trundle, Singleton, West Sussex: view from the north east, showing the bold ramparts and ditch of the 'developed' Iron Age hillfort, and the Neolithic causewayed enclosure within the interior.
(Photograph: Cambridge University Collection: copyright reserved.)

defences (although Torberry has suffered badly from ploughing). At Cissbury and the Trundle the circuit of the defences involved a massive rampart and ditch which enclosed the crests of their respective hills (in the case of the Trundle the earthworks enclose the site of the Neolithic causewayed enclosure – see Ch. 3). In contrast, at Torberry there were three phases in the development of the defensive circuit: the first phase consisted of a rampart (with a simple gap entrance) which cut off the neck of the promontory defining the original defended area; the next phase involved the continuation of the defences around the summit of the hill; and the third phase saw the abandonment of the Phase 1 defences and the extension of the Phase 2 defences in order to enclose an additional 1–2 ha (Cunliffe 1976*b*). The Phase 3 defences had a new and more sophisticated entrance (which involved a defended corridor), but this was later remodelled on a massive scale (Phase 4). Investigations at both Cissbury and the Trundle have also produced evidence for various phases of refortification of the entrances, particularly so in the case of the east gate at the Trundle, where three periods of construction were recognized (Curwen 1931).

Having established the defensive qualities of the three enclosures, we must consider what they were designed to protect. Unfortunately, there have been only very limited investigations of the forts' interiors, but the investigations at the Trundle (which were mainly intended to investigate the Neolithic aspects of the site) revealed a number of Iron Age pits and large quantities of artifacts (Curwen 1929; 1931). One of the artifacts was an iron latch lifter and indicates that there were probably also houses inside the fort. Other finds included much pottery, bones (both animal and a few human), bone objects (including tools and a weaving comb), spindle whorls, loom weights, large quantities of fire-cracked flints, quern fragments, oyster shells, daub, a mass of raw clay, various iron objects (tools, weapons, etc.), iron slag, sling stones (beach pebbles), one clay 'sling-bullet', flintwork, parts of two Kimmeridge shale bracelets and part of a blue glass ring.

The animal bones include examples of cattle, sheep/goat, horse, pig, deer, dog and cat (cat was also present in a Late Iron Age pit at Bishopstone). This varied assemblage of finds, together with the pits, indicates that activities carried out within the hillfort included habitation, storage and craftwork (spinning, weaving, metallurgy, (?)pottery and (?)leather and woodworking). In addition, some of the finds (such as the shale bracelets, the glass ring and the querns) show that the settlement had networks for obtaining goods from outside the locality. Obviously these discoveries are only from small areas of the forts and may therefore not be typical (other areas might be 'empty' of features and finds). The available evidence suggests, however, a fairly intensive use/occupation of the site. The range of finds from Torberry tends to duplicate that from the Trundle.

In the absence of a more extensive investigation of the interior of one of the Sussex Developed hillforts, we must look outside the county. At Danebury (Hants) very large-scale excavations (approximately half of the interior) have provided us with a detailed picture of life within a Developed hillfort (but obviously such a picture need not be typical of all such forts). The impression obtained is of a large resident community which occupied the site over a considerable period of time (Cunliffe 1984). The settlement was planned and included roads, housing zones, storage and activity areas and (?)religious structures. Significantly it does not appear to have 'empty' areas for such activities as the keeping of stock. In addition to undertaking normal domestic activities, the inhabitants of the fort were also involved in long-distance trade and the production of various types of goods.

Such forts were the most complex form in a hierarchy of settlement types and Cunliffe has suggested that they were nucleated centres which provided services for the surrounding territory. He has also pointed out that the order apparent in the layout of sites such as Danebury, and the massive nature of their defences 'implies a degree of sustained coercive control by a central

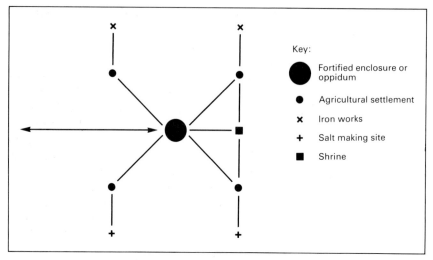

Key:

● Fortified enclosure or oppidum

● Agricultural settlement

✕ Iron works

+ Salt making site

■ Shrine

Figure 5.9 Theoretical model to show the possible relationship between different elements of the Iron Age settlement pattern.

power'. These forts were 'the central pivots for the articulation of all major social and economic systems' (Cunliffe 1976*b*: 141). It is further suggested that the Developed hillforts occupied central positions in large, often naturally defined, territories and that they achieved their position as the focus of the region by gradually gaining supremacy over other centres (Fig. 5.9).

How does this model fit the Sussex data? The discoveries at the Trundle possibly hint that this site at least may have contained a large community which undertook domestic, craft and trade activities (but so did most of the farmsteads). All three of the Developed hillforts had massive defences, the construction of which (particularly Cissbury) must have required a substantial input of labour, thus implying the coercive control of a large number of people. The distribution of the forts is also suggestive, each being located on a block of Downland between the main rivers. But although the forts were constructed during the period when most of the 'Early hillforts' were going out of use, there is no evidence to suggest that they were gaining supremacy over the sites being abandoned. Indeed, if the emergence of dominant forts was the cause of the abandonment of earlier enclosures, why are there no Developed hillforts east of the River Adur? (Note also the differences in the main functions of the two phases of enclosure: the keeping/protection of stock, and the protection of a large settlement.) In addition, although finds from the Developed hillforts indicate earlier Iron Age activity on these sites, there is no evidence that such activity involved an enclosure. Perhaps the location of the Developed hillforts, which are basically different to the Early hillforts, depended upon different criteria, particularly those of defence (as the massive earthworks suggest). Such defences imply the possibility of violence, perhaps due to social unrest, warfare or raiding. Possibly the underlying cause of such troubles was population pressure (see above).

All three of the Developed hillforts in Sussex appear to have gone out of use by about 100 BC. It is possible that these abandonments may have been linked to changes in political or economic power associated with the development of an *oppidum* on the Coastal Plain (see below). Only Torberry has yielded possible signs of a violent end: the deliberate slighting of the gate.

Although there were no typical Developed hillforts on the South Downs to the east of the river Adur, defended enclosures were a feature of this region during the period following the abandonment of the forts to the west. The main example of these *Late hillforts* is Mount Caburn (1.4 ha), but other possible examples are the promontory fort known as the Devil's Dyke (15 ha) and Castle Hill, Newhaven (size unknown). Each is located on a separate block of Downland, and they all appear to have been occupied in the last century before the Roman Conquest (Bedwin 1978*a*). Unfortunately, only the Caburn (Plate 5.5) has been the subject of archaeological investigations.

The sequence of occupation at the Caburn starts as an enclosed farmstead during the sixth and fifth centuries BC. Later (first-century BC) the site was fortified by a ditch and simple dump rampart. Finally, in the first half of the first century AD, perhaps as a response to the Roman invasion, the site was refortified (the new defences include a wide, flat-bottomed ditch of the Fécamp type). One result of these two phases of hillfort construction is that today the site appears to be multivallate, when in fact it should probably be viewed as two univallate forts, one succeeding and containing the other. The fort appears to have gone out of use soon after the Conquest and the reason for this may be linked to 'distinct evidence of burning' in the gateway (Wilson 1939). Was this fort perhaps attacked or compulsorily abandoned after the Roman invasion? Possibly the inhabitants may have moved to the foot of the Downs at Ranscombe, where a settlement was established at approximately this period (Bedwin 1978*c*).

Fairly extensive excavations have been undertaken within the interior of the Caburn and some 140 pits, which were fairly evenly distributed within the enclosure, have been excavated (Pitt-Rivers 1881; Curwen and Curwen 1927). The excavations produced a large quantity of finds and these, together with the possible storage pits and the lynchetted field systems, indicate that the settlement had a mixed farming economy, but was also involved in various craft activities including spinning, weaving, metallurgy (the manufacture of both iron and bronze objects) and the making of items from antler. Although the excavations failed to reveal any features which could be attributed to buildings within the fort, the discovery of three iron latch lifters indicates the former presence of such structures. Long-distance contacts are evidenced by the presence of various items including a Kimmeridge shale bracelet, glass beads, and 12 Class I Potin coins (the main distribution of such coins is centred on the Thames and North Kent – see below).

155

Plate 5.5 Mount Caburn, Beddingham, East Sussex: view from the east. The massive rampart and wide 'Fécamp' type ditch of the later refortification appear on the right.

How do we explain the role of this strongly defended site, particularly at a time when defended hilltop enclosures were being abandoned in West Sussex? Firstly we should consider the size of the Caburn. Its relatively small size (1.4 ha), and the evidence for its basically mixed farming economy, can perhaps best be interpreted as indicating a well defended, permanent and prosperous farming settlement as opposed to a refuge for people from a large territory. The contrast with the Downs of West Sussex might also be explained in terms of the two regions having by now different social and economic systems. Possible evidence in support of this idea is provided by differences in pottery between the two areas (see above) and by the presence in the region between Lewes and Eastbourne of a relatively large number of Class I Potin coins (Rudling 1979), which is in marked contrast to the situation in West Sussex. Perhaps by this stage parts of East Sussex were becoming more involved in the social systems to the north, than with those to the west. Such a shift of interests may have continued and thus explain the re-defence of the Caburn before the conquest: a possible anti-Roman action which would contrast with the presumed pro-Roman sympathies of West Sussex (see below).

Moving northward to the hillforts of the Weald and the surrounding Greensand, there has been a recent survey of the Iron Age sites in the Weald (Money 1978) and a report on excavations at three of the Surrey Greensand sites (Thompson 1979). Seven sites with enclosures have been recorded in the High Weald. Of these only the site at Castle Hill, where there were two forts, can be dated to the middle part of the Iron Age (Money 1976). The first fort, a bivallate earthwork enclosing 1.8 ha, was built in the fourth century BC, but appears to have been used for only a brief period before being (?)destroyed/abandoned. Later, during the third century BC, a univallate fortification enclosing 1.01 ha was built to the south-west of the first fort. Again this enclosure appears to have had only a short period of use before being abandoned.

Three hillforts in the High Weald have been dated to the Late Iron Age: High Rocks, Garden Hill and Saxonbury. Excavations at High Rocks have indicated that parts of the area were occupied/farmed prior to the construction of the first enclosure (Money 1968). The first fortification, which consisted of a single bank and ditch enclosing 9.71 ha, was soon abandoned. The next phase of activity at the site appears to have involved farming and possible iron-working, but later the old enclosure was refortified with double banks and ditches. Occupation may then have continued into the Roman period.

The univallate earthwork at Garden Hill encloses 2.7 ha (Money 1977). The site has been the subject of eleven seasons of excavations, and the final report is being prepared. Inside the defences, a smelting furnace, a forging hearth, an oven and a hearth have all been dated by archaeomagnetic tests to the first century BC (*Britannia* Vol. XI, 400; Vol. XII, 364). Other traces of Iron Age occupation include the remains of two round houses. During 1985 a small earthwork (Chelwood Gate) in the vicinity of Garden Hill was found to contain evidence of occupation dating to the Late Iron Age. This site has been tentatively identified as a small farmstead (Wickenden 1986).

At Saxonbury the earthwork has a single bank and ditch and encloses a mere 0.6 ha (Winbolt 1930). Near to this site is the (?)contemporary open settlement at Eridge Park (Money 1979).

Two other enclosures in the High Weald may also be Late Iron Age hillforts. At Dry Hill Camp, extensive excavations (Winbolt and Margary 1933) and two watching briefs (Margary 1946; Tebbutt 1970) have failed to produce any definite dating evidence for their multivallate earthwork, which encloses 9.6 ha. The only finds made were possible Iron Age sling stones (rounded pebbles) and iron slag. The situation is even worse with regard to the 7 ha univallate fortification at Philpots. No dating clues have been discovered, and a trench across the interior of the enclosure failed to reveal any features (Hannah 1932).

Situated on the Greensand on the borders of the Weald are a number of hillforts. Three of the Surrey examples have recently been sampled and dated to the Late Iron Age (Thompson 1979). At Anstiebury (4 ha) there were three banks, although the outer defences were apparently never completed and the main rampart seems to have been deliberately demolished. Three miles to the west at Holmbury, discoveries within the bivallate enclosure (3.6 ha) included hearths and possible signs of forced abandonment (deliberately broken querns). Six and a half miles away at Hascombe, the univallate enclosure (2.5 ha) has yielded traces of domestic activity (pits, hearths, a loom weight, a spindle whorl, querns and grain). This site has also yielded signs of possible enforced abandonment (deliberate demolition of the defences and the (?)breaking of querns). None of the three sites has produced much evidence for settlement, but all have yielded quantities of sling stones/clay 'bullets'. Thompson has pointed out that the multivallate defences at two of the sites (and elsewhere) may be a consequence of sling warfare.

Dating evidence for the forts includes: radiocarbon dates (310 ± 100 bc Birm-591) for a pit in the interior of Holmbury; and 290 ± 70 bc (HAR-1968) and 170 ± 70 bc (HAR-1699) respectively for samples from below the bank and from the core of the entrance at Hascombe, archaeomagnetic dating at Holmbury (later than 70 BC and earlier than AD 50), pottery (*c.* 200–50 BC) and three Class I Potin coins (mid first century BC) at Hascombe. Recently a much larger (9 ha) Late Iron Age univallate enclosure has been discovered at Feldry, about one mile to the south of Holmbury. Sample excavations have been undertaken (Field 1985).

To the east in Kent, two large enclosures situated on the Greensand are of particular interest. At Oldbury there is a vast (50 ha) strongly defended multivallate enclosure. Excavations by Ward-Perkins (1944) indicated that there were two structural periods, the first dating to the first half of the first century BC, whilst the second phase, a time of refortification (including the making of a Fécamp-type wide, flat-bottomed ditch) was Claudian. Recently, further excavations have been undertaken at Oldbury (Thompson 1984; 1985). These provided no evidence in support of the earlier theory of two phases at the site, and Thompson is of the opinion that 'the suggestion of a Belgic refortification seems untenable'. He suggests that the site was rapidly constructed on a massive scale, that it was never permanently occupied and was abandoned by *c.* 50 BC. Whilst the original excavations had failed to reveal any traces of settlement, the recent fieldwork has located a few features, including hearths and a pair of linked smelting furnaces. Finds from the site have included six gold coins of the mid-first century BC, pottery, querns, sling stones, a whetstone and glass beads.

In the Upper Medway Valley at Quarry Wood, Loose, a univallate earthwork (about 12 ha) was constructed on the valley side. The defences are perhaps of two phases, the latter period possibly including a Fécamp-type ditch (Kelly 1971). The precise dating of this Late Iron Age enclosure is not certain, and nothing is known about its interior. Finds include an imported Dressel 1B amphora. Evidence for linear dykes, 'defensive outworks' (Kelly 1971) has been noted in the vicinity of the site and the area in general has yielded a high concentration of Late Iron Age sites and findspots (Rodwell 1976).

Again we are faced with the problem of trying to explain the main functions of these Wealden and Greensand hillforts. It will be noted that they vary considerably in size (from 0.6 to 50 ha) and that few sites have yielded any signs of occupation. Most sites, however, are dated to the Late Iron Age, and many have produced 'shot' suitable for sling warfare. A popular theory is that this group of enclosures were temporary 'centres of refuge for a large, scattered population ... and ... that they were erected in times of stress in response to some external danger' (Ward-Perkins 1944: 149). Currently the main advocate of this explanation is Hugh Thompson, who has also suggested that the builders of the forts were the agriculturalists on the Downs and that the Weald did not seem to attract settlement until the Roman period (Thompson 1979). Thompson has tried to link the building of the hillforts with the known historical threats: Belgic invaders and the two landings of Caesar. He favours the Roman invasions as the main inspiration behind the construction of the forts (Thompson 1984). On this defence theme we should also note Caesar's (*Gallic War*, Book V) comments about the Briton's 'strongholds ... densely wooded spots fortified with a rampart and trench, to which they retire in order to escape the attacks of invaders'.

Another popular explanation for the Wealden hillforts is that they may be a response to an internal stress situation caused by population growth on the Downs (see above). It has also been suggested that one solution to this stress situation would have been to make better use of marginal or previously unproductive land, such as the Weald and Greensand areas (Cunliffe 1982). Certainly there is little sign of Iron Age activity in these areas during the Early Iron Age, but in the later period there are the various defended enclosures and a few possible farmsteads, such as Chelwood Gate and Eridge Park (a relative lack of fieldwork and the practical difficulties of undertaking surveys in many parts of the Weald may be major factors behind the small number of recorded Iron Age sites in the region, and a likely bias towards the large earthworks). Others, however, have expressed doubts about a shift of settlement off the North Downs until the very end of the Iron Age or the early Roman period (Thompson 1979; Hanworth 1987). The general lack of settlement evidence from within the Wealden hillforts tends to confirm this argument, and is also data in favour of the interpretation of the forts as temporary refuges.

Other functions for the forts are possible, however, and their range of sizes probably indicates that we should expect a range of functions as well. The enclosures may be linked with the expansion of trade, both long distance and local. Some of the sites (such as Quarry Wood Camp) are well positioned to control and benefit from trade routes. Other sites may have been located in order to aid or control the local redistribution of specific commodities. Rosamond Hanworth (1987) has suggested three such commodities: timber, querns and iron. Timber would certainly have been important, especially since intensive farming on the Downs would have removed many of the trees in that region. Querns were also very important and are found on most Iron Age sites. The Weald provides a variety of suitable sources of stone for querns and the occurrence of two such sources close to Holmbury has led to the suggestion that quern production could have been a local industry (Hanworth and Tomalin 1977). The Holmbury enclosure has also yielded querns made from a source in the Petworth-Midhurst area (Thompson 1979), thus demonstrating the possible size of the catchment area of such sites. Possibly the most important commodity associated with the forts, however, is iron. The Weald is exceptionally rich in sources of iron ore and many of the fort sites have yielded pieces of slag. In particular, at Garden Hill there is now evidence for both smelting and forging activities. Perhaps a major function of some of the Wealden forts was as a centre for the collection and primary processing of iron ore, which when smelted was then traded/redistributed to the farming communities on the Downs.

Another possible major function of some of the forts was as seasonal pastoral enclosures. This might help to explain the size of some of the earthworks and the lack of evidence for settlement. Unfortunately, there is very little information available concerning local environmental conditions around the forts during the Iron Age, and this is clearly a high priority for future research. Even without clearance of the woodland for pasture, the area would have been ideal for swine pasturage (Hanworth 1987). In addition, the woodlands would also have provided good hunting prospects.

Thus it can be seen that there are a large number of possible explanations for the defended enclosures of the Weald: defence, pastoral farming and as centres for trade and the obtaining of materials and food from the woodlands. The fact that many of the forts were constructed in places a long way from the areas of intensive settlement (the Downs), and the size of some of the defences implies a well developed system of control of communal labour. Perhaps, as Hanworth (1987) suggests, the forts should be regarded as the 'frontier posts' of the territory.

The third group of hillforts in the South-East (those to the north of the Weald) are a very mixed lot. There are a few defended enclosures on the North Downs, such as War Coppice, Surrey and Caesar's Camp, Keston, Kent. Very little work has yet been undertaken on these enclosures, but that at Keston has yielded some interesting environmental data which suggests that the site was in dense oak forest with bracken becoming more abundant (Dimbleby *in* Piercy-Fox 1969).

Of the defended enclosures located off the Downs, the multivallate 5.5 ha fortification at St George's Hill, Surrey (near the Brooklands site discussed above) may have been used, perhaps intermittently, for a long time, possibly from the Late Bronze Age to the end of the Iron Age (Hanworth and Tomalin 1977). St George's Hill is a source of iron ore, and perhaps one of the main functions of this hillfort was with regard to the exploitation and redistribution (to sites such as Brooklands) of this raw material.

In Kent, the large (14 ha) multivallate enclosure at Bigbury is the most easterly known example of a hillfort. Finds indicate that there was occupation on the hill prior to the construction of the fort, which probably occurred during the late second or early first century BC. Various excavations have been undertaken at the site (Jessup and Cook 1936; Thompson 1983), but only relatively small areas of the interior have been sampled. The most recent excavations revealed some traces of activity within the fort: a probable hut, a hearth, a 'waterhole', gullies and a smithy area within the 'annexe' which forms part of the earthwork complex. The site has yielded an exceptionally large number of metalwork finds (agricultural and forestry equipment, carpenters' tools, items connected with the use of ponies and chariots, cooking equipment and slave chains and fetters) and Thompson has suggested that the abandonment of so many items may indicate that the inhabitants were forced to evacuate the site, perhaps following defeat by Caesar (Bigbury has been a popular candidate for the stronghold known to have been stormed by the Seventh Legion). Possibly the settlement moved to Canterbury, where traces of a major Late Iron Age settlement are now being discovered (e.g. Blockley and Day 1979).

Oppida

A feature of the Late Iron Age settlement patterns in some areas of the South-East are sites referred to as *oppida*. Although the term *oppidum* was used by the Classical writers to describe both hillforts and the larger, dyke-enclosed complexes of Southern Britain, it is today used with regard to large, nucleated centres (defended or undefended) which exhibit characteristics appropriate to an urban or proto–urban organization. Precise definitions, and sometimes also identifications, have proved difficult, and these matters form the subject of a specialist book (Cunliffe and Rowley 1976). Several writers (e.g. Cunliffe 1976*a*) have suggested that some of the British Developed hillforts should be regarded as having urban characteristics, whilst others (e.g. Collis 1976) have disagreed. Agreement has proved much easier, however, with regard to the Late Iron Age 'Belgic' nucleated centres, which have been classified by Cunliffe (1976*a*) into three types: *Enclosed oppida*, which are often in excess of 10 ha and located on valley sides, are protected on all flanks by natural or artificial defences. These enclosures represent the last stage of 'hillfort' development in the South-East. In contrast, *Territorial oppida* are very large areas of land, partially defined by discontinuous lengths of linear earthworks. Finally there are *Undefended oppida* which are densely settled sites with no identifiable defences. Most *oppida* are situated on fairly low-lying land in positions clearly chosen in order to command major route ways (e.g. river crossings) and thus presumably of trade networks.

In the South-East a number of sites have been interpreted as *oppida*. In the case of Enclosed *oppida*, possible examples are three of the 'hillforts' described above: Oldbury, Quarry Wood Camp, and Bigbury. All these sites dominate important river crossings and appear to have been constructed during the first century BC None of the sites, however, has yet been demonstrated to possess the functional criteria of *oppida*, and recent trial excavations at two of the enclosures have failed to convince the excavator that the sites are anything more complex than 'strongholds' (Thompson 1983). Only large-scale investigations of the interiors of these enclosures will clarify the situation.

Cunliffe (1982) has suggested that two of the Kent enclosed *oppida*, Quarry Wood Camp and Bigbury, may have been replaced by new, open *oppida* at Rochester and Canterbury respectively. The evidence for extensive pre-Roman levels at Canterbury has been mentioned above, and at Rochester finds have included examples of Iron Age type—coin moulds (such moulds have been found at a number of *oppida* sites, but in themselves need not indicate the location of an *oppidum*). Hopefully, future research will shed light on the relationship between these various sites.

The only example of a Territorial *oppidum* in the South-East is in West Sussex. The Chichester Dykes (or Entrenchments) form one of the largest systems of Late Iron Age defensive earthworks in Southern England. These larger linear dykes, which run across the northern edge of the Coastal Plain just to the north of Chichester (Fig. 5.10), have an overall length of 10 km from east to west, and measure 4.5 km from north to south. Other boundaries may have been marked by natural features, such as the River Lavant and the stream running into Bosham Harbour. The total area involved is potentially enormous, especially so if it included Selsey. A survey has suggested that the dyke complex is the result of three major phases of defence, protecting progressively smaller territories (Bradley 1971*b*). In 1982 the east terminal of the eastern dyke of Phase 1 was excavated, and the results indicate that this stretch of the defences was probably constructed in the Late Iron Age, although is is impossible to rule out an immediately post-Conquest date (Bedwin and Orton 1984).

What then was the purpose of these major earthworks, the construction of which must have involved a vast amount of labour and organization? It has been suggested (Frere 1967) that such defences might mark the limits of large tracts of settled land (note that the Oving settlement lies within the area defined by the dykes). In addition, the entrenchments may also be the outer defences of a more concentrated type of settlement (*oppida*), perhaps including the tribal capital. No such settlement nucleus is known, but possibilities include Selsey and the Fishbourne area. For many years Selsey was the most popular choice, but a recent examination of the evidence shows that there are various major

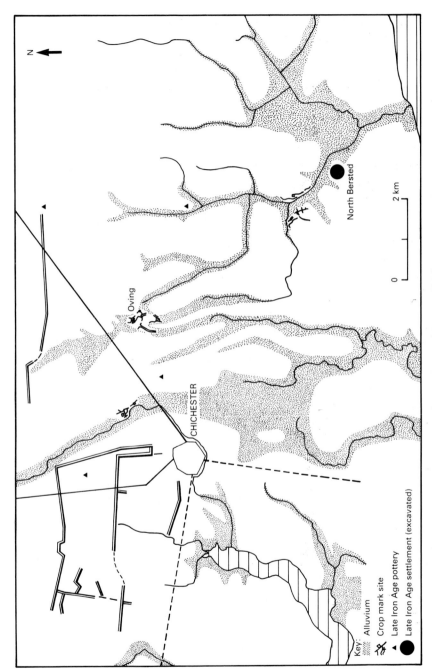

Key:
Alluvium
Crop mark site
Late Iron Age pottery
Late Iron Age settlement (excavated)

N

CHICHESTER

Oving

North Bersted

0   2 km

Figure 5.10 The Chichester Dykes, Late Iron Age settlement sites and Roman Chichester.

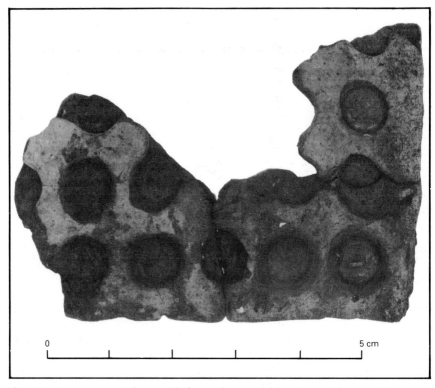

Plate 5.6 'Iron Age type' clay moulds for producing gold coin blanks. Recovered from early Roman contexts during the excavation of a settlement site adjacent to the easternmost terminal of the Chichester Dykes system, West Sussex.

problems with regard to both its location and the 'evidence' it has yielded (Bedwin 1983). Others have noted that the dyke system focuses on an area around the head of Chichester Harbour, and it is thus perhaps in the Fishbourne area that an *oppidum* might have been located. The Chichester area is another possibility, and recent excavations at the Cattle Market Site have produced evidence of Late Iron Age occupation, including three round huts (Down 1982). A major mystery is the discovery of several coin moulds (Plate 5.6) at Boxgrove, on a Roman settlement adjacent to the excavated dyke terminal referred to above. These are the only 'Iron Age type' coin moulds from Sussex, but their possible post-Conquest dating, and their findspot at the eastern end of the dyke system, do not make them useful as indicators of the postulated 'tribal capital'.

Houses

Well defined house types are fairly rare, and this is probably because most excavations have been undertaken on ploughed sites where shallow features have been destroyed. Where remains of houses have survived, they include both round and rectangular structures. Very little is known about the super-structure of these buildings, but the various discoveries of latch lifters indicate a degree of sophistication for the doors.

The round house typical of the late second and early first millennium BC (chapter 4) continued to be constructed throughout the Iron Age. Frequently only traces of such huts are found, particularly ring gullies (which functioned either for eaves-drip drainage or as bedding trenches for upright posts), circles of post holes and floors. In contrast to the huts of the Bronze Age, many Iron Age examples of round houses have been found without associated post-holes and it is therefore considered that these buildings may have been stake-built.

Evidence for rectangular and subrectangular buildings is found from the beginning of the Iron Age (example Heathy Brow). The remains of such houses are usually limited either to traces of floor levels (as at Heathy Brow) or to rectangular surface depressions rich in domestic debris (e.g. Park Brow). The absence of post-holes associated with many of these buildings suggest that the method of construction used allowed them to stand on the ground surface or to have very shallow foundations. Such building techniques may have involved the use of timber frames or walls of cob.

Other rectangular buildings with more substantial foundations have been found in Canterbury (Rodwell 1978). In Whitehall Road one structure (in excess of 13 m long and about 7 m wide) combined two methods of wall construction: trenches for timbers and individual post-holes. Another building had a sunken floor (about 5 m square) which was edged with stake holes. We should also perhaps consider the various multi-post structures found on many of the settlement sites. Whilst the larger structures (6 or more posts) have often been considered as buildings (e.g. Bishopstone and Park Brow), some of the four-post structures (which are usually regarded as 'granaries') could be the remains of buildings, perhaps even houses. There is some evidence to suggest that rectangular buildings became more common by the end of the Iron Age, and Warwick Rodwell (1978) is of the opinion that in the South-East there is a correlation between the demise of circular huts and the emergence of the Belgic dynasties.

Burial and Ritual

Death and the disposal of the dead are extremely important topics, since these matters usually have prominent places in the ideologies of most cultures. Funerary customs are therefore likely to provide a fairly reliable indication of Cultural continuity or change, and in the case of Iron Age Britain, their study is thus potentially useful for testing theories of Continental immigration or insular evolution (Whimster 1981). Unfortunately, for most periods and places during the Iron Age in Britain, there are no specific burial sites, and until recently it was often assumed that no major burial tradition could be identified prior to the very end of the Iron Age.

The known ways of disposing of the dead during the first part of the first millennium BC include both cremation and inhumation, but the number of discovered burials is fairly small and there may have been more common techniques which leave no archaeological trace (Whimster 1981). In the South-East, at the beginning of the Iron Age, there were a few cases of the continued practice of in-urned cremation burials (e.g. at the Caburn and Park Brow), but generally this method was apparently abandoned, unless the burnt remains were not systematically buried, until the first century BC (see below).

Much more common in the South-East are inhumation burials, and also finds of disarticulated human bones. Whimster (1981) has made a study of all the examples of Iron Age burials in Britain that had been discovered up until 1976, and has been able to identify various regional inhumation traditions. At least two of these traditions were present in the South-East on settlement sites: inhumations in pits (examples: Broadstairs in Kent, Bishopstone (Fig. 4.11) and Slonk Hill) and inhumations in ditches (e.g. Bishopstone). Most of the bodies were lain on their sides, with the head orientated to the north and the legs flexed or crouched. Although Whimster records that most Iron Age inhumations were without grave goods, several examples in the South-East were accompanied by objects (such as a shale bracelet and an involuted brooch with Grave 2 at Slonk Hill) or possible 'ritual deposits' (at Slonk Hill the body in Grave 1 lay on a layer of sea shells which contained a fossil sea urchin). The total number of pit and ditch burials, however, is not very large (the odd one or two per settlement) and it is thus hard to accept that these methods were the normal way of disposing of the dead. Whimster has suggested that such graves may have been '*ad hoc* burials of social outcasts', and their frequent occurrence in 'rubbish' contexts tends to support this theory. If so, it is interesting and significant that over large areas of Britain these 'rubbish burials' conformed to certain 'rules' or preferences (such as context, and orientation and arrangment of the body) and thus indicate an extensive and powerful body of *insular* common tradition.

What happened then to the bulk of the population? It seems likely that the main method of disposal of the dead was by a method which leaves little or

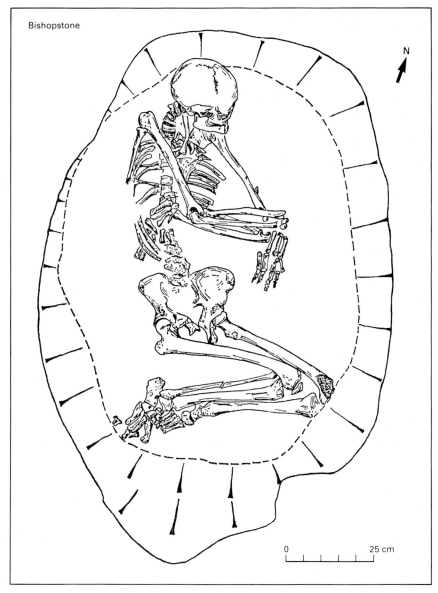

Figure 5.11 Crouched burial in a disused storage pit at Bishopstone, East Sussex. The skeleton is that of a male aged about 30–40 years old.

no trace in the archaeological record. It is important here to point out that most settlement and 'hillfort' sites in the South-East (where soil conditions permit) have yielded fragmentary and complete examples of human bone. These finds imply either a form of exposure burial (perhaps on some of the four-post structures – see Ellison and Drewett 1971), or very shallow graves, in or around the domestic area.

The region has provided one particularly interesting and unusual inhumation from Deal, Kent (Woodruff 1904). This burial, of a female whose extended body was laid on her back, had a pair of bronze spoons (one marked with a cross, the other with a small hole) placed on either side of the head. A parallel for this unusual burial type was found at Burnmouth in Berwickshire, and pairs of such spoons have been found in various parts of Britain (Cunliffe 1978*a*).

In parts of the South-East the rite of cremation became common during the first century BC. This method, which normally involved the burial of the ashes of the deceased in a pottery urn (or sometimes more exotic vessels) in a well-defined cemetery, is usually regarded as an intrusive La Tène burial custom, and its introduction has been linked with the 'Aylesford-Swarling Culture'. In our region the main concentration of such burials is along the northern and southern edges of the North Downs in Central and Eastern Kent (Whimster 1981). To the west and south, however, no in-urned cremations have yet been definitely dated to the Late Iron Age (although they are widespread in these areas by the late first century AD).

Although there were some cremation burials without an obvious container (some of these may have been placed in receptacles made of materials which have since decayed), most cremations were accompanied by containers, and often other grave goods as well. The burials show marked variations in displayed wealth, and thus presumably of status within society. In Kent there are none of the extremely rich 'Welwyn' type burials that occur on the other side of the Thames, but some sites, notably the type-sites of Aylesford (Evans 1890) and Swarling (Bushe-Fox 1925) have produced a number of rich burials which involved various exotic items such as iron-bound or bronze-plated buckets, elaborate fibulae, and Italian bronze vessels. Within the cemeteries the graves, which were presumably marked, were carefully arranged, sometimes in lines (as at Stone) and sometimes in rings (as at Aylesford).

Possibly the cremation rite and the new methods of pottery manufacture were introduced into parts of Kent by immigrants from the Continent (where both techniques, and also the range of objects often chosen to accompany burials, were well established traditions). Alternatively, the *ideas* and *technologies* of cremation and wheel-made pottery may have been brought across the Channel by traders and/or returning mercenary soldiers (see below).

Other than burials, there is little evidence in the archaeological record for Iron Age ritual. Part of the problem in this respect is the nature of Iron Age religion, the centres of which were often natural locations such as streams, rivers, ponds, groves of trees and even individual trees (Ross 1967). One example is almost certainly the River Thames, which has yielded a large number of valuable weapons and parade pieces (see above). The nature and numbers of these objects indicates that they were probably

168

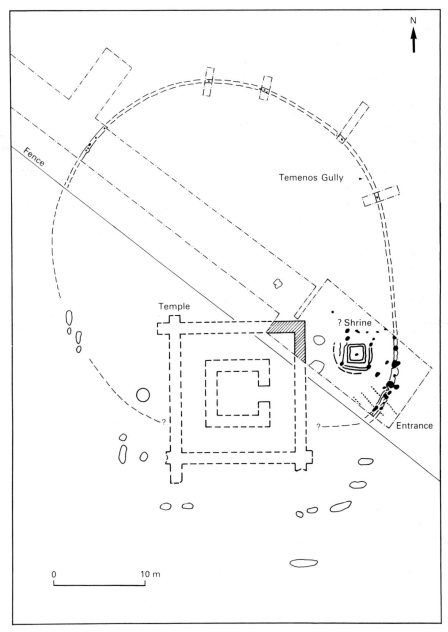

Figure 5.12 Lancing Down, West Sussex: general site plan. The principal features include the late Iron Age 'shrine', the Romano-Celtic temple, and the temenos gully.

ritually placed or thrown into the river as opposed to being accidentally lost.

In addition to natural locations there were also some shrines, and in several instances these sites can be shown to have continued into the Roman period. One of the best examples of such continuity is at Lancing Down, Sussex, where excavations have revealed what is thought to be a small, square, wooden Late Iron Age shrine (Fig. 5.12) adjacent to the Romano-British temple (Bedwin 1981*b*). Prior to the recent excavations, the site had yielded Late Iron Age pottery and coins. A similar case of continuity of religious activity seems to have occurred at Worth, Kent, where the Iron Age levels beneath the Roman temple yielded several votive model shields (Klein 1928). In addition, at Farley Heath, Surrey, the site of the Roman temple has produced examples of Iron Age coins and may therefore also have been an Iron Age religious centre. At Wanborough, Surrey, a similar story appears to be emerging following the discovery there of an exceptionally large deposit of Iron Age coins. Sadly, this important site has been badly damaged and looted by treasure hunters, but rescue excavations have shown that the coins came from a layer below what appears to be a square Romano-Celtic temple (Bird 1986).

Other signs of Iron Age ritual practices have been found on some of the settlement sites. These practices include unusual deposits or the placing of items in pits. An example of such activity is at Findon Park, Sussex, where the skull of an ox was found in the centre of a ring of flints on the floor of one of the pits (Fox and Wolseley 1928).

Industry

During the Iron Age, in addition to the various home-based crafts (such as weaving, pottery, metallurgy, and bone, wood and leatherworking), examples of larger-scale specialist industries developed, especially with regard to high-quality metallurgy (see above), Late Iron Age wheel made-pottery (see above) and the production of iron, querns and salt.

How extensively iron was used at the beginning of the Iron Age is difficult to assess, but by the middle and late periods, objects made of iron are fairly common finds on settlement and hillfort sites (see above). But whilst traces of forging activities have been discovered on a number of farmstead sites (suggesting that smithing was either a home craft or the work of itinerant smiths), very few settlements have produced evidence for smelting iron. The exceptions include sites such as Brooklands, which for part of its history may have been the homestead of a specialist smith.

We have also seen that several of the Wealden hillfort sites have produced forging slag, and that at Garden Hill, ironworking features included a smelting furnace. It is possible that some of the hillforts were specifically located in order to exploit local sources of iron ore. Other than the hillfort sites the Weald has so far yielded a few other traces of possible 'ironworking' (Money 1978). In addition to the archaeological evidence from the Weald, we must also consider the writings of two of the Classical authors who mention Britain as a source of Iron. Thus, with regard to the 'Maritime region' (the South-East), Caesar (*Gallic War* V) informs us that it produced iron, but only in small quantities. Writing later at the turn of the millennium, Strabo (*Geography*) lists iron as one of Britain's exports, thus implying a considerable expansion of the industry since the time of Caesar (mid first century BC). Thus the archaeological evidence and the historical sources suggest that the exploitation of Wealden iron was on a fairly small scale during the first century BC, but that it quickly became more important. Perhaps by the time of the Conquest, the production of iron had sufficiently developed to make the existence of the industry one of the reasons for the invasion (Cleere and Crossley 1985).

Other specialist industries may have included the quarrying and production of stone querns (see above) and salt manufacture. The South-East, with its long stretches of coast and estuarine areas, would have been suitable for the obtaining of salt from sea water. Traces of such activities include various discoveries of fragments of briquetage, and at Chidham, Sussex, excavations revealed a single pit (possibly an evaporating pan) which was part of a badly eroded Early Iron Age salt-working site (Bedwin 1980*b*). At the end of the Iron Age a new specialist craft would have been the production of coins (see below).

Coinage

For many years, the interpretation of the earliest Celtic coins in Britain was based on the theory of a series of invasions from the Continent (Belgic Gaul), each wave of new immigrants bringing with them a distinctive type of gold coinage. Six main types (A-F) of Gallo-Belgic coinage were recognized by Derek Allen (1961) and their distributions were plotted with the aim of detecting the movements and areas of contact of the immigrant groups. This historical approach has continued to be developed, in particular by Warwick Rodwell (1976) who used the data to suggest several areas of primary Belgic settlement centring on Northern Kent, Essex and parts of Hertfordshire.

Recently however, research by John Kent (1978; 1981) has upset Allen's long-accepted scheme, although it is still agreed that Gallo-Belgic A (Plate 5.7) and B coins were the first to reach Britain, most probably in the pre-Caesarian period. The Gallo-Belgic B coins are of particular interest since in their home-

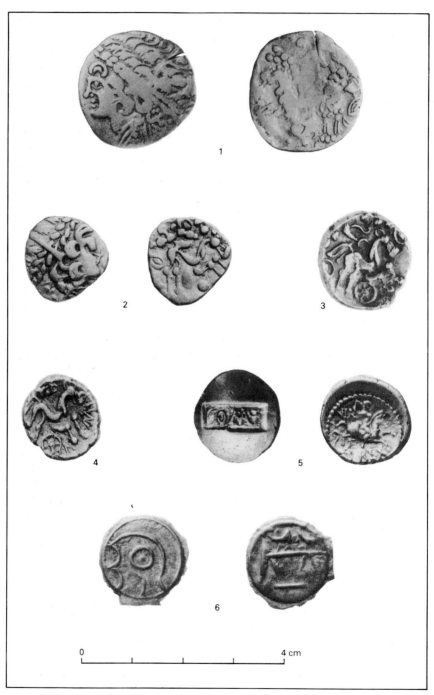

Plate 5.7 Iron Age gold and Potin coins. Gold staters: 1: Gallo-Belgic A; 2: Gallo-Belgic C; 3: British Q; 4: Cummius; 5: Verica; Potin: 6: Class I. (Photographs: Ashmolean Museum (1–2, 4, 6); Sussex Archaeological Society (3).)

land, the Department of Seine-Maritime, the coinage consists of quarter-staters only. Kent has suggested that the staters found in Britain (which cluster in the Lower Thames Valley, especially in the area of present-day London) may have been 'struck for export only'. Is this perhaps further proof that the spread of an idea and the discovery of items of Continental origin need not imply a movement of people, but could be the result of trade or payment for services rendered? Kent has also drawn attention to the early importance of another, probably pre-Caesarian category of currency, the locally produced Class I Potin coins (Plate 5.7). Cunliffe (1982) has taken up this point and suggests that these Potins, whose distribution indicates their likely production in Kent, may have been in use alongside Gallo-Belgic B staters, and that the two types of coin may represent the initial stages in the development of a market economy in Britain. Although Class I potins are the earliest locally produced coins in Britian, their role (as small change or as units of higher value) has been the subject of controversy (Collis 1974; Rodwell 1976).

Gallo-Belgic C (Plate 5.7) and E coins are now dated to the time of Caesar's Gallic Wars, and Kent has suggested that they may have reached Britain as payment for the 'reinforcements' that Caesar (*Gallic War* V) records were supplied by the Britons to his enemies. There is a wide distribution of both types of coin (especially of type E), and they became the inspiration for the first British derivative issues, British A. Kent has also made the interesting suggestion that Allen type Xc2 gold quarter staters (with the letter Λ on the obverse), which are mainly found on the Sussex Coast, may be connected with the flight to Britain in 52 BC of the Atrebatic King Commius. Another coin type which is often linked with the migration to Britain of members of this Atrebatic tribe is Gallo-Belgic F, which gave rise to British Q (Plate 5.7), which in turn developed into the inscribed issue of Commius (Plate 5.7).

The use of coinage spread rapidly, and in the main zone developments occurred quickly, such as the issue of new, smaller denominations and inscriptional types (Plate 5.8). The latter form a complex series of dynastic issues, which have been studied in detail by Rodwell (1976). The interpretation of the rapid changes in coin types and the distribution patterns of the various types is not fully understood, but is likely to involve both political and economic factors (Cunliffe 1981). Although coin distributions need not represent political dominance, they continue to be of use in helping to indicate the likely extent of the different tribal territories in lowland Britain.

Physical proof of coin manufacture in the South-East is limited to the discovery of Iron Age type coin moulds at Rochester and Boxgrove, near Chichester (but here the moulds could date to after the Conquest). In addition, the distributions of various coin types indicate their likely production in specific areas. Thus Kent appears to be the origin of issues of Eppilus, Vosenius and Dubnovellaunus. West Sussex may have been the origin of various issues of the Atrebatic Kings (Commius, Tincommius and Verica), but other locations (such as to the north-west) within the kingdom are also possible.

173

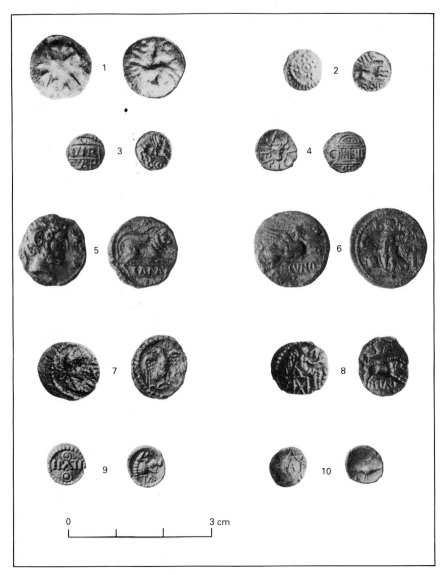

Plate 5.8 Late Iron Age silver and bronze coins from post-Roman invasion levels in the north-west quadrant, Chichester, West Sussex. ATREBATES silver coins – 1: Tincommius (*c.* 20 BC–AD 5); 2–4: Verica (*c.* AD 10–40); CATUVELLAUNI bronze coins – 5–6: Cunobelin (AD 10–40), 7–9: Epaticcus (AD 25–35); CANTIACI silver coin – 10: Aminus (*c.* AD 15). (Photograph: Chichester District Archaeological Unit.)

174

Social and Economic Change, *c.* 100 BC to AD 43

Our knowledge of society in the South-East at the end of the Iron Age is considerably better than that for the earlier periods, and this is partly due to more distinctive and informative elements in the archaeological record (such as pottery types, coins and burial practices) and the existence of contemporary Roman written sources, especially Caesar's *Gallic War*. It seems likely that society was stratified into an aristocratic warrior upper class, the peasants (the bulk of the population) and the religious leaders known as the Druids. At the beginning of this period, the population in the South-East was apparently divided into a number of small tribes, and in the case of Kent, Caesar records four 'kings'. By the time of the Conquest, however, some of the small 'king-doms' may have merged to form larger tribal groupings: the Atrebates of Sussex and parts of Surrey (and also other areas to the west) and the Cantiaci of Kent. In addition, areas in the north of Surrey and the Thames Valley may have belonged to the Catuvellauni, whose main territory lay to the north of the Thames.

A major problem with the Late Iron Age is in trying to assess whether parts of the South-East should be regarded as 'Belgic' territories. Of all the postulated invasions during the Iron Age, only that of the Belgae is supported by a reasonable body of archaeological data, including wheel-made pottery, cremation burials, and the use of coinage (although the introduction of all of these could have other explanations). The invasion is also supported by Caesar, who informs us that the coastal areas were inhabited by 'Belgic immigrants who came to plunder and make war ... and later settled down to till the soil.' In addition, Caesar later records a further example of Belgic migration to Britain with regard to the flight of Commius. The problem, then, is really one of assessing the size and impact of Belgic migration.

In the case of Sussex, it is interesting that the refugee Commius appears to have not only been accepted by the local people, but also made their king. The name of the tribe is also that of Commius' tribe on the Continent, and it is thus possible that there were close kinship links between these areas before Com-mius' flight from Caesar. Subsequently, under Commius and his successors, the development of coinage occurred in this region. Other economic and political changes seem to have happened after *c.* 100 BC, especially with regard to the demise of the West Sussex hillforts and the development of the Coastal Plain, including the building of a territorial *oppidum*. Although there were also significant changes in pottery styles, it is perhaps surprising that cremation burials do not appear until after the Conquest.

In Kent there are various types of evidence, such as wheel made pottery, cremation burials and coinage, which have been taken to indicate settlement by Belgic immigrants (e.g. Rodwell 1976). The data is particularly concentrated in areas of East Kent. Kent east of the River Medway is also a region free of hillforts (assuming Quarry Wood and Bigbury to be *oppida*), and may thus have had a different socio-economic system to that present in the west (Cunliffe 1982). A further contrast between these two areas of Kent can also be detected with regard to Late Iron Age pottery styles. Cunliffe has used the archaeologic-al data to suggest a number of socio-economic territories and he assumes that by this stage the river valleys had become the centres rather than the frontiers of territories (in the cases of the two easternmost regions, *oppida* at Quarry Wood and Bigbury are located adjacent to such rivers).

Of Caesar's well-known invasions of 55 and 54 BC, both of which landed in Kent, there is no direct evidence. It has been suggested, however, that the burial of hoards (including several in the South-East) dating to this episode may have been caused by the invasions or the threat of such invasions (Rodwell 1976). In addition, we should also bear in mind Thompson's theory that many of the late hillforts were constructed in response to the Roman threat (see above).

The outcome, however, of Caesar's Gallic Wars, including the 'inva-sions' of Britian, had much longer-lasting effects. Thus we have already seen that the wars on the Continent were probably responsible for the introduction (as payment for mercenaries) into Britain of large quantities of Gallo-Belgic gold coins, and that these coins helped to inspire developments in local coin-age. The conquest of Gaul would have affected the Britons' Continental trading partners, such as the Veneti, and it has been suggested that following Caesar's campaign in Britain in 54 BC, favourable trading treaties might have been arranged with the pro-Roman tribes, such as the Trinovantes (Cunliffe 1982). Subsequently the volume of trade between 'Belgic' Britain and the Roman World increased significantly, but the rewards of such trade seem to have mainly benefited the communities to the north of the Thames. Possible reasons for the relatively unfavourable situation to the south of the Thames include the suggested favourable (perhaps monopoly type) trade treaties men-tioned above, the opposition of the Kent tribes to Caesar's forces, and a little later, in the case of the area of the Atrebates, the presence of a strongly anti-Roman ruler, Commius. The situation in the Atrebates' region may have improved after about 16 BC, when Commius' successor, Tincommius, seems to have become pro-Roman. Perhaps such a change of policy may have had economic benefits, and the area around Chichester is gradually producing evidence that at least this region was able to share in the wine trade (fragments of Dressell 1B amphorae have been found at Oving, Carne's Seat and Box-grove). In terms of exports, the South-East, perhaps indirectly via the Belgic areas to the north, could have supplied many of the items mentioned by Strabo (*Geography*), including iron, corn, cattle, hides, hunting dogs and slaves (note the discovery of slave chains and fetters at Bigbury).

It remains to set the scene for the Roman Conquest. The ninety years between the invasions of Caesar and Claudius appear to have involved various struggles for power, both within and between tribes, and the main political

176

events have been documented elsewhere (Cunliffe 1978*a*). By about AD 10, two rulers seem to have emerged to dominance in Belgic Britain: Cunobelin in the North and Verica in the South. Of these two kings it has generally been assumed, based largely on coin distributions, that Cunobelin had expansionist territorial ambitions; but the coin data would also have economic implications (Cunliffe 1981). Whatever the situation, by external or internal pressure, *c.* AD 42, Verica fled to the protection of Rome.

Chapter 6

A Colony of Rome, AD 43–410

The coming of the Romans to Britain resulted in dramatic alterations in the social and economic environments. The results of these changes, together with equally major changes in technology, make the period of Roman occupation one of the most distinctive and dynamic episodes in the history of the South-East. In our region, the trends noted for the Iron Age with regard to an expansion of population and gradual movement of settlement into areas of previously marginal or unused land continued, and were accelerated thanks to a combination of technological innovation and new economic possibilities.

Pax Romana, the introduction of a major road network, new and expanded focuses of economic demand (towns, the military market, and taxation), the ending of the postulated earlier 'restrictive' trading treaties between Rome and certain areas and tribes, a highly developed coinage system and a limited but important inflow of people (soldiers, administrators, traders, entrepreneurs, and settlers) of different cultures from throughout the Roman Empire are just some of the new forces which helped to foster fundamental changes in the movement of people, goods and ideas, social relations, economic strategies and settlement types and locations (Fig. 6.1). Although many aspects of local culture continued, especially so in the countryside, almost all areas of the South-East can be shown to have quickly experienced some of the ideas and products of their conquerors' culture, including new pottery forms and wares, a dramatic increase in the use of iron, especially nails, the introduction of new building techniques and materials, especially tiles/bricks, and Roman coinage.

Peace under the Romans meant that defended settlements were no longer necessary, and in certain areas the resources available to the native aristocracy were used instead to pay for impressive houses in more agreeable and convenient locations. In addition to the building and furnishing of luxurious houses, there was also a variety of other ways in which the aristocracy could display their status and wealth, including the consumption of wine and exotic foodstuffs imported from the Continent, and by serving as officials within the Roman system of local government (although such positions could prove very

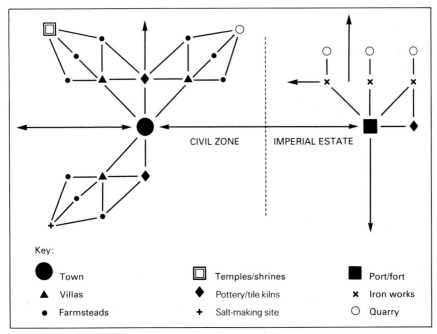

Figure 6.1 Theoretical model to show the possible relationships between different elements of the Roman settlement pattern.

expensive and may often have been only reluctantly undertaken). The four centuries of Roman rule saw the introduction of many religions, both those of Rome itself and also those from further afield, including Christianity. The archaeological evidence, however, suggests that such religions may have had little impact outside the more cosmopolitan centres (the towns and military establishments) and the bulk of the native population probably continued their traditional cults, although sometimes adopting new features, such as temples with masonry footings.

The period from AD 43 to 410 is not, in terms of Roman culture, a continuous period, and as elsewhere in the Empire, there are great differences between the early period in Roman Britain (first–mid-third century) and the later period. These differences include such aspects as major changes in the army, in administration, in ritual and in the economy. In Britain the economic changes are especially obvious in the late fourth century, which is characterized by the collapse of the low denomination coinage system and thus presumably also of the market economy and ultimately of large-scale industry. The decline of towns, which in some cases had started much earlier, became more widespread at this time. The late fourth century also witnessed major reductions in the army defending Britain and, in addition to the weakening of the defence system, these withdrawals of troops to fight on the Continent would have had serious repercussions for the economy. A recent general history of Roman Britain has been provided by Peter Salway (1981).

The archaeological evidence for the Roman period in South-East England is considerable, and traces of settlement and utilization are found in most areas (Fig. 6.2). This widespread pattern of settlement is partly due to a genuine increase in population and land utilization, but is also due to the fact that traces of Roman occupation (especially distinctive and well-fired types of pottery, tile, and building stone) have often survived better, and are easier to recognize, than traces of earlier periods. General interest in this period has also helped to ensure that Roman archaeology has always done well in terms of archaeological research and public awareness. Yet, despite the extensive database and the long history of investigating Roman sites, there are still large gaps in our understanding of the South-East during the Roman period.

A major problem has been a strong bias towards the more 'spectacular' types of site, especially the towns, villas, domestic buildings, forts and temples, and a relative neglect of landscape studies, the 'peasant' farmsteads and industrial sites. Even with the categories of sites which have been extensively studied, our knowledge is far from complete. This is mainly due to the general inadequacies of the older excavations in terms of detailed recording of the stratigraphy and features, the failure in many cases to recognize traces of timber construction, a general lack of interest in the recording and keeping of all types of finds, especially the less 'attractive' types of pottery and food remains together with a serious shortage of environmental analysis. In addition, as with the archaeology of other periods, a number of excavations have unfortunately resulted in either very inadequate or no publication. In some instances, the examination in detail of the findings of older excavations has led to major re-interpretations of well-known sites, an example of this being Ernest Black's recent study of the villa at Bignor (Black 1983).

Since the 1960s there have been many excavations of Roman sites, especially under 'rescue' conditions, and there has happily been a general improvement in field techniques and strategies, with a resulting increase in the types and quantity of information available for study. Lately, in addition to the publication of site reports and studies of particular topics, there has also been a healthy flow of more general treatments of the Roman period in the South-East, including several books (Cunliffe 1973; Detsicas 1983; Black 1987) and 'County Summaries' (Rudling 1982a; Blagg 1982; Bird 1987). Given this extensive literature, the remainder of this chapter is designed to be an updated summary of the major topics.

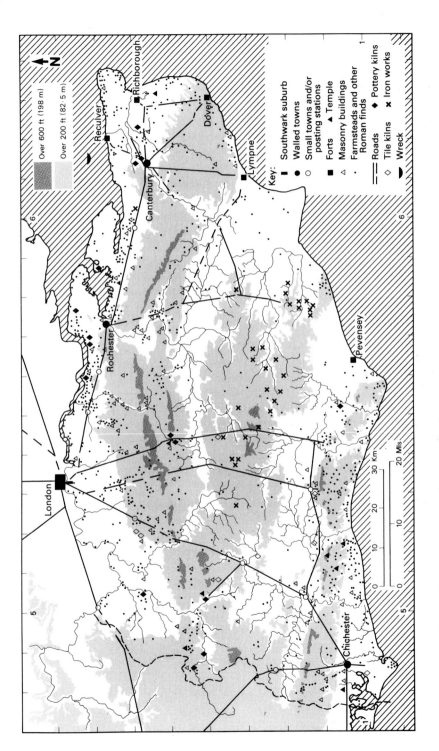

Key:

━	Southwark suburb		
●	Walled towns		
○	Small towns and/or posting stations		
■	Forts	▲	Temple
△	Masonry buildings		
·	Farmsteads and other Roman finds		
╌╌	Roads	◆	Pottery kilns
◇	Tile kilns	✕	Iron works
◗	Wreck		

Over 600 ft (198 m)

Over 200 ft (82·5 m)

Figure 6.2   The distribution of Roman sites in South-East England.

Conquest and Consolidation

The flight from Britain of the pro-Roman king Verica provided the new Emperor, Claudius, with a convenient diplomatic reason for invading Britain. Although the reinstatement of Verica to his kingdom may have been useful to Rome in terms of supporting its policy of alliances with friendly rulers on the frontiers of the empire, there were probably a number of other factors which were equally, if not more important in influencing the decision to invade Britain (for a discussion of some of these factors see Salway 1981).

Although it is known that the invasion force of four legions plus auxiliaries (a total of perhaps some 40,000 men) set sail from Boulogne, it is not definitely known where they landed. We are not even sure if we should be looking for one or more landing places, since Cassius Dio's account of the invasion informs us that the expedition sailed in three divisions so as not to be hindered in landing. Possibly they may all have landed at one place, but in three stages. It is likely, however, that at least some, and perhaps even all, of the forces disembarked at Richborough, Kent (Plate 6.1), a location that would have provided the Romans with safe anchorage and which has yielded traces of a Claudian defended camp (although this is too small to have accommodated the entire invasion force). If all the expedition did not land at Richborough, various other possibilities have been suggested for additional landing points (Dudley and Webster 1965) including Dover and Lympne in Kent; or the Fishbourne/Chichester area of West Sussex (which has also yielded traces of a Claudian military presence), a move which would at least have been consistent with the official reason for the invasion and would presumably have enabled the Romans to enlist the help of friendly native forces. Given the available evidence, however, such suggestions can only be speculative.

Nevertheless, it is clear that the main force was in Kent and that the first serious confrontation with the British opposition occurred at an unknown location on the River Medway. After a two-day battle, the eventually victorious Romans crossed the river and moved on to the next major barrier, the River Thames, which in turn was crossed (again the precise location is not known) enabling the invading army to march on towards Camulodunum, the capital of anti-Roman 'Belgic' Britain. Thus, within several months of landing in Britain the Roman forces under the command of Aulus Plautius, and briefly under Claudius himself, had succeeded in crushing the main opposition of the South-Eastern tribes. The next task was to consolidate Roman control of the newly conquered territories. This was achieved by various methods, including the disarming of the tribes that had surrendered, the construction of some forts, supply depots and roads, and the establishment of a client kingdom in part of the territory of the pro-Roman Atrebates tribe. With South-Eastern Britain quickly secured, the Roman forces were soon able to continue the invasion into more distant territories.

Plate 6.1   The Roman fort at Richborough, Kent: view from the north. The photograph shows a section of the ditch of the Claudian camp, the third-century triple ditches surrounding the foundations of the Monument and the walls of the Saxon Shore fort and its outer ditches. (Photograph: Royal Commission on Historical Monuments.)

There is, therefore, very little archaeological evidence for the immediate effect of the Roman invasion in the South-East. The main site of this initial period is the beach-head fortified camp at Richborough. Here an area of about 4 ha of the promontory was protected by two parallel defensive ditches and a rampart, with at least one well-built entrance (Cunliffe 1968). The nature of these defences suggests at least semi-permanent occupation, but only a few features in the interior have been definitely dated to this phase.

Within a fairly short time (probably less than a year) the site of the camp was cleared, its ditches filled in and a new, enlarged, unenclosed permanent military supply-base constructed in its place. The basis of this settlement was a regular grid of metalled roads, of which the main example also formed the beginning of 'Watling Street', a major road which ultimately connected Richborough with various important centres, including Canterbury, Rochester and

London. To the north and south of this road terminal were various *insulae*, those to the south being used for storage buildings (most probably granaries), and those to the north for timber buildings which may have mainly had administrative and accommodation functions, including perhaps a *mansio*. This military establishment continued with various modifications, including a possible reduction in its grain storage capacity, until about AD 85, when the site was again partly cleared, this time in preparation for the construction of the *quadrifrons*, an impressive imperial monument covered in marble.

Donald Strong (1968) suggested that the *quadrifrons* may have been started by the Emperor Domitian, possibly following the recall of the Governor, Agricola, and the subsequent abandonment of the 'forward policy' in Northern Britain. The monument may therefore have been a symbolic entrance (at a major channel port) to the Province of *Britannia*, the conquest of which might by then have been considered to be complete.

Traces of a second Claudian fort have been discovered at Reculver (Philp 1969), and another is suspected at Canterbury, where excavations have revealed lengths of a V-shaped ditch dating to the mid-first century (Tatton-Brown 1977). Other, perhaps temporary, camps are likely, especially in the very early stages of the Conquest, but the general lack of substantial forts in the South-East probably indicates that the inhabitants of this region were not considered by the Romans as being either particularly troublesome or needing close supervision.

Another military supply-base, and perhaps also a fort, was in the Fishbourne and Chichester areas of West Sussex. The supply-base was located at Fishbourne in order to take advantage of the good natural harbour facilities of this district. Evidence of this depot was first found during the excavations of the famous Flavian Palace site (Cunliffe 1971). The Claudian military remains included three timber storage 'granary' buildings. As at Richborough, these buildings were also well served by gravelled roads, one of which leads eastwards towards Chichester, where there was perhaps a fort (see below). There were a few associated military artifacts including an iron ballista head, and last century a legionary's helmet (Plate 6.2) was dredged out of the nearby creek. Recently, excavations by Alec Down in the field to the east of the Palace have revealed further traces of timber structures dating to the Claudian period (*Britannia*, Vol. XV, 328). The military depot at Fishbourne is presumed to have been built by the Second Legion, under the command of Vespasian (the future Emperor), in preparation for the legion's campaign in the hostile South-West, during the second half of AD 43. Obviously the establishment of such a supply-base in presumably friendly territory, and with good communications and transport by sea, would have had many advantages.

Of the postulated camp at Chichester there are as yet only a few traces. The discovery *outside* the Eastgate of lengths of large 'military-style' ditches has been interpreted as indicating an early defensive enclosure on the east side of the later town (Down 1981; *Britannia*, Vol. XIV, 332–3). From within the

Plate 6.2 A legionary helmet found in Chichester Harbour, West Sussex.
(Photograph: Sussex Archaeological Society.)

area of the later town have come quantities of military equipment, and excavations in the north-west quadrant have revealed the remains of timber buildings associated with Claudian pottery. The ordered layout of these buildings, together with their style of construction, has led to the suggestion that they are the result of military planning, but whether they should be regarded as part of a military or civilian (perhaps *vicus*) settlement is uncertain (Down 1978*a*). The evidence from Chichester therefore suggests the presence of a Claudian military settlement linked with the supply-base at Fishbourne. Neither site is likely to have been needed for very long (perhaps for a year or two at the most) since despite fierce resistance, the South-West was fairly quickly subdued. Before AD 50 there were major alterations at the Fishbourne site and its military role was replaced by a civilian settlement (see below).

Additional early forts and supply-bases are likely to have been built in the South-East, and several sites have been suggested, although definite proof is lacking. Thus, in Surrey for example, it has been suggested (Bird 1987) that there was a 'full-size fort at Staines' where early Roman finds include a few military objects, including a cavalry helmet.

Other traces of possible early military activity in the South-East are the major roads, some of which have associated posting stations. The principal Roman roads in our area include Watling Street (see above), Stane Street which links Chichester with London, and the roads between London and Silchester, London and Hassocks, London and the Lewes area, and Hastings and Rochester. The precise dating of these roads is uncertain, but some at least (such as

185

Watling Street) probably date to the first few years after the invasion. It will be noted that many of the major roads in the South-East converge on London. There is no known Iron Age predecessor to Roman London and it is now thought that the settlement came into existence *c.* AD 50 (Merrifield 1983), the initial capital of the province being at Colchester. If this dating is correct, it is likely to have a bearing on the dating of some of the major roads in the South-East. There are many other proven or suggested Roman roads in the counties currently under examination, some of which clearly date to after the initial stages of Roman occupation. The whole subject of Roman roads in Britain, and especially those in the South-East, formed the basis of a lifetime of research by the late Ivan Margary, and the reader is referred to the published results (Margary 1965; 1967).

At regular intervals (approximately a day's march apart) along several of the major roads were *mansiones* or 'posting stations'. In addition to forming part of the imperial communications system, these sites would also probably have served various other functions, including the provision of accommodation for official travellers, and perhaps 'local policing' and the collecting of taxes. One of the best-known examples of such a road with associated posting stations is Stane Street. The system here would have involved four posting stations, but only the sites of two of these, at Hardham and Alfoldean (both in Sussex) are known for certain. The camp at Hardham is situated some 13 miles to the north of Chichester and nearly 12 miles to the south of the next station, at Alfoldean. There has been much speculation as to the locations of the two stations in Surrey, but in terms of spacing criteria, possible locations include the Dorking or Burford Bridge areas and the Merton area (Neale 1973).

Both of the known *mansiones* on Stane Street have been partly, but unfortunately poorly, excavated. The site at Hardham (Winbolt 1927) consisted of a rectangular earthworth enclosing some 1.6 ha. Pottery finds (including wasters, which suggest the local production of some of the pottery) indicate occupation from the mid-first to mid-second centuries. After this period the site was apparently abandoned as a settlement, and part of it was used as a cemetery.

The *mansio* at Alfoldean also consisted of a rectangular earthwork, but was smaller in size (1 ha) than the site at Hardham. Another difference between the two sites is that at Alfoldean, occupation continued much later, to at least the late-third century (Winbolt 1923; 1924). Excavations in 1922 and 1923 revealed various features, including traces of buildings, inside the enclosure. Despite the problems caused by the poor quality of the excavations and recording, Ernest Black (1987) has recently undertaken a useful re-examination of the available evidence from Winbolt's investigations and has suggested that the north-east quadrant of the site is likely to have been the residential part of the *mansio*. Although it is uncertain as to whether the buildings were constructed of timber or had masonry footings, signs of elaboration include tessellated floors, painted wall plaster, window glass, and

186

box-flue and roofing tiles. At some stage, possibly in the late-third century, these buildings were demolished and replaced by several new timber-framed structures. Other changes at this time seem to have involved the fortifications. The coin evidence from the site may indicate that there was little or no settlement during the fourth century.

Recently the recording of a trench dug across and beyond the Alfoldean enclosure has provided further traces of occupation within the earthwork, and also traces of extra-mural settlements extending up to 600 m to the south of the station (English and Gower 1985). The extra-mural remains are of particular interest and include various features such as a possible iron furnace, a path at right angles to Stane Street; an area of concentrated occupation material, a succession of floor layers, and various pits and ditches. The investigators have posed the interesting problem of whether this extra-mural settlement was limited to the sides of Stane Street (ribbon development), or whether it is more extensive and spreads away from the road. If the latter, there may therefore have been a fairly large settlement and perhaps industrial area (in addition to the possible furnace, the finds included 'much iron slag') attached to the posting station. The pottery finds indicate that the main periods of occupation were the late first and second centuries (there were only a few sherds dating to the third or fourth centuries).

Just to the north of the posting station Stane Street had to cross the River Arun, and this was achieved by means of a bridge based on wooden piles, the remains of which were found during a period of drought in 1934 (Winbolt 1936). The Alfoldean station was obviously specifically located in order to control and/or benefit from the meeting point of the road and the river, and Judie English and John Gower have suggested that there may also have been a wharf near the bridge.

Other important methods of helping to consolidate the Romans' position in Britain after the Conquest included the establishment or recognition of semi-independent client kingdoms (see below), and the creation of regional tribal units which were largely the responsibility of trusted members of the local upper classes. Thus the tribes of Iron Age Britain were re-organized into a number of *civitates*, to which various administrative functions were delegated. In the South-East an area approximately that of modern-day Kent formed the *civitas* of the *Cantiaci*; much of Sussex (especially the areas to the south of the Weald) belonged to the *Regni*; parts of northern Surrey were likely to have formed part of the *territorium* of the major settlement at London (which later became the capital of the province); other areas of Surrey were probably split between the *Cantiaci* and the *Atrebates* of the Berkshire area (who, like the Regni, were previously part of the original Atrebates tribe) and/or the Regni; whilst part of the Weald may have been separately administered as an Imperial Estate (see below). Although the precise boundaries of these administrative regions are not known, several possibilities have been suggested (Cunliffe 1973; Detsicas 1983; Bird 1987). Each tribal region had its own capital,

Canterbury for the Cantiaci, Silchester for the Atrebates and Chichester for the Regni.

The Client Kingdom

Soon after the invasion the Romans established in Southern Britain a client kingdom consisting of part of Sussex, and perhaps also other areas to the north and west. The Roman practice of using client-kings to govern parts of newly conquered territories or areas on the borders of the Empire, was already well-established, and was especially useful in the early stages of conquest since it helped to economize on Roman manpower for administrative and 'policing' requirements. There is no record that the first ruler of this client kingdom was Verica, the Atrebatan king who had so conveniently fled to the safety of Rome in AD 42. If, however, he was restored as king, it is perhaps possible that some of the coins bearing his name were actually struck *after* the Conquest. We have already seen (Ch. 5) that moulds for gold and silver coins have recently been discovered in an 'early Roman' ditch at Boxgrove, whilst the excavations in Chapel Street (Down 1978*a*) have yielded previously unrecorded coin types of Verica (although these were admittedly found together with pre-Conquest issues of other rulers) from *post*-Conquest contexts. Possibly, if Verica did return to power, he may only have done so for a short period, and he perhaps died or was replaced within a few years of the invasion. In any case, the only historical information about a client king in our region concerns one Tiberius Claudius Cogidubnus.

There are two definite ancient references to Cogidubnus, the famous passage by Tacitus (*Agricola*, 14) and the appearance of his name on a dedicatory inscription (Plate 6.3) (*RIB* 91) from a temple of Neptune and Minerva located at Chichester. There is also still the possibility that the legend CRAB which appears on two romanized 'Iron Age type' silver coins may be an abbreviation of Cogidubnus' name and titles (Black 1987).

Remarkably little is really known about Cogidubnus, and the various theories and sources of information have formed the basis of two very useful recent papers (Barrett 1979; Bogaers 1979). Nothing is known about the king's origins, although it is generally assumed that he was a member of the original Atrebatic dynasty (but see Salway 1981). Barrett's work suggests that Cogidubnus became King between AD 43 and 52 and that he was dead or had retired before AD 78, and probably before the end of Nero's reign in AD 68. According to Tacitus, the King remained loyal to the Romans for a long time, and it is clear from the archaeological evidence from Sussex that during his reign he was fairly successful in introducing elements of Roman culture into his kingdom.

Plate 6.3 The Cogidubnus Inscription from Chichester, West Sussex. The inscription is the dedication of a Roman temple thought to have stood at the junction of North Street and Lion Street, where the stone was found. (Photograph: R. L. Wilkins and N. Pollard.)

As to the extent of the client kingdom, there is much uncertainty. The discovery of the temple dedication at Chichester demonstrates that this area of Sussex must have been part of the kingdom, but not necessarily the centre of it. Tacitus informs us that Cogidubnus was given 'certain *civitates*' (probably at least three, thus implying that the territory was likely to have been quite extensive). Barrett suggests that the kingdom may have consisted, in part at least, of the old Atrebatic kingdom of the Commian dynasty, and that after the death or retirement of Cogidubnus the client state would have been absorbed into the province and then divided into the three Roman *civitates* referred to by Tacitus. Such a theory receives some support from archaeological discoveries at Silchester (Boon 1969), where during the first century there were two defensive systems, at least one of which was *post*-Conquest, and during the Flavian period the town layout was reorganized following an earlier and less rigidly planned phase of urbanization (which nevertheless included public baths). Possibly this Flavian period of reorganization at Silchester may mark the conversion of the settlement into the capital of the new *civitas*.

In Sussex, in addition to the general, widespread acceptance and distribution of products of Roman manufacture, such as pottery and coins, there are various other archaeological discoveries which also shed light on the processes

189

of Romanization during the period of the client kingdom, especially so in Chichester which was clearly developing as a Romanized centre. The dedicatory inscription referred to above is proof that there was a temple to Neptune and Minerva (classical deities) and that this was erected with the permission of King Cogidubnus, and paid for by a guild of artisan craftsmen. The date of construction of the temple is unfortunately unknown. Another dedicatory inscription (*RIB* 92), now lost, can be dated to AD 58, and was apparently associated with a building, or perhaps even a statue of the Emperor. In the north-west quadrant of the town the Claudian 'military' timber buildings (see above) were superseded by new timber-framed buildings and extensive areas of industrial activity, including the manufacture of Gallo-Belgic style pottery, bronze working, enamelling and ironworking (Down 1978*a*). This concentration of craft work may indicate a developing civilian market.

A large and mid–late-first-century ditch was recently discovered outside the eastern edge of the later walled town (*Britannia* XIII, 363; XIV, 332–3). Alec Down has suggested that this feature might be part of a previously unknown defensive system around the early town, possibly during the time of Cogidubnus, or perhaps during the subsequent early stages of the *civitas* capital.

At Fishbourne the military supply base was replaced by an extensive civilian element (Cunliffe 1971). Possibly once the army had left the site, it would have become an attractive location for merchants and traders owing to its proximity to the Roman harbour works. One building of this phase was unusually elaborate for its date, and had at least six rooms, painted walls and a veranda. The function of this building is uncertain but could be residential. It may be associated with another nearby timber building which served as a workshop.

Towards the end of the Neronian period, part of the settlement at Fishbourne was cleared, and an area fenced off prior to the creation of an elaborate masonry house on an open site to the south of the demolished timber buildings (including the two structures mentioned above). Referred to as the 'proto-palace', this spacious and sophisticated dwelling had such luxuries as a colonnaded courtyard, a suite of baths, painted walls of exceptional quality, floors of *opus sectile* and mouldings of Purbeck marble. Clearly, the planning, construction and decoration of this building were well beyond the expertise of local craftsmen, and would thus have required the importation of Continental workmen. The suggested date of construction for the proto-palace is about AD 65 to 70. Also assigned to this period are the remains of a second, unfinished masonry building which was found beneath the West wing of the Flavian palace, and also the masonry footings of another building which were recently revealed during the excavations to the east of the palace (*Britannia*, Vol XV: 328–9). The function of both of these buildings is unknown.

The building of the proto-palace complex, and also of the earlier timber buildings which it replaced, implies a wealthy owner or a prestigious person who was able to borrow substantial sums of money. Possibly the progression from an elaborate timber house to a sumptuous masonry establishment may represent a gradual increase in wealth and status. Cunliffe (1971) has suggested that the owner of both phases of buildings might have been King Cogidubnus. There are other possibilities however, including foreign traders or businessmen (*negotiatores*), or other members of the local aristocracy. That the latter could afford such Roman luxuries is suggested by the discovery of a relatively large number of 'early villas' in Sussex, of which the Angmering and Arundel (Tarrant Street) sites have yielded parallels to the distinctive tile types used in the baths of the proto-palace at Fishbourne (Black 1985). The dating of the proto-palace and contemporary elaborate houses may also be too late (*c.* AD 65–70) for Cogidubnus (see above). Other even earlier masonry houses have been suggested for Sussex, however, and these sites (Borough Farm, Pulborough; the Shepherd's Garden, Arundel, and somewhere in the vicinity of Westhampnet Church) presumably must have belonged to the reign of Cogidubnus. Again the dating and linking of this group of sites is largely derived from an analysis of the tile finds (Black 1987). It is interesting that a fair number of the early Sussex villas are sited near to the River Arun, and Black has pointed out that the location in this area of the pre-Flavian villas may help to explain why the Arun is named in Ptolemy's *Geography* (the only other named river in the South-East is the Thames).

In about AD 75 to 80, a massive programme of rebuilding was started at Fishbourne and the proto-palace was incorporated into a considerably larger complex, consisting of four ranges of rooms placed around a large, central garden (Plate 6.4). The main approach was through an Entrance Hall in the east wing, and was apparently served by a road leading directly to Chichester. This new building is the famous 'Palace', an interpretation based on various factors, such as its huge size, the exceptional richness and grandeur of its decorative features, and the suggested 'official' functions of some of the rooms, especially the large room in the centre of the West wing which Cunliffe (1971) identified as an 'audience chamber'. Cunliffe has suggested that the palace was the residence of King Cogidubnus, a romantic but extremely unlikely theory given the dating involved (see above).

Others have suggested that the palace might have been the official residence of a high-ranking member of the Roman administration of the Province, possibly an official required to deal with the problems of integrating the client kingdom into the province (including perhaps the postulated division of the kingdom into the three separate *civitates*) following the death (or perhaps retirement) of Cogidubnus. It may be no coincidence that two special legal commissioners (Salvius Liberalis and Javolenus Priscus) were in Britain in the period immediately after AD 80 (Salway 1981).

It should be noted that a possible major problem with regard to the various historical interpretations of both the proto-palace and palace at Fishbourne is the precise dating of the periods of construction and occupation of

Plate 6.4 A reconstruction of how the Flavian Palace at Fishbourne, West Sussex, may have looked at the height of its development: viewed from the east.
(Photograph: Sussex Archaeological Society.)

these buildings. Currently, for instance, Ernest Black (pers. comm.) is suggesting slightly later dates for the construction of the two buildings: *c*. AD 75–80 for the proto-palace and *c*. AD 90–110 for the palace. These changes in dating are largely based upon the theory that the material in the make-up of the palace should be treated as providing a *terminus post quem* and not the actual date of construction. Such a change of emphasis in turn affects the dating of the occupation of the proto-palace. Professor Cunliffe assigned this phase to *c*. AD 65/70–75/80 on the basis of the *terminus ante quem* thought to be given by the material in the make-up layers of the palace. It may be possible however, to re-interpret some of this material; for instance, Ernest Black suggests that the relatively large number of Vespasianic coins found in the make-up of the palace may reflect the activities of the work force used to build the proto-palace rather than its successor. The significantly later date range for the palace is suggested by the fact that similar types of roller-stamped flue-tiles have been found associated with both the construction of the palace and also the public baths in Chichester. Tiles stamped with these dies (the 'London-Sussex' group) are presumed to be fairly contemporary. At Chichester such tiles were found in contexts which have been dated to the Late Flavian period or slightly later (Down 1978*a*, 142–4).

A new approach to the ownership of Fishbourne has been put forward by

Ernest Black (1987). Black suggests that the complex need not be interpreted as a 'palace'. Instead he uses John Smith's (1978) unit system approach to suggest that the buildings might have been the residence of up to four families of similar status. The large 'audience chamber' is also re-interpreted as a large, formal dining room. Black appreciates that the owners of such an establishment must either have had considerable wealth, or have been regarded as sufficiently creditworthy to borrow considerable sums of money. He suggests that perhaps 'one generation of joint heirs determined to rebuild their father's house on a grandiose scale'. Possibly Cogidubnus was that father. The contemporary but smaller villa at Southwick, the design of which is presumably based on that at Fishbourne, is also viewed as a multi-unit house (for two families). Such a radical reinterpretation of these two villas involves Black in interesting speculation about the local social system, which he suggests included partible inheritance.

Other insights into the post-Conquest social scene in Sussex may be obtained from a consideration of the large number of elaborate first-century villas in this region. If these villas are the homes of members of the indigenous aristocracy, it is interesting that they are widely dispersed at Fishbourne, Westhampnet, Borough Farm (Pulborough), Arundel (2), Angmering (2), Southwick, Newhaven and Eastbourne, and perhaps also at Preston (Brighton). Since many of these locations were clearly not chosen with the specific aim of capitalizing on urban markets for farm produce, it is possible that their distribution corresponds to the pattern of nobles' farms at the end of the pre-Roman Iron Age and during the client kingdom. Indeed, it is reasonable to assume that, in the politically favourable conditions of the client kingdom, the local landowners would have remained in possession of their lands (in contrast to the situation in some of the other regions), and Black argues that the capital or repayment of loans necessary for the building of the early villas in Sussex is likely to have come from the traditional exploitation of the peasants by the nobles. These nobles may also have been able to use their favourable relations with the Romans in order to obtain profitable military contracts for their farming surpluses.

The Classis Britannica

From the time of the Conquest until the mid-third century, parts of Kent and Sussex were used by the Roman fleet known as the *Classis Britannica*. Unfortunately very little is known about the fleet, either from historical or archaeological sources, but the fragmentary evidence has recently been reviewed by Henry Cleere (1977). The fleet was established by Claudius (or perhaps Gaius) in preparation for the invasion of Britain. Its main functions at the time of the Conquest were the transportation of the army, the supply of stores and materials, and the provision of an important maritime communications network.

Probably the fleet's earliest base in Britain was that established at Richborough, which has yielded a single example of a tile bearing the fleet's *CL BR* stamp. Elsewhere in the South-East the fleet may also have been involved with the Claudian military supply depot at Fishbourne, but evidence is lacking. After the relatively rapid consolidation of the lowland zone of Britain, the *Classis Britannica* appears to have continued to carry out a primarily supportive role for the army units in the military zones of the North and West. It also continued, however, to maintain bases on the coast of South-East England, and became involved in the iron industry of the Weald.

During the 1970s, the remains of two forts of the *Classis Britannica* were discovered at Dover (Philp 1981). These forts were both located on a spur overlooking a tidal estuary (of the River Dour) at the shortest crossing point from the fleet's continental base at Boulogne. The earliest fort, which enclosed about half a hectare, was started but soon abandoned. Features belonging to this phase, which is dated by the excavator to *c.* AD 117, consist of the foundations of the fort's wall, at least three barracks, and a possible store building. In about AD 130–140 the fleet returned to Dover and constructed a much larger (1 ha) fort. This had a stone defensive wall, a ditch on three sides, at least three gates, a metalled forecourt leading to the waterfront, granaries, barracks, a possible *principia*, well-metalled roads and elaborate drainage and water systems. Brian Philp has estimated a total garrison of perhaps 600–700 men. The fort was abandoned *c.* AD 154–55, but was repaired and re-occupied about ten years later. Another period of abandonment occurred after *c.* AD 180, prior to the fort's last period of rebuilding and occupation *c.* AD 190–200. The fort was finally abandoned about AD 208. Philp has suggested that the periods of abandonment may be linked to episodes when the fleet was involved in major campaigns in the north. In addition to the forts, the *Classis Britannica* also constructed at Dover major harbour installations and two masonry lighthouses. A civilian settlement (see below) developed to the north of the forts.

Other *Classis Britannica* forts may have existed at Lympne and Pevensey. These sites, which were both later the locations of Saxon Shore Forts, have yielded stamped tiles of the British fleet. The case for a fort at Lympne is further strengthened by the discovery of an altar dedicated to Aufidius Pantera, prefect of the *Classis Britannica* (*RIB* 66), which was found built into the east gate of the later Shore Fort. Additional hints of an earlier fort at Lympne include other examples of reused masonry, a coin of Antoninus Pius and several pieces of pottery (Cunliffe 1980). Although these various discoveries need not prove that there was a fort at Lympne, the site's strategic importance at the mouth of the Rother estuary would have made it a logical choice. The discovery of *CL*

194

BR stamped tiles at a villa at Folkestone, and also at a possible port at Bodiam, have been interpreted as indicating an involvement of the fleet at these two sites.

Elsewhere in the Weald the fleet's stamped tiles have been found at three sites (Bardown, Beauport Park and Cranbrook) connected with the iron industry. At Beauport Park about 1,600 *CL BR* tiles were found in association with a well-preserved six-roomed bath-house (Brodribb 1981; Cleere and Crossley 1985). The large number of stamped tiles clearly demonstrates the connection between the fleet and the bath house, which was presumably used by the work force of the adjacent large ironworking complex. The bath house, which was rebuilt and enlarged at least twice, dates from the early second to the mid-third century. Henry Cleere considers that the discovery of *CL BR* tiles at various ironworking sites, which form a distinct *eastern* group, indicates the direct involvement of the British fleet in part of the iron industry in order to secure supplies of iron for military purposes. He further argues that this involvement supports the case for these having been an Imperial Estate based on the ironworks of the Weald, with direct state participation in the eastern region, and private entrepreneurs controlling the western group of ironworks.

The *Classis Britannica* disappears from the archaeological record during the mid-third century. Although it is possible that the fleet continued and that no further references to it have survived (unfortunately the practice of stamping tiles appears to have ended by this period), there is some evidence to support the theory that the unit under its former organization may have ceased to exist. At Dover the large fleet base was by now finally abandoned, and the important ironworking establishments at Bardown and Beauport Park came to an end. Henry Cleere has suggested that one reason for the sudden end of the eastern group of large ironworking sites may have been that these sites were threatened by raiding, and were thus abandoned in favour of the more secure setting of the Forest of Dean. The military response during the third century to increasing raiding on the coast of South-Eastern England (see below) may also have led to a major re-organization of the naval forces, with perhaps the reallocation of the personnel and vessels of the *Classis Britannica* to the army units used to establish the new Saxon Shore Fort defence system.

The Saxon Shore Forts

During the early third century the east coast of Britain became threatened by pirate raiding. This threat was to be an increasing problem during the rest of the Roman occupation. The initial response was to build forts at Brancaster on the Wash and at Reculver (Kent) at the mouth of the Thames estuary. Subsequent improvements to the coastal defences included the construction of further forts, four of which (Richborough, Dover, Lympne and Pevensey) are located in the South-East. These fortifications have become known as the 'Saxon Shore' forts since in the *Notitia Dignitatum* (a fifth-century handbook of military and civil offices) the forts are listed under the command of the 'Count of the Saxon Shore' (*comes litoris Saxonici*). The naming of the coastal defence system after this officer's title may be confusing, however, since the title and command are unlikely to date to before the late third century, and are possibly much later (Salway 1981). In addition, it is uncertain whether the title means that the shore was attacked by and/or settled with Saxons. Whatever the case, the coastal forts have been the subject of two recent books and the reader is referred to these for detailed information (Johnson 1976; Johnston 1977). It is important to note, however, that the forts represent an evolving system which should be considered alongside the contemporary Roman coastal fortifications on the Continent.

All five Shore forts in the South-East have received some archaeological attention. The earliest of these forts is that at Reculver, which dates from the early third century. It was nearly square in shape with rounded corners. It also had masonry walls, two ditches and four gates, and is typologically very similar to the contemporary fort at Brancaster. Excavations within the interior (Philp 1969) have revealed various buildings including the *principia*, barracks and baths. Although occupation was not necessarily continuous, the fort remained in use until the second half of the fourth century. Traces of civilian settlement have been found adjacent to the fort.

At some time between AD 200 and 280 the site at Richborough (Plate 6.1) was re-occupied by the army, and 1.1 acres around the *quadrifrons* was enclosed by a rampart and triple ditch (Cunliffe 1968). Although no remains of any internal buildings have survived, it is thought that the monument was converted into a defended look-out post and signal station. During the late third century the earth fort at Richborough was replaced by a much larger stone-built fort which was rectangular in shape, with two gates, rounded corner turrets, regularly spaced projecting rectangular bastions (Plate 6.5), and two ditches. Unfortunately little is known about the interior features of the fort, but the foundations of the *quadrifrons* are thought to have been used as the base for the *principia*, and other buildings included wooden barrack blocks, a small bath house, two other masonry buildings, and a Christian church which is thought to date to the early fifth century. Of definite early-fifth-century date are a number of coins which indicate that the site was still an important centre of activity at this period. Outside the fort have been found an 'amphitheatre'/'arena', two Romano-Celtic temples and traces of civilian settlement.

The Shore Fort at Dover was built across part of the abandoned *Classis Britannica* fort. Only part of the fort has so far been located, but the shape appears to be trapezoidal. There were corner turrets, a single ditch and bastions, at least some of which were later additions to the original scheme. As yet

Plate 6.5 Part of the wall and one of the projecting bastions of the Saxon Shore fort at Richborough, Kent. The photograph shows the use of double tile-courses and small ashlar blocks to face the walls.

little is known about the interior of the fort. Its irregular plan and the provisional dating of the associated finds indicate that the fort dates to the late third century.

Another late-third-century Shore Fort is that at Lympne, which has subsequently suffered greatly from ground subsidence. The distortions resulting from these major landslips have caused serious problems with regard to the reconstruction of the fort plan. For many years it was thought that the fort was polygonal in shape, but excavations by Professor Cunliffe (1980) produced evidence which suggested that this was not necessarily the case and that it may have had a regular, rectangular plan, similar to those of the contemporary forts at Richborough and Porchester. Subsequently however, a combined archaeological and geotechnical project has shown that the fort was in fact polygonal (Hutchinson *et al.* 1985). At Lympne the defences incorporated rounded corner turrets, semicircular bastions, a main east gate and a northern postern gate. Features found within the interior of the fort include what is thought to be the *principia*, a bath house and traces of two other masonry structures. The dating evidence suggests that the fort was abandoned by *c.* AD 350.

The Shore Fort at Pevensey (Plate 6.6) differs in a number of important respects from its neighbours in Kent. Firstly it was built much later than the

Plate 6.6 Pevensey Castle, East Sussex: view from the north-west. The outer curtain wall with its gates and projecting bastions originally formed part of the defences of the Saxon Shore fort. The defences in the south-east corner of the site are Norman and Medieval. (Photograph: Royal Commission on Historical Monuments.)

others, probably *c.* AD 340. It also incorporates a number of significant improvements in terms of the fort's defences. Its shape is roughly oval and the curtain wall follows the contour of the slightly higher ground upon which it was built. Instead of being placed at regular intervals (as at the earlier forts) Pevensey's U-shaped bastions were strategically placed so as to be intervisible each with the next. The fort had a main west gate, a smaller east gate, a north postern gate, and a ditch. Despite various excavations earlier this century, very little is known about the interior of the fort. A port and civilian settlement was probably located to the west of the fort (discoveries of Roman material have been made at Westham). Finds from the fort indicate that occupation continued until at least the late fourth century. One particular source of evidence for a late occupation at Pevensey, however, can now be rejected. Until fairly recently it was thought that the discovery of two tiles stamped HON AUG ANDRIA represented a period of building at Pevensey during the reign of Honorius. These tiles have now been shown to be forgeries, and are almost certainly the work of the mischievous Charles Dawson (infamous for the 'Piltdown Man' hoax). Other finds of third-century date suggest that there was also an earlier phase of occupation at Pevensey (note also the discovery of *CL BR* tiles referred to above).

Although historical sources (Hassall 1977) provide us with some information about the official garrisons of the Shore Forts, not all of the occupants were necessarily regular army personnel. The precise roles of the forts are also not fully understood. Thus at Porchester (Hampshire), the only Shore Fort which has been excavated on a large scale under modern conditions (Cunliffe 1975) there is evidence to suggest that throughout the fourth century a wide range of activities was carried out within the fort and that the inhabitants included women. Although it is possible that these women may have been the wives of members of the garrison, it is also possible that during part or all of the fourth century, some of the Shore Forts may have been occupied by a civilian community, among whom may have been billeted an official militia. Future excavations at various Shore Forts may help to indicate how typical is the social situation revealed at Porchester.

The ultimate fate of the Saxon Shore Forts is also uncertain. Most of the sites appear to have been occupied during the late fourth century and probably continued into the fifth century. Although troop withdrawals at the end of the period of Roman occupation will presumably have weakened the garrisons of the forts, the local communities may have continued to maintain their strongholds, perhaps with local militia or mercenaries.

Urban Settlement

Towns were a major characteristic of Mediterranean culture and an essential part of the Roman way of life. They functioned as centres for administration, trade, religion, entertainment, education and protection. The development, form and history of towns in Roman Britain may thus provide an indication of the degree of success by which certain fundamental elements of Roman culture were imposed upon, or assimilated into, the indigenous regional communities.

We have already seen (Ch. 5) that in the South-East during the late Iron Age there were already a number of large, nucleated 'urban' or 'semi-urban' settlements. Two of these, the sites at Rochester and Canterbury, continued in use after the Conquest and developed into towns, with Canterbury being chosen as the Tribal Capital of the Cantiaci. The other Tribal Capital in the South-East, that of the Regni at Chichester, may have been a new foundation within the area of the Late Iron Age territorial oppidum (Fig. 5.10). The development of London and its suburb at Southwark would have served a large area of northern Surrey and north-west Kent. A number of 'small towns' (nucleated settlements which usually lack the organization, sophistication and amenities of the major towns), developed alongside some of the major roads (examples: Springhead, Kent; Staines and Ewell, both in Surrey) and ports (e.g. Dover). Other smaller nucleated centres (e.g. Seaford, Sussex) may also have been minor urban settlements, perhaps providing local markets. Access to, and distance from, the larger 'Romanized' towns in the South-East varied considerably from area to area, and some regions, especially East Sussex and the rest of the Weald, are very isolated from major towns (Green 1980). Such isolation is likely to have had important economic and cultural implications.

Published information about Roman urban settlements in the South-East is mainly confined to the two tribal capitals, London/Southwark (not covered by this volume), and only a couple of the smaller nucleated settlements. The smaller 'towns' are therefore a priority for future research, and their potential has been highlighted by recent excavations at Staines, Ewell, Springhead and Dover, and the recent observations at Alfoldean (see above). The decline and end of Roman towns in the South-East is discussed in Chapter 7.

Roman Chichester (*Noviomagus Regnensium*) has been the subject of many excavations, and in recent years regular reports have been published as a series (Down and Rule 1971; Down, 1974; 1978a; 1981). In addition, Alec Down, who has been in charge of most of the recent investigations in Chichester is in the process of writing a book on the Roman town. It is therefore only necessary to provide a short account of the main aspects of the settlement's development.

The earliest phases of urban occupation at Chichester have been discussed above. These are presumed to belong to the period of the Client Kingdom of Cogidubnus. During Flavian times there was a phase of demolition and levelling, followed by building work and the establishment of a new street grid. Possibly this episode represents the demolition of the native town and its rebuilding as the *civitas* capital of the Regni, presumably following the death or retirement of Cogidubnus. Few traces of public buildings dating to the Flavian period have been found, but one such discovery is of a major bath suite, probably the public baths of the city. As yet no remains have been found for the forum and basilica, which presumably occupied the prime site at the junction of the main north-south and east-west streets. Another major public building was the amphitheatre, which lay on the eastern edge of the city (White 1936). Other public works may include an earthwork defensive circuit (see above). During the late first and second centuries evidence for domestic occupation covers a large area, including areas outside that defined by the later town walls (Down 1978b). By about the middle of the second century some of the domestic houses began to be rebuilt in masonry, and this trend possibly reflects increasing prosperity. At this period there was one major cremation cemetery outside the later east gate, and another possible cemetery near the south gate.

The first indisputable system of town defences at Chichester was constructed in the late second century; a time when many other comparable towns in Roman Britain also acquired defences (possibly for prestige reasons or as a reaction to the depletion of the British garrisons to support the personal aspirations of Clodius Albinus). At Chichester the defences originally consisted of a pair of V-shaped ditches with a bank on the inside. Later, perhaps in the early third century, the bank was cut back and a wall erected in front of it. There is some evidence to suggest that the town gates may have been constructed at the same time as the original earthbank (Cunliffe 1973). Unfortunately there is little evidence available about the gates, none of which remains above ground level. The town defences did not enclose all the earlier areas of settlement, and during the third and fourth centuries, settlement continued to occur outside the east and south gates. At the north gate, however, it appears that a cemetery (inhumation and cremation) was established which spread across part of the earlier town.

In the late third or early fourth century significant modifications were made to the town defences. A number of D-shaped bastions were added to the walls and the earlier ditches were filled in and a new, wider ditch dug further away from the wall. Such defensive improvements are probably part of a widespread response (including the Shore Fort system) to the threat of raids in South-Eastern Britain. The bastions, which were functionally designed for the use of artillery, suggest that by now the town may have been defended by a permanent garrison.

The results of excavations in the north-west quadrant of Chichester (Down 1978a; 1981) indicate that during the late third and fourth centuries this area of the town was very prosperous and witnessed the building, and sometimes subsequent rebuilding or enlargement, of substantial masonry houses. In addition, during the first half of the fourth century one of the town sewers was repaired and several of the roads were resurfaced. In the second half of the fourth century, however, although initially masonry construction continued, there are signs of gradual neglect and decay. Outside the city walls occupation (which involved ironworking during the late fourth century) may have continued at the Cattlemarket site until the early or mid fifth century (*Britannia* Vol. XIV, 333). In addition, a late Roman inhumation cemetery was established on the south side of St Pancras.

The study of Roman Canterbury (*Durovernum Cantiacorum*) has occurred in three main phases: the first during the laying of an extensive drainage system in the 1860s, the next as excavations on bomb sites after the Second World War, and most recently by rescue investigations by the Canterbury Archaeological Trust. The results of the post-War excavations and observations are beginning to appear as a monograph series (*The Archaeology of*

Canterbury). Recent general summaries about Roman Canterbury have been produced by Blagg (1982), Detsicas (1983) and Bennett (1984). These publications make it necessary here only to outline some of the main developments of Roman Canterbury.

We have noted that after the Conquest the already established nucleated settlement at Canterbury was chosen as the tribal capital for the Cantiaci. Earlier, at the time of the invasion itself, Canterbury may have been selected as the site for a fort to guard the River Stour crossing, but definite proof is lacking. Little is known about the layout of the first-century Roman town, but new house types include both timber-framed and masonry examples. The settlement may have had an early major setback since excavations (Tatton Brown 1977) have produced possible traces of human slaughter dating to the time of the Boudiccan revolt.

Recent research (Bennett 1984) suggests that the topography of the town did not really become established until the early second century, and that the street grid developed gradually and was not a planned regular chequerboard grid as had previously been postulated. In the early second century part of the town was cleared and a network of interconnecting streets formed. At the centre of this new street pattern were the major public buildings: the theatre, the temple precinct, the forum, and the public baths. At the end of the second century the baths underwent substantial alterations, and in the early third century the theatre was rebuilt. The first theatre, which was possibly elliptical in shape, was replaced by a new and enlarged construction based on the conventional semicircular plan of the Classical Roman theatre (Fig. 8.5). Such changes to public buildings may indicate increases in the prosperity and population of the *civitas* capital. Other signs of prosperity are suggested by the various discoveries of mosaics and tessellated floors associated with the remains of private housing in the town.

Given the apparent wealth of Roman Canterbury it is surprising that it apparently did not acquire defences until *c.* AD 270–90 (contrast with the situation at Chichester, and also at nearby Rochester). Possibly at Canterbury an earlier defensive circuit still remains to be discovered. The late-third-century defences, which enclosed an area of about 50 ha, consisted of a flint wall backed by an earth rampart. The wall had a number of contemporary square interval towers attached to its inner face. Later, perhaps in the late fourth century, the defences appear to have been strengthened by the addition of external wall-towers, and perhaps also by the digging of a wide ditch. The remains of four gates are known, and at least two more are postulated. With the exception of the Ridingate, all the other gates apparently consisted of only a single unimpressive, but defensively utilitarian, portal.

The construction of the town defences resulted in the exclusion of parts of the former settlement area, the inclusion of areas presumably previously outside the town (such as areas used for burial), and changes in the street pattern. As previously, burial grounds continued to be located outside the settlement area. Of the pre-wall burials there are several examples of burial mounds, although none has so far been excavated. The area outside the town has also produced various traces of industrial activity (metalworking, pottery, and tile manufacture) and these indicate the presence of industrial suburbs.

Although overshadowed by the much larger Roman town at Canterbury, the settlement at Rochester (*Durobrivae*) continued after the Conquest as an important centre and port, perhaps with administrative responsibility for the western part of the *civitas*. Unfortunately, very little is known about Roman Rochester except for its defences, which enclosed an area of about 9.5 ha. The first defences, an earth rampart and ditch, were constructed during the second half of the second century. Later, probably in the third century, the defences were modified by the construction of a stone wall. Recent excavations near the Norman Castle (Flight and Harrison 1978) have yielded large numbers of Late Roman coins, which may indicate a possible market area.

Of the various smaller, nucleated 'urban' centres in the South-East, mention will be made of just a few sites (summary details are available for all the sites in the respective county articles/books referred to above). The site at Springhead, Kent is of particular interest since it has received a large amount of archaeological investigation. Although some excavation reports have appeared, the main general summaries are by Penn (1965) and Detsica (1983). The settlement is a typical example of irregular ribbon-development along Watling Street. The main feature of the settlement is an important temple complex, which probably provides the explanation for the town's location, growth and prosperity. Other aspects of the settlement include domestic buildings, industrial workings and a walled cemetery.

At Dover, in addition to the military forts discussed above, there was also an extensive civilian settlement and port. The site had various major attractions, including its safe natural harbour and its proximity to the Continent. The establishment of the military presence would also have been an important stimulus for urban development. The civilian settlement included a large bath house, various domestic buildings including the famous Painted House, a shrine, and several cemeteries. The growth of Dover (*Dubris*) as a port has been linked to the second-century decline of Richborough.

Roman Staines (*Pontes*) has been the subject of extensive fieldwork in recent years. The town possibly originated as either a 'posting station' at an important river crossing (see above) or perhaps as a civilian settlement alongside a fort which may have been located there during the early stages of the Conquest (Bird 1987). Although the settlement has produced traces of occupation from the first to the fourth century, the archaeological data indicate that its development had a number of set-backs, including what has been claimed to be evidence of destruction at the time of Boudicca's revolt, and also a period of decline between the late second and the mid third centuries (Crouch 1978). Whilst in the early (1st century) stages of the settlement, the buildings were made of timber and clay; during the later stages there were also some masonry buildings. During the late first and early second centuries one aspect of the economy of the town or the surrounding area may have been the production of sophisticated pottery (lead glazed and mica-dusted wares).

Despite the fairly large number of archaeological excavations which have been undertaken in Roman towns in the South-East, there is as yet very little published data regarding the economic and environmental aspects of the investigated towns. Such data is extremely important, not only because it can provide a valuable insight into the functioning of the various towns, but also because it enables comparisons to be made with the findings obtained from nearby rural settlements and other nucleated centres. The range and relative proportions of different types of food are likely to be of particular comparative interest. At Canterbury, for example, the published excavations document the remains of cattle, sheep, goat, pig, horse, deer, hare and various types of birds, fish and marine molluscs. The potential for such studies, however, is demonstrated even better at an urban settlement just outside the area covered by this book, that at Southwark. Here, in addition to all of the food range listed above for Canterbury, excavations (Sheldon 1978) have also proved the presence of fig, grape, raspberry, blackberry, plum, cherry, damson, apple or pear, lentils, peas, the cabbage family, coriander, mustard, dill, millet, flax, wild boar and badger. At both Canterbury and Southwark, dogs and cats were also present and represent household animals.

Rural Settlement

The basis of the wealth of the Roman economy was land, and its exploitation by farming had to produce sufficient surpluses to support the more sophisticated aspects of Roman life: the towns, the sumptuous country and seaside homes of the rich, large-scale manufacturing industries (such as pottery and iron production) and the army. It is therefore surprising that, given its importance, there has been relatively little detailed examination of the *farming* aspects of the countryside, especially land use and settlement patterns, field systems, methods of drainage, sources of information about the crops and domesticated animals, and farm tools and buildings. There has, however, been a considerable amount of time and resources spent on the study of one specific aspect of the Roman countryside, namely the 'villas'.

The precise definition of the term 'villa' has been the subject of much discussion, but most would probably agree that it refers to a rural house which exhibits a significant degree of the Roman style of life. In practical terms this assessment is usually determined by the discovery of masonry footings; concrete, tessellated or mosaic floors, clay tiles/bricks, and sometimes hypocaust heating systems and bath suites. Most of these establishments are presumed to be the centres of farms, but other functions are occasionally possible, as at the ironworking site at Garden Hill (Money 1977). Given the frequent lack of information about the economic aspects of villa type sites, it is perhaps wise to have a more general usage of the term for Romanized masonry houses in the country.

The majority of the farming settlements in the Roman countryside however, were the less wealthy and less sophisticated native 'peasant' settlements. Despite their vast numerical superiority, and the fact that many of these sites span the entire period of the Roman occupation (many sites originating in the Late Iron Age, and some perhaps continuing into the fifth century), they have received remarkably little attention. This situation is especially disappointing in the areas containing villas, and the relationship between the two types of settlement in these areas is unclear (perhaps landowner and tenant, or owner and employee, or both independent). Much remains to be learnt about peasant settlements, and although it is rare to find traces of houses, the sites and surrounding landscapes can provide much useful information about settlement patterns and history, farming practices, and the effects of Romanization on basically traditional 'Iron Age' communities. Surely this important topic deserves considerably more than the odd page or paragraph, as presented in recent general studies of specific areas of the South-East (see Blagg 1982; Detsicas 1983; Bird 1987). Hopefully, the following discussion about several sites on the South Downs will indicate some of the potential for non-villa rural studies in other parts of the South-East.

'Peasant' Settlements

One of the classic examples of a 'native peasant' settlement is the Late Iron Age/Romano–British site on Park Brow. We have already discussed (Ch. 5) the separate and earlier pre-Roman Iron Age settlement, which in turn replaced a Late Bronze Age site. Although there are three distinct occupation areas of different periods, they may represent continuous occupation with the occasional relocation of the habitation area. The entire complex is also closely linked by trackways and field systems, which again may have been in continuous use for a considerable period of time (Fig. 5.4).

The Iron Age/Romano–British site lay within a roughly triangular area amongst the fields, and the excavators during the 1920s (Wolseley *et al.* 1927) revealed three possible successive boundary ditches, various pits, and five rectangular 'house sites' which varied in size from 7.2 x 5.9 m to 9.8 x 7.9 m. One of these houses was totally excavated. Its walls were shown to have been constructed of vertical timbers and infilled with wattle and daub, which was internally decorated by the application of plaster painted red. The discovery of roofing tiles, window glass and a door key are other indications of the degree of sophistication and 'Romanization' of this building. Further evidence at the site for Roman influence and contacts includes some of the pottery finds, such as Samian ware and amphorae.

In the absence of good dating evidence it is difficult to interpret the five huts, since it is not known how many were in use at any one time. Possibly they represent successive 'single hut houses'. Or if some huts are contemporary 'individual houses', they may form a 'hamlet of cottages' (Cunliffe 1973; 98). Alternatively, contemporary huts may have been used by one family for different purposes (as in the Later Bronze Age – see Ch. 4). Recently, Ernest Black (1987) has suggested that the huts at Park Brow fall into two groups, each with a principal building which is approximately the same size in each group. He further suggests that the groups were not contemporary and that they 'look like two discrete houses'.

On Bullock Down, Beachy Head, an intensive multiperiod settlement project located two Romano–British sites which are linked by a double lynchet trackway, and extensive traces of associated field systems and other trackways (Rudling 1982*b*). One of the settlements, Site 16, has surface depressions suggestive of fairly level 'house platforms'. There were nine possible platforms and these were arranged in three pairs and a probable fourth pair (or perhaps a group of three). A geophysical survey failed to show any substantial anomalies, while the total excavation of one of the platforms revealed a definite terrace with a possible fence line, several pits, a number of isolated post-holes, but no obvious structural evidence for there having been a building. The large quantities of domestic pottery suggest, however, that there might have been a dwelling. If so, it must have been of a type which did not leave any trace in the archaeological record, or if it did, this has subsequently been destroyed by ploughing.

As with similar situations in the Iron Age (Ch. 5), possible explanations for such 'vanished' buildings include forms of timber framing and/or the use of either turf or cob walls. It is therefore possible that at Site 16 there were four separate 'houses', each formed of two huts. It is also likely that such houses were contemporary, since they are fairly evenly spaced out within an area set back from the double lynchet trackway which borders the settlement on its south side. If they are contemporary, the settlement is presumably of the 'hamlet' type. Again, precise chronology is lacking, but finds from the excavated area and the plough soil indicate occupation from the first to third centuries.

Site 16 is very unusual in that over the years it and the adjacent field (down slope from the settlement) have yielded a large number of metal objects, some of which are quite exotic (Fig. 6.3), and at least five third-century coin hoards. Three of the coin hoards were discovered within a few metres of each

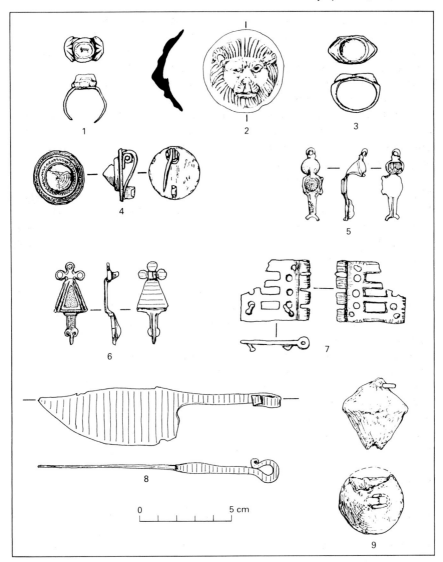

Figure 6.3   Romano-British metalwork from Bullock Down, East Sussex. Silver: 1: finger-ring; Copper-alloy: 2: lion's head terminal; 3: finger-ring; 4: gilt brooch with glass boss; 5: brooch with enamel inlay; 6: brooch with a zoomorphic head and enamel inlay; 7: belt-plate; Iron 8: knife; Lead: 9: Steelyard weight.

other (just to the east of Site 16), suggesting that they were probably all buried by one person or group of people. A detailed study of these particular hoards suggests that they represent two 'savings' hoards and one 'currency' hoard (Bland 1979). In addition, the comparative lack of irregular coins has been taken to indicate the acumen of the hoarder. A further point of interest is that the 1973 hoard was buried in a Hemmoor type bronze bucket, a Continental type which is extremely rare in Britain (the only other definite example is from Ramsgate, Kent).

Thus, if all the exotic objects and coins found near Site 16 actually belonged to the inhabitants of the settlement, we would have to conclude that the inhabitants were very accustomed to Roman material culture, that they recognized the problems of the mid-third-century currency system, and that they were living well above the subsistence level! Alternatively, some of the objects and coins may have come (legally or otherwise) from a more Romanized settlement, perhaps the nearby villa at Eastbourne, which, together with other coastal settlements, may have been troubled by coastal raiding at about the same time as the date when the latest of the Bullock Down hoards was 'closed', *c.* AD 274. Other possible connections between the two Bullock Down Romano–British sites and the villa at Eastbourne include the discovery at Bullock Down Site 44 of fragments of roller-stamped flue tiles of types known to have been used at the villa (Rudling 1987*a*). Given that on the Downs such tiles are extremely unlikely to have been used for the purpose they were made for, it is probable that they were brought to Bullock Down by one of two methods. Either they came along with manure and general rubbish from a villa, such as Eastbourne (Fig. 6.4), to be spread on the fields (thus suggesting either direct management or a tenancy arrangement between the downland sites and the villa) *or* they were 'salvaged', probably along with other re-usable building materials, from a destroyed or abandoned villa (many peasant sites have yielded pieces of Roman tile/brick which were clearly used for a variety of 'unorthodox' purposes).

Excavations on the other Romano–British settlement site on Bullock Down (Site 44) were mainly focused on a possible farmyard area just to the east of a ditched enclosure which is thought to have contained the settlement area. Features associated with the 'farmyard' included fence lines, some of which might have formed compounds for animals; two 'corn-drying ovens', one of which was adjacent to a structure which is thought to have been used for the threshing of corn (Fig. 6.5), various pits, isolated post-holes, and a possible beacon.

Recently, there has been much debate concerning the function of 'corn-drying ovens', a feature found on many rural sites (both peasant settlements and villas). It was originally suggested that such ovens were used to dry grain prior to storage. Recent experimental work, however, has failed to demonstrate that the ovens could have been efficiently used for drying large quantities of corn. The experiments have, however, shown that an alternative function might have been connected with malting (Reynolds and Langley 1979). Another possible use of the ovens was for the domestic rather than economic task of drying small quantities of grain in preparation for grinding, and in the South-East various 'corn driers' have been found in association with querns and/or large storage jars or granaries (Black 1987). The ovens on Bullock

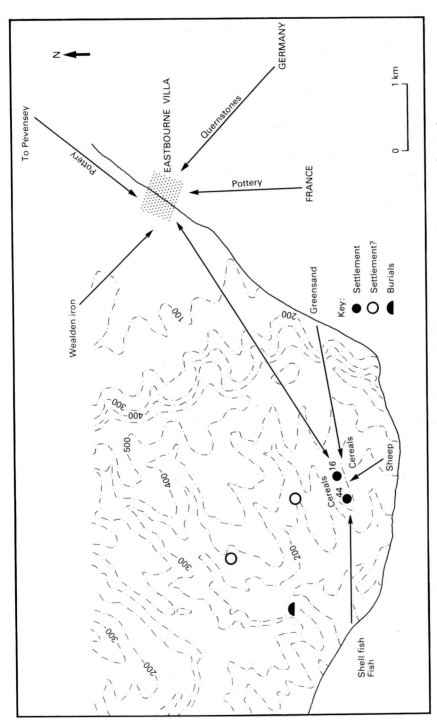

Figure 6.4 The Romano–British settlements on Bullock Down, and the Roman Villa at Eastbourne; adjacent sites and natural resources.

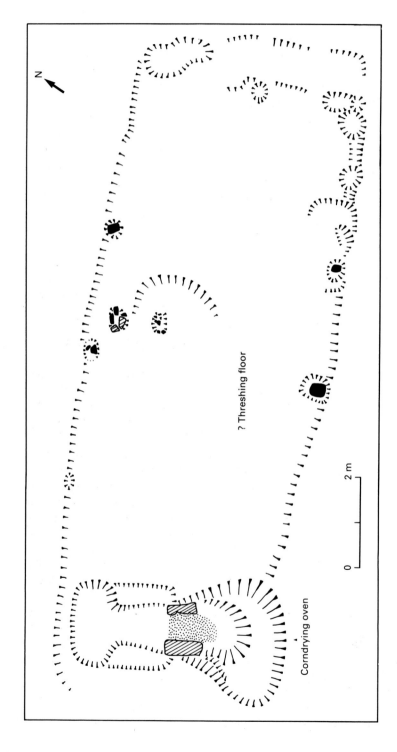

Figure 6.5 Site 44, Bullock Down, East Sussex: plan of corn-drying oven and adjacent building (possibly used for threshing corn).

Down conform to this general pattern and a quern was found in the fill of the small T-shaped structures, and fragments of a large Thundersbarrow Ware storage jar were found in the fill of the large keyhole-shaped oven (Fig. 6.5). The latter also contained quantities of carbonized grain, almost all of which was either spelt wheat or six row barley.

To the west of the farmyard area were located two sections of a probable enclosure ditch, which were separated by a possible entrance. A resistivity survey undertaken by the Ancient Monuments Laboratory unfortunately failed to detect the shallow ditch, and it was therefore not possible to trace the full extent of the enclosure. Traces of activity just within the enclosure (which was otherwise not sampled) included several pits and post-holes. The pits, together with a similar example found outside the enclosure, are vertical-sided and flat-bottomed. They may have been used for the storage of grain.

The economy on Bullock Down was mixed farming. Evidence for arable agriculture includes the associated field systems and marling pits (both of which have been sampled for dating and environmental evidence), the possible threshing floor, the 'corn-drying ovens', carbonized seeds, quernstones, the possible grain-storage pits, and three steelyard weights which may have been used to weigh grain (by whom is uncertain, perhaps by the inhabitants, land owners, traders, or government officials).

Animal husbandry is attested mainly by animal bones, but also by the possible animal enclosures and pens at Site 44, pottery cheese presses and spindle whorls. The faunal remains indicate a predominance of sheep, and the bone specialist, Terry O'Connor (in Drewett 1982) suggests that Site 44 may have been in an area of sheep production. The sheep remains include one complete skeleton of an old ewe, and also the 'trimmings' of a butchered carcase. These findings suggest that sheep were being bred on the farm, kept for their wool (note the spindle whorls), and butchered on the site for meat. The paucity of cattle bones and the scarcity of pig bones suggests their presence as food remains. The relative quantities of sheep and cattle bones contrast strongly with the evidence obtained from the villa at Newhaven (Bell 1976). As Martin Bell has pointed out, it is likely that such differences can be explained by the fact that the waterless Downs are better suited to sheep, whereas the villa situated in a river valley would have been capable of supporting a bigger head of cattle.

Other types of meat eaten during the Roman period on Bullock Down include a variety of marine molluscs (especially limpets, periwinkles, mussels and oysters), fish (although in spite of extensive sieving only one unidentified fishbone was recovered), and birds (including dove). The absence of bones of wild land animals (such as deer or boar) and the small quantities of fish and bird bones probably indicates that hunting was only a minor activity. A single horse bone was found at Site 44. The only other evidence for economic activity includes the discovery of iron forging slag at Site 16. It is also possible that

211

some of the local East Sussex Ware pottery may have been made at, or in the vicinity of, the settlements.

The date range for Site 44 is first to fourth century *or later*. As for Site 16, Site 44 has yielded traces of *early*-first-century occupation. The two sites contrast in terms of their later histories since Site 16 appears to have gone out of use during the third century, whilst Site 44 clearly continued at least into the late fourth century. As is general elsewhere in Roman Britain, the bronze coinage sequence ends *c*. 370–80 (there was a total of five coins of Valens, *c*. 364–78). There were, however, reasonable quantities of late fourth-century pottery types, including the locally produced Pevensey Ware, Thundersbarrow Ware and East Sussex Ware. The dating of the ends of these three traditions has not been established, and all or some could have continued into the fifth century (all three wares were present in the filling of the large corn-drying oven).There is no sign of a violent end to this settlement, and the absence of early Saxon material from anywhere on Bullock Down (approximately 300 acres) may suggest that there was no reason why occupation should not have continued into the fifth century.

At Bishopstone a rectangular enclosure (0.35 ha) was laid out early in the Roman period, in the north-east corner of the early Iron Age enclosed settlement (Ch. 5). It was divided into two parts by a cross ditch, the northern part being approximately twice as large as the southern part. The enclosed ditch had become silted up by the late second century and Martin Bell (1977) suggests that there may have been a reduced level of activity on the site during the third century, followed by a more intensive occupation in the fourth century when a corn-drying oven was in operation. Other features included pits and post-holes. Some of the latter were in groups suggesting structures, but nothing which can be definitely interpreted as a domestic building. The economic data are similar to those described for Bullock Down. Roman occupation at Bishopstone may also have lasted into the fifth century, before being replaced by a Saxon settlement. There is, however, no definite proof to suggest direct continuity between the two settlements.

At Slonk Hill, occupation at the Iron Age settlement site (Ch. 5) was not resumed until the late first or early second century, but once established again continued until the end of the fourth century and perhaps into the fifth century (Hartridge 1978). This site is somewhat unusual, and probably even had ritual functions, since the two Bronze Age round barrows on the site appear to have been 'regarded as monuments worthy of respect'. It is possible that the area surrounding the barrows was defined by a ditch, and later (in the fourth century) both barrow ditches were filled in and a square structure of posts built around one of the mounds (see below). Other features include pits and post-holes and the economic data is similar to that at the other downland sites, but also includes an iron shoe possibly from a primitive plough. It also appears that in comparison with the economic data from the Iron Age occupation of the site, there was an increase in the importance of pig and a change in shellfish preference from mussel to oyster.

To conclude, the material culture of the Downland 'peasant' settlements discussed above shows both continuity with the past (including the well-established field systems and settlement sites, and the possible use of pits for storage), and various signs of Romanization, especially in the case of the relatively elaborate hut at Park Brow: the acceptance of the coinage system, and the acquisition of various manufactured goods. There is also a very noticeable increase in the use of iron, especially in the case of nails. Finally, it is clear that at least some of these settlements may have continued to be occupied into the fifth century.

Villas

As already mentioned, Roman masonry houses have attracted considerable archaeological interest, and they were chosen for some of the earliest 'excavations' (e.g. Samuel Lysons' investigations at Bignor in the early nineteenth century). Unfortunately, despite the long history of villa studies, there has been and still is an incredible obsession with the investigation of the residential areas of villa settlements, and generally very little attention has been paid to the subsidiary buildings (a notable exception is the site at Bignor) or the areas immediately surrounding the main building complexes (such areas may contain traces of activity areas, for example for farming practices, craft production or burial). In addition, in many cases (mainly in the past) excavators of villas have been particularly guilty of ignoring various potentially interesting and useful types of evidence, especially those relating to the economy and environment. The study of villa estates is still in its infancy and is a major priority for future research.

The villa buildings of the South-East have been well featured in several county surveys (Cunliffe 1973; Rudling, 1982*a*; Blagg 1982; Detsicas 1983; Bird 1987) and are also the subject of a major regional study (Black 1987). Given the amount of recent publication on the subject and the size of this chapter, it would be both impossible and unwarranted to undertake a detailed examination of the many villas in the South-East. I therefore recommend the reader to consult the publications mentioned above and shall confine myself to providing a few general observations and discussing three specific case studies which now warrant updated summaries from those provided in earlier surveys.

Ernest Black's survey of mainly published reports on Roman villas in the South East includes a list of 161 definite or possible villa sites for the counties of

Kent, Surrey and Sussex (Black 1987). Whilst not all of the sites on Black's list need be villas, there are probably many other unpublished examples. Clearly we are dealing with a large number of sites which vary considerably in date, size, complexity, wealth and economic possibilities. Many of these villas can be seen to have 'grown organically' out of native farms, a pattern which is normal for many areas of Britain (Applebaum 1966). Such growth often involves a gradual development, with usually a change from a farm built in timber to a single masonry building of much the same size, to which occasionally luxuries such as small baths and simple mosaics might be added. Some villas were further elaborated, usually during the fourth century, but only a very few achieved luxurious proportions.

In some situations, however, there is a sudden, sometimes major development, as is the case of the large early villas in Sussex. Possible reasons for such sudden developments or the appearance of new villas might include major changes in economic possibilities (such as the availability of loans or the development of new markets), the combining of two or more previously separate farms (perhaps in order to benefit from economies of scale), and immigration into the area (including land owners and farmers from overseas, and retired soldiers). With so many possibilities available, any attempt to explain major changes in villas will require a detailed understanding of the chronology and fortunes of other sites: rural, urban and military, in the area. Unfortunately there are few instances where such wider investigations have been undertaken, but examples include the Chilgrove Valley (Down 1979) and Lullingstone, where three Late Iron Age sites located within 1.5 km of the villa seem to have been abandoned at about the same time as the earliest phase (mid-first century AD) at the villa (Meates 1979).

The distribution of villas (Fig. 6.2) is very important and they concentrate in certain areas: the coastal plain of West Sussex, just to the north of the South Downs (especially on the Greensand ridge, which has very fertile soils and various springs), the corresponding southern edge of the North Downs, and the area to the north of the North Downs. In all areas river valleys or locations with easy access to the major roads were particularly popular locations. In the case of the former, in addition to the need of water for domestic and farming purposes, many of the rivers would have been useful for transport and perhaps for hunting (water fowl and fish). Communications by road or water, and access to suitable markets were clearly major considerations, probably more so than the quality of the land on which the villas were built.

A major exception to the normal pattern of a dense clustering of villas around a major town is the Canterbury area. It has been suggested (Blagg 1982) that this might be a cultural rather than an economic situation, with the major land owners of East Kent preferring to reside in Canterbury (Blagg has further suggested that, as at Silchester and Cirencester, the town properties of such land owners may have functioned as working farms, with barns, corn-drying ovens, etc.). If this theory is correct (and there is no archaeological proof

214

as yet), there would have been no reason for the land owners to build expensive houses on their estates, and the only settlements in such areas would therefore be those of their tenants or perhaps their servants.

The developmental history of villas in the South East has been examined by Ernest Black (1987), who suggests that there was a gradual trend towards integrating small structures into larger ones. This theory is based on an earlier idea by Professor Rivet (1964) that the individual huts on Iron Age and Roman–British 'peasant' sites should be regarded as the equivalent of a single room in a villa, and that a number of such huts (as at Park Brow) might have been grouped to form a house. If this theory is correct, it helps to bridge the gap between life in a hut, and life in a multi-roomed unit. If we take the integration theory one stage further, it is possible to suggest that discrete accommodation units (or houses) could have been combined to form larger and more complex multi-family establishments (the unit-system approach). Such integrations may have been attractive propositions due to the sharing of costs and economies of scale (e.g. for bath suites). Whilst the ideas outlined above need not apply to all villas, they do at least provide an interesting social and economic approach which can perhaps be tested by very careful excavation and interpretation of individual rooms, groups of rooms, and the overall constructional history of villas.

Since it is generally assumed that most of the villa owners in the South-East were the descendants of the local Iron Age communities, it is interesting to try and identify the stimuli behind the 'integrating' trend discussed above and the general development of villas. The large early villas in Sussex are exceptional and are clearly derived from Italian-style villas. They may represent a deliberate policy of encouraging aspects of Roman (Mediterranean) culture. Elsewhere the stimulus might have been the houses being built in the towns (Rivet 1964), but Black (1987) favours the introduction of the idea of villas by Gallic immigrants. It is possible that such immigrants, and also veteran soldiers, may have settled in areas of the South-East, such as in parts of Kent, where there may have been confiscations of land following local resistance to the invasion. In particular Black suggests that the normal early villa types in the South-East may be derived from Gallic 'hall-villas'.

The economic basis of most of the villas was mixed farming and many villas were situated at places suitable for the exploitation of several environments, including good arable and grazing lands. Various villa complexes have revealed ancillary farming buildings and features, including barns, granaries and corn-drying ovens (there were no less than eleven such ovens at West Blatchington, Sussex), and farm tools. Discoveries of carbonized seeds and animal bones indicate the same range of domesticates as for the 'peasant' settlements. Again hunting appears to have provided only a small proportion of the meat diet, although many villas have yielded evidence for the consumption of marine molluscs, especially the famous oyster shells. Some villas may also have been involved in other ways of making money, including perhaps the

215

quarrying of stone (for building purposes and the making of querns), pottery manufacture, saltworking, forestry and iron working.

Finally, I wish to consider briefly some of the major economic and social factors which may have affected the fate of villas in various parts of the South-East. As we have already seen, in the first century the favourable economic and political climate in Sussex was conducive to the building by the wealthy of large, sumptuous houses, the cost of which is likely to have been met by the taking of large loans. The repayment of these loans was probably based on a combination of the exploitation of the peasants and the sale of agricultural produce to the military, who at that stage were mainly in the north of Britain. Payment of debts and high maintenance costs may not always have been possible, however, and the subsequent contraction of some of these large villas, as at Fishbourne and Southwick, may be examples of such difficulties.

The large military market in the North and the local development of urban markets would have been major factors behind the emergence of other early villas in the South-East, especially in West Kent. It has been suggested by Ernest Black that the emergence of some of these villas may be linked to the combining of several small farms to form a larger enterprise with resulting economies of scale, and hence the resources with which to invest in more expensive forms of housing.

By the late third century many of the villas in the South-East show signs of decay or abandonment. This situation, which is especially evident on the coastal plain of West Sussex, can perhaps be linked both directly and indirectly with Saxon and pirate raiding. In addition to the Saxon Shore Fort system (see above) possible indications of troubled times include signs of burning and destruction at some of the villas (e.g. Fishbourne) and the widespread burial of hoards of coins. Black (1987) has suggested that a major inhibitor for villa life at this period in the South-East was the presence of large numbers of troops associated with the coastal defence system. He argues that whilst the military market is good news for villas and potential villas located at a distance from the army centres, agricultural communities in the hinterland of the forts would be particularly vulnerable to the requisition (as opposed to contract purchase) of supplies by the military. The favourable economic circumstances which had previously benefitted the farming communities of the South-East were apparently now enjoyed by the areas to the west of our region, and it is especially in these areas (away from the army) that villas flourished in the late Roman period.

Although certain parts of the South-East continued to have villas, especially in the catchment areas of the still significant London and Chichester markets, other areas may have witnessed major changes in the agricultural system. Possibly some of the villa owners may have moved to the safety of the towns, and it is probably significant that the early fourth century in Chichester was a period of prosperity, expansion and of major rebuilding in stone. Such absentee land owners may have left the day-to-day running of their estates to a bailiff, or perhaps have made new arrangements with their tenants. Some of the peasant farmers may also have been experiencing a change to a more nucleated type of settlement, the village, the development of which appears to be particularly associated with the late Roman Period (Cunliffe 1973).

The end of villa life in the South-East is uncertain, but many fourth-century villas show signs of destruction or decay, usually during the second half of the century. With the collapse of the market economy it is likely that, in addition to a reduction in convertible wealth derived from the land, there would also have been a major contraction or end to the specialist building and 'interior decorating' service industries (perhaps one reason for the apparent decline in 'standards' at a number of late villas). Some villas may, however, have lasted into the early fifth century, but definite proof is lacking.

Turning to individual case studies, I wish to examine two recently investigated villa complexes in Sussex, and one in Surrey. The first of these is Fishbourne, where over the last five years various excavations have been undertaken. To complete the summary of the original excavations, at the end of the first century the palace underwent a series of major changes and contractions which gradually converted it into a much smaller, but still impressive villa. Possibly these alterations were due to a drastic change in its function (for example *if* it had previously been used as a palace), or changes in ownership. In particular it was the north wing of the Flavian Palace, the area interpreted by Professor Cunliffe (1971) as the possible residential unit for visitors rather than the suggested 'private range' (south wing) that became the core of the later villa. For nearly 200 years there were many changes, including the building of new bath suites and the laying of elaborate mosaics (Plates 6.7; 6.8), and there is evidence to suggest that yet further changes were being undertaken when parts of the villa were destroyed by fire in about AD 280–90.

Despite the fact that the aisled hall and the east-wing bath suite escaped the fire, there was no attempt to rebuild the villa, which was then apparently abandoned and robbed (possibly in two stages) of its building materials. Perhaps some of these materials were used during the major building work which occurred at this time in nearby Chichester. Although there is some archaeological evidence to suggest that the east-wing bath suite was probably demolished at the same time as the north wing, there is less good evidence for dating the end of the aisled hall. It is not even certain whether the hall was still standing at the time of the fire, but equally there is so little evidence, the floors having been 'kept very clean', that one cannot necessarily say that this building did not continue in use. Signs of habitation in three rooms in the east wing have been interpreted as temporary occupation by workmen involved in the demolition of the villa. Alternatively, however, there could possibly have been a very limited continued agricultural occupation of parts of the site. It is perhaps worth noting the various items of farming equipment (including iron sheep shears and iron sickles or reaping hooks) found in the destruction levels and robber trenches. Could such a phase of post-fire occupation, which need not

Plate 6.7 Detail of a sea-horse which forms part of the second-century 'boy-on-a-dolphin' mosaic at Fishbourne, West Sussex. (Photograph: Sussex Archaeological Society.)

have lasted very long, explain the apparent period of abandonment between the initial and later phases of demolition?

It is not known what caused the fire at Fishbourne, but possibilities include an accident or coastal raiding. If the latter, the owners, if they survived, may have decided to move to the greater safety of Chichester. Several other Sussex coastal villas may also have been abandoned or destroyed at about the same time as at Fishbourne (Rudling 1985c). Cunliffe (1971) has suggested that one possible reason why the Fishbourne villa was not rebuilt was that the site appears to have been increasingly subject to the problems of flooding.

Information concerning the diet at Fishbourne consists of both direct evidence (animal and bird bones) and indirect evidence (especially amphorae). The animal bones for all periods include cattle, pig, sheep/goat, horse, deer and dog. Of these the main sources of meat were pig, sheep and especially cattle, which increase in importance throughout the use of the site. The relative importance of pig is particularly striking and may be a reflection of the wealth of the owners of the establishment. Thirteen species of bird are represented and of these, three species (common fowl, grey lag goose and mallard) were possibly domesticated. Of the remaining species at least some (common partridge, wood pigeon and stock dove) are likely to have been killed for the table.

Plate 6.8 General view of the late third-century hypocaust at Fishbourne, West Sussex. (Photograph: Sussex Archaeological Society.)

The lack of fish bones is surprising from a site so close to the sea, especially since the robber trenches yielded two bronze, barbed fishhooks. Unfortunately, no carbonized grain was recovered and no report is published on the marine molluscs.

Of the new fieldwork at Fishbourne, a recently discovered site on the western shore of Fishbourne Creek, about 500 m to the south-west of the palace is of particular importance. Excavations revealed traces of two successive buildings (Rudkin 1986). The earlier of these structures was of timber and consisted of one rectangle inside another. It has been variously interpreted as either a building with four wings around a central open courtyard, or as an aisled building. The latter seems the more likely explanation and Ernest Black has pointed out to me that the plan of the building is similar to that of the aisled building found at Wingham, Kent (*Journal of Roman Studies* Vol. 58, 205). Features within the Fishbourne Creek building consisted of a tiled hearth and a small room, within which was a depression containing a 'store' of used tesserae. The purpose of this building is not certain, but the associated finds, which include the tesserae, roller-stamped daub and perhaps the painted wall plaster found in the Period 2 foundations, and the site's proximity to the harbour edge, may indicate both accommodation and storage functions. It is suggested that the building was constructed during the last quarter of the first century and it was destroyed by fire in the middle of the second century.

The burnt timber building was replaced by a large masonry aisled barn, which was constructed at right angles to the earlier structure. This new building later underwent various changes, including the construction of internal sub-divisions (perhaps indicating the provision of rooms for accommodation) and a sequence of three extensions, including a projecting corner tower, to the north end. At the southern end there was a substantial flint platform which may indicate a base for either some form of lifting or loading apparatus, or a large entrance porch, perhaps with an upstairs loading bay. Internal features include a T-shaped corn-drying oven, five hearths, a gully, and a large rectangular pit which was designed as an 'under-floor heating system'. Although it is possible that this hypocaust was for domestic purposes, perhaps even as part of a bath suite (Ernest Black, pers. comm.), the excavator favours the idea that it was used for the drying of large quantities of grain.

The precise functions of the aisled building are therefore not certain, but were probably similar to those of the Period 1 building. It is probably an example of an Aisled Villa, a type which became common in the Later Roman period (see Black 1987). It is possible that the barn was abandoned somewhat later than the Palace, perhaps in the early fourth century. The only direct economic data retrieved from the site were animal bones and included cattle, sheep, pig, horse, deer (?)dog, and unidentified bird bones.

The dating of the two Fishbourne Creek buildings and their proximity to the Palace has led to the suggestion that the two sites might have been connected, with the newly discovered structures providing some of the missing agricultural elements of the palace complex. However, both of the Fishbourne Creek buildings have yielded traces of fairly sophisticated domestic occupation, and the site may therefore have been independent of the palace. The absence of subsidiary farm buildings for the palace site suggests that there should also be other possible candidates awaiting discovery.

Other traces of Roman activity at Fishbourne are currently being investigated by Alec Down's excavations to the east of the palace. Discoveries dating to the occupation of the palace/villa include several roads, including the main roadway leading towards Chichester. To the north of this road are three phases of drainage ditch and bedding trench complexes. The bedding trenches vary in shape from straight lines to circular arrangements, and are sometimes associated with lines of post-holes, either actually in or beside the trenches. Alec Down (pers. comm.) is of the opinion that these bedding trench complexes, which cover several acres, indicate some form of horticulture.

The second case-study is of the famous villa at Bignor, which is situated on the southern slope of the Upper Greensand Shelf, just north of the South Downs. In addition to being located on very fertile arable land, the villa was well placed to exploit grazing lands on the nearby Downs, and perhaps also the woodlands of the Wealden clays. It is close to Stane Street and was therefore advantageously positioned for good communications with the markets at Chichester and the possible minor urban settlement in the Hardham–Pulborough area.

The site was discovered and extensively excavated in the early nineteenth century by Samuel Lysons (1817*a*; 1817*b*; 1821) whose main plan of the villa and its farmyard is very well known (Fig. 6.6). Recently, however, our understanding of this villa has changed considerably due to various re-excavations and re-interpretations. The first major re-examination of the site was by Professor Frere, whose excavations between 1956 and 1962 were in parts of the west, north and south wings of the courtyard villa (Frere 1982). This work showed that there were some inaccuracies in Lysons' plan and also provided useful information about the earlier development of the site. Thus it was shown that the Roman settlement was established in an area that had previously been used for lynchetted fields. There was some evidence to suggest that a farm was probably established on the site by the end of the first century AD. At the end of the second century a timber-framed building (the Period I house) was constructed, and this lasted until *c.* 225–50 when it was destroyed by fire. It was then replaced on the same site by the first masonry house, a rectangular building with probably four rooms (27–30). Soon after its construction a channelled hypocaust (which was perhaps used as a corn-drying oven) was added to the south side of the roughly north–south orientated building. Later additions include a portico (34) on the east side, wing rooms (one of which, 33, contains the only mosaic belonging to this period of the villa) and one other room (31). The various developments in this relatively modest Period II house span the second half of the third century.

At the end of the third century the villa was dramatically transformed by the rebuilding of the Period II house, and the addition to the east of it of the great courtyard with its north, south and east wings, and the outer yard with its farm buildings. Frere subdivided the Period III villa into two phases, A and B. The first phase involved the laying out of all four wings of the courtyard house, whilst the second phase witnessed the addition of more rooms to the north wing and the laying of the fine mosaics in that wing.

Later, however, Ernest Black used Frere's findings together with a re-examination of Lysons' plan to suggest a more complicated sequence (Period III: I–III) for the development of the fourth-century villa (Black 1983). Black notes that in the north wing there were constructional differences between the walls of Rooms 16–24 and those to the west, and that at this change in the character of the masonry there was also a wall dividing the corridor fronting the wing. He suggests that this change of masonry and the dividing wall may represent part of the original (Period III: I) east end wall of the wing. He also suggests that at this stage, Rooms 18 and 65 formed part of a large, separate rectangular building, similar in size to the aisled barn (70–74). It is further

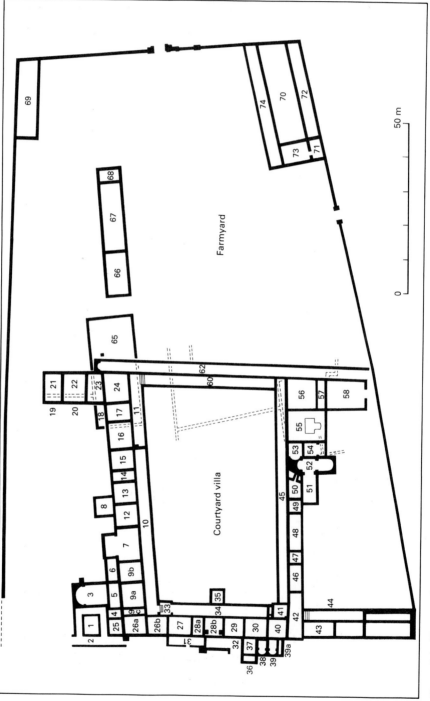

Figure 6.6 Bignor Villa, West Sussex: revised version of Samuel Lysons' general plan.

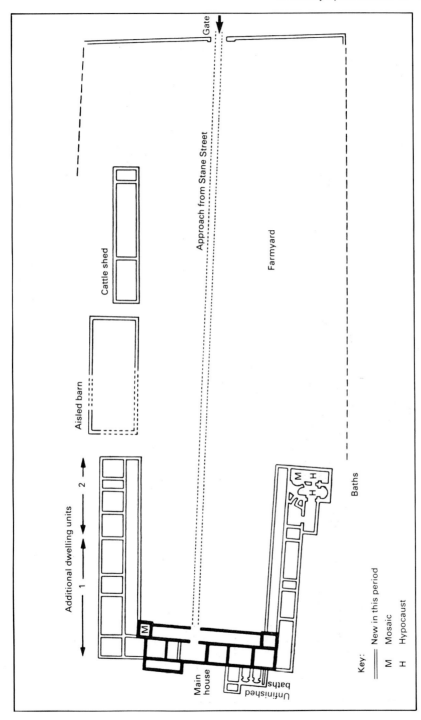

Figure 6.7 Bignor Villa, West Sussex. Plan of Period III: 1.

suggested that the other separate block (66–88) was contemporary with building 18/65. During this phase elaborate baths (50–58) were constructed at the eastern end of the south wing, and these replaced baths (36–39) which had not been completed in the west wing (Fig. 6.7).

In period III: II (Fig. 6.8) Black suggests that building 18/65 was demolished and the north wing extended eastwards by the addition of a 'unit' of three rooms (16, 17 and 24). A second unit (19–23) was added at right angles to this, and was designed to balance rooms 56–58 in the south wing, thus creating a symmetrical effect when approached from the east (which at this period was still the main approach to the villa). Possibly the east portico (60–61) was built during this phase. There should also have been a complete remodelling of the outer courtyard, with the demolition of building 66–68 and the construction of two new buildings (69; and 70–74), new north and south enclosure walls and new gates (75 and 77).

The final phase (III: III) sees the addition of further rooms and the famous mosaics to the north wing: the building of the ambulatory (62–64), which would probably have cut off access to the inner courtyard from the east, and the construction of western entrances into rooms 23 and 38b.

In addition to suggesting different developmental schemes, Frere and Black also offer contrasting interpretations of the villa during the fourth century. Thus, Frere argues against an earlier theory (Smith 1978) that Bignor was a 'unit-system villa' and instead suggests that it 'remained a unity revolving round a single great household'. In contrast Black followed up Smith's unit-system approach and proposes that in phase III: I the villa might have been occupied by three families, one in the west wing (at this stage perhaps the main residential quarters since this was the site of the Period II house), and two in the north wing. The reasoning behind the idea of two 'houses' in the north wing is the identification in Period III: I of two 'units' of four rooms (Rooms 26a, 9a/c, 9b, and 7; Rooms 12–15), each unit having the same arrangement of rooms. The two additional units of Period III: II in the northern wing, which showed no signs of comfort, may have been slave or servants' quarters. It is suggested that the large, elaborate bath suite in the south wing would have been used by all three households living in the villa.

It has already been suggested that in Period III: I the main residence may have been in the west wing. By Period III: III however, the most elaborate rooms were now in the most westerly of the postulated 'houses' in the north wing (this 'house' was also considerably enlarged at this stage). Black suggests that the development of these luxurious quarters may represent the emergence, linked to economic functions, of one family above the others. Thus, in contrast to earlier theories (such as change of ownership or a substantial economic improvement) the scheme and theories put forward by Ernest Black provide an attractive new explanation, based on economic and social evolution, for the exceptional developments that occurred at Bignor during the fourth century. If Black's theory is correct, however, many problems still remain to be answered,

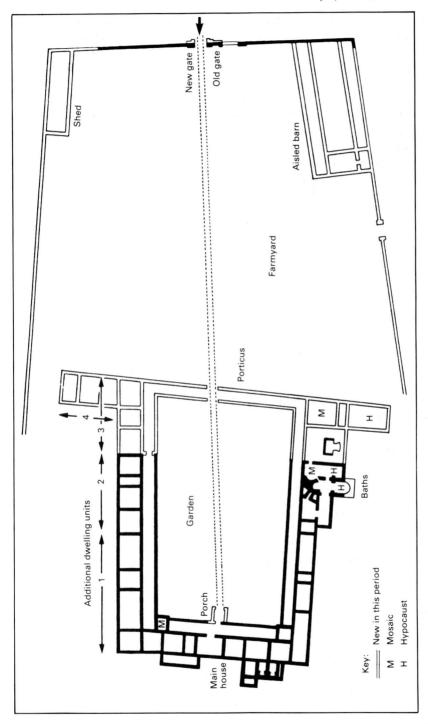

Figure 6.8 Bignor Villa, West Sussex. Plan of Period III: II.

such as *where* did the two new households come from, and *why*? Was it, as Black suggests, a voluntary unification of three smaller farms into a larger estate? (In which case two nearby abandoned farms presumably await discovery.) Also, *how* did one family achieve greater economic success than the other families?

Black's scheme for Bignor during the fourth century also has important implications for previous interpretations of the villa's economy based on identifications of the various buildings found by Lysons in the outer courtyard (or farmyard). In particular, this aspect of the villa has been discussed by Professor Applebaum (1975), who uses his building identifications to make suggestions about such things as the numbers of plough-teams at the villa, and then by implication the acreage of land on the villa estate which is likely to have been ploughed. One of the major problems here is that Applebaum assumes that all of the buildings in the outer courtyard are contemporary, whereas Black's scheme suggests that there were two successive sets of agricultural buildings. Black (1983) has re-examined the evidence for the farmyard buildings and made various revisions to Applebaum's identifications and economic implications.

In 1985 new archaeological fieldwork was undertaken at Bignor (Aldsworth 1986; Rudling and Aldsworth 1986). This work included a new survey of the site, a plough-damage assessment investigation of some of the areas of the site which were normally cultivated, and a partial re-excavation of the bath suite in the south wing. Of particular interest was the discovery that Rooms 18 and 65 were in fact parts of an aisled barn which was demolished when the north corridor was extended eastwards. This helps to confirm Black's scheme for Period III. The investigation of the courtyard wall revealed further inaccuracies in Lysons' plan, and excavations in and around part of the aisled barn which forms the south-eastern corner of the farmyard revealed various previously unrecorded features including three ditches, a gravelled(?) path, and a possible earlier lynchet. Work in the bath house also exposed several unknown phases of construction. In addition, the results of the current analysis of the finds from the 1985 excavations will produce the first systematically collected and studied evidence about the villa's economy.

Thus at Bignor we have an example of a masonry villa which first developed out of a modest timber-framed farmhouse, and was later dramatically enlarged, perhaps as a result of the merging of three farms. The reasons for the villa's success and wealth during the early fourth century are not known, but may include economies of scale following the postulated merging of the smaller farms, the villa's relatively safe inland location (in contrast to the villas on the Coastal Plain), and perhaps its access via Stane Street to the important market at Chichester, which at this period shows signs of rising prosperity (other villas in the vicinity of Chichester, such as those in the Chilgrove Valley (Down 1979), also show signs of large-scale improvements at this time). The recent investigations have demonstrated that there is still much to be learnt from previously excavated sites. In the case of Bignor many problems remain unresolved, not least of which concerns the end of the villa, which is not securely dated (perhaps late fourth or even fifth century).

The Surrey case-study is the villa at Beddington. Since its initial discovery in 1871, the villa has had a long history of excavation and chance finds (Adkins and Adkins 1986; Adkins *et al.* 1986). Until recently the site was used as a sewage works, but is currently being destroyed by sand and gravel extraction. In advance of the destruction of the site, rescue excavations have taken place in order to record more fully the surviving traces of Roman and prehistoric occupation. As a villa the site is of particular importance since it is the nearest known example to Roman London south of the Thames.

The results of the recent excavations suggest that the site of the Beddington villa was probably farmed throughout the period from *c.* 700 BC to the Roman invasion in AD 43, and during the Roman period as well. Evidence for Iron Age occupation includes various ditches, at least four round-houses, possibly a burial, and finds of pottery, loom weights and metalwork. As yet no definite traces of the subsequent early Romano–British (pre-*c.* AD 180) farm-buildings have been found, and it is probable that structures associated with this phase of the site were made of timber.

In about AD 180 part of the land previously used as fields was turned into a large courtyard area, and on this courtyard were constructed the first masonry buildings. These structures included the villa-house and a detached bath-house. The house, which consisted of a long corridor with rooms opening off it, had painted wall plaster and a roof of clay tiles. The bath-house consisted of a line of rooms ranging from a cold room, through a warm room, to the hot room. Traces of three other buildings belonging to this phase were also discovered. All were made of timber; a probable farm outbuilding, and two buildings (one of which had a ceiling of painted plaster) of uncertain functions. A further three timber buildings, including a large aisled barn, were discovered during additional excavations in 1984–85. The dating of these buildings, and also that of a Roman well (which was lined with blocks of chalk and tufa), has not yet been published.

In the late third century the villa-house was enlarged by the addition of a wing at each end of the corridor. The western wing, which had the luxury of an underground heating system, may have functioned as the main living room. Other signs of sophistication include the discovery of pieces of window-glass and components from simple tessellated floors. During the third century the bath-house was also enlarged and altered. The alterations to both the villa-house and bath-house presumably reflect an improvement in the financial status of the villa estate. By about the mid-fourth century the economic position of the villa may have changed again, since by now the bath-house had gone out of use. Finally in the early fifth century the villa-house was abandoned and robbed of its building materials.

Economic data from the site includes: the bones of domesticated animals (cattle, sheep and pigs), the bones of hunted animals (deer and hare), marine molluscs, and spindle whorls. The final report on the first phase of recent excavations at Beddington (1981–83) has been submitted for publication (Adkins and Adkins (forthcoming)).

Religion

A major aspect of the culture of Roman Britain was that of religion. The study of this is very complicated however, since it involved a mixture of Classical religion of the Graeco–Roman world, indigenous cults, and imported non-Roman cults.

The early importation of Classical gods is demonstrated by the famous dedicatory inscription from a temple of Neptune and Minerva at Chichester. This inscription records that the building of the temple was undertaken with the permission of King Cogidubnus (see above), thus indicating the acceptance (or toleration) of Classical religion during the period of the Client Kingdom. Also from Chichester is another inscribed stone which possibly refers to the god Jupiter. Such discoveries in the very Romanized environment of a tribal capital are not surprising, and similar temples and inscriptions can also be expected at Canterbury and perhaps some of the other nucleated settlements. Other indications of Classical religion include many of the themes depicted on mosaics, such as the popular head of the goddess Medusa (examples at Fishbourne and Bignor). The choice of such themes for mosaics, however, does not necessarily indicate the worship, even knowledge of, these religious deities or stories. More definite evidence for the worship of Classical deities in private residences (both town houses and villas) is the discovery of cult figurines, such as the base of a statuette of Fortuna found at the Chilgrove 1 villa (Down 1979). Perhaps the most common way in which Classical religion was introduced to the mass of the population was through coinage, since the reverses of many Imperial coins bear representations of Classical deities.

Of the indigenous cults, the main sources of evidence are 'Romano–Celtic' type temples, ritual pits and shafts, and figurines. Typical Romano–Celtic temples consist of two concentric squares: a simple *cella* surrounded by an ambulatory. They are often located within an enclosure or *temenos*. Such temples occur in various parts of the South-East, both in towns and rural settings (Bedwin 1980*b*; Blagg 1982; Bird 1987). At Springhead a typical Romano–Celtic temple is the earliest religious building so far discovered at the important temple complex (Detsicas 1983).

Some Romano–Celtic temples were constructed on the sites of earlier shrines or centres of ritual activity, as at Lancing Down, Sussex (Bedwin

228

1981*c*) and Worth, Kent (Klein 1928). At Lancing recent investigations revealed a small square wooden structure adjacent to the masonry footings of the Roman temple (Fig. 5.12). The excavator has suggested that this structure might represent a Late Iron Age shrine. It has also been suggested that this structure (or structures) may have been connected with burials, at or above ground level (Black 1986). Other evidence for Iron Age activity includes finds of pottery and coins. At Worth an Iron Age context below the Roman temple yielded votive model shields. The possibility of continuity of cult worship is suggested by the discovery in Roman contexts of what is thought to be part of a war-god cult statue.

Generally, the nature of the cults practised at Romano-Celtic temples is poorly understood, and discoveries of cult statues or relevant epigraphic evidence are rare. Usually insights into some of the ritual practices are limited to finds of votive offerings, such as coins and small 'model' objects, and discoveries of animal bones and marine molluscs, which may either have been used for various rites or else represent food, perhaps eaten in connection with religious events. Some of the votive model objects suggest a certain type of cult belief. An example of this is a clay model of a human leg found at the circular timber 'temple' structure at Muntham Court, Sussex (Bedwin 1980*b*). This object may be connected with a healing cult. Another important find at Muntham Court was a bronze plaque depicting a boar: an animal which may have been of particular religious significance since the Muntham Court plaque is just one of a number of miniature bronze representations of boars which have been found at various rural sites in the South-East. Of particular interest, therefore, are the finds from the temple on Farley Heath, Surrey, which include a priest's crown and sceptre binding (Goodchild 1938). The latter has been interpreted as depicting representations of the Celtic deities Sucellus, Nantosuelta, and Taranis, and probably the Celtic equivalent of Vulcan (Goodchild 1949). This important temple site has yielded evidence to suggest continuity of use from the Iron Age to the end of the Roman period. The recently investigated temple site at Wanborough, Surrey, has also yielded items of priestly regalia, including crowns and sceptre handles (Bird 1986).

Another important category of features connected with Romano–British activity are various pits and shafts. Two recent discoveries have been made in Kent at Deal and Keston. At Deal a chalk-cut shaft led into a small underground chamber which had a rectangular niche level with its roof (Parfitt 1986). This niche may have been for a chalk figurine which was found in the fill of the chamber. If so, the excavator suggests that the chamber may have been an underground shrine (a type previously unrecorded for the South-East). The location of the underground chamber is of considerable interest since it appears to have 'existed as one element of a typical rural settlement'. At Keston an approximately 5 m deep shaft contained the remains of more than twenty-five animals, mainly dogs but also three complete horse skeletons which had been carefully laid out and arranged around the shaft (Philp 1985). Ritual shafts/pits/wells are a fairly widespread phenomenon in Roman Britain (Ross 1967; 1968).

A more unusual example of Romano–British ritual was discovered at Slonk Hill, Sussex (Hartridge 1978). In the late first or early second century the two Bronze Age barrows on the site appear to have been regarded as monuments worthy of respect and the area surrounding them was defined by a ditch. During the fourth century, both barrow ditches were filled in and a square of posts, perhaps a fence, was built around one of the mounds. The nature of the Romano–British activity associated with the barrows is uncertain, but one possible trace of ritual behaviour connected with the tumuli may include a cut into the Roman filling of the unfenced barrow. This cut contained a deposit of leg bones from lambs and piglets. Another possible ritual deposit in the vicinity of the same barrow are twelve fourth-century coins found in a 'post-hole'.

The archaeological record suggests that in the countryside the local cults continued to flourish and were able to absorb new material elements from Roman culture. In contrast, the towns show much less evidence for local cults and were presumably more subject to the religious influences of the Roman authorities, and also of traders and travellers from different parts of the empire.

The South-East has produced various types of evidence for the import of non-Roman cults. These are likely to have been introduced by a mixture of immigrants, traders, travellers and army personnel.

Of fairly widespread distribution throughout the South-East are Romano–Gaulish clay figurines (Plate 6.9), which were perhaps associated with cults introduced from Gaul. In Gaul many native deities may have been equated with imported Roman deities which were believed to have similar functions (Jenkins 1957). Thus the *dea nutrix* figurines (a matron suckling infants) might have been connected with a Gaulish mother goddess or fertility cult. A similar association may also be true for the more common 'pseudo-Venus' figurines (Jenkins 1958).

Of the more exotic cults imported from the eastern part of the Empire there are various possible cases of influence or worship. One example is a bronze Ibis head found at the Chiddingfold Villa, Surrey (Cooper 1984) which may be related to an Egyptian cult. Another example is the discovery at the Rapsley Villa, Surrey (Hanworth 1968) of five stylized terracotta pine cones. Such cones were perhaps associated with the worship of Atys (Green 1976).

Ultimately the most successful of the imported eastern religions was that of Christianity. Prior to the fourth century, however, there is very little evidence for Christian worship in Britain and the religion did not become more common until after it became the official religion of the Empire, following the conversion of Constantine the Great. Even then the evidence is not very plentiful, and it appears that the faith may only have proved popular with specific groups of people. The evidence for continued use of temple sites (for example, Farley Heath) and local ritual customs also indicates that Christian-

Plate 6.9   Romano-Gaulish clay figurine from Chichester, West Sussex. The figurine may represent a deity or votive offering, although other purposes have also been suggested (Taylor 1944). Height: 141 mm. (Photograph: Chichester District Museum.)

ity failed to oust the popular pagan cults amongst large sections of the population.

The main evidence for Christian worship during the Roman period in the South-East has been found in Kent. The most famous site is the Lullingstone Villa, where a chapel or 'house church' replaced a pagan basement cult-room (Meates 1979). The Christian complex consisted of a suite of first-floor rooms which were separated off from the rest of the villa. Paintings on the walls of the chapel include both Chi-Rho monograms and also scenes of *orantes* (humans in the act of prayer). The chapel, which may have served a private, household, estate or even larger congregation, dates to the end of the fourth century (from *c.* AD 380). The residential areas of the villa also contain a mosaic floor which has possible Christian associations (Smith 1969). The theme of this mosaic is the Greek myth of Bellerophon killing the Chimaera.

Another very late Roman church has been identified at the Richborough Saxon Shore Fort (Brown 1971). Its interpretation is based on a new identification of a nearby six-sided plaster-lined basin, which from continental parallels can now best be interpreted as a font. Of the church itself only a few traces have been recorded: two lines of well-spaced stone blocks. These blocks are presumed to be the foundations of a free-standing timber building. Other evidence for Christians at Richborough includes the discovery of a gold ring which bears a Chi-Rho symbol on its bezel, and also a bowl with an incised Chi-Rho graffito (Hassall and Tomlin 1977, 442–3).

Other Chi-Rho symbols have been found on several items which formed part of a Late Roman silver hoard found just outside the city walls at Canterbury (Potter and Johns 1983). In addition, the reference by the Anglo-Saxon chronicler Bede with regard to a Roman church at Canterbury, together with the remains of Roman brickwork at the extra-mural church of St Martin indicate that Canterbury may have had one or more churches in Roman times.

Another important discovery which indicates Christian worship is a lead cistern found in the marshes at Wiggonholt, Sussex (Curwen 1943). The cistern is decorated with a Chi-Rho monogram and may have been used in the rite of baptism.

Burial Practices

Another type of evidence which sometimes provides an insight into the religious beliefs of the inhabitants of the South-East is that of burial. As in the case of cult worship, Roman burials in the South-East fall into two main groups: Classical practices and Romano–British customs. The latter category predominates and is the subject of a recent survey by Ernest Black (1986). Since little new evidence has come to light following the completion of Black's survey, it is only necessary here to outline some of the main trends detectable from the recorded burials.

The evidence for Iron Age burial customs has been discussed above (Ch. 5). For much of the Iron Age the remains of burials are fairly rare and it seems likely that the majority of the dead were subjected to some form of exposure burial rite. At the end of the Iron Age, however, the practices of cremating the dead and subsequently burying their remains became popular in certain areas of the South-East. After the Conquest the rite of cremation became common throughout the region, and was also the burial custom practised by the Romans. Cremation was to remain the principal funerary practice until the late third and fourth centuries, when inhumation burials gradually became the norm.

Generally both rural and urban burials were located in distinct cemeteries, enclosures or structures. According to Roman law, urban communities had to bury their dead outside the settlement area, and fairly large burial grounds, such as that at St Pancras, Chichester (Down and Rule 1971) developed just outside the towns and alongside the major approach roads. At the St Pancras cemetery, and also at many other Roman burial grounds, there was very little destruction of earlier burials by later ones and this implies some system of marking the graves.

In the countryside of Kent several examples are known of walled cemeteries (Jessup 1959). Of these, that at Borden is particularly interesting. It contained a circular Mausoleum which was surrounded, both within and outside the walled enclosure, by 'satellite' burials which span a period of perhaps two centuries. Other examples of mausolea, which are sometimes referred to as 'temple-mausolea', have been discovered at several villa sites such as Lullingstone (Meates 1979). Possibly they were also constructed at many other villas, but that their detection has not been made is due to such factors as their peripheral locations with regard to the main villa complex, or the use of alternative building materials, especially timber.

Unfortunately, very few burials/burial grounds have been found associated with rural 'peasant' settlements. One example, however, is at Kings Wood, Sanderstead, Surrey, where a small Late Iron Age/Early Roman cremation cemetery was located just outside the settlement enclosure (Little 1961). All the interments were those of babies and young children, and there was thus presumably at least one separate area or site for adult burials.

It should be noted that not all dead infants were necessarily given the adult form of burial, and an example of this is at the Frost Hill site, Bullock Down, Sussex, where a baby was buried in the upper fill of a rubbish pit (Rudling 1982b). It is possible that this infant had died at or around birth.

During the Roman period a fairly rare structure used for burials is the earthen round barrow, and several examples are known, especially from Kent (Jessup 1959). Possibly the construction of round barrows during the Roman period helps to explain the contemporary interest shown in the two Bronze Age round barrows at Slonk Hill, Sussex (see above). Perhaps the square timber structure associated with one of these barrows may have been connected with some form of mortuary practice.

In addition to the nature and location of the burial grounds or structures, the actual burials themselves can provide us with various types of information. Thus the bones, especially when unburnt, can yield valuable data concerning such matters as the age or sex distribution within a cemetery, and details of stature, illnesses, periods of malnutrition, and injuries. Similarly the way in which the human remains were treated and buried, such as cremation or inhumation, body orientation, type of container (if any), and any accompanying grave goods, can be indicative of status, religious beliefs, and perhaps even in some cases of ethnic origins. Unfortunately as yet in the South-East there have been very few detailed scientific and pathological studies of Romano-British human remains, and the large-scale excavation and study of a major inhumation cemetery is a high priority. Fortunately, however, there is much more information recorded about burial practices, and the data can be compared from different sites (Black 1986).

In the case of cremations some burial sites have yielded evidence which is either definitely or possibly associated with the actual rite of cremation. Thus at the St Pancras cemetery, Chichester, excavation revealed several areas of extensive burning which might represent the locations of funeral pyres (Down and Rule 1971). At the Holborough barrow, Snodland, Kent, evidence was obtained which provides a rare insight into ritual behaviour associated with a high-status funeral (Jessup 1955). The primary burial, of a male aged about forty, was contained in a coffin. A folding stool was amongst the items found associated with the human remains, and it has been suggested that the deceased may have been cremated sitting on the stool. After the cremated remains had been put into the grave, five amphorae were ritually smashed beside the burial. Finally, the barrow was constructed over the grave.

There were a number of different forms of cremation burial and many cemeteries contain a mixture of types. Thus at the St Pancras cemetery, Chichester, the excavator was able to identify two main types of cremation burial: single-vessel burials with the bones placed in the urn, and burials (Plate 6.10) with food and drink vessels (Down and Rule 1971). In addition, the Type 2 burials were divided into six sub-types: box burials, tiled cist burials, food vessel burials, crescentic burials, burials where one or more of the vessels were inverted, coin burials, and pipe burials. While most cremation burials in the South-East were placed in fairly small grave pits, there are also a number of burials in very deep pits or shafts, as at Hardham, Sussex (Boyd Dawkins 1864). The social and religious implications of the complete range of variations in burial customs is not always very clear, although poverty and low status are often suggested for the most simple types of burials with no associated grave goods. Where grave goods are present they are often useful for indicating the status of the deceased.

Grave goods can also sometimes shed light on religious beliefs. At the St Pancras cemetery, for example, 14 per cent of the cremation burials had lamps (Plate 6.11) or lampstands, and the excavator suggested that the finding of such items indicates that they were thought to be needed to light the deceased on their journey to the underworld. Alternatively, however, the lamps might also be interpreted as being needed to provide the dead with light within the grave. It is possible that either or both of these explanations is correct, since grave goods were intended to be of use to the dead in 'two distinct locations: within the grave itself and in the other world' (Black 1986). Other common

Plate 6.10 Cremation burial group, St Pancras Cemetery, Chichester, West Sussex. (Photograph: Chichester District Archaeological Unit.)

grave goods include food containers and unburnt shoes, which respectively indicate that the dead were thought to continue to need nourishment and were about to set out on a journey. The widespread practice of depositing coins in burials has usually been interpreted as indicating the Roman belief that the souls of the dead were ferried across the Styx by Charon, who required payment for his services. Whilst this theory sounds very attractive, the custom of depositing coins with burials may in some instances, especially where a number of coins are involved, have links with a pre-Roman indigenous tradition of providing offerings to a Celtic deity. Another widespread type of belief can be detected from some examples of both cremation and inhumation burials. The burials in question show signs of concern for 'confining the dead within the grave'. Probably the most well-known sort of evidence for this idea are the various decapitated inhumation burials, such as that from Cuxton, Kent (Tester 1963). Another possible example is at Plaxtol, Kent, where a large stone was placed upon the chest of the deceased (Jessup 1959). There are also many other examples of the covering of bodies or cremations with heavy objects such as tiles or stones. Ernest Black (1986) has suggested that these

235

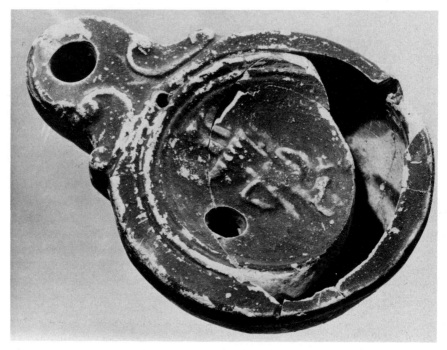

Plate 6.11   Pottery oil lamp from a cremation burial group; St Pancras Cemetery, Chichester, West Sussex. The upper surface of the lamp is decorated with the moulded figure of Anubis. Length: 108 mm. (Photograph: Chichester District Archaeological Unit.)

various practices were intended to confine the dead to their graves until the time came for them to travel to the other world.

Although cremation was common during the first and second centuries, there were also a number of contemporary inhumation burials. At the St Pancras cemetery, Chichester, there were nine inhumations out of a total sample of 260 burials. Although it is possible that most or all of these inhumations may date to the period when cremation burial was going out of fashion, at least one example (no. 158) was overlain by a cremation burial. Of the nine inhumations, two were placed in the crouched position and the rest were extended. As with the cremations, grave goods were put with some of the inhumation burials at Chichester and also elsewhere in the South-East. The use of grave goods appears to have remained fairly popular until the mid-fourth century, when it became much less frequent (Clarke 1979). During the third century, inhumation gradually became the most popular form of funerary practice and by the late fourth century there were very few cremation burials.

Ernest Black (1986) has made a study of the orientation of Romano–British burials in Southern England and where the relevant data has been adequately recorded the grave orientations appear to conform to certain regional patterns. As an example, at the St Pancras cemetery the two crouched burials were orientated north-west–south-east, and of the inhumation burials three were orientated approximately north-east–south-west and one was laid north–south. Whilst the numbers involved are small, the St Pancras inhumations share several traits, posture and orientation, with Iron Age inhumations in the region. At nearby Fishbourne four inhumations date to after the demolition of the palace in the late third century (Cunliffe 1971). Of these burials three were orientated north–south and one was laid west–east. Two Late Roman inhumation cemeteries have recently been investigated at Chichester (Down 1981; 1986). All the complete burials were extended and the majority were orientated west–east, with just a few graves aligned north–south. At the Eastgate cemetery seven out of the ten west–east burials had the head at the west end. Some of the bodies were buried in coffins, which were usually made of wood, but in one case (at the Westgate cemetery) was made of lead. In both cemeteries there was a marked scarcity of grave goods.

Other examples of lead coffins are known from South-East England and include a recently published example (Figure 6.9) from Beddington, Surrey (Adkins and Adkins 1984).

The main Late Roman burial trends discernible in the Chichester area are fairly typical of those of the South-East in general. The major changes in funerary practices during the Late Roman period still require adequate explanation, but need not necessarily imply a general change of religious belief (note our own culture's dramatic change in funerary custom during the last hundred years: from 100 per cent inhumation burials to over 50 per cent cremation burials with no linked change in religion). The gradual decline in the custom of grave goods and the major shift from predominantly north–south to west–east orientation burials with the head at the west end, has often been interpreted as indicating the gradual adoption of Christianity. If this popular hypothesis is to be accepted however, it is necessary to more thoroughly investigate and date the various changes in funerary custom. Should the theory be correct, the exceptions to the general late-fourth-century burial pattern may indicate that not all of the population were converted to the new official religion.

The Wealden Iron Industry

During the Roman period the most important industry in the South-East was that of iron-making. We have already seen (Ch. 5) that iron was being made in the Weald during the Late Iron Age. The potential of this local industry may have been appreciated by the Romans, and was perhaps one of the attractions

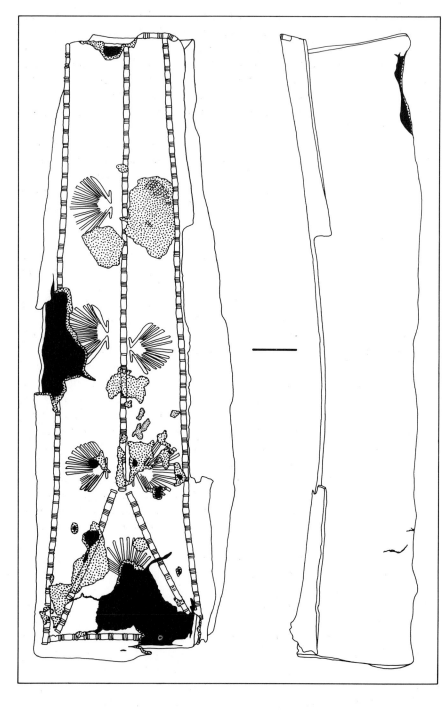

Figure 6.9 Lead coffin found *c.* 1870 near St Mary's Church, Beddington, Surrey. The lid of the coffin is decorated with scallop shells. Length: 140 cm.

of conquering Britain. The Roman iron industry of the Weald has recently been reviewed by Henry Cleere (Cleere and Crossley 1985). About sixty iron-working sites have now been definitely dated to the Roman period, and there are others which are also thought to be Roman. These sites are found in two main areas, in the High Weald and near the coast. They have been divided by Cleere into two main groups, a western group orientated on the major north–south roads, and an eastern group with a main outlet by sea from the estuaries of the Brede and Rother.

The *Classis Britannica* was connected with the eastern group (see above), although its precise role is not properly understood. It is uncertain as to whether the Roman fleet was actually involved in the production of iron, or was merely responsible for the acquisition and transportation of iron. If the latter, the use of CL BR tiles at various iron-working sites may represent military building projects, especially bath houses, as encouragements and rewards to local ironmaking communities. In contrast, the western group of ironworks lack CL BR titles, and are therefore thought to have been run by civilians, who used the road system to transport their products to the London area to the north and the agricultural areas of the Downs to the south.

Although a number of iron-working sites were in operation during the first century (some of which were started before the Conquest), there appears to have been a major expansion of the industry during the second century, with many new sites coming into use. One possibility for the apparent slowness in developing the Wealden iron industry is that if the Weald had formed part of the territory of King Cogidubnus, its iron industry may not have come under direct Roman control until after the death of the client king (Cunliffe 1973). Various writers have suggested that once the Weald was under Roman control it may have formed an 'Imperial Estate'. Some of the evidence given in support of this hypothesis includes the fact that in theory all mineral rights were owned by the state, parallels with other mining areas of the Empire, the 'presence' of the Roman fleet at various iron-working sites, the absence of major urban settlements, and the lack of 'villas' in the High Weald. With the exception of the iron-working establishments, the apparently sparse Roman occupation of the High Weald is certainly hard to explain, and the possibility of an Imperial Estate remains an attractive theory.

Information concerning the nature of the iron-working sites is unfortunately rather limited since, although several sites have been excavated on a large scale, they have not been published in full. The sites vary considerably in size, from large establishments such as Beauport Park (8–10 ha) to individual furnaces with their associated slag heaps. The site at Beauport Park may have been the headquarters of a large concern. It was equipped with a six-roomed bath house, and nearby were discovered traces of possible masonry buildings. In the vicinity are massive slag heaps, which demonstrate the grand scale of the iron-working activities undertaken at this complex.

Another 'headquarters' type establishment is that at Bardown, where there were discrete residential and industrial areas, and slag-metalled roads. Features associated with iron-working include ore pits, slag heaps, roasting furnaces, forges, and a charcoal-burning hearth. Although it appears that at the beginning of the third century iron-working activities ended, the site continued to be occupied and it is thought that iron production was switched to satellite sites, such as Holbeanwood, which lies some 2 km from the main settlement. The reason for moving the iron-workings may have been the exhaustion of local supplies of raw materials. Henry Cleere (1976) has tried to use the evidence of slag heaps at the Bardown complex in order to estimate the quantities of iron produced and raw materials used. He has, for example, estimated that some 40–45 tonnes of iron would have been produced annually at the main site, and that this would have required the product of 0.15 km^2 of iron ore extraction, and timber from 13–15 ha of woodland (possibly less if coppicing were practised). The production of iron in the Weald during Roman times would thus have had a major effect on the environment.

Similar nucleated ironworks are also found in the western group of sites. Thus the unexcavated Great Cansiron site, Hartfield, consists of a large (2 ha) area of blackened soil and slag. The site has yielded large quantities of pottery and building materials. In addition, the range of products made at a recently discovered nearby tileworks (see below) suggests that the ironworks at Great Cansiron may have had a bath house.

After the Conquest the Iron Age hillfort site at Garden Hill (Money 1977) continued to be involved with iron-working. Although industrial activities at Garden Hill were only on a fairly small scale, the site may have acted as a 'headquarters' for local bloomery sites. The site had a modest bath house and at least several rectangular buildings.

The later history of Roman iron-working in the Weald is not fully understood. By the mid third century the ironworks connected with the British fleet had been closed down. By the end of the third century, only Oldlands and Broadfield in the western group and Footlands in the eastern group were still functioning, and there is only a little evidence for activity at these sites during the fourth century. The reasons for the decline in the 'private' zone are unknown, but possibilities include over exploitation of resources or major changes in the economy.

Other Industries

In addition to farming and iron-working, other major Roman industries in the South-East included the manufacture of pottery, tiles and salt, the quarrying of stone, forestry, and the 'harvesting' of oyster beds. Of these industries we know most about those which produced durable products, such as pottery. The economic importance of such industries, however, has tended to be over-emphasized at the expense of those such as forestry, for which little evidence remains.

Pottery manufacture was undertaken in various parts of the South-East, and the whole region received quantities of imported pottery from elsewhere in Britain and from the Continent. In one large area (mostly present-day East Sussex) the Late Iron Age tradition of the local (?domestic) hand-making and bonfire-firing of grog-tempered ware vessels continued throughout the Roman period. Even by *c.* AD 300 over half of all the pottery vessels used in East Sussex were still of this Iron Age type (Green 1980). The contrast in the pottery types used by the Romano–British inhabitants of East and West Sussex is very marked, with the River Adur acting as the approximate boundary of the two ceramic zones. In the Late Roman period another distinctive handmade tradition occurred in East Sussex: the manufacture of very large storage jars of a type known as Thundersbarrow Ware.

Elsewhere in the South-East the Conquest was followed by the production of 'Romanized' pottery vessels and the widespread use of the potter's wheel and kiln. In West Sussex early pottery industries were established at Chichester. The Hardham–Pulborough area of West Sussex was also an important area for early Roman pottery production, and one unidentified workshop produced a type of Samian Ware, whilst other potteries at Wiggonholt specialized in making flagons (Evans 1974). A very late pottery industry in Sussex was established during the second half of the fourth century, probably in the Pevensey area (Fulford 1973). This industry concentrated upon the production of red colour-coated imitations of Oxfordshire Ware bowls. The potential of pottery studies for the investigation of Romano–British marketing patterns in West Sussex has been demonstrated by Martin Millett (1980).

The production of pottery in Kent has recently been reviewed by Pollard (1982), Detsicas (1983) and Monaghan (1983; 1987). There were three main groups of potteries in Kent: Canterbury, the Upchurch Marshes and the western Cliffe Peninsula. Other sites were mainly small-scale general producers or specialist manufacturers, as at Eccles. In West Kent and parts of Surrey grog-tempered 'Patch Grove Ware' may have had Iron Age origins (and possible links with East Sussex Ware?). In Surrey important pottery centres existed at Staines (see above), and in the Farnham/Alice Holt Forest area. The Farnham industry started in the early Roman period and expanded into a major production centre during the third and fourth centuries (Lyne and Jefferies 1979).

Another important ceramic industry was that of tile making. The manufacture and use of tiles/bricks was introduced to Britain by the Romans, and throughout the period of occupation, tiles were a major category of building materials. Tiles were extensively used on most of the more Romanized types of site (such as towns, villas, and bath houses), but they also occur, although often in relatively small quantities, on most 'peasant' type settlements. An example of such use is at Park Brow (see above) where it is thought that at least one of the huts had a tiled roof.

Various tile kilns have been found in the South-East. Most would have been located on suitable clay deposits near a major source of demand for tiles, since the transportation of such heavy commodities over any distance would have been an expensive and difficult undertaking. It is likely that in the countryside many of the tilemakers were itinerant manufacturers who would have been commissioned to produce specifice consignments for particular building projects. Many 'one-off' tileries presumably remain to be discovered.

An example of such a short-lived tilery was recently discovered near the large iron-working site at Great Cansiron, Hartfield, Sussex (see above). Excavations have shown that in addition to the tile kiln, the tilery also comprised two ancillary structures, one of which is thought to have functioned as an open-sided drying-shed, and the other, which contains a tile-built hearth, as a workmen's hut (Rudling 1986). The kiln (Fig. 6.10) has been dated by archaeomagnetic dating methods to *c.* AD 100–130. The products of the tilery included roofing tiles, 'flat' tiles/bricks, and box-flue and voussoir tiles used in heating systems. All the flue tiles were keyed on at least two of their faces, usually by combing but sometimes by roller-stamping. The latter is of particular interest, and the die appears to be of a type classified by A. W. G. Lowther (1948) as Group 1, die 5A. The known distribution of 5A and related dies includes sites as widespread as Essex, Herts, Hants, Surrey and now Sussex. This wide distribution, together with the presumed short life of the Hartfield kiln, suggests that at Hartfield one is seeing a temporary mobile brickyard. The most obvious source of demand for the products of the Hartfield tilery is the nearby large iron-working site, which may perhaps have an as-yet-undiscovered bath-house complex.

Details of other Roman tile kilns in the South-East have recently been reviewed by Alan McWhirr (1979). Of these an exceptionally large, almost square kiln was discovered near the Eccles villa, Kent. At Wykehurst Farm, Cranleigh, Surrey, there was a kiln whose plan is fairly similar to that of the kiln found at Hartfield. As at Hartfield, the Wykehurst Farm kiln produced both roofing and building tiles (but no roller-stamped flue-tiles), and also red-brick *tesserae* cubes. At Ashtead, Surrey, traces have been found of a major tileworks with a number of tile clamps (Hampton 1977). This tilery appears to date mainly to the first century and produced a wide range of tiles, including some very sophisticated types. It has been suggested that the Ashtead tileworks may have supplied a large market throughout the South-East. If so, the production of tiles may have been an important aspect of the economy of the Ashtead villa. At Itchingfield, Sussex, excavations revealed a building which has been interpreted as a tilemaker's workshop (Green 1970; 1979). This building may have had specific activity areas used for the storage of raw clay, the preparation of the clay, the making of tiles and the drying of tiles.

242

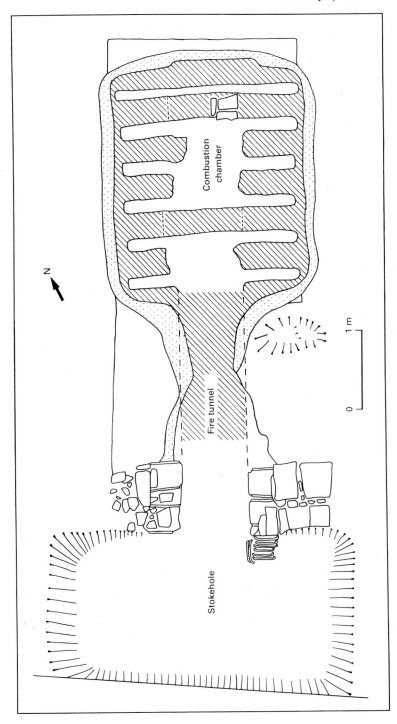

N

Combustion
chamber

Fire tunnel

Stokehole

0   1 m

Figure 6.10 Plan of the Roman tile kiln found at Hartfield, East Sussex.

Recently a surface artifact-collecting survey, a geophysical survey and trial excavations have been carried out on the site of a tilery at Dell Quay, Chichester Harbour, Sussex (Rudling 1987*b*). Of particular interest were the results of the magnetometer survey, which located a large anomaly which is thought to be a tile kiln.

A recent petrological examination of some of the *Classis Britannica* stamped tiles suggests that they were produced in two brickyards on either side of the Channel (Peacock 1977). The more important tilery was the British one, which was located somewhere in the Southern Central Weald, probably on an outcrop of the Fairlight Clay.

Research, including petrological analysis, is currently being undertaken with regard to one specific aspect of Roman tile production in South-Eastern Britain: that of relief-patterning ('roller-stamping'). At present the main published study of these very distinctive tiles is still that produced by A. W. G. Lowther in 1948. More recently there have been two general reviews of this group of material, which is particularly important for dating purposes (Johnston and Williams 1979; Black 1985). As research continues, the number of known dies has grown from the 46 recorded by Lowther to 86 as at July 1986 (Ernest Black, pers. comm.). The new data is being used by the Relief-Patterned Tiles Research Group to produce a new corpus and classification of roller-stamped tiles.

Another important aspect of the construction industry was the exploitation of building stone. Various kinds of suitable stone are available in the South-East and types used included flint, chalk, greensand, ferruginous sandstone, mixon limestone, ragstone and tufa. Of these, Horsham sandstone provided a suitable local alternative to clay tiles for roofing purposes, and Kentish ragstone was exported to London and Essex. Although most of the constructional building stone was available locally, occasionally stone was imported from outside the area, such as the limestone from the Isle of Wight which was used at Fishbourne. Stone used for decorative purposes included 'Sussex marble', Wealden mudstone, and imported marbles, especially Purbeck marble from Dorset. The whole subject of Roman building materials in the South-East has been reviewed by J. H. Williams (1971). In addition to its use for building purposes, some types of sandstone in the South-East were also used for making quernstones.

The extraction of salt from sea-water continued to be of great importance to many areas of Kent and Sussex. The methods used involved the formation of salt crystals either by the natural evaporation or boiling of sea water. Hearths and fragments of clay vessels (*briquetage*) used in this industry have been found on various coastal and estuary sites. In particular, extensive evidence for the manufacture of salt has been found on the lowlying areas of the Thames and Medway marshes (Detsicas 1983; 1985).

The sea and estuary environments would also have supported other important industries, especially the collecting of shellfish (particularly oysters,

244

cockles, mussels and limpets) and presumably fishing, although as yet surprisingly few traces of fish or fishing equipment have been found or reported from Roman sites in the South-East. The collection of seaweed, which has various uses (e.g. as a fertilizer) may also have been extensively practised.

Many other specialist and part-time industries and trades would also have been carried out during the Roman period. Such activities include smithing, the building industry (including specialist craftsmen such as mosaicists), spinning, weaving, tanning, woodworking, the retail trade, milling, baking and the entertainment industry. Of these, important evidence for milling has recently been discovered at Ickham, Kent (Young 1981; Spain 1984).

Chapter 7

The Early Anglo-Saxon Period, 410–650 AD

The end of the Roman authority in Britain and the arrival of the Anglo-Saxons has often been written of in terms of a collapse of classical values and a relapse into barbarism. This view of a fifth-century moral and social apocalypse is one which was first expressed by the early historian Gildas and has coloured much archaeological and historical thinking since. It does not fit, however, with the re-evaluation of the historical sources for the period and with the growing archaeological evidence. A vision of catastrophe, even in the heavily Romanized South-East which was exposed to Anglo-Saxon raiding and settlement appears less convincing. Placed in a broader context, the changes which occurred around 410 appear as a culmination of the developments of the previous century rather than anything entirely new.

Two important developments of the fourth century may be recognized in retrospect for their consequences in the early fifth century. From 383 the army in Britain was gradually reduced as units left to support pretenders to the post of Emperor. From this point on, the interests of the army in Britain were directed less towards the defence of the province and increasingly to events in Gaul and Italy. The army was as significant, of course for its role in maintaining security, peace and Imperial authority, and also indirectly for its effect on the economy of the country. It was through the payment to the army that coinage was introduced into Britain and as the army withdrew, money ceased to reach the country and fell out of circulation as it was lost or hoarded. As the monetary system failed, the production of goods which required coinage as a medium of exchange to be traded ceased. Pottery, for example, manufactured in the main at a few, centralized 'factories', stopped being made by the first decade or so of the fifth century. As the mechanisms of production, exchange and taxation simply stopped operating, the period of Roman culture in Britain came to an end.

The second of the long-term trends which became significant in the early fifth century was the shift of power, wealth and population from the towns to the countryside. Many towns had begun to contract in size during the third century and in the countryside new villas and farms had been built. Roman merchants, having made their money in commerce in towns, moved out into the country and took from towns their wealth and patronage. The towns were left as gradually declining service centres with a reduced population. They stood in a surrounding territory of wealthy farms and villas. The change towards the dispersed rural settlement pattern of post-Roman Britain began before the end of Roman rule. The final urban collapse of the fifth century was simply the terminal event in a prolonged process of decline in towns (Reece 1980).

In archaeological terms this decline can be traced in Roman towns by the spread of layers of dark, humic soil over the final Roman occupation layers. The soil is found covering the base of walls and on the floors of buildings and overlying streets. The dark earth was formed mainly of rubbish matter from the final years of Roman urban life and also from decayed organic remains, the thatch from roofs, the daub from the walls and timbers of collapsed buildings. In Southwark, on the south side of the Thames, dark soils appeared as early as the third century when the suburb of London, experiencing a major economic crisis, suffered from depopulation and contracted in size. Dark soil was brought into the town and dumped over the remains of former buildings to create large, open spaces between the surviving structures. These areas were then cultivated as market gardens and agricultural land, or were just left as waste ground (Yule 1982). Flooding higher up the Thames at Staines in the third century overwhelmed houses on the south side of the main street. Some reconstruction took place, but the spaces between the new buildings were left and used to grow food, probably to sell within the town. Settlement in Staines continued into the fourth century, although in a reduced form, with further dark soil accumulating until the town was finally abandoned (Jones 1982).

The dark soils of Southwark and Staines began to develop at a relatively early date. In other Roman towns the soil occurs as a fifth-century layer above the last evidence of Roman occupation. The two *civitas* capitals of Chichester and Canterbury show signs of decline only in the late fourth century. Excavations in the north-west quadrant of Chichester have shown a period of decay in the formerly prosperous area of the town. In two Roman town houses, the falling standards of living conditions were evident. One of the buildings was subdivided by partitions to create smaller rooms and in the other house, an oven was dug through the floor. As the buildings fell down, lean-to shelters were built against the walls within the shells of the town houses. Outside in the streets, silt and rubbish accumulated on the worn surfaces of the roads which were no longer maintained or swept, and the town's sewers were gradually allowed to silt up (Down 1978*a*; 45, 83). Urban authority appears to have been no longer able to keep up the services of the Roman town.

The coin series in Chichester ceases before the end of the fourth century, and it is uncertain how much longer after that urban life continued. A layer of dark earth developed in Chichester between the fifth and eighth centuries from the decaying remains of buildings, during a time when there is almost no evidence for activity in the city. Only a single find of a gold solidus of Valentinian III (425–55), one of the latest Imperial coins found in Britain, shows any continued activity within the walls of the town.

Canterbury gives a similar impression of urban decay, but occupation in the town lasted for a few decades longer than in Chichester. Construction work on new buildings continued up till the end of the fourth and into the fifth century. Behind the Roman theatre on the Marlow Car Park site I, a new masonry building of coursed flint and brick with a tessellated corridor was erected in the late fourth century. It was not used for long because within a few decades dark earth had begun to accumulate on the floors. Nearby on site IV, the structure of two substantial Roman buildings was robbed out, but within the remains of these, timber buildings were erected. In one room a deposit of occupation debris 1 m thick formed, and the building was repaired or recon-structed on four occasions, which suggests that occupation continued well into the fifth century. By the middle of the fifth century, dark earth layers began to form in the town. On the east side of the Roman forum, within both the destruction layer of a Roman courtyard and the dark soil, fragments of a goldsmith's hoard were found. Included in the hoard was a Visigothic gold tremissis dated to post 480. In Canterbury, as in Chichester, an odd gold coin marks the final datable activity in the remains of the decaying Roman town.

Historical Sources

The flowing narrative of events that historians have given for the last years of Roman Britain and the subsequent arrival of Germanic settlers appears to be a convincing story. The Roman army in Britain, depleted by the withdrawal of troops to support the pretender to the Roman Empire, Magnus Maximus in 383, by Stilicho in 401 to fight Alaric, and by Constantine in 407 to defend Gaul, can barely have been a viable fighting force by 410. A letter dated in that year from the Emperor Honorius, apparently in reply to a plea for assistance against the barbarians, told the cities of Britain they would have to look to their own defence. About this time the people of Britain rose up and expelled the last of the Roman officials. They established their own constitution and, taking arms on their own behalf, expelled the barbarians from the country. The Britons were faced with continuing problems as the story of the visits of Germanus, Bishop of Auxerre, to Britain in 429 and *c.* 437 shows. He is said to have led the Britons in a battle against the Picts and Saxons. The Britons ambushed the Saxons and shouting 'Alleluia' three times, routed the invaders in a bloodless victory which was almost identical to the biblical success of Joshua and the Israelites at Jericho.

The achievement of the Britons was short-lived, for they continued to suffer from attacks. The council in Britain led by the 'proud tyrant' Vortigern decided to invite Saxon mercenaries into the country to help defend them. Initially three boatloads arrived and were established in the eastern part of the country, but when more mercenaries landed, they could not be supplied with rations. They rose in revolt, led by Hengest and his brother Horsa, and defeated the Britons in Kent. Vortigern was forced to cede Kent, Sussex and Essex to them. The Britons appealed to Aetius, Consul in Rome for the third time and *Magister Militum*, for assistance but the appeal was not answered and the Gallic Chronicle of 452 records that Britain fell under the control of the Saxons.

Though this forms an impressive story, modern critical scholarship has left very little of the narrative secure and immune from considerable doubts. The events which were once thought to be independently recorded in a number of texts are now known to be based on limited evidence which was copied by one ancient historian from another. The very date 410, which archaeologists and historians have used confidently as the end of Roman Britain, has been shown to be doubtful. The date is given by the sixth-century historian Zosimus when he says that the Emperor Honorius sent letters to the cities in *Bruttium* ordering them to guard themselves. The cities of *Bruttium* were for many years understood by historians to refer to Britain. It is now thought likely that this is a misreading of the text. The context of the passage makes it more likely that the letter was sent to cities in an area called *Bruttium* in Southern Italy, and not to Britain at all. The date 410 therefore becomes of less significance.

This is not the only passage in which it has been necessary to reconsider Zosimus's history. In 409, it is reported, the Britons took up arms and freed their cities from the barbarians who were pressing on them. But an alternative translation would understand this entry to refer not to barbarian attackers, but to loyal barbarian troops who at that date formed a large part of the Roman army. The passage, construed in this way, describes a revolt by the Romano–British against units of the Roman army stationed in their cities, and thereby avoids any suggestion of a Saxon invasion (Bartholomew 1982). This alternative view has not convinced all historians, but it has raised queries about the traditional interpretation.

The story of the visit and military success of St Germanus of Auxerre comes from a life of the saint written by Constantius. Like all works of hagiography, the life attributes splendid, if not miraculous works, to the saint. The biblical parallel with Germanus's victory raises particular doubts about its historicity, for writers of the period including even Bede, were fond of describing events which echo those of the Bible. The life of Germanus is a work of allegory, according to one interpretation, intended to instruct Patiens, a fifth-century Bishop of Lyons. Though employing an historical setting, it was not intended as an accurate narrative of events (Wood 1984).

While these criticisms have raised doubts about the details of events in the early fifth century, the most fundamental objections have been levied against Gildas, historian of *De Excidio Britanniae*, whose work has guided the archaeological interpretation of the fifth-century Anglo-Saxon settlement. To modern eyes, his history lacks conviction. It reads as if it is a story which has been pared to its bare essentials so that its historical message stands out in black and white. Indeed, the work has less value as a work of history than as a moral tract, for Gildas was not writing for the benefit of modern historians, but as a prophet of the Old Testament sort. He was using the past as a vehicle to reveal the errors which had taken place and denounce the present order. The rhetorical sequence of events which he employs is one depicting disaster, recovery and then decadence, and the happenings he describes have been selected to fit this pattern.

If the purpose of Gildas's work is understood and its limitations appreciated, it might be thought that it could still be used as a source for fifth-century events. Unfortunately, even with these reservations, Gildas may not be accepted as a reliable historian, for his text contains all the signs of being derived not from recorded or well-remembered events, but from legend and oral tradition. The three ships in which the first Anglo-Saxons arrived place this event in the genre of origin legends. In these myths, the founders of a nation typically set sail in a small number of boats to a new land. Likewise the first leaders of the Anglo-Saxons belong to the same type of story. The names of the brothers Hengest and Horsa may be translated as 'stallion' and 'horse', which makes them appear to be a pair of horse deities rather than historical personages. The story of two brothers who led the Anglo-Saxons against the Britons and founded the nation appears to be a reworking of the same type of myth that made Romulus and Remus founders of Rome. The events of the fifth century recounted by Gildas become an interesting record of Anglo-Saxon legend, but they have little worth as an historical record (Sims-Williams 1983a).

Gildas is unfortunately vague with dates and places which makes it difficult to check the events of his history. He does refer to an appeal made by the Britons to *Agitus ter consul* in Rome which is the one fixed point in his work which may be compared with external evidence. Historians identify the recipient of the appeal with Aetius, who began his third consulship in 446 and died in 454. Gildas was able to quote from this letter which seems to have been the sole documentary source available to him. The letter complains that 'the barbarians push us back to the sea, the sea pushes us back to the barbarians; between these two kinds of death we are either drowned or slaughtered'. This letter used to be associated with an entry in the Gallic Chronicle which noted that in the 440s the provinces of Britain came under Saxon control. This entry, it has been suggested, may be an interpolation. Though this view is not universally accepted, it is possible that it is a later addition to the text, and therefore of doubtful authenticity (Miller 1978).

It remains to consider the other source from which the history for the Germanic settlements has been drawn. This is the work of Bede, particularly his *Historia Ecclesiastica*. Bede, writing in the eighth century, had few sources for the fifth and sixth centuries beyond those available to the modern historian. In default of any better, he had to use Gildas's account, though he carefully prefixes certain events with the phrase 'it is said that ...' and avoids committing himself to their historical authenticity. Modern historians have been able to examine Bede's account in turn and take it apart to show where he misunderstood Gildas. Bede was dependent for further detail on ecclesiastical informants in Kent, the West Saxon kingdom and elsewhere, but there is no reason to think that they were able to pass on more than traditions current in their day. They are unlikely to have had written records from the fifth and sixth centuries (Sims-Williams 1983*b*).

The historical sources for the events of the fifth century provide poor material on which to construct an interpretation of events. It is now being appreciated that the written records barely give a coherent or credible account of the fifth century, and that it is difficult to describe the events of the Germanic invasions from the written sources alone.

The Archaeological Evidence

The historical sources have had a strong influence on the interpretation of the archaeological evidence and few attempts have been made to examine the period from the excavated material without the prejudice of the documentary sources. But discussions of the Early Anglo-Saxon period have also been affected by the assumptions of the Invasion Hypothesis. For many years archaeologists considered that prehistoric cultural change was the result of the arrival of successive waves of people from the Continent. They brought with them, it was thought, cultural innovations which were gradually spread throughout the country before they in turn were superseded by a subsequent wave. This view of change is now discredited in prehistoric archaeology, but it continues to be influential in the conception of the Anglo-Saxon settlements where, ironically, there actually is good evidence for a movement of people from abroad to Britain. It is no longer certain, though, how far this was in reality an invasion, nor if the cultural changes which occurred conform with the assumptions of the Invasion Hypothesis. Terms such as 'refugees' and 'boat people' have begun to replace the older ideas of Germanic mercenaries and warriors arriving in Britain.

A number of the indicators formerly thought to distinguish the Germanic Anglo-Saxon period from the preceding Romano–British culture seem less certainly to have originated with one group or the other. Hand-made grass-tempered pottery found in the Early Anglo-Saxon period has a wide distribution in the areas occupied by Germanic settlers, but also in the unoccupied west of England. In Sussex and perhaps Kent, such pottery can be regarded as essentially a continuation of prehistoric hand-made pots and the hand-made pottery of the Roman period such as East Sussex Ware. Anglo-Saxon buildings in England seem to owe something to both Romano–British traditions of building and to Migration Period styles found in the Germanic homelands. This is not to suggest that nothing distinctively Germanic was introduced into Britain, for most brooch types and pottery forms of the post-Roman period can be matched by similar artifacts in the Anglo-Saxon homelands, but there might have been a greater blending of cultures than has been acknowledged in the past.

Metalwork decorated in Quoit Brooch Style is one example of a number of cultural influences present in a single group of artifacts. Belt-fittings and brooches in this style with shallow chip-carved decoration, so named from its similarity to methods of wood-working with semi-naturalistic animals, are known from a number of fifth-century graves (Fig. 7.1). Clearly displaying both Germanic influence in decoration and Gallo–Roman animal style and use of chip-carving, the hybrid origins of the style are apparent. In the past it has been suggested that this metalwork was made by Romano–British craftsmen and continued to be manufactured after the Anglo-Saxons arrived. The prevailing view now sees Quoit Brooch Style metalwork as having its origins in the Germanic animal style of the third and fourth centuries, but displaying the influence of late fourth and early fifth-century Gallo–Roman artifacts, in short a mixed product of Continental art styles (Ager 1985).

The collapse of Romano–British culture in Britain cannot be attributed to a violent Anglo-Saxon settlement. Romano–British culture collapsed at the same time as, or more probably before, the arrival of the Germanic settlers and the two events are not necessarily linked as cause and effect. The Romano–British culture was closely associated with the economic system which produced and sustained it. When the economy failed at the end of the fourth and in the fifth century, a cultural vacuum was created. The surviving sub-Roman population became archaeologically invisible, for they must have resorted to artifacts which are indistinguishable from those of the Anglo-Saxons, or which could be simply produced and were made of organic materials which leave no trace at all. The Germanic settlers brought their own culture, which was more closely adapted to the emerging patterns of production and exchange and very quickly this became firmly established as dominant in South-East England.

The Invasion Hypothesis and its view on the diffusion of culture has also underlain the view of the spread of Anglo-Saxon settlement within England. In general terms it is true that the Anglo-Saxons did gradually move out from the areas in the East and South-East which were first occupied, into the west of the country, but on a local scale this pattern is more complex. Within the South-East some areas such as Central Sussex were settled from an early date, but the western part of the county and the eastern end were occupied somewhat later.

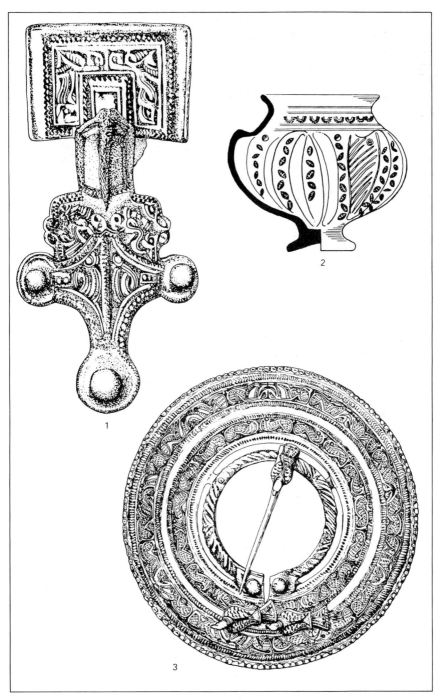

Figure 7.1 Early Anglo-Saxon artifacts. 1: a small square-headed brooch dated to the sixth century from a cemetery at Mitcham, Surrey (1/1); 2: a bossed zoomorphic pot from Alfriston, Sussex, made in the late fifth or early sixth century, possibly in a local workshop (1/4); 3: a silver quoit brooch from Sarre, Thanet in Kent (1/1).

The settlement of the Anglo-Saxons and their relationship with the Romano—British population is more complicated than simple ideas of conquest and invasion might suggest. This relationship between the existing population and the new arrivals has been interpreted by a study of settlement patterns. Though only a few settlements have been discovered, it is likely that they were situated close to the cemeteries which are known in some numbers, and can be fairly well dated. The earliest Germanic sites are known from Kent, where they often occur in coastal situations. Such sites may have been chosen because they were most like the lands the Anglo-Saxons had left on the North German and Frisian coast, or because they were the places first reached on landing in England. The Anglo-Saxons had rowed their way around the North Sea, along the Continental coast and then across the Channel to England. The sea level on both sides of the English Channel had begun to rise in the fourth and fifth centuries, and on the coastal margins of their homelands in Germany and Frisia the fields and settlements of the Anglo-Saxons were submerged under the rising waters. As their farms began to disappear under water, 'boat people' fled across the sea to the nearest land on the east coast of England, where they settled.

Early Germanic settlement sites in Kent have been found alongside the Thames at Milton Regis and Chatham and close to the Wantsum Channel which separated Thanet from the mainland at Ozengell near Ramsgate and Dumpton Gap near Broadstairs. They cluster around the creeks which lead into the Thames. Sites have also been found in the river valleys leading down to the sea, at Westbere for example in the Great Stour valley below Canterbury, and in the Little Stour at Bekesbourne and Howletts and right up the valley as far as Lyminge at its head. Indeed, this area of North-East Kent was occupied fairly densely by the incoming Anglo-Saxons. It contains some of the lightest and most fertile soils in the county and was served by a good network of Roman roads. They took over this land which had been cultivated by Roman villas and farms, apparently without any significant opposition.

The Germanic settlers appear to have avoided the towns in Kent generally, though at Canterbury finds indicate some activity in and around the city from around the middle of the fifth century onwards. In the Roman cemeteries outside the walls of Canterbury the number of artifacts discovered suggests that they were adopted for use or were revived by the Anglo-Saxons. The largest concentration of material is known from Martyrs' Field cemetery on the south side of the town, indicating that the Roman burial ground remained in use in the later fifth and into the sixth centuries. The sunken huts found inside Canterbury and containing so-called Anglo-Frisian pottery can no longer be certainly dated to this period. Within the town the find of a fifth-century firesteel is the sole piece of metalwork suggesting a Germanic presence (Kent 1974). These few finds do not indicate continuity of settlement. After the mid-fifth century, much of Canterbury may have been deserted, the streets became blocked and abandoned, and weeds grew up among the ruins. The

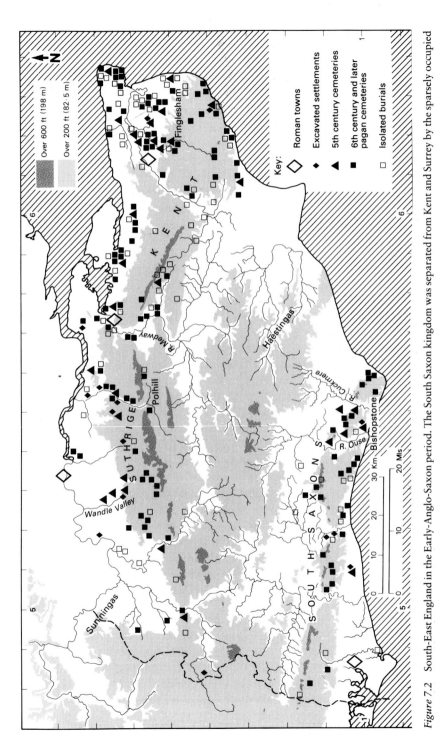

Figure 7.2 South-East England in the Early-Anglo-Saxon period. The South Saxon kingdom was separated from Kent and Surrey by the sparsely occupied areas of the Weald and Romney Marsh.

River Stour, which flows through the town, flooded a large part of the western half of Canterbury and rendered it uninhabitable.

Bede identifies the Germanic settlers in Kent as Jutes who also occupied the Isle of Wight, and he distinguishes them from the Saxons who settled elsewhere in the South and East of England. Archaeology has confirmed this identification and shown that many artifacts in Kentish graves have a close connection with those found in Jutland, while those from Sussex and Surrey are better matched on the Continent in the area to the west of the River Elbe. The division between the areas of the peoples in South-East England is roughly along the line of the River Medway. West of the Medway the density of settlement is much lower and the cemeteries are also quite distinct from those of East Kent, more like the Saxon cemeteries of Surrey. Here too the finds have a coastal or riverine distribution, occurring on the Cray at Orpington and St Mary Cray and also along the Darent Valley at Dartford and Horton Kirby. The pattern continues into Surrey where all the Anglo-Saxon cemeteries of the fifth century lie within the major river valleys. In the Wandle Valley are a group of cemeteries at Mitcham, Beddington and Croydon, lying in a line along a short stretch of the river about 8 km long near the headwaters. The site at Croydon lies close to a Roman road and wayside settlement. The other fifth-century cemeteries were situated on the Rivers Mole and Wey. They have been found on Guildown outside Guildford and at Fetcham. Some of these cemeteries are so large that it has been suggested that they may not have served only the adjacent community, but may have been the burial ground for the surrounding area. The cemeteries are situated generally in areas of better soils, but there is not the density of occupation that is found in Kent. The concentration of three of the cemeteries in such a small area in the Wandle Valley may suggest that this may have been a ghetto district for the incoming refugees, or perhaps an area of settlement agreed with the existing population.

Sussex too shows a concentration of fifth-century settlements within a small area. With one exception, all the cemeteries lie in a block of land between the Rivers Ouse and Cuckmere. This was well away from the most Romanized areas on the most fertile soils of the Coastal Plain around Chichester. There were few villas in the Ouse–Cuckmere area and it was occupied mainly by peasant farmers. The Romano–British authorities may have chosen to grant this convenient area to the incoming settlers by a treaty agreement. A memory of such an agreement may be preserved in the Anglo-Saxon Chronicle, which contains a reference to a battle fought by Aelle, the supposed leader of the Saxons in Sussex, in 485 near the banks of the 'Mearcredesburna', the 'river of the frontier agreed by treaty'. Ignoring the date, which may have no authority, and without taking these events too literally, it is possible that this record does recall the breakdown of a settlement agreement between the Britons and Saxons (Welch 1971).

Without the crutch provided by the historical sources, the events of the fifth century are extremely difficult to interpret. The evidence of archaeology is not particularly suitable material from which to construct a political history of the period, and the relations between the Ango-Saxons and the native population remain very uncertain.

The Kingdom of Kent

A distinct sense of identity was one of the reasons for Kent emerging as the first recorded Anglo-Saxon kingdom in England. It was also a compact and well-defined tract of land. Its borders were naturally defined by the coast and the Weald, which separated it conveniently from Sussex to the south-west. On the western side, its boundary lay along the line of the River Medway. Cemeteries in West Kent are culturally more similar to Surrey than to the east of the county. The frontier was guarded by large, well-armed communities known from cemeteries at Rochester where the Roman road crossed the Medway, and at Aylesford where a track along the North Downs entered the kingdom. While the early cemeteries occur on the east side of the Medway, there are no signs of burials on the western side and indeed, Western Kent was not as completely settled as the eastern part.

Kent had been particularly densely colonized in the fifth century by the incoming Anglo-Saxon settlers, among whom Jutes apparently played a leading role. The best land was rapidly occupied and taken over, perhaps directly from the Romano–Britons who had been farming it. The area east of Canterbury was particularly favoured and Germanic cemeteries occur at the head of almost every creek leading into the Thames estuary or Wantsum Channel. On Thanet, the cemeteries lay on the slopes of coombes leading down to the sea, at the bottom of which were places to beach boats. Inland, along the valley of the Little Stour, there was a string of early Anglo-Saxon cemeteries. The soils in this region are particularly light and fertile and formed some of the best farmland. Many cemeteries were also situated in the other fertile area of Kent, at the foot of the North Downs in the Vale of Holmesdale, running eastwards from near Sevenoaks. All the best lands in Kent were therefore occupied within a short period.

From the fifth century the wealth of the Kentish kingdom and the high status of the Germanic settlers is clearly established. The finds from the cemeteries show that the Jutish arrivals included some of the aristocracy, the warrior elite of Jutland. These, to judge by the continuing receipt from Jutland of prestige goods such as relief brooches, maintained links with their homelands. The Jutish products may have been brought to Kent either as rich gifts, as items of trade or arrived with further settlers, perhaps brides for the aristocracy (Hawkes and Pollard 1981). From about 500, new and no less rich settlers arrived in Kent. These were Franks who had come across the Channel from northern France and their influence can be very clearly identified from the new and elaborate style of jewellery which begins to be found in Kentish burials. They are found buried in some of the most important cemeteries in Kent, around the royal vill at Lyminge for example, and in the rich cemetery in the princely vill of Finglesham. It seems probable that the Franks were accepted directly into the royal household of Kent without prejudice for their ethnic origins.

The arrival of Franks in Kent initiated links across the English Channel. Just as the Jutes had maintained contact with their homeland in Jutland, so did the Franks with Northern France. Many of the richly endowed female burials in Kent may be of brides who had crossed the Channel to marry. The movement was not one way, for Kentish jewellery is also found in the cemeteries of Northern France, brought by women who had married abroad. The intermarriage of the two peoples consolidated the connection between the kingdoms in France and in Kent. The association of these two areas was definitely established when, in *c.* 560, King Æthelberht of Kent married the Merovingian princess Bertha, daughter of King Charibert of Neustria. The marriage was significant not only in social and economic terms, but also politically. When the king of a minor people married into the ruling family of a major kingdom, he became, by social convention, their dependent.

This match confirms other evidence for the exercise of overlordship by the Merovingians over the kingdoms of Southern England. It also reflects in harsh terms the relative wealth and importance of Kent. By comparison with Continental power and wealth, Kent was not of significance, and the importation of high-status Frankish goods into the kingdom indicates the superiority and prestige value of products from abroad. But within England the comparative importance of Kent was very evident and the marriage to Bertha no doubt reflected this. Bede names Æthelberht as one in a list of the kings who had *imperium* or lordship over the lands south of the Humber. The meaning and implications of this title are not understood, and it may be that this power came from the recognition of Æthelberht by the Merovingians (Wood 1983).

Burials between 535 and 560 were richly equipped with the recent imports from France and the old heirlooms from the original Jutish settlement of Kent. About the middle of the sixth century the supply of jewellery from the Frankish territories begins to decrease. Though links with the Continent remained very strong and many other commodities continued to be imported, almost all jewellery found in burials thereafter was manufactured in Kent. The change of custom appears to conclude a period of migrations into Kent and marks a new sense of self-identity.

258

Social Structure

Evidence for the organization of society and its ranking in the Early Anglo-Saxon period comes from the discoveries from excavations and is also contained in some later documents which cast light on the earlier situation. An insight into the world and mentality of the warrior aristocracy of the upper classes of society in the sixth and seventh centuries is given by the poem, *Beowulf*. Though only surviving in a later copy, it describes a heroic society in which the elite were armed with weapons by their lords. In return they were expected to fight loyally, win treasure and capture the arms of their enemies. On their death they were given a ceremonial burial with their weapons. The poem reflects the same heroic values as the mythological genealogies of Anglo-Saxon kings. These trace the ancestry of kings backwards to legendary figures in the past, including Caesar, Noah and the god Woden.

The earliest laws, written in Kent in the first years of the seventh century, show a hierarchical society firmly divided into a number of classes. The warriors depicted in *Beowulf* were at the top of a complex society of free and unfree men and women. Though the laws give a formalized view of the social hierarchy, it is a view which archaeology for the most part confirms. Among the free there were two or maybe three ranks, there were three for the half-free (*laets*) and there were even divisions among the slaves. The status of men in Anglo-Saxon society was indicated by their possession of weaponry. It was the right and duty of all free men to carry arms and when they were buried, their weapons were positioned around them in the grave, or sometimes they were placed grasping their weapons. Weapons were a mark of status in life as well as death, and the giving and possession of them played an important part in social relations.

The most important men could expect to own a sword which was a symbol of high status. Swords were of such value that they were sometimes not buried, but handed down as heirlooms. The majority of freemen would not have owned a sword but would have possessed a spear, which was the most common weapon for the early Anglo-Saxon warrior. It was not used for throwing but carried and used to stab the enemy. Some spearmen, to defend themselves, also carried circular shields which were made of wood and leather, often with a central iron boss. Knives often found in graves were not weapons but were carried as a general tool for eating or cutting. They occur in the graves of unfree men and also with burials of women and youths.

The composition of Anglo-Saxon society can be studied through the finds from graves, for if the weapons and other artifacts buried with the dead reflect their rank in life, then the distribution of grave goods in a cemetery should mirror society generally. We may take Anglo-Saxon graveyards to be the ritualized counterparts of living society. The character of Anglo-Saxon cemeteries varies widely with some having a higher proportion of well equipped arms-bearers, others with less well armed males and others still with few arms at all. As Christianity began to spread more widely through society and replace the pagan cults in the later seventh and eighth centuries, weapon burial declined. Polhill in west Kent is a cemetery belonging to this period and only 10 per cent of the burials contained weapons. This compares generally with the graves of the better recorded cemeteries of all dates in Sussex and Kent in which the average proportion of armigerous males was about one fifth of the total number of burials (Arnold 1980: 86–90). Women were never buried with weapons and nor were children and youths who, if buried with grave goods at all, were often given goods such as knives or pots which do not characterize gender. It may be estimated on the basis of these figures that males and females of free status therefore made up perhaps one half of the population. The remainder were semi-free or slaves.

The social analysis of Anglo-Saxon society through a study of the cemeteries is a current area of research. In the next few years analyses of more cemeteries, especially in Kent, should become available, but at present only the cemetery at Alfriston, Sussex has been examined in detail. About 165 graves were excavated there in 1912–13 and more burials probably still remain to be found. The cemetery was in use from the second half of the fifth century until the first half of the seventh century, a period of perhaps 175 years. It was the burial ground of no more than a small community which would have lived close by in a hamlet. The skeletal remains have not survived from the excavation, but the sex of many of the burials could be determined from the associated grave goods. One third were identified as male and one quarter as female. The male weapon-holders fell into three roughly equal categories. The most prestigious had a sword or an axe, which in the later fifth century appears to have served as a comparable status marker. Some of the sword-bearers also had spears and shields as well. 'Middle-class' free male burials had shields and sometimes spears. The least well-equipped burials had only spears. The numbers of shields may be under-represented as some shields were made entirely of organic materials and no trace of these may have survived the period of burial.

The social analysis of female burials at Alfriston is more complex. While males were buried with a limited range of grave goods, the variety of artifact types in female graves was much larger. Thus the social status of males in Anglo-Saxon society would have been clearly identifiable because of the small number of indicators they used. The ranking of males was very firmly stratified, with little chance of social mobility. Though women also used personal goods to indicate their status in the social hierarchy, there was no well-defined stratification. This difference is shown in a study of wealth scores of grave goods from selected cemeteries in Kent (Fig. 7.3a). The graph of male graves shows two extended plateaux produced by society. The female grave graph is quite different. It is a curve showing continuous gradation between the poorest and the richest (Shepherd 1979).

The social status of women buried at Alfriston can be determined only

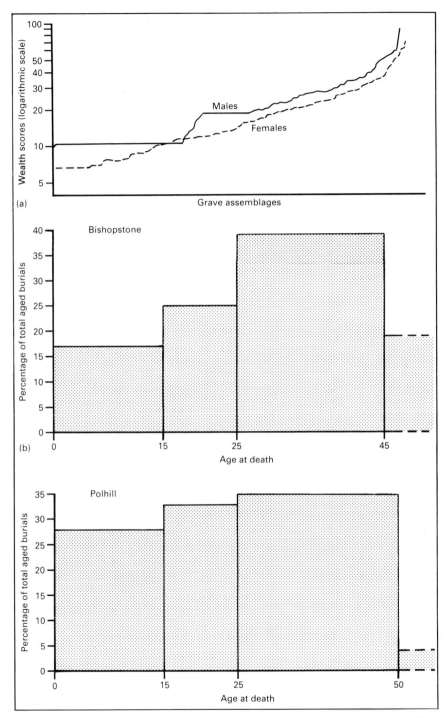

Figure 7.3 (a) Male and female wealth scores based on graves from seven cemeteries in Kent (after Shepherd 1979); (b) Age at death of cemeteries at Bishopstone, Sussex and Polhill, Dunton Green, Kent. The comparative longevity of the Bishopstone population is evident from the greater proportion that survived into 'old age'.

approximately. It is possible to pick out six rich females who represent one or two families. They appear to match the axe- or sword-bearing males. Likewise nine women with pairs of brooches correspond to the ten 'middle-class' males and the poorest male burials can be linked with an almost equal number of least well-equipped females. Two and perhaps three of the richest female burials have grave assemblages which are very similar. These have been interpreted as close relations, sisters or sisters-in-law. But with perhaps these exceptions it is not possible to pick out groups which might represent families from the cemetery. Indeed, an analysis of the plan of the cemetery at Alfriston for the distribution of graves of similar periods, sex or wealth, shows that there were no significant concentrations (Welch 1983: 188–211).

Few Anglo-Saxon cemeteries have been excavated so completely that the social composition might be studied. Many are known only from the accidental finds made during building work, often found during the nineteenth century when a few graves were disturbed. The cemetery at Finglesham in East Kent was discovered when human bones were noted over a number of years of chalk quarrying. A local farmer excavated 38 graves in 1928 and since 1959 another 215 have been carefully dug (Fig. 7.4). Apart from a small area lost in the quarrying and a few graves now inaccessible under the adjoining road, the entire cemetery has been recorded. It is regular in plan and must have had well-marked boundaries on the east and south-east sides. The Whiteway, an ancient track, formed the western limit. The cemetery lies above the head of a creek to the south of the Wantsum Channel and is a short distance from the royal vill at Eastry. The place-name Finglesham, 'the prince's manor', suggests it was land held by an aristocratic family who are presumably buried in the cemetery.

Many of the earliest and richest graves were situated on the north edge of the cemetery on the highest land. Seven male burials in this group were probably inhumed under barrows, although these had been ploughed flat by the time they were excavated and the largest of these, over grave 204, was thought to have been 12 m in diameter. Grave 204 was probably the founder's grave; a male aged 25 years who was buried in *c.* 525 with a sword, spear, an elaborate buckle and glass claw-beaker. His wife may have been buried some distance away in grave D3. A small skull of a child had been added to the grave after her burial and may have been that of their son or daughter, placed in its mother's grave at a later date. The woman in D3 was buried with her heirlooms from Jutland, more recent Frankish radiate-headed brooches and some jewellery made in Kent. She, like her husband, had a claw-beaker and had also an iron weaving sword which was a symbol of a wealthy woman.

The sixth-century burials represent members of a few generations of probably just a single wealthy family. The cemetery may have gone out of use for a few years in the last quarter of the sixth century and when burial resumed, the grave goods were less rich. Some of the seventh-century burials imitated the barrow burial custom of the earlier graves. The later barrows are often smaller

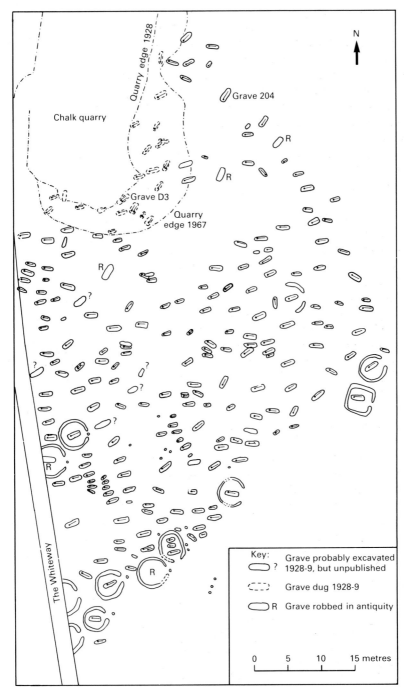

Key:

⬭ ?	Grave probably excavated 1928-9, but unpublished
⟨⟩	Grave dug 1928-9
⬭R	Grave robbed in antiquity

0   5   10   15 metres

Figure 7.4 The Anglo-Saxon cemetery at Finglesham, Kent, 1928–29 and 1959–67. The earliest graves adjoin the quarry edge and some of the richest were buried under barrows. Though the barrows were ploughed flat at the time of excavation, their extent is indicated by the area surrounding isolated graves unoccupied by other burials. Later burials were often surrounded by penannular gullies, dug to construct barrows over the dead.

and surrounded by panannular gullies which are found more commonly in the later period. The flat graves can sometimes be seen to cluster around the barrow burials. The ditched barrows are concentrated at the opposite corner of the cemetery from the sixth-century burials. Analysis of the cemetery will indicate the significance of these patterns (Hawkes 1958: 1982*b*).

The Finglesham burials are likely to show the two features common to many Anglo-Saxon cemeteries. Grouping of graves in family plots has been suspected in other cemeteries such as at Abingdon in Berkshire, but the pattern is often confused by the way in which burials in cemeteries are made progressively across the graveyard. This practice produces a 'horizontal stratigraphy' of the graves so that the earliest and latest burials may lie at opposite ends of the cemetery. These two factors create a complex cemetery pattern reflecting the elements of date of inhumation, status and the family of the burials.

Anglo-Saxon cemeteries suggest a strong contrast between the male warriors buried with their weaponry and the richly dressed females inhumed with their jewellery. The wealth of so many female burials is indicative of the importance of women in Anglo-Saxon society. The finds in women's graves clearly associate their activities with domestic work in antithesis to the weapons and shields of the male graves. Control of the household was apparently vested in women, in whose graves iron keys or latch lifters are often found. The excavations at Polhill in east Kent located five female burials with keys, but these were not the graves that contained jewellery. In the Polhill community there was a distinction between the lady of the house and the housekeeper buried with her key to the door of the house or to a chest within the building (Hawkes 1973). The key-bearer had a major responsibility and the key was a symbol of this. Later laws mention a fine to be imposed on a freewoman who abused this role. Key-shaped objects called girdle hangers are also found in some graves at, for example, Alfriston and Croydon, though they are rare in the South-East. These had a purely symbolic function, but again evoked the female association with the house.

Other grave goods in female graves link women to the work of sewing and weaving. The weaving sword or panel beater found at Finglesham has already been mentioned, but iron tools of this type are rare and found only in the graves of the highest status. The more common type of panel beater was made of wood, and these have survived only rarely. Thread boxes were a similar symbolic and prestigious version of a utilitarian item linked to textile work. They have been found in a number of seventh-century graves in some of the major cemeteries of Kent. Where the contents of these cylindrical boxes have survived, they are found to have held small bits of cloth and a few strands of thread. The boxes are elaborately made and decorated and were equipped with rings so that they could be suspended from the waist. These were not purely functional, and indeed may not have been intended for practical use at all, but were worn as status symbols.

The role of women in Anglo-Saxon society was clearly well differentiated from the male role. No doubt it would have varied according to the status of the individual. The work of women was not unvalued. The associations of these grave goods imply the high worth given to the work of housekeeping and textile production. Women had a more nearly equal status with their male counterparts in Anglo-Saxon society than they did after the Norman Conquest. Archaeology suggests that it was a different role, though not necessarily a lesser one (Fell 1984).

Below the armed freemen and women with jewellery were the semi-free and the slaves. The seventh-century laws of the West Saxon king Ine distinguishes two groups among the slaves. Those of lower status were Britons, presumably the descendants of the Romano–British population. One must conclude that the slaves of higher status were either derived from the serfs brought across when whole Germanic communities moved and settled in England, or freemen who had been deprived of their liberty. Many of the Britons were enslaved by the Anglo-Saxons and the Old English term for 'foreigners' used by the incomers for the Britons was *walas*. This developed in due course the secondary and derogatory meaning of a 'slave' or 'serf' which must reflect a common Anglo-Saxon perception of the Britons. The word is also found in the names of settlements such as Wallington in Surrey and Walton in Sussex. These place names were given to identifiable communities of Britons who often lived close to the important Anglo-Saxon settlements. The contact between the Germanic and British groups is also indicated by place-names. The vast majority of places in South-East England were renamed by the Anglo-Saxons with names in Old English. A cluster of names derived from Celtic or Latin survived in north Surrey: Penge, Caterham and Croydon are examples. There may well have been a significant proportion of Romano–Britons in this area who were able to pass on the traditional names of places.

Interaction between the two populations is also implied by the historical evidence and not all Britons were fated to become slaves. The West Saxon genealogy includes a king with a Celtic name and among the South Saxon rulers, Aethelwalh's name suggests he had some Celtic blood. With intermarriage taking place at this level in society, it is not possible to be certain that all those who were inhumed with Anglo-Saxon rites and with Anglo-Saxon artifacts were ethnically German. In a few centuries of the settlement of England, though there remained some distinct British communities, many of the Britons merged with the Anglo-Saxon population. As attitudes changed and 'Britons' were increasingly equated with 'serfs', there can have been few who wished by choice to remain distinguishable from the main body of society.

Population, Settlement and the Micro-economy

Current assessment of the population trend during the Anglo-Saxon period suggests that in the early centuries the number of people was declining. From the large population which archaeologists now ascribe to Roman Britain, the numbers fell as living standards deteriorated. Studies of the Romano–British population suggest that they had a high average life span. It was greater than the preceding prehistoric peoples and longer, too, than the early Anglo-Saxons.

The reason for the decline in population numbers is not clear. The historian Gildas makes much of the pestilence which he reports as striking England in the first half of the fifth century, but plagues are a common rhetorical device among moralising writers. Classical authors are silent; they record no widespread epidemics in the 200 years up till the Justinian bubonic plague in *c.* 540.

In South-East England the cemeteries give valuable evidence of the size and demographic structure of the population. The pattern of mortality was fairly typical of pre-industrial western societies. Fertility was high, but was balanced by a correspondingly high death rate. The population level was therefore likely to alter most rapidly with changes in mortality. Disease and health were probably the most important determinants of the level of population. The high birth rate and the risk of disease were particularly significant for women, who had a lower life expectancy than males. They faced the repeated hazards of childbirth and subsequent infection. This is graphically illustrated by the skeleton of a woman from Kingsworthy in Hampshire who had already had children, but died during labour of a further baby. The excavated bones from cemeteries do not correctly reflect the likely high infant mortality. Young infants were apparently not buried in the same cemeteries and with the same rites as adults or even children (Brothwell 1972). The most detailed evidence of the character of the population comes from two cemeteries, Bishopstone dating to the fifth and sixth centuries and Polhill which is seventh century. They give a very similar impression. The under representaion of infant burial is clear in both places. The greatest period of mortality indicated by the skeletons in the cemeteries was for young adults between 15 and 25 years. This was a hazardous period and at Polhill and Finglesham about half the population died before the age of 25, but those who survived this time in their lives often lived to a good age (Fig. 7.3b).

The smaller Anglo-Saxon population reduced pressure on the land which had been so extensively cultivated in the Roman period. Anglo-Saxon barrows on Farthing Down in Coulsdon, Surrey and on Breach Down, Kent where there was also an adjacent cemetery, overlie fields which had gone out of use. On some areas of agricultural land, scrub and woodland may have overgrown the fields which were no longer cultivated. It should be possible to trace any such changes through pollen analysis, which can be used to study the past vegetation of a local area. Few samples have been taken which cover this period in the South-East, though in silts taken from Gatcombe Withy Bed on the Isle of Wight the expected rise in arboreal (tree) pollen can be seen. The pollen diagram shows an increase in the pollen from ash trees. The spread of scrub and trees would have given rise to secondary woodland in which ash is an important component, but ash is not a prolific source of pollen and the rise in the collected pollen at this level is therefore particularly significant (Scaife 1982: Fig. 5).

The results more generally from Southern England do not show significant ecological changes in the period after the Roman withdrawal. The pollen diagrams, though, may not reveal the full details of change in the vegetation, for they may not distinguish between cereal and grass pollen. A change from an arable regime to a more pastoral regime therefore, would not be reflected. This might provide an explanation for a lack of increase in woodland, even though the population had fallen and demand for agricultural products decreased. Alternatively, Anglo-Saxon agriculture may have been less efficient than Roman methods and achieved a smaller harvest, while still cultivating large areas.

The Anglo-Saxons probably arrived in the South-East to discover fields which were either still being cultivated by the sub-Roman population or had very recently been abandoned. At Bishopstone, Sussex for example, there may have been a gap of some years before a late fifth-century settlement and cemeteries were established on the fields below a Romano–British farm which had been worked up to at least the end of the previous century. There is no suggestion of continuity, for the Saxons built their houses over many of the long-established features of the earlier farm enclosures. Buildings were constructed on the partially silted ditches and over trackways without regard.

Bishopstone is the most completely excavated site from the early Anglo-Saxon period in South-East England. In total 22 buildings were found, but a dense scatter of Anglo-Saxon pottery extended beyond the area excavated and suggested that in the whole settlement there could be up to 60 buildings (Fig. 7.5b). Not all of these buildings were occupied at any one time, and the settlement at Bishopstone was probably of hamlet or small village size. It stood on a chalk promontory surrounded on three sides by water and looked out over the English Channel (Fig. 7.5a). The most common type of building found was a rectangular hall with posts set in individual post-holes. The halls had two doorways in the middle of the long walls. Internally they may have been divided by partitions, though little trace of these remained in the eroded chalk. The larger halls conformed to a double-square plan, their length being twice as long as their breadth, which is typical of buildings of this period and may, in part, be derived from a Romano–British building tradition (Fig. 7.6a).

Three Sunken Featured Buildings (SFBs) or *Grubenhauser* were found during excavation (Fig. 7.6c). These have been discovered on many Anglo-Saxon sites and because they were small huts built with their floors below ground level, they gave rise to the view that the Anglo-Saxons lived in squalid

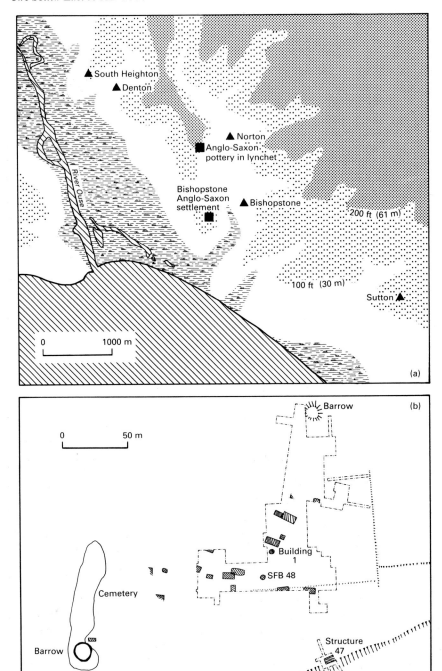

Figure 7.5 a. The Early Anglo-Saxon settlement at Bishopstone, East Sussex.
b. Excavations uncovered part of a hamlet standing on the lynchets of a Romano-British field system.

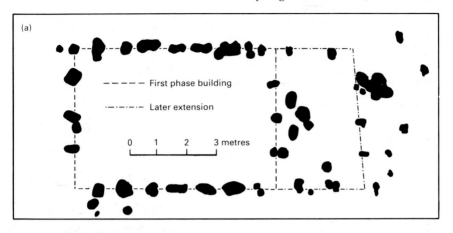

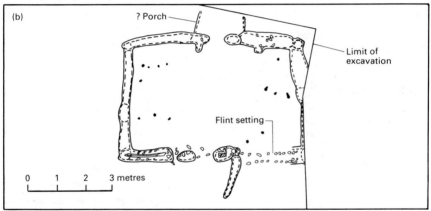

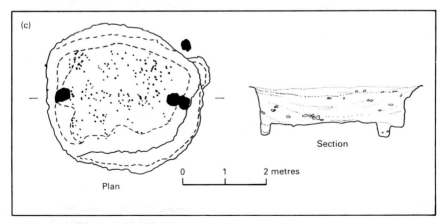

Figure 7.6 Early-Saxon buildings from Bishopstone, East Sussex (after Bell).
a. Plan of Building 1, a post-built hall.
b. Plan of Structure 47, a continuous trench building.
c. Plan and section of Structure 48, a Sunken Featured Building.

holes in the ground. It is now clear that SFBs were used for craft work and other specialized activities, but were not intended as dwelling quarters. Though none was found at Bishopstone, a frequent find in SFBs is that of clay loom weights, sometimes discovered in rows where they fell from the loom after the hut was abandoned. Textile work is likely to have been carried out in the Bishopstone SFBs as spindle whorls, the teeth from bone combs and a needle were all found in the huts.

One building of 'boat shape' was found partly overlying another structure. Buildings of this type are so called from their bowed long walls which are wider in the centre than at the ends. This building also had paired posts set a regular distance apart. In some of the post-holes evidence was found to suggest that the inner posts leant slightly inwards. These posts may well have held cruck blades and a cruck construction has now been argued for other Anglo-Saxon buildings (James *et al.* 1984).

Set some distance apart from the other structures, building 47 was originally interpreted as belonging to the Roman farm because it is quite unlike the other Anglo-Saxon buildings (Fig. 7.6b). It had a continuous trench for the wall posts instead of individual holes for posts. In one of the trenches was a charred timber which was interpreted as a sill beam. It is possible that the trench may have held close-set vertical posts like buildings of this plan found on other sites. This type of building is generally given a later date than the buildings with post-holes. It is significant that at Bishopstone this building was set at some distance from the others and was associated with a quite different assemblage of pottery. The vast majority of all Saxon pottery found at Bishopstone (84 per cent) had a hard sandy fabric. Smaller quantities of Fabrics 2 and 3, tempered with flint, were found. Yet around Building 47 two-thirds of the total numbers of sherds of Fabric 3 were found and a reasonably high proportion of Fabric 2.

It seems probable at Bishopstone that only part of the settlement was uncovered and this was of the earlier buildings. The different ceramic assemblage and the continuous trench method of construction used on building 47 argues that the later buildings are likely to have lain further south on the area of the unexplored hill slope. The movement of early Anglo-Saxon settlements within a small area has been commonly noted. As the timbers of the buildings were set in the ground they would have become rotten and it would have been necessary to rebuild them at regular intervals. The reconstruction could have been made in the same spot or might be placed in adjoining land and in time settlements could drift one way or another.

Bishopstone is one of an increasing number of settlement sites which have been found adjacent to a contemporary cemetery. This seems likely to have been the normal pattern in the pagan period. With this in mind, it is possible to reinterpret the finds from the excavations at Highdown, further west along the Sussex coast. Within the hillfort and near to the Saxon graves two buildings similar to the Bishopstone structures were found. One had paired posts and the other had posts set in a foundation trench. In the original report these were considered to be Iron Age and Roman, but it is now clear that they were Anglo-Saxon (Bell 1977). On very few occasions have sufficiently large areas been excavated to establish the relationship of the cemetery and settlement. Most finds of both types of sites have been made by accident and either the cemetery or the settlement has been found.

Excavations on the Roman villa at Eccles in Kent found both burial and traces of buildings in close association. The villa was occupied up till the end of the fourth century, but was then abandoned and the buildings allowed to fall down. Some time later, ditches were dug close to the villa through the debris from the collapsed buildings, and these ditches were still visible in *c.* 650 when graves were cut into the ditch silts. Burial continued through the eighth century with bodies carefully inhumed in an east west orientation and with very few grave goods. One of the burials was equipped with a buckle and plate with a fish decoration on the reverse. This apparently Christian symbol suggests that the burials were of people who converted to the newly introduced religion. The people lived in a settlement close by. Many stake and post-holes were found cut through the rubble from the Roman buildings and domestic refuse from the villa, but it is unfortunate that a large enough area was not opened up to find the full extent of the settlement (Detsicas 1975; 1976; 1977).

Eccles is one of a number of Roman sites in Kent which have now produced evidence for Anglo-Saxon occupation. Around the bath house of a villa or inn at Proverest Road in Orpington the cremations and inhumations of a mixed community of men, women and children were found. The Roman buildings had gone out of use in *c.* 370 and some time had elapsed before the first burials were made in *c.* 450 (Palmer 1984). On the opposite side of the River Cray and only 400 m away, a contemporary Anglo-Saxon sunken hut was found, which was part, no doubt, of a larger settlement. This SFB at St Mary Cray was cut into a second- to third-century ditch with unabraded pottery, suggesting that there was a Roman settlement nearby. On the villas of Lower Warbank in Keston and Franks in Farningham, further SFBs have been located, while at Darenth excavations on the villa found a timber building as well as sunken huts (Philp 1984).

The number of Anglo-Saxon settlements now found on Roman sites in this small area of West Kent is surprisingly large, but it reflects the concentration of recent excavations on Roman sites in this part of the county. Earlier excavations on villas probably missed any vestigial traces of Anglo-Saxon settlement in clearing the overburden to reveal the Roman layers. The Anglo-Saxon finds on a Roman villa at Wingham in the east of the county suggest that the pattern is typical of Kent more generally, though, the evidence must often have been missed when less systematic methods of digging were used.

Taking these finds from the Kent villas and the number of Anglo-Saxon cemeteries which lie in the areas of some of the best soils in the county, it is clear that the land of the Roman villa estates was taken over without any significant opposition from the British population. There is, however, no direct evidence for continuity from Roman villa to Anglo-Saxon farm. The final period of Roman activity cannot be dated accurately enough to show that, and indeed, at Eccles and Orpington there was a clear gap between the two phases of use. Though the villa buildings may not have been continuously occupied, it is hard to avoid the conclusion that some farmland must have remained in cultivation if only to feed the surviving population, albeit reduced in numbers. It is impossible to demonstrate continuous usage of land by archaeological means, but it is possible to point to areas where the field boundaries appear to have survived from the Roman period down to the nineteenth century. The preservation of boundaries must carry some weight in arguing for continued cultivation.

Blair has pointed to the area of Ashtead in Surrey as a possible example of a surviving field pattern. It lies a little to the south of a villa complex where, perhaps coincidentally, Early Anglo-Saxon material has been found. A Roman enclosure lies to the south of the fields and a Roman road passes close by. A pattern of lanes divides the land in six or perhaps nine irregular squares which are aligned on the Roman road. These squares are respected by both the parish boundary and Medieval property boundaries (Blair forthcoming). A second area of possible Roman land division lies north of the Roman town of Rochester, at Cliffe, where the rectilinear pattern of the fields appear to conform to a Roman standard of measurement (Nightingale 1952).

The reoccupation of the ruinous Roman sites by the Anglo-Saxon communities in Kent reflects a conscious attitude, for they not only took over the fertile land which had been cultivated, but also chose to occupy the very settlement sites of their Roman predecessors. There was a general and perhaps superstitious interest in the past on the part of the Anglo-Saxon who sought out pots, coins and other trinkets from Roman sites. Graves may contain collections of these finds which were carried in bags, and are thought to have been treated as amulets (Meaney 1981). This identification with the past occasionally led to the use of Roman cemeteries for burial. Outside Canterbury, in an extensive Roman burial ground at Martyrs' Field, finds indicate that the cemetery was in use by the Anglo-Saxons during the fifth and sixth centuries and in Deal, graves of the two peoples have also been found close together. The choice of villas for settlement sites was also part of the identification with the Roman past, but more specifically it also allowed them to represent themselves as the heirs and successors of the Romans and legitimate their present status. The choice of a place of settlement and burial was perhaps then not just a matter of selecting the best ground, but had ideological implications as well.

The Saxons in Surrey and Sussex do not appear to have used Roman sites in this way, though the lack of modern excavation on villas may conceal the extent of the later activity there. Only a small number of Roman villas in Surrey show any sign of Anglo-Saxon use. The proximity of the villa and cemetery at

Beddington may be significant and at Ashtead, Saxon pottery and a knife were found in a Roman bath house mentioned above. Very few Anglo-Saxon cemeteries or settlements can be shown to be significantly close to Roman villas. The notable exception is Highdown where the Romano-Britons and Saxons may have been buried alongside one another in a cemetery close to a possible villa.

Though the Anglo-Saxons may have followed Roman practices to the extent of settling on the same land and even on occasion in cultivating the same fields, the economy of their settlements was very different. The Roman settlements were engaged in the production of food for the market place, but the Anglo-Saxon farmers were not involved in trade except of a limited kind and were largely self-sufficient. The utilitarian items of the Anglo-Saxon farm, the pottery and clothing were made within the settlement and not brought in. Items which could not be obtained locally such as iron for tools would have had to be acquired by exchange. The elaborate jewellery and weaponry found in the burials were the product of specialist workshops and must have been acquired from outside the settlements, but these were not necessarily bought, but may have been received through gift exchange or donation. Certain very elaborate pots may also have been made in workshops. Cremation vessels decorated with zoomorphic bosses have been discovered at Alfriston and Highdown in Sussex, Northfleet in Kent, London and Mucking in Essex on the Thames estuary and appear to be the product of a single centre (Myres 1978: 69, 78). There is little evidence otherwise for specialist settlements producing particular commodities which could be traded within a market economy. The level of economic activity at the micro level of the settlement was very low indeed.

Anglo-Saxon society may be visualized as a typical subsistence peasant society. The unit of production and land holding was the family. Land was assessed in hides, though these were not consistent areas of land. Bede implies that the hide was the land held by one free family. He does not define the character of this family, but it seems likely that it was a nuclear family comprising just the parents, grandparents and children. They were assisted in working the land by their dependents, the half-free *laets* and serfs. The hide was the land which could be cultivated by one plough team. The equivalent term for the hide, used only in Kent, was the sulung which is derived from *sulh*, plough. Within the family the land was cultivated, harvested and consumed, but the family was related to a wider circle of kindred who probably lived on adjoining farms and on certain occasions the kindred may have acted together. For most purposes then, the family was the unit of production and consumption and were the owners of the means of production. Economic interaction with similar groups was very limited because each settlement was to a large degree autarchic. In sum, society consisted of a large number of identical units of production with a barely developed settlement hierarchy (Fig. 7.7).

The settlement at Bishopstone provides the most detailed evidence for the economy practised by Anglo-Saxon settlements. This hamlet or small village probably consisted of a number of households whose buildings were separated from one another by fenced enclosures. Traces of some of the fence lines were detected during the excavation, but such a pattern is much more clearly indicated in the settlement at Chalton in Hampshire. There, the fences enclosed curtilages containing a number of buildings, presumably representing farm houses and their outbuildings (Addyman and Leigh 1973).

Bishopstone was situated in a suitable position to get access to the resources of the surrounding land and the sea. Some indication of the extent of the land cultivated by the settlement is given by the discovery of pottery identical to the material from the site in a ploughed-out lynchet 1 km from the settlement (Allen 1982 and pers. comm.) (Fig. 7.5a). This pottery was probably deposited on the fields with manure carried out from Bishopstone and must indicate the minimum extent of land under cultivation. The only evidence of the crops grown is from three impressions of barley found in sherds of Anglo-Saxon pottery. A number of carbonized seeds were found around a hearth and had been gathered along with the cereal crops during harvesting from the weeds growing in the fields. Among the bones from the site, sheep bones predominate and represent 39 per cent of the total. Cattle, though less numerous forming 25 per cent, would have had the greater meat weight. A smaller number of pig bones were found and horse, red and roe deer, goose and fowl were also present. Pig and deer bones, though not very common, suggest access to the resources of woodland. Domestic animals would have fed within the village as well as in the fields. Land snails, which are good indicators of environment, show that the area between the buildings was closely grazed grassland. The resources of the sea were also exploited by the villagers. Marine molluscs were very common finds and the bones of conger eel and whiting were also discovered.

The economy of Bishopstone was clearly very eclectic, utilizing a large range of resources, some of which were in the immediate vicinity and others at greater distance. Analysis of the clay used in the pottery indicated that the nearest source for the raw material occurred north of the Downs, in the Weald. The more limited faunal assemblage from the sunken hut at St Mary Cray gives a similar impression of the use of a variety of environments and contrasts with the bones from the Roman layers on the site, which are typical of a simple, pastoral or mixed regime. This rather sparse archaeological record of the microeconomy can be supplemented from charters of a slightly later date. These record the transfer of land, but occasionally the charters make clear that not only land, but all the appurtenant rights which go with the land are granted too. A late-eighth-century charter to found a monastery at Farnham in Surrey mentions the pieces of land 'with everything belonging to them, fields, woods, meadows, pastures, fisheries, rivers and springs' (Sawyer 1968: no. 235).

Organisation of the Kingdoms

By the end of the fifth century or the beginning of the sixth, Kent had emerged as a stable Anglo-Saxon kingdom. It occupied an area smaller than the present-day county and was bounded by natural frontiers. On the west it extended as far as the River Medway, on the south as far as the forest of the Weald and the Romney Marsh, and on the other two sides it faced the sea. At the point at which Watling Street, the Roman road from London crossed the Medway and entered the kingdom there is a cemetery of a well-armed community and another cemetery stands beside the Pilgrims' Way track, a little to the south guarding the approach. Sussex, separated from Kent by the Weald and settled by Saxons rather than the mainly Jutish settlers of Kent, developed as a distinct kingdom. It fronted on to the West Saxon kingdom on the west. Near to the present county boundary, between Sussex and Hampshire, is the place-name Marden, meaning the 'boundary down' and recalling the frontier between the kingdoms.

A seventh-century tribute list, the Tribal Hidage compiled for the Mercian kingdom, lists the early tribal groupings of Southern England. The various peoples named may be divided into three categories according to size. The kingdoms of Sussex with 7,000 hides and Kent with 15,000 hides are among the middle rank of peoples, but Surrey is not mentioned by name. Somewhere in South-East England lay the two peoples called the *Noxgaga* (5,000 hides) and *Ohtgaga* (2,000 hides). Nothing more is known of these peoples, but together they too make up a medium-sized unit which must have lain in Surrey and perhaps eastern Berkshire. A charter of the late seventh century was issued by a sub-king of a province of Surrey which was then under the domination of the Mercians. The name Surrey, *Suthrige*, means 'the southern region' which can only imply it was part of a larger block of land lying to the north. This places Surrey as part of the Middle Saxon kingdom recorded in the county name of Middlesex. Remarkably, old rights of the people of the Middle Saxon kingdom appear to have survived in the privileges of the men of London in the twelfth century. They claimed to have the right to hunt over an area bounded by the south and west borders of Surrey, the River Cray in Kent and the Chilterns. West Kent would have therefore lain within the lands of the *Suthrige*. The land of the Middle Saxons was disputed between the larger kingdoms of the East Saxons, Mercians and the West Saxons in the seventh century and the land partitioned between them.

The kingdoms of Kent and Sussex were both divided at times into two smaller sub-kingdoms. Ruling over these parts were separate kings, though neither of the kingdoms was partitioned in a permanent fashion and one king was always senior to the other. The evidence for the division of the kingdoms is later than the Pagan Anglo-Saxon period, but it is so common in the succeeding two centuries that it must have already been well established. The two dioceses of Rochester and Canterbury within Kent formed in the early years of the seventh century are particularly interesting because the pattern elsewhere was for one diocese per kingdom. The ecclesiastical division of Kent probably corresponded to the two existing sub-kingdoms. In the seventh century Kent was certainly divided between one king in the east and a junior king in the west of the county whose particular responsibility may have been to protect the frontier with Surrey. The kings were closely related, either a father and his son or two brothers. Of the nine kings between Æthelberht I and Æthelberht II who died in the mid-eighth century, all but two can be shown to have ruled jointly for at least part of their reign (Yorke 1983).

The kingship in Sussex may have been similarly divided between two branches of the royal family. Some of the kings had names beginning with *Os-* and others use the element *Aethel-* for their names. Anglo-Saxon families often took alliterative names with a common root so that two separate groups are suggested here. Traces of the two parts of the kingdom may be found much later in Domesday Book which gives an equal value in hides to the two halves of the county divided along the line of the River Adur. The division may even correspond in general terms with the two counties of East and West Sussex which are perpetuated today.

Though poorly recorded, there were also in South-East England minor groups living in distinct territories within the larger kingdoms. The identity of these groups was gradually submerged as they fell under the direct control of the kingdoms. They are often known only from incidental references and place names. To the north-west of Surrey was the province of the *Sunningas* who are remembered in the places-names Sonning and Sunninghill, now in Berkshire. Some of the place-names in eastern Berkshire link this region with Surrey and suggest that that kingdom once stretched farther westwards. When Frithu-wold, the sub-king of Surrey, granted land which ran 'as far as the boundary of the next province which is called Sonning' he did not seem to imply that the province was outside his kingdom (Sawyer 1988: no. 1165). On the west side of Sussex was another group. Bede records that the South Saxons briefly held control of the *Meanware* province, now the Meon valley in Hampshire. On the opposite side of the kingdom were the *Hæstingas* who were finally incorporated into Sussex. They gave their name not only to Hastings, but also to Hastingleigh in Kent and perhaps to Hastingford in north-east Sussex. Their remote situation helped them to retain their identity as late as the eleventh century, when it is recorded that the *Hæstingas* were harried by the Danes.

It is significant that the *Sunningas*, the people of *Meanware* and the *Hæstingas* all lay on the periphery of kingdoms. This position may have helped them keep their unity for a little longer than other groups. The kingdoms of Anglo-Saxon England were not composed of homogeneous groups of people, but were an amalgam of many different peoples who had been mixed up on the Continent before the migration. In England, when they settled they interbred with the existing Romano-British population. The group identity of these peoples would have needed to be suppressed to emphasize the internal unity of the kingdoms. Kent may have emerged at an early date because ethnically and culturally the people were more dissimilar to the surrounding Anglo-Saxons than they were to each other. Surrey and Sussex, on the other hand, were part of a larger Saxon 'cultural province' which stretched across the remainder of Central Southern and South-East England. The problem for the emerging kingdoms in the sixth century was to create an internal cohesion and a sense of identity, and conceal the heterogeneity of the peoples. The foundation myths of the kingdoms in the Anglo-Saxon Chronicle were part of this process. They were part of an ideology which gave identity and explained in heroic terms the origin of kingdoms.

The administration and boundaries of the early Anglo-Saxon kingdoms are not well understood. Incidental references, place names and the distribution of cemeteries suggest that every kingdom was divided internally into a number of districts, each based on a royal centre which controlled the surrounding area. In Kent the royal centres can be identified because they often had names which end in the archaic Old English *gē*, district. Eastry (*Easterge*) was the centre for the eastern district and Wester Linton near Maidstone may have been the corresponding centre on the west side of the kingdom. Two other capitals are named after rivers: Lyminge, the Limen district and Sturry, the Stour district. There were probably other important centres at Milton, Faversham and perhaps Wye. The king travelled between these *villae regales*, staying at each one for a few days and administering the surrounding area. One of the duties of the district was to provide a food rent to sustain the king and his household.

Clustered around many of these district capitals were rich graveyards in which members of the aristocracy residing in the centres were buried. Around Eastry there were no less than four cemeteries. Though most of these have not been properly investigated, it is clear that the cemetery at Updown to the south of Eastry, a site now protected by law, was particularly wealthy. In 1976 a number of burials was excavated and twelve graves with penannular ditches were found, but aerial photographs of the cemetery show other clusters of graves with further ditches (Plate 7.1). Around Lyminge two cemeteries have been identified and in the vicinity of Milton five cemeteries or groups of burials are known. The cemetery at Faversham lies in the significantly named King's Field and is among the richest in Kent.

The royal centres were also important in maintaining the control exercised by the king of trade reaching the kingdom. This was particularly important for Kent as a major trading kingdom. The position of some of the vills seems especially relevant for this. Sturry lay immediately opposite, on the other side of the Stour estuary from Fordwich, which became an important trading port by the middle of the Anglo-Saxon period. It may have been operating as such at an earlier date or could have replaced Sturry as a port. Both Milton and Faversham are also known as later ports and there is little doubt that they served this function in the pagan period too. Eastry lay on an inlet which may have given access to boats, but its importance must also have derived mostly from its position astride the Roman road to Dover. Sturry likewise stood on the road to Reculver, and Faversham and Milton lay just a little to the side of Watling Street.

By their position and from their administrative role, the *villae regales* dominated and controlled the surrounding districts. The districts were large areas of land which resembled the later divisions of Kent called lathes. It is very likely that the earlier districts of Kent developed directly into the later lathes. The lathes are matched in Sussex and Surrey by similar divisions. Though there is very little evidence for the antiquity of the division in these other two kingdoms, an early origin seems quite possible. The divisions of Sussex are called in Domesday Book rapes, and reference is made there to land which is described as *foris rapum* or 'outside the rape'. The expression recurs in later Medieval documents where it is called *forraēpe* land. It is also used in a charter granting land in Surrey in 947 (Jolliffe 1933: 83–4). The implication is that there were districts called rapes in the Anglo-Saxon period and that they were found in both Sussex and Surrey. In contrast to the position in Kent, it is not possible to identify with any certainty the capital of most of these districts, although there are several possible candidates. In Sussex it is also not very certain where the boundaries of these rapes lay, or even how many there were. In Surrey the boundaries of four districts have been identified and they resemble in size and shape the lathes of Kent (Blair forthcoming).

Macro-economics

The economy of the Anglo-Saxon settlements suggests that there was a low level of trade activity in the kingdoms of the South-East. The evidence from the cemeteries shows, on the other hand, a continuing flow of prestige goods and raw materials necessary to manufacture jewellery, which came from the Continent. This discrepancy between the micro and macro levels of the economy may not be contradictory for it would be wrong to assume that all foreign imports were items of trade. Some may just as likely have been bride wealth payments and gifts given to promote friendship. But these extra-commercial transactions cannot explain the sheer number of imported goods, for the graves of Kent in particular are full of luxury items.

The quality of these imports is symptomatic of the nature of trade between England and the Continent. The items that were crossing the Channel were not imported for general consumption, but for elite use. In the first half of the sixth century high-quality jewellery was traded in both directions across the sea. The importation of Frankish jewellery declined in the second half, and it is not possible to know from the inadequately excavated French cemeteries how much metalwork continued to be exported abroad. Nor is it possible to be certain of many of the other types of traded goods. These may have been more mundane items, perhaps the traditional exports from Britain of iron, slaves, corn and hunting dogs which have left no identifiable trace in the archaeological record. They are all items which could be collected from rural communities and assembled for export and which required no specialized processing.

The wealth of the Kentish cemeteries has alerted archaeologists to the importance of trade in the kingdom. Kent was naturally well situated to participate in trade with the Continent, but it appears to have been so successful in Continental commerce that it quickly established a monopoly from the early sixth century onwards and excluded the other emerging South and Middle Saxon kingdoms. The Frankish connection with Kent, implied by the small-scale immigration of aristocrats in the sixth century, was consolidated and on the basis of the relationship trade connections were established leading to the importation of Frankish metalwork. The marriage of Aethelberht, the king of Kent to the daughter of the Neustrian king, Charibert, recognized the importance of the link between the two kingdoms and at the same time strengthened it. The trade by Kent was not only with the Frankish territories but also with Frisia and lands further east, including Scandinavia. Contact with Provence is attested in a hoard of gold coins found at St Martins, Canterbury which includes issues from there. Indirectly Kent also received goods from the Mediterranean, Byzantium and as far afield as the Red Sea. This does not suggest immediate contact with these distant sources, but down-the-line exchange seems more likely, by which the goods were passed from their source through a series of middlemen to the eventual recipient.

In turn Kent too acted as a staging post in the transmission of goods through to other kingdoms in England. Whether by trade or by gift, goods were dispersed across southern England. The Thames Valley received relatively large quantities of goods conveyed from Kent. Prestigious bronze Coptic bowls were passed on to be buried in the 'princely' graves at Cuddesdon and Taplow, and a further bowl was placed in the ship burial at Sutton Hoo. Kent acted as a manufacturing centre as well, converting the imported gold and precious stones into jewellery and releasing them to the other kingdoms. The character of the apportionment of goods from Kent is evident from the distribution of the prestigious disc brooches. Avent's type 2.1 is concentrated in east and southeast Kent and types 3.2 and 5 in the west, suggesting perhaps two centres of production within the kingdom. The fall-off curve in numbers of brooches with increasing distance from their source shows however, that the dispersal was very limited outside their kingdom of manufacture (Arnold 1980: 99). Kent, though acting as a channel through which goods were introduced into England, absorbed most of the imports within the kingdom itself.

Some of the ports through which trade with the Continent may have arrived have already been discussed. The Wantsum Channel between Thanet and mainland Kent formed a fine natural haven for shipping. Though no site of a trading station has been found on the Wantsum, it is possible to point to Sarre as one of the major ports. Certainly it was used as a port in the eighth century, when tolls charged on shipping there and at Fordwich were remitted by the king of Kent. At Sarre is a large cemetery with inhumations accompanied by imported pottery, Merovingian and Byzantine coins. The burials include a very high proportion of well-armed males with a large number of swords which exceeds even the number commonly found in aristocratic cemeteries, and several graves with scales. These were apparently the officials who guarded and administered the port, and merchants trading there. Sarre may be compared with the similar community represented by a cemetery at Buckland above Dover. Both in the cemetery and down in Dover itself imported wheel-thrown pottery has been found. The pottery bottles appear to have served as containers for wine or oil which was imported from Northern France. Again the trade appears to have been in a prestige commodity and it is interesting to note that the pottery vessels buried in graves often are very worn, as if they have been used for a long period of time, no doubt serving as a status symbol themselves. Single bottles have also been found on the coast at Folkestone and at Lympne, showing limited trade at these places too.

The ports of trade were closely supervised by royal officials. Heavily armed communities at Buckland and Sarre were present to enforce royal control and later documentary evidence clearly shows the involvement of kings in the exercise of trade. It was important for the head of the kingdom to regulate the flow and distribution of the items of trade because they were symbols of status and power. Possession of these material goods was closely related to social position, as has already been discussed. The custom of burial, however, required that many of these appurtenances of rank were disposed of with the deceased and not passed on to his heirs. A continuing demand was set up, for each new generation had to acquire once again the goods that were appropriate to their status. The king in control of the distribution of the products of trade created a dependency on his munificence. It was an important part of the king's role that he should hand out gifts to his followers, be seen as a generous giver and not hoard them himself. The principle of reciprocity in social relations among the Anglo-Saxons required that those who received gifts should give service in return. The roles of the king and his followers were articulated through the medium of the giving of the products of trade. Likewise, external relationships between kingdoms could be expressed in the granting of gifts (Fig. 7.7).

The unanswered question in this discussion of Kentish society and macro-economy is what goods were traded in return for the high-status products arriving at the ports? This is the question posed at the beginning of this section for it has an important bearing on the nature of social relations in Kent. If the exports from Kent comprised primarily agrarian products, then we must

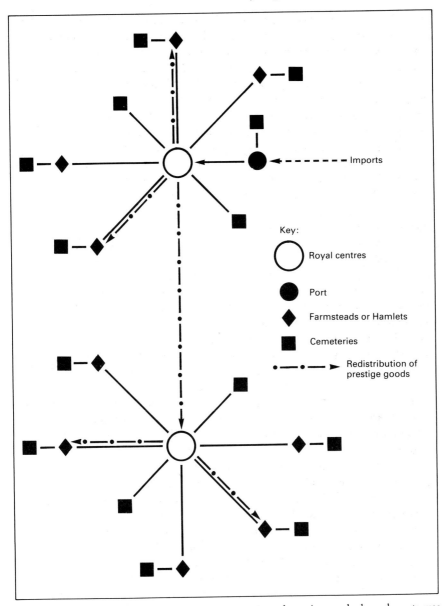

Figure 7.7 Early Anglo-Saxon society. The importation of prestige goods through ports was under strict royal control. Goods were then redistributed to other kingdoms or lower-order settlements in the same kingdom, enhancing the status of the king and creating a debt by the recipient.

visualize a complex society. To extract agrarian goods implies that the rural settlements were able to grow a surplus product and argues for a social order in which the elite can mobilize this surplus for their own use and concentrate

281

them at a port ready for export. Such a society is on the road towards a full-scale market economy with a high level of internal trade, some communities producing specialist crops for exchange, and urban settlement with permanent markets. If, however, the exports from Kent were like the imports, also of prestige goods, then the nature of trade and organization within Kent were quite different. Essentially such a trade would involve the elites on either side of the Channel exchanging status symbols and need have no profound implications for the organization of the rest of society.

Burial and Belief

For no other period in British archaeology have so many graves been excavated, and few other cultures have left such evident remains of the complexity of belief connected with the rites of death. The Early Anglo-Saxon period provides copious evidence for burial and belief, but the quantity of graves excavated has not always been matched by the quality of the excavation and the methods of recording. Only in the more recent excavations have the finer aspects of the burial rite become apparent.

The Germanic settlers brought with them the practice of cremation burial, which was the established rite in the Continental homelands. In Britain the native custom was inhumation burial, which had been growing in popularity since the third century. North of the Thames the Anglo-Saxons continued to dispose of their dead through cremation, but in the South-East, though cremation was used throughout the fifth, sixth and seventh centuries, the Roman custom of the inhumation burial was gradually adopted. Cremation burial with the ashes interred in an urn is known from the areas of early settlement, particularly in Kent at Howletts, Westbere and Hollingbourne and in Surrey at Beddingham and Ewell, but also now from some of the later cemeteries such as Apple Down in West Sussex too. Ploughing and nineteenth-century methods of excavation have probably destroyed the evidence of other cremation cemeteries. The two rites were used alongside one another in all but the earliest pagan burial grounds. Excavations at Appledown have found the two rites used for adjoining burials, perhaps even by members of the same family (Plate 7.2). In a further grave there, evidence for the continued late Romano-British custom of inhumation with a pot and a single coin to pay the ferryman across the River Styx was found in a grave, possibly of a descendant of the enserfed population.

The rites of burial used may have been dependent on both individual preference and local custom, for the cemeteries of the South-East display considerable variation in their material remains, and the rituals accompanying

Plate 7.1   Graves and penannular ditches of an Anglo-Saxon cemetery at Updown, near Eastry in Kent. The site lies close to a Roman road which ran more or less on the line of the modern road. (Photograph: Cambridge University Collection: copyright reserved.)

Plate 7.2 The Anglo-Saxon burial site at Appledown, Marden, West Sussex. Both cremation and inhumation burials have been discovered here. The inhumations in the photograph cut, and therefore are later than, the cremation burial with its encircling ditch.
(Photograph: Alec Down, Chichester Excavation Unit.)

the disposal of the dead which have left no physical remains may have been even more diverse. Barrow burial, for example is confined in Kent mainly to the eastern part of the county where a large number of barrow cemeteries are known from Breach Downs in Barham, Updown (Plate 7.1), Chartham Downs and Wye to list a few. Some barrow cemeteries are recorded from West Kent but the proportion is smaller. In Sussex, barrow cemeteries predominantly cluster around the River Ouse. Other customs are displayed in only a few cemeteries, such as the use of charcoal in burials noted in twenty graves at Riseley, Horton Kirby where yet other burials were surrounded with large flints to form cists, and at Bourne Park, Kent. Some of the variation in funerary custom may be due to social status rather than religious belief. Wooden coffins, where they have been noted, are found in the richer graves, and barrows are often found over the more wealthy burials within a cemetery.

Towards the end of the sixth century the rites of inhumation changed and burial structures became more common. At the same time in Southern England, outside the wealthy area of East Kent the quality and quantity of jewellery buried in female graves declined. This second development may not reflect religious rite, but the impoverishment of the South-East at the expense of the kingdom of Kent or the change in dress fashions which no longer required metal brooch fasteners. The decline in grave goods does foreshadow the increasing influence of Christianity in the seventh century, which discouraged the burial of artifacts. Barrow burial and burial structures, which are found with increasing frequency from the late sixth century, may have been employed as an alternative means of indicating status in the stead of grave goods, though this cannot have been true in East Kent where they augmented personal artifacts rather than replaced them. The above-ground markers were a more visible and ostentatious marker of past social position than goods placed with their bearer beneath the soil.

Anglo-Saxon barrows had the simple form of a penannular gully surrounding a circular or sub-rectangular mound constructed from the soil scooped out of the ditch. At the break in the encircling ditch a marker post was often placed. At St Peters, Thanet evidence was found in one gully suggesting that it had once held a close-set stake fence, while at Ozengell in Ramsgate, traces of a wickerwork fence were found in the similar ditches. Barrow burials often occur in clusters towards the edges of the cemetery and at Polhill, Dunton Green they are situated at the highest point at which burials were made. A funerary hut of sixteen post-holes was found at Polhill close to the barrows. A more common type of cemetery building is the four-post structure which has been found in other graveyards in close association with barrows and also with flat grave inhumations. At St Peters, where the traces of the post-pipes have survived, one building appears to have been a wooden tent-like structure which covered the grave. Some of the recorded four-post structures did not stand over burials but to one side, and these may have been mortuary houses or platforms for exposing the dead.

Not all barrows used for Anglo-Saxon burial were newly raised. In all the counties of the South-East examples of inhumation in existing Bronze Age barrows are recorded. The recognition of the function and the re-use of prehistoric barrows argues that the Anglo-Saxons wished to place themselves in a direct relationship to the people of the past to the extent of being buried alongside them. At Bishopstone this may have been particularly significant, for the Anglo-Saxon settlement was built over the traces of the Roman farmstead. A prehistoric barrow formed the focus of the Anglo-Saxon cemetery, and though at the time of its excavation it was ploughed almost flat, it may formerly have contained a secondary burial. The flat graves in the cemetery clustered round the barrow and extended out to the north. In the Bishopstone cemetery, as in many others, a number of the graves contained Roman artifacts, which though often broken and in a fragmentary state, seem to have had a particular fascination for the Anglo-Saxons. Openwork objects seem to have been particularly favoured by the collectors of antiques for these could be strung together and suspended from the waist, and they may have had an amuletic use (Meaney 1981).

The barrows and mortuary buildings are but some of the types of above-ground structures, for recent excavations have recorded an increasing number of these, particularly in East Kent and also elsewhere (Hogarth 1973). They have been consistently found in cemeteries dating from the end of the pagan period, but if the construction of more elaborate funerary structures might imply the strength of religion at this period, other evidence could suggest the contrary. Within seventh-century cemeteries, and particularly in the proto-Christian cemeteries of the late seventh and early eighth centuries, there is a decline overall in grave-goods, but an increase in the provision of pagan amulets. Ritual practices such as the decapitation and stoning of corpses increases, which has been interpreted as symptomatic of uncertainty of the efficacy of the new religion of Christianity. Burials display an ambivalence about their affiliations and include symbols of both pagan cults and Christianity and pagan practices continued for some centuries, for the church authorities issued warnings and threats against them.

Chapter 8

The Middle and Late Anglo-Saxon Periods, 650–1000 AD

The politics of the period from the late sixth century are complicated by a series of wars between the English kingdoms south of the Humber. In Southern England no single kingdom was sufficiently strong to maintain sovereignty over the others for any length of time. It is possible that this period of sporadic warfare began even earlier and that the inadequate historical sources do not mention it. The kingdoms of the South-East were normally engaged in warfare not with each other, but against the larger kingdoms of Wessex and more frequently with Mercia, which came to dominate Southern England. Mercia came into conflict with the small but wealthy kingdom of Kent, for both had territorial ambitions in Surrey, part of the Middle Saxon kingdom. From at least 568 when Wessex defeated Æthelberht, king of Kent and drove him back, Surrey was disputed between Kent, Wessex and Mercia.

The dominance of Wessex in the south was brief, for after 584 Caewlin, the Wessex king, won no further victories and Bede records Kent's Æthelberht as having lordship over the area south of the Humber, though the nature of this power is not clear. Æthelberht certainly appears to have been the overlord of the East Saxon kingdom, which was ruled in the early seventh century by his nephew, Saberht. Later on in the century the roles were reversed, and Kent came under East Saxon domination. The East Saxon kingdom considerably extended the area under its lordship during the course of the seventh century. The kingdom itself consisted of lands north of the Thames in Essex and eastern Hertfordshire, but Middlesex, London, and possibly Surrey were brought under its control and by c. 688 Kent had also been conquered. The East Saxons were in turn eclipsed by the rising power of the Mercian kingdom in Southern England and Kent fell under Mercian domination and remained so sporadically, though retaining its own kings till 756 (Yorke 1985).

The following year, Offa came to the Mercian throne and began a prolonged campaign, which decisively subdued the kingdoms of the South-East. So effective was this that after 772 he is referred to in charters as *Rex Anglorum*, king of the English. He had already completed the subjugation of the South Saxon kingdoms and reduced their kings to mere *Duces*, and in 771 also conquered the *Hæstingas* at the eastern end of Sussex. The Kentish kingdom continued to oppose control by outside powers and at the battle of Otford in 776 defeated the Mercians, who could not regain control of the kingdom for ten years. Only then was Kent finally brought under Mercian rule.

These territorial disputes left a number of defensive linear earthworks, particularly in the contended territory of Surrey. Four lengths of banks and ditches have been recognized and these can be divided into two groups. The first pair both run parallel to a major river and appear to have served as a secondary defence against any invader who should cross their waters. They are also both mentioned as bounds in Anglo-Saxon charters, which allow them to be attributed to this period with greater certainty. The *Fullingadic* mentioned in a document of AD 672–4 has been identified with a line of ditches on St George's Hill, Walton and an intermittent bank running across Wisley and Ockham commons (Fig. 8.1a). The earthwork runs close to the River Wey from just above its confluence with the Thames for a distance of about 5 km or more. It was already described as an 'old ditch' in the late seventh century and may date back to the early part of that or the previous century (Blair forthcoming). Though used as a boundary mark, it seems improbable that this earthwork had been built only as a temporary division, for the River Wey itself would have served as a boundary equally as well. It is likely its primary purpose was as a defence.

The *Fullingadic* stands in a similar position to a second bank and ditch which lies on the eastern side of the Cray Valley in Kent near Bexley, and in 814 was appropriately called the *Faestendic* or 'strong dyke' (Fig. 8.1b). About 2 km from the river, it faces towards Surrey and must have been erected by the kingdom of Kent as a defensive line against armies coming from the west. Like the Wey ditch, it runs just below the crest of the hill and follows the contours of the land to enclose the head of a valley. Much reduced now by soil movement, and with its full length obliterated by agriculture on the north and south sides of the wood in which it is preserved, this was a major earthwork. Even in its present form it runs for about 3 km. It lies to the south of Watling Street and may have been part of a larger defensive scheme to prevent movement along that Roman road into Kent (Hogg 1934).

The second group of linear earthworks act as defensive barriers at roads. A ditch and bank on the boundary between the parishes of Epsom, Ashtead, Walton-on-the-Hill and Headley in Surrey is undated by excavation, but must pre-date the parish boundary which runs along it (Fig. 8.1d). Originally at least 3 m high and 10 m wide and running for 2 km, it is more substantial than the usual bank built to mark a boundary between parishes and, significantly, it lies across the line of the Roman road of Stane Street and also across Langley Bottom Road which was certainly used in the Medieval period, when it was called the Portway, and perhaps before (Nail 1965). It is not clear, though, how this earthwork, which appears to have served to block or control access along these roads, fits into the political events of the Anglo-Saxon period.

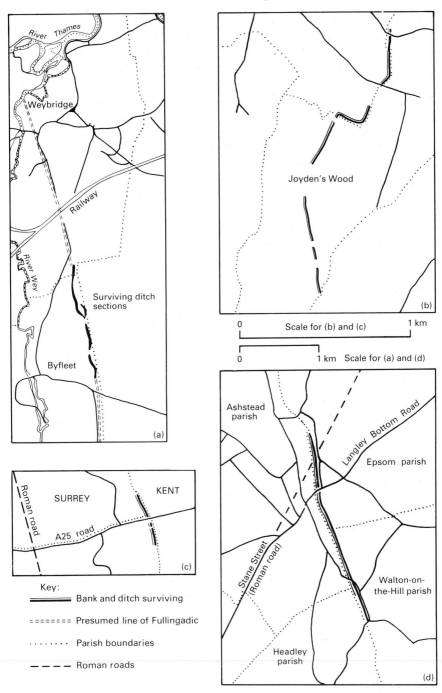

Figure 8.1 Linear earthworks.
a. *Fullingadic* near Byfleet, Surrey (after Blair (forthcoming))
b. *Faestendic* near Bexley, Kent (after Hogg 1934)
c. Bank and ditch near Westerham on the Surrey–Kent border (after Clarke 1960).
d. Bank and ditch near Ashstead, Surrey (after Nail 1965).

An even larger bank and ditch lies across the old trackway which, for the most part, ran along the Greensand ridge (Fig. 8.1c). The route now is more or less followed by the present A25 road. This earthwork, which is 300 m long, cuts the trackway at a point where it runs through a valley between two hill slopes. The earthwork crosses the small valley near Westerham and controls movement along the trackway from the west. It lies exactly on the present county boundary between Surrey and Kent. Like the *Faestendic* this earthwork must have been built by the people of Kent as a defensive measure against invasion from the Surrey direction by the hostile kingdoms of Mercia and Wessex (Clarke 1960).

The concentration of linear earthworks in Surrey and Western Kent is notable (Fig. 8.2). In neither Eastern Kent nor Sussex have any traces of defensive banks and ditches of this period been found. Only in East Hampshire, where there is a confusing series of earthworks known as the Froxfield dykes, might there have been a defence for the South Saxon kingdom against Wessex. But it has been noted that the Froxfield dykes are of uncertain date, have an unknown role, and it is not even clear that all the earthworks belong to a single group. The implications of those banks and ditches in Kent and Surrey that do come from this period are particularly interesting, for they suggest that the Anglo-Saxon kings could mobilize a labour force to carry out large communal works. Though the business of fighting was limited to the upper echelons of Anglo-Saxon society, a larger number of people must have been involved in the physical work of constructing such defences. This implies a degree of centralized power and organization which is not otherwise apparent from the archaeological record.

Middle Anglo-Saxon Rural Settlements and Their Economy

Any estimate of the population of South-East England during the Middle and Late Anglo-Saxon period must be made by starting from the figures given in Domesday Book and working backwards. This eleventh-century survey lists a population of 10,400 in Sussex, 12,200 in Kent and only 4,400 in Surrey, though this last figure seems unduly low. To convert the enumerated figures into a total population it is necessary to use a multiplier which will take account of the numbers within a family. A factor of four or five is generally used. Taking the higher figure would produce a population for the South-East of 135,000. To place this number in context it may be calculated that this would have allowed each individual to have held an area of 8 ha (20 acres) of land.

Estimates such as these give some idea of the level of exploitation and settlement at the end of the period in question. Though much of the area would have been dense woodland, unreclaimed marshland or unattractive, infertile soil, there was no shortage of land. The increase in population between 650 and 1000 can only be guessed at. Bede, writing in the early eighth century, says that there were 7,000 families in the kingdom of the South Saxons. The figure may not be taken too literally, for this round number was a standard size for a medium-sized kingdom and may have been simply a symbolic figure, for it was also the area of land given to Beowulf (Welch 1983: 261). The clearest evidence for the growth of population is the remarkable expansion of settlement which occurred during these centuries. Few archaeologists have been prepared to follow a recent suggestion that the land in the seventh century was exploited almost as completely as it was in the eleventh. On the contrary, there was a very apparent intensification of land usage.

The colonization of the countryside is most evident in the growth of settlement in the Weald. This large block of woodland lay across the centre of all three counties in South-East England. No Early Anglo-Saxon remains have been found in the area except at the peripheries, but by the eleventh century the Weald was thoroughly, though sparsely, settled. The Weald has been envisaged as a frontier zone comparable to the Middle West of the United States in the nineteenth century. Decade by decade, the frontier of settlement, it is imagined, moved inwards away from the surrounding older settled districts towards the centre of the Weald (Brandon 1978).

This diffusionist view of settlement is contradicted by the evidence of place-names which show that at an early date Anglo-Saxons occupied areas at the very centre of the Weald. It is more likely that the expansion of Middle and Late Anglo-Saxon settlement was not, for the most part, a physical movement into entirely new territory. It involved an increasing density of population and an infilling of the gaps between settlements. It has been suggested above that the subsistence strategy of the Early Anglo-Saxons involved the extensive use of a very wide area which had access to a range of resources. But as the area exploited became more densely populated, it was necessary to define the rights of the users of the land and record boundaries more precisely. The first Anglo-Saxon charters were typically vague in their descriptions of land granted. A charter of Hlothhere, king of Kent, refers just to land in Thanet, marked 'by the well known bounds indicated by me and my reeves' (Sawyer 1968: no. 8). One may doubt if in fact these bounds were defined with any precision at all.

The rights of use of commonland during this phase were also very unspecific. The commons were open to use by the people of a large area. The occupants of the Lympne district of Kent held an area of common woodland called the *Limen weara walde* in the Weald and it is known that there were similar areas belonging to the people of the Canterbury, Rochester and Wye districts. Altogether the land divisions of the Kingdom of Kent, the lathes, divided up the Weald into a total of twelve woodland commons. Each district of well-established settlement on the north and east beyond the Weald had a corresponding area of woodland common. The Rapes of Sussex served a similar purpose, and the land divisions of Surrey apportioned the Weald there and the western end of the county in a similar fashion. This allowed use of the wooded areas by settlements situated at some distance, practising a strategy of extensive exploitation. Settlements may have been separated by up to 50 km and more from their woodland pastures.

From an early date there was a tendency to divide up the common resources further and allot them to specific settlements or lordships. This allowed better control of the commons to be exercised and enabled the land to be exploited more intensively and even settled. A number of charters from the eighth century and later granted named pieces of the Wealden common in Kent to religious bodies. In Sussex, a similar process of dividing the commons may be traced through place-names. The people of Poling, based in a village on the Coastal Plain, gave their name to the lands they used in the Weald at Pallingham, Pallingfold and *Palinga schittas*, but the association of these areas of common with the particular settlement may have been through habitual usage rather than prescriptive right. The last of these places is mentioned in a charter of the tenth century, when it was no longer held by the people of Poling and was then granted to Felpham, another coastal settlement. Through the Middle and Late Anglo-Saxon periods, many of the common pasture lands would, like this, have been re-allotted as patterns of exploitation altered and the commons were used more fully and older customary rights were no longer exercised.

The woodland and the commonland in the South-East was not confined to the Weald. Forests extended over parts of the fertile coastal fringes and over areas of the North and South Downs. Large areas of the Downs of East Kent in particular are covered by Clay-with-Flints, an infertile soil which has always been difficult to work. Initially, settlement in this area was in the river valleys with many of the early places taking the names of the adjacent river. Thus along the Cray were St Mary Cray, St Paul's Cray, North Cray and Crayford, and in the Darent Valley were North and South Darent and Dartford. The river valleys formed the basis of estates exploiting the adjacent woodland on the Downs either side, but as the population increased, settlement expanded up the valleys and then on to the Downs. The place-names Sibertswold, Womenswold, Walderchain and others from this area contain the element *wald*, of which 'Weald' is a form, indicating that these areas were once wooded. The forest on the Kent Downs once must have stretched for 30 km, from Waltham near Wye to Ringwould south of Deal and extended almost as far north as Canterbury (Everitt 1977). Even on the fertile coastal fringes there were areas of woodland. Bede describes a monastery on the Sussex Coastal Plain at Bosham as surrounded by woods and the sea, and there were other woods nearby at Manhood, the 'common wood', and the forest of Broyle north of Chichester.

Woodland was one of the resources required by every Anglo-Saxon community. It had a value not only for the timber used in building houses and in making ploughs and other tools, but also as pasture for stock. Many animals are happy to feed in woodland, on the pasture in glades or to browse on the foliage of the trees themselves. Acorns and mast, the fruit of beech trees, provide a valuable autumn food for pigs. In the Sussex Weald pigs were widely grazed as the very many early place-names which refer to them suggest, names such as Boreham, the 'boar enclosure'. Cattle, sheep and goats are mentioned in a few names, though they occur far less frequently. So important was the woodland that it was probably carefully managed and exploited. A pollen diagram from Epping forest, just north of the Thames, has indicated that certain tree species were promoted to provide fodder for the animals. Elm trees were selectively felled during the Middle-Anglo-Saxon period and burnt, and oak and birch were encouraged (Baker *et al.* 1978).

Though few Middle-Anglo-Saxon sites have been extensively excavated, their economy seems to have resembled those of the pagan period. They continued the extensive, eclectic subsistence strategy of the earlier sites, exploiting all available resources. A group of settlements facing the sea along the West Sussex coast demonstrates this. The largest is a settlement 150 m long at Medmerry Farm near Selsey which was discovered as the coast eroded. Bones found on the site show the presence of all the main stock animals and also domestic fowl. Cereals were consumed and a number of rotary querns for grinding grain were found. As at Bishopstone, the resources of the sea and seashore were also exploited by the occupants of Medmerry. The place-name which means the 'middle island' suggests its setting. Large middens of oyster, winkle, cockle, limpet and mussel shells and the bones of cod were found. The unusually wet conditions of the site preserved wooden objects, including timbers which have been recently identified as part of a boat and the top of a barrel (Damian Goodburn, pers. comm.). A similar economy is suggested by a nearby contemporary site at Becket's Barn, Pagham where carbonized grain was found near to a cobbled path leading down to Pagham Lagoon. The path was probably for pulling up fishing boats. A third Middle-Anglo-Saxon site at Sampton in Kent appears to have been very like the other two, though the details of the excavation are unpublished. Finds from the site included all the usual stock animals and part of a spade and also fish-hooks.

The interest of the pattern of exploitation of the environment by these rural sites is brought out by comparison with an urban site of the period. Urban sites necessarily will have a higher level of economic interaction. Their inhabitants would spend at least some, and perhaps a good part of their time in work which was unconnected with the direct procurement of food. They would have relied on trade in products, some of which were brought in from the surrounding area, to obtain their food. Hamwic, Saxon Southampton, for example occupies a similar position to the two sites described and could have had access to similar resources. The faunal and molluscan remains, however, show a concentration on the products of husbandry rather than the hunted and gathered foods. Though deer, fish and marine mollusca are present, they formed only a small proportion of the total (Bourdillon and Coy 1980).

The Middle-Anglo-Saxon buildings were similar to those of the earlier period. The settlements consisted of both timber halls and sunken-featured buildings used for weaving, such as the one found at Old Erringham (Shoreham, West Sussex) on the floor of which was a row of loom weights, or at West Marden (Plate 8.1). They were also comparatively short-lived and the location of settlements tended to drift as new buildings replaced old ones in different position, or they might move to an entirely separate place. Excavations have taken place in and around the present settlement of Selmeston in East Sussex over a number of years, and the results have shown how the site of a settlement may shift. The present buildings lie just below a ridge of Lower Greensand which has been occupied since the Mesolithic period and overlooks much wetter, though not infertile, clay soils. In East Sussex the Lower Greensand produces a light, not too acidic soil. Two Roman roads intersect near the village church and a probable Roman site has been noted on aerial photographs along one of these, a little further east. Certainly the quantities of Roman pottery found in excavations show that there was a settlement nearby. Close to the village was a pagan Anglo-Saxon cemetery which was used from the fifth to the early seventh centuries and it is very probable that an associated settlement was located nearby. The Middle- and Late-Anglo-Saxon finds, however, come from further up the slope, indicating that the settlement had then moved. No plans were recovered of Anglo-Saxon buildings in the recent excavations, but earlier unpublished work found hearths in association with Middle-Saxon pottery. In the Medieval period the area of occupation must have shifted yet again, as finds from the excavations show that the top of the ridge was brought under cultivation (Rudling, 1985*a*).

The largest concentration of Middle-Saxon rural settlements in the South-East has been found in the Thames valley above London. Here at Thorpe, Egham, Shepperton Green, Stanwell and Staines a series of settlement sites has been discovered along the river during housing development and gravel extraction (Fig. 8.2). The soil is light and fertile and has been extensively cultivated since at least the Bronze Age. A number of Early-Anglo-Saxon cemeteries have also been located, but there was no direct continuity between the pagan and Middle-Anglo-Saxon sites. Throughout the Anglo-Saxon period the position of settlements shifted around. At Shepperton Green occupation began in the sixth century, and decorated pagan pottery was found in ditches. The earliest structure discovered was a sunken-featured building associated with grass-tempered pottery and a bronze pin of the eighth or ninth century. A rather surprising find on this site, which appears to have been no more than a

---

Plate 8.1 A sunken-featured building excavated at North Marden, West Sussex. This is probably just one of a number of buildings from a Middle Anglo-Saxon farmstead or hamlet situated high on the chalk Downs. Finds from the hut included pottery, whetstones and two spindle whorls.

farm, was a coin of Offa minted probably at Canterbury in *c.* 792–6 and another of the tenth century. The inhabitants of the community here were buried locally in a small graveyard, which contained more than twenty individuals inhumed in a Christian fashion, aligned east-west and without grave goods. There was a break in the occupation of the site, but by the Saxo-Norman period a small farmstead with ditched enclosures was cultivating the area (Canham 1979).

These farmsteads along the Thames have to be placed in the context of the nearby site of Old Windsor, just over the county boundary in Berkshire. Excavations in the 1950s discovered a site which began like the others as no more than a farmstead. By the early ninth century a large and sophisticated water mill with three vertical wheels driven by water from leet 1 km long had been built. Close by was a stone building with glazed windows and a tiled roof. Though apparently similar to a church and almost without parallel in a secular context, the excavator suggests that this was a domestic building. Given the later history of Old Windsor and the scale and rarity of the structures, it is very probable that these were the buildings of a royal vill. Pollen analysis associated the period of construction of the mill and leet with major deforestation as the area was developed, perhaps to grow the quantities of grain which are implied by the size of the mill (Wilson and Hurst 1958: 183–5).

An enterprise of this scale resembles the estates of Carolingian France listed in the *polyptiques* or looks forward to the 'federated grain factories' that were the great Medieval manors. It is of a different size to the small farmsteads lower down the river, yet all the settlements on the Thames are characterized by their wealth and wide-ranging contacts. At Old Windsor imported Rhenish pottery decorated with tin-foil, called Tating Ware, was found and even on the more modest farm site at Yeoveney near Staines, Ipswich-type Ware from East Anglia occurred. Taking this with the imported querns and whetstone mentioned above, the wealth and imports of this area are outstanding. They are of a level normally to be found in towns. The settlements here were not farming on a subsistence basis, but were producing food for the market place and their position close to an important waterway along which goods could be transported and above London are both relevant. The royal estate at Old Windsor may also have been participating in this commerce for the requirements of a peripatetic king and his household could not justify the scale of production implied by the excavated buildings.

Economy and Coinage

By the seventh and eighth centuries the initial contacts Kent had established with the Continent had developed into full-scale trade. On both sides of the

Channel, ports of trade grew up to handle the increasing volume of transactions. Kent was well placed to trade with the Neustrian kingdom based on the court at Paris, and while this remained the major source of imports into the country, Kent was able to maintain a virtual monopoly on commerce. But trade with the Austrasian kingdom in the Rhineland developed in the seventh century and was directed towards the nearest part of England, East Anglia. Excavations at Ipswich have found that Rhenish imports were arriving there from the early part of the century.

Kent was able to limit the participation by other kingdoms in Southern England to foreign trade during the seventh century, but it was not able to exclude them. Up to the 670s Kent appears to have had control of trading activities in London and presumably also in Southwark on the south side of the river, which is alluded to in a charter granting land 'near the port of London, where ships tie up'. A royal reeve supervised the Kentish merchants at the port from a hall within London. Finds of Continental wheel-thrown pottery from the late sixth or early seventh centuries demonstrate that the port was operating from that date. During the 670s, however, Mercia was able to extend its power in this area. It gained control of London itself in 670, had extended its domination to Surrey by 672–4 and in 675 held Essex as well. Kent therefore lost an important port, and by the following century was facing severe rivalry from a new port in Wessex.

The foundation of the Anglo-Saxon port at Hamwic, Saxon Southampton a little downstream from the old Roman fort at Clausentum on the River Itchen, has been associated with the Wessex king Ine, who established the kingdom as the leading power in Southern England. The coin finds at Hamwic show that trade began at a low level in the first quarter of the eighth century, but in the following twenty-five years expanded very rapidly, decisively breaking the hold that Kent still maintained on trade. Hamwic was one of a number of ports which grew up on either side of the North Sea with names ending in *-wic*. London was called *Lundenwic* in the eighth century, and the modern place-name Aldwych may recall the area of the mid Saxon port (Vince 1984). In Kent there were the ports of Sandwich and Fordwich and along the Thames were perhaps Woolwich and Greenwich, although in neither place has the site of a port been identified (Fig. 8.2). The now lost place-name Wyke is recorded from Dover in the area of the harbour. On the east coast of England were the ports of Ipswich, Norwich, Harwich and Dunwich and on the continent were Wijk bij Duurstede (Dorestad) in Holland and the recently located Quentovic near Etaples in France.

There is a curious gap in the string of ports between the trading centres of Kent and the port of Hamwic at Southampton. Nowhere along the Sussex coastline has a port of comparable size been found, and the South-Saxon kingdom may have been effectively excluded from direct participation in Middle-Anglo-Saxon foreign trade by the large and successful competitors to the west and east. The kingdom does appear to have been economically

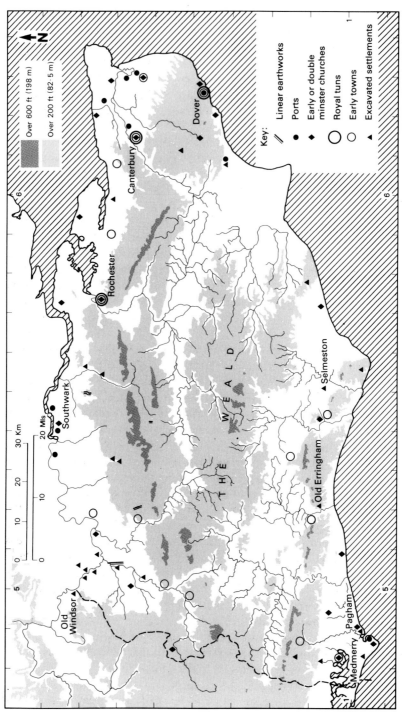

Figure 8.2 South-East England in the Middle Anglo-Saxon period. Comparatively few sites of this date are known. The density of settlements in the Thames valley would have been typical of other fertile areas. The number of minster churches shown is also less than the number which would have been in use.

underdeveloped at this period, with no trace of a pottery industry which may be taken as a sign for growing specialization of production. Only around the Selsey and Pagham Harbour area is there any indication of even low-level activity. Finds of coins called sceattas are concentrated around the Selsey peninsula where they may have been minted (Metcalf 1984).

The archaeological evidence for many of these ports is very sparse indeed. At neither Fordwich nor Sandwich has pottery from this period been found, and they are known as ports only from the documentary records. Sandwich is recorded as the landing place of St.Wilfrid on his return from the Continent in 664–5 and two charters of the mid-eighth century record the exemption of ships belonging to religious bodies from tolls at Fordwich. Only at Dover have excavations been carried out in Kent which have revealed the character of the ports. The Middle-Anglo-Saxon settlement there was established inside the walls of the Roman Saxon Shore fort, though earlier cemeteries outside the fort suggest that there had been just a small shift in an already existing community. Traces of halls, sunken-featured buildings and remains of the minster church which was founded in the 690s have been discovered in the area of Queen Street and Market Street. Excavations suggest that the town was destroyed by fire in the eighth or ninth centuries, but was rebuilt. The results of the excavations are not yet reported in detail, but the finds included quantities of imported pottery, decorated bone work and a gold finger ring set with garnet which must have belonged to an important person, perhaps a royal official with responsibility for controlling trade.

The church appears to have actively participated in foreign trade, using its contacts on the Continent. Goods such as wine, necessary for religious rituals, would have needed to have been imported. Many of the early churches were on the coast and were well situated to engage in commerce. Not only in Dover, but elsewhere in Kent a number of churches were placed within Saxon Shore forts, the walls of which made convenient monastic enclosures. At Lympne an imported bottle has been found, while at Richborough and at Reculver there were minster churches in or close to the forts. In the latter two places, large numbers of sceattas have been found and at Reculver many seventh-century gold tremisses have also been recorded. At Richborough the coins have been discovered in the area of the chapel and at Reculver eroding out from cliffs, and although this concentration has been explained as finds from graves, the problem still remains as to how the deceased came to possess so many coins in the first place (Rigold 1977). An imported pot was also found, having fallen from a cliff near to Reculver. In Sussex likewise, a number of large ecclesiastical estates were situated around the possible port of Pagham, and in Surrey the churches of Bermondsey and Chertsey faced the River Thames. The charters mentioned above, exempting the Abbess of St Peter's, Thanet and Reculver church from tolls at Fordwich and Sarre, suggest a much wider involvement in trade.

Not all finds of imported goods are evidence of commercial transactions and equally they do not indicate direct contact with the Continent. The role of gift exchange, ransom payments and gifts to avert conflict between kingdoms may have been just as important, or more so, in the movement of goods as the action of traders. Reciprocity of gift exchange was the principle on which personal relationships were based. It required that all gifts must be answered by counter-gifts or by a render of services. It has been suggested too that the existence of coinage should not be taken for an indicator of trade, but that coins were another medium in which the donation of a gift could be answered (Grierson 1959). It is a small step between answering a gift with a counter-gift of coins, to paying for the 'gift' with money, and no doubt the first developed gradually into the second. Even so, trade in the Middle-Anglo-Saxon period hardly represents a state of incipient capitalism. The motivation behind trade was the acquisition of goods which were not otherwise obtainable. The prime impetus was to import, not to export. Royal control was maintained over the movement of objects into the country, for in this way the king was able to continue to play his traditional role as distributor of wealth within the king-dom and outside. By handing out largesse to his subjects or allies, he enhanced his prestige and created a debt to be answered by a reciprocal gift or act of service (Fig. 8.5). The wheel-thrown imported pottery found up the East Anglian coast may then be interpreted as the result of secondary distribution of goods imported first into Kent and later passed on, especially since the royal families of Kent and Essex were related by marriage.

The distribution of goods within the country is best illustrated by locally produced pottery, which had a low value and was rarely re-used. In most of the South-East the Middle-Anglo-Saxon pottery was made in a domestic context to supply the local community and perhaps adjoining communities, and there was no identifiable industry as such. The products were hand-made and consisted mostly of globular cooking pots tempered with quartz or more commonly flint (Fig. 8.3). So-called grass-tempered pottery found in the Pagan period continued to be produced and may have been used up to the eleventh century. In fact such pottery was tempered not only with grass, but also straw, chaff, bracken and dung on occasions, and was fired in simple bonfire kilns. But in eastern Kent, the Southampton area including the western part of Sussex and around the Thames valley, production was on a larger scale and supplied a wider area. Pottery industries in these regions served a district in the radius of a day's walk. It is significant that these industries were all based on centres engaged in foreign trade. An interpretation of this would be that the foreign commerce had stimulated a low level of exchange between settlements within the country and created a situation in which an industry producing pottery could develop.

The exact role of the coinage in commerce both within the country and for exchange for Continental imports is clearly very uncertain. It is impossible to know when it changed from being a primitive source of wealth which could be stored or exchanged, to being treated as cash. As the burial custom changed

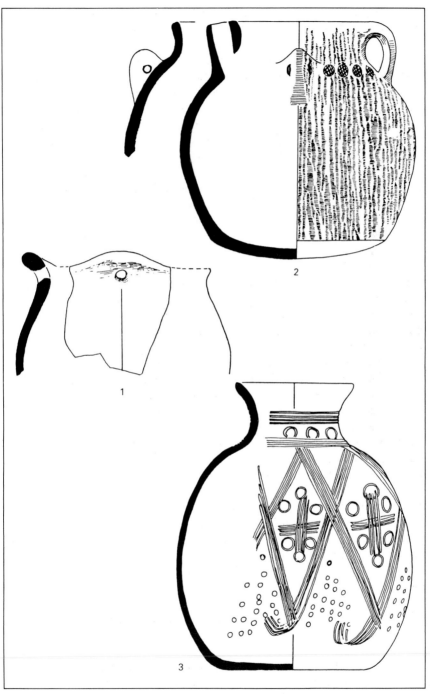

Figure 8.3 Domestic pottery such as the cooking pot from Friston, East Sussex (1) is often poorly made. Better quality vessels show the continuing use of stamps and other decoration, such as those from Pagham, West Sussex (3) and Richborough, Kent (2). The latter displays Continental influence in its sagging base form (all ¼).

with the spread of Christianity, and smaller quantities of wealth in the form of gold and silver were inhumed with the dead, more bullion became available for conversion into coinage. Not surprisingly it was in Kent and London that some of the first coins were minted in England, for they were among the few areas which had access to adequate bullion. The first coins imitated closely the Continental gold tremisses which arrived in the country through the ports of trade. They were minted from before the middle of the seventh century, but were in use for only a short period before the supply of gold diminished and the coins were replaced both in England and on the Continent by silver sceattas and deniers. The earliest, primary series of sceattas was minted in East Kent from *c*. 680 and circulated mainly in the South-East. During the first quarter of the eighth century the secondary sceattas appear, minted in a larger number of kingdoms, suggesting a broader based access to bullion and reflecting a wider participation in foreign trade. Sussex was among the kingdoms producing coinage, possibly from a mint near Selsey where the finds of Series G sceattas are concentrated. The distribution of coinage, though, still attests the importance of Kent as a trading centre. The Midland sceattas, for example, are concentrated in the region in which they were struck and also around the Wantsum Channel in East Kent, but with few finds in between. Midland trade must therefore have been passing through the Kentish ports, even though there was access to the sea nearer at hand.

From 730 the sceattas became progressively debased, either because of a decline in the supply of bullion to the country, or because there was a slump in overseas trade with England. When the situation revived, coin production again started in Kent. The new coins were heavier-weight pennies which imitated the Continental coins of Pepin III. They were produced first on a small scale in about 765, and then twenty years later in much greater volume and formed the basis of the coinage in England for the remainder of the Anglo-Saxon period.

The First Towns

In no town can occupation be shown to have continued directly from the Roman period through to the Middle Anglo-Saxon period without a break. The layers of dark earth sealing the final Roman deposits are convincing evidence of a hiatus in use. The earliest post-Roman towns are usually divided into two groups. There were the coastal trading sites through which goods were imported and the administrative centres or burhs, the royal centres from which goods were redistributed. Trade was the prime impetus behind the urban renaissance of the Middle-Anglo-Saxon period, for it brought people together, stimulated exchange and provided an alternative livelihood, but it is not certain to what extent the trading and redistributive centres were truly urban. Stenton suggested that an Anglo-Saxon town should have a wall, a mint and a market, but if these criteria were applied to the South-East, the discussion would be limited to Rochester, Canterbury, perhaps Dover and a few other places at the very end of the period. A more satisfactory way to look at towns may be to take a bundle of criteria and find places that satisfy at least some of these.

There is little to separate many of the towns from rural settlements. The people who moved back into the walls of Canterbury in the late sixth or seventh centuries did not immediately give up farming and become traders. Just as parts of the late Roman towns had been given over to agriculture, so too were parts of Canterbury. The western half of the city was liable to flood from the River Stour; it was not built on, and continued to be cultivated even as the population was becoming quite dense in the other half of the town. As late as the thirteenth century this land was unoccupied, and was eventually used for the site of a Franciscan friary. The inhabitants of Canterbury had further land outside the walls and ninth-century charters commonly grant with a haw or burgage plot in the town an area of land in the fields and meadows on the north, east and south sides beyond the town walls. They had the usual rights of pasturing their pigs and other animals and cutting timber within a common wood. Inside the walls and out, archaeologists have found evidence for agriculture as late as the end of the Saxon period. On sites dug at Stour Street near the river within Canterbury, a thick layer of 'turned over' loam was found containing pottery, showing that it was cultivated up to the Saxo-Norman period and a similar layer was found while digging in the outer court of St Augustine's Abbey just beyond the walls, which satisfactorily confirm the historical evidence.

The -*wic* ports of Sandwich and Fordwich were probably very similar, though in neither place have excavations been carried out. Trading was a sporadic, and perhaps seasonal activity which did not engage the inhabitants in full-time work. Land outside the ports was, as with Canterbury, associated with plots inside the town. A tenth-century charter grants two haws in Fordwich, together with a meadow. Full publication of the results of excavations in Dover should show the character and extent of occupation in that trading port and the area in the walls of the town used for agriculture. But Dover was in many ways not a typical trading centre. The presence of an early minster church within the town indicates that it was a royal centre, comparable to Canterbury or Rochester, from which goods were also redistributed. Though some of the later minster churches also participated in water-borne trade, in no other place was an early seventh-century minster founded in an already existing trading post. It was a unique settlement combining the functions of trade and redistribution from a very early date.

The relationship of the church and the re-emergence of urban settlement

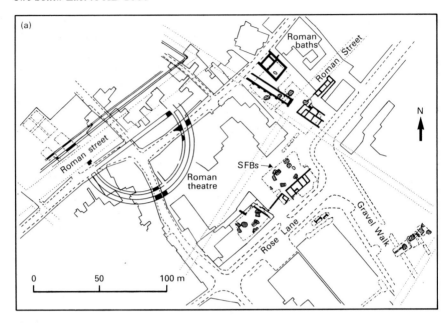

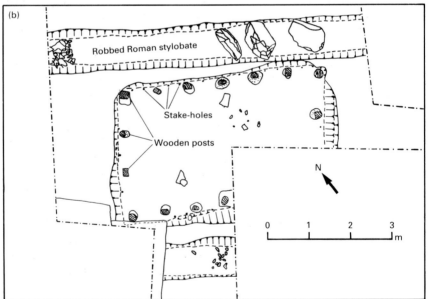

Figure 8.4　a. Central Canterbury showing the results of forty years' excavation in the city. Roman buildings are indicated by solid lines and Anglo-Saxon huts are cross-hatched (after Bennett 1981).

b. A Late Anglo-Saxon sunken building set inside a Roman building from excavations at 69a Stour Street, Canterbury. The stake-holes around the edge of the building suggest it was lined by wicker-work (after Bennett 1980).

is complex. The re-occupation of Canterbury has been attributed to the arrival of St Augustine, who founded his first church just outside the city and later churches within the walls. It has been suggested, though, that Augustine would not have chosen a place which was otherwise deserted to establish the first church, and it is notable that the other seventh-century minster churches were founded for the most part at known and existing royal centres. Bede hints at some activity in the area of the town before St Augustine's arrival: Bertha, the Frankish wife of King Æthelberht of Kent and a Christian, had worshipped at an unnamed church, probably St Martin's, to the east of Canterbury. Professor Brooks in an imaginative interpretation, would like to see the Roman theatre which survived as a dominating structure till after the Norman Conquest as the meeting place of the *Cantware*, the folk of Kent during the pagan period (Brooks 1984; 25) (Fig. 8.4a). Canterbury means 'the fortress or stronghold of the Kent people'. No Early-Anglo-Saxon remains have been excavated within the theatre and archaeology can be of little help, for it can only place the earliest post-Roman occupation in the walls within the date bracket of the late sixth to the early seventh centuries. The influence of the church on the urban renaissance may not have been seminal, but with churches established in the town there was a further stimulation to growth.

Behind the Roman theatre in Canterbury more than twenty Sunken Featured Buildings (SFBs) from the early years of urban settlement have been found cut into the dark earth loam (Fig. 8.4a). As on rural sites, the huts would have been ancillary to above-ground post-built halls, though few of these have been discovered because they are more difficult to identify on complex urban sites. At Stour Street, post-holes representing a flimsy timber structure of the eighth century may have been such a hall. The SFBs were similar in form to those found on rural farms and were mostly placed in the open spaces between Roman buildings or cut into Roman streets. The walls of the Roman buildings were still standing, but their roofs had collapsed and plaster had fallen from the walls. Some of the SFBs, though, were dug through the destruction debris onto the Roman floors inside buildings. One hut at Watling Street was cut through the wall of a Roman building on to a tessellated floor below. This more ambitious SFB also had a porch-like entrance to the north (Plate 8.2). The huts contained loomweights, confirming that they served much the same function as rural SFBs, pottery and decorated brooches, which give a date of the late sixth to seventh centuries. More remarkable, in one hut was the fully articulated skeleton of a wolf, perhaps a discarded trophy from hunting in nearby woodland.

Within the Roman town walls of eighth-century Canterbury were numbers of huts and timber halls in the shadow of the standing theatre and scattered among the walls of former Roman buildings. Bede was able to call the town a metropolis, for it had its own mint and a market-place (*forum*) recorded in a charter of 762. Canterbury was burnt down in 754 and for the fire to have spread across a sizeable part of the city there must have been a sufficient density

Plate 8.2 An Anglo-Saxon hut of the sixth or seventh century found at 16 Watling Street, Canterbury. The hut was cut through the collapsed wall of a Roman building and re-used the Roman tessellated floor. The post- and stake-holes at the centre of the photograph are from a possible porch at the entrance to the hut. (Photograph: Canterbury Archaeological Trust.)

of buildings at that date. It did not cause long-term damage to the town's prosperity, for the mint there continued to function. Some of the coins from the mint have been found within the city, in for example the upper layers of a pit in Castle Street. In the same pit was a unique Anglo-Saxon bronze fitting and round about were quantities of iron slag, suggesting craft activity. Ninth-century charters provide sufficient incidental detail to show that the town was flourishing. There was an active land market and pressure on building space was such that a local bye-law stated the distance to be left between properties for an eavesdrip. Merchants are mentioned in a context showing that some were of lowly status and they may have been among the many poor who were granted alms of bread in recorded wills (Brooks 1984: 29–30). The emergence of an urban poor is a convincing sign of the development of a town.

Canterbury was perhaps the first post-Roman town and is the best documented and among the most widely excavated. The second capital of

Kent, Rochester, is less well covered by historical sources and has not been extensively excavated. Like Canterbury, the land within the Roman walls was re-occupied and a minster church constructed in 604, inside which those newly converted to Christianity were buried. The charter granting land to the church suggests that the land within the walls was hardly, if at all, occupied. Excavations in the nineteenth century uncovered evidence for the east end of the early church and further work has found scattered finds of the period, but no structures. The strategic position of Rochester at the boundary of the kingdom of Kent and close to the surviving, though perhaps ruinous Roman bridge across the Medway, was one reason for its continuing importance during the Early-Anglo-Saxon period. Bede refers to it in connection with a Synod of 673 as a *castellum*, but it cannot have been very secure, for it was ravaged by the Mercians three years later, though this also suggests that the town had developed sufficiently to be worthy of the attention of the invaders. The contrary case is suggested by the discontinuous occupation of the Bishopric during the seventh century, which hardly indicates a flourishing community; one bishop resigned because of the poverty of the See. A rare metalworker's die of the mid-seventh century, found redeposited in a Medieval pit, is evidence of specialized production and other finds of the period have included a spearhead, pottery and a sceat. By the ninth century Rochester was more securely established as a settlement and had the attributes of an urban centre. It had a mint and a market, and although its coastal position made it vulnerable to Viking raids, it was protected behind its Roman walls and was expanding.

There are few signs of urban growth in Surrey, which has no direct access to the sea, or in Sussex, which remained a backwater barely participating in long-distance trade, in spite of an extensive coastline and some suitable harbours. At Chichester, pottery has been found of this date, though almost always redeposited in later pits. The pottery, dated to the period between the eighth and early tenth centuries, occurs in small quantities and does not suggest that the settlement was very considerable. Coins once thought to bear the inscription *R-x Cic*, which might be expanded as King of, or King at Chichester, and dated to the period 670–750, have now been reconsidered. It seems more likely that they were minted in France and do not refer to Chichester (Welch 1983: 118). If then, there was an extensive settlement in Chichester, excavation has been in the wrong place to locate it.

The evidence, even if incomplete, sets apart the expanding Middle-Anglo-Saxon towns of Canterbury and Rochester from the settlements which barely merit the name of a town, such as Chichester. These are perhaps better called proto-urban centres. Kingston-on-Thames is another likely example of a proto-urban settlement. It was an important royal centre, probably in the ninth century and certainly by the early tenth, when it was the site of the coronation of six kings. Excavations around the church have discovered two fragments of stone with ornamentation, probably dating to the eighth century and more recently, restricted work in Eden Street has found grass-tempered pottery and

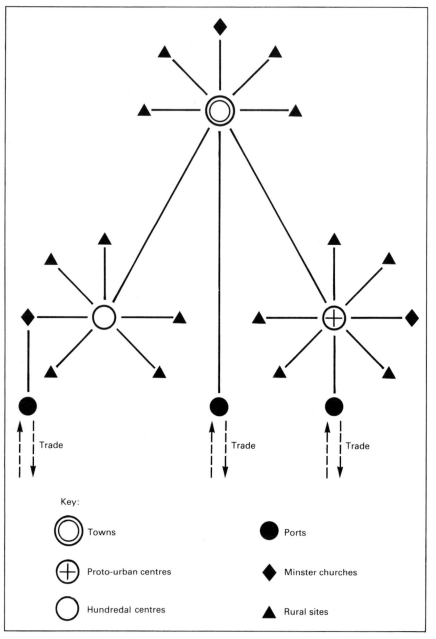

Key:

◎ Towns   ● Ports

⊕ Proto-urban centres   ◆ Minster churches

○ Hundredal centres   ▲ Rural sites

Figure 8.5 Middle Anglo-Saxon society: the redistributive economy of the Early Anglo-Saxon period was gradually changed as trading and the use of coinage became more widespread. Continental trade was an important spur to the development of the economy.

in Thames Street a property boundary of the ninth/tenth century. Given the limited nature of excavation in the town, these results are very interesting.

The proto-urban centres lie in the hierarchy of settlement between the towns proper and a lower order of centre which had no urban pretensions. This class can often be recognized retrospectively through documentary evidence, but rarely through excavation. These places stood at the centre of a hundred and had the rights of that hundred attached to them. They were often held by the king, though some had been granted out to major landowners, particularly the church. The King's reeve sat in these centres, collected food rent and administered the King's justice to the surrounding district (Fig. 8.5). Minster churches were often founded at these hundredal centres and they too served the encircling area. The administrative districts called hundreds, are mentioned in Anglo-Saxon laws in the tenth century, but it is certain that there must have been similar districts before that, perhaps with a different name (Cam 1932).

The centres within the districts acted as collecting points from which the surplus produce could be gathered from the adjoining area and mobilized for the use of the King or the estate owner. The agrarian wealth of the South-East was channelled through these centres, so that it could be made available for consumption by the landowner and his household, or exchanged in the course of trade to buy utilitarian or prestige items. As centres of collection and exchange, it is not surprising that some of these developed into towns themselves in the Late Anglo-Saxon period.

Christianity and Churches

King Æthelberht of Kent would already have been acquainted with the new religion of Christianity before Augustine landed in 597. He had married a Frankish wife, Bertha, with the agreement that she could continue to practise Christianity, and with her priest, Liuhard, she had used an old Roman church, probably at St Martins, outside Canterbury. Augustine arrived from the Continent and following the route of boats trading with the kingdom of Kent, landed at one of the ports near Thanet. He was welcomed, cautiously at first, by the King but within the year of Augustine's arrival, Æthelberht himself had become Christian and by Christmas time the missionaries were converting large numbers of people.

Success in Kent opened the way for the spread of religion to other kingdoms. Æthelberht as overlord had some influence over other kings south of the Humber and may have encouraged them to convert too. He was able to use his position to arrange a meeting between Augustine and the Celtic bishops of Wales, though this ended inconclusively with the bishops unwilling to acknowledge the authority of Augustine. In Kent, though, a second bishopric was established in Rochester and a third in the kingdom of the East Saxons at London. After this initial expansion though, the missionaries faced greater problems. Æthelberht failed to have his son and heir baptised and some of the converts, such as King Raedwald of East Anglia, were equivocal about their new religion. Raedwald continued to worship pagan deities in his temple in which he also kept a Christian altar. On the death of Æthelberht in 616 or 618, his son Eadbald resumed pagan practices and at about the same time Mellitus, Bishop of London, was driven from the East Saxon kingdom. From this low point the missionaries were able gradually to recover their position. Eadbald was converted to Christianity and East Anglia was recovered in the 630s.

The conversion of the South Saxons may have taken place very late. Bede attributes the introduction of Christianity into the kingdom to Wilfrid, who arrived in Sussex in 681. He also mentions, though, that there already was a Christian presence in the kingdom, at Bosham where a monastery was led by an Irish monk, Dicuill. The role of the Irish mission is minimized by Bede, but it is significant that Bosham is later recorded as a royal vill. It is known that the king of the South Saxons, Æthelwalh and his wife had already been converted and some of their subjects may also have become Christian before Wilfrid arrived. The accounts of the introduction of Christianity into Sussex in the 680s given in the *Life of Wilfrid* and by Bede are very partisan and confused. They have tried to over-emphasize the role of Wilfrid and perhaps exaggerated the level of paganism in the kingdom. As a result we lack a reliable history of the conversion of the South Saxons (Kirby 1978).

It is fortunate that so many churches from the early years of Christianity should have survived. The greatest damage to them has often been from antiquarian investigation in the last and present centuries, which has been grossly destructive and added little to an understanding of their structural history. It is, however, from this antiquarian work that the plans of many of the churches have been recovered. From these it is possible to identify a distinctively Kentish group which belongs to the seventh century and some of which were built by the original missionaries in England. They are all immediately striking because of their small size. Only a very restricted congregation could have attended a service within the church, but for most of the year they would not have been used by the whole community. In the first centuries, many public services would have taken place in the open air, perhaps around an isolated cross, wherever there was a group of Christians. Only on the major feast days would there have been a service for the whole community at the church. The churches were otherwise intended principally for the use of the minster priests themselves.

The monastic church dedicated to Saints Peter annd Paul and now part of St Augustine's Abbey in Canterbury (Fig. 8.6) is typical of these early churches. Begun soon after 597, it consisted of a nave, a stilted semi-circular apsidal chancel and porticus or chapels on the north and south sides. It was constructed almost entirely in re-used Roman brick. In these porticus were buried King Æthelberht and Bertha and many of the early archbishops, including Augustine. Eadbald, Æthelberht's son began a second, smaller church immediately to the east of Saints Peter and Paul. Unfortunately, little of this survives today except for a west wall, but in plan it was probably similar to its neighbour. A third church lay on the same axis, 80 m further east. This is the better-preserved church of Saint Pancras. In plan it is strikingly similar to Saints Peter and Paul, but had a polygonal rather than semi-circular nave. Recent excavation here has clarified the character of the first phase of the church. It was built of Roman brick with foundations of flint and had a clay floor and walls of white plaster. The first structure either became ruinous or was demolished, and in the late seventh or eighth centuries was reconstructed with external porticus built against the north and south walls of the nave and a third porticus on the south of the apse. Between the apse and chancel an arcade was inserted with three arches. Later, a further chapel was built, also in the same line, to make a series of churches spread out on an alignment 135 m long. The axial arrangement of churches is characteristic of early monasteries and may be in conscious imitation of Saint Peters, Rome.

The remains of the east end of the church at Rochester were discovered in 1889 underneath the west front of the cathedral. The plan recovered was sufficiently similar to the Canterbury churches, but a second structure was later found between the south transept and aisle and either of these buildings could be the seventh-century church. The most impressive church of the group of early Kentish churches would have been the church perched on the edge of the sea at Reculver. Sadly, this was pulled down in 1805 at the wish of the vicar's mother, in an act of almost unparalleled vandalism. The remains of the church were excavated in 1927 and have been re-examined more recently, though the latter work is unpublished. The church had the usual nave and apsidal chancel with two porticus north and south. The floor was made of *opus signinum*, crushed brick dust set in mortar and is related to the eighth-century extension to the church. On this was found the base of the altar set in the nave forward of the chancel arch. The chancel arch itself had the form of a triple arcade, similar to that in the second phase at Reculver, which may be related to the first construction of the church. To this earliest phase may also belong an east apse made of sandstone blocks and a wall of similar construction at the west end, found in the 1969 excavations.

These five Kentish churches together, with one other at Lyminge which has been poorly recorded, form a distinct group. They are defined by their small size, apsidal chancels and, in some of the churches at least, the presence of porticus and triple arcading between the nave and chancel. Recent excavations have shown that this group is less homogeneous than was once thought and some of the churches were not single-phase structures and have complex constructional histories. The plan of the early churches was derived from Continental buildings and it is almost certain that the masons who constructed

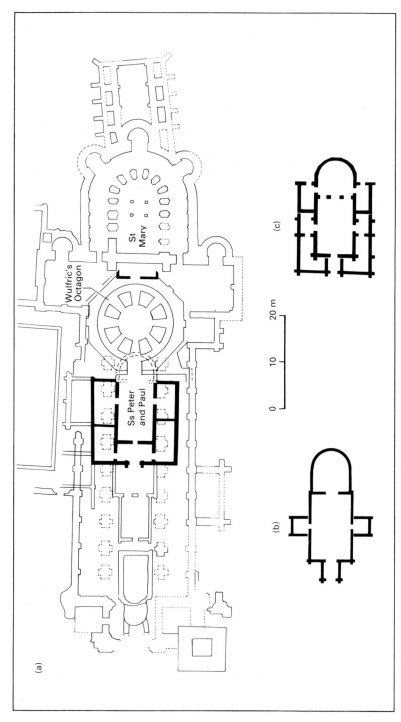

Figure 8.6 a. The medieval abbey of St Augustine, Canterbury overlies the seventh-century churches of Saints Peter and Paul and St Mary. An octagonal rotunda was built to join them in the eleventh century.
b. A third church, St Pancras, lies directly to the west.
c. St Mary's, Reculver has a very similar plan.

them came from abroad. The Continental influence is apparent in the details of the churches. A column capital and base from the chancel arches at Reculver preserved from the nineteenth-century demolition closely resembles those from late Roman and Byzantine ecclesiastical buildings and the column base from St Pancras, Canterbury, once thought to have been re-used from a Romano–British building, was inspired by the same source (Blagg 1981).

It is not difficult to imagine the effect in the seventh century of the construction of the first masonry buildings in England for 200 years in a design in the Roman tradition. Situated outside Roman Canterbury, the juxtaposition of the ruins of the old buildings and new churches must have been striking and the use of arcading, columns, Roman brick and the semi-circular apse cannot have failed to evoke the past. Whether intentionally or not, the buildings of the Christian missionaries placed them as the inheritors of the Roman tradition. But the adoption of Christianity was part of a broader renaissance in the kingdom of Kent in which a number of aspects of Roman culture were adopted. In the first few years of the seventh century, writing was re-introduced, which made possible the first written laws and the first charters recording grants of land to the church. Bede records that Æthelberht's laws were made after Roman models, though historians suggest that they owe more to Merovingian laws. The Roman town of Canterbury was re-occupied as a capital and the principal church was constructed to a similar plan to St Peters in Rome. Bede says that Æthelberht had *imperium* or lordship over the area south of the Humber, a power which may have been intended to allude to aspirations to claim a role as an inheritor of Roman authority in England.

The churches in Anglo-Saxon England were divided according to importance into cathedrals or head minsters, ordinary minsters, lesser churches with graveyards and field churches. The cathedrals in the South-East were at Christ Church Canterbury, Rochester discussed above, and Selsey which served a diocese coterminous with Sussex. Christ Church Canterbury was destroyed in a fire in 1067, the old foundations were robbed out and it was replaced by a Norman cathedral. Should excavations ever be made on the site and traces of the Anglo-Saxon minster survive, its plan is likely to be no less complex than that of the Old Minster uncovered at Winchester during the 1960s, located beside the cathedral there. The Winchester Old Minster was a building of many phases and unusual form. Documentary evidence shows that Christ Church certainly was an elaborate building with apses at opposite ends and a ring crypt beneath the eastern one. It was repaired and modified on a number of occasions, including perhaps in the tenth century when Christ Church was one of the centres in the reformation of monastic life. A number of attempts have been made to reconstruct the plan of the cathedral on the basis of the documentary evidence, but the sources are open to differing interpretations.

No physical remains of an Anglo-Saxon cathedral still stand at Selsey, south of Chichester either. The estate of Selsey was given to Wilfrid when the South Saxons were converted to Christianity and a cathedral was constructed at Church Norton. This was replaced after the Norman Conquest by a cathedral within the city of Chichester and the old cathedral was downgraded to a simple parish church. An indication of the former status of the foundation at Church Norton is given in the fourteenth-century will of a bishop of Chichester, which expressed his wish to be buried in the church at Selsey, 'formerly the cathedral church of my diocese'. The buildings of the surviving church are early thirteenth-century in date and fragments from an Anglo-Saxon stone cross, now built incongruously into the Selsey war memorial, are the only remnants of the cathedral above ground (Aldsworth 1979).

Below the cathedrals were the minster churches, which served a much wider area than the parish churches of the Middle Ages. They were staffed by a group of priests who travelled out to preach to congregations in the surrounding area or *parochia*. Services were given at wayside crosses in the open air, or in the small field churches, which were gradually built at settlements within the *parochia*. Many of the *parochiae* had been established within a century of the conversion to Christianity and divided up the country so that few places were more than a morning's journey from the central church or minster. In neighbouring Hampshire this meant that nowhere was more than 10 km from a minster church. That county, like much of central Southern England including the western end of Sussex, had a particularly high density of minster churches, but even so in the South-East, except in the area of the sparsely populated Weald, the distance to a minster church was rarely much more (Fig. 8.8).

The priests lived a communal life at the minster church. In the grounds of the church they would have had rooms and would have lived a life not unlike Medieval mendicant monks. Few excavations have uncovered the ancillary buildings attached to the minster churches, though it seems probable that buildings were not arranged in the claustral plan familiar from the Middle Ages. Within a bank, ditch or wall which surrounded the minster precincts were many cells occupied by the priests and in some places there was a similar number of small chapels around the minster church. There is little evidence for these in the South-East, but in Hampshire it is recorded that there were nine small churches and canons' houses besides the former minster at Christchurch Priory. When the antiquarian Leland visited Reculver in about 1540, he noted monastic ruins still visible above ground and recorded beyond the minster church a neglected chapel, which may have been one such priest's church. Old engravings show that, although this was partly of thirteenth-century date, it had features characteristic of early Anglo-Saxon churches. Of the other buildings connected with a monastic establishment, only a small structure of the eighth century on the north side of Saints Peter and Paul, Canterbury has been found, which was perhaps one of a number of buildings there.

Somewhat different from most minster churches, which were bases for missionary activity, were the double minsters for nuns and priests. These were founded by, or for, ladies of princely rank and acted as places of retreat from the world for women of high status. Minster-in-Sheppey was founded by

Seaxburh, daughter of the king of the East Angles, who retired to serve as abbess after she had acted as regent in Kent for her son Ecgberht. The double minster at Lyminge was established by King Eadbald for his sister, when she was widowed on the death of King Ædwine of Deira. There were other double minsters at Folkestone, Minster-in-Thanet, Hoo and possibly at Eastry in Kent, but the phenomenon of minsters for both priests and nuns did not spread much beyond that kingdom, though there was one possible double minster at Aldingbourne near Chichester in Sussex (Rigold 1968) (Fig. 8.2).

Ordinary minster churches, like double minsters, often owed their foundation to grants of land made by the king. Minster churches were usually situated at royal vills and the minster often served a *parochia* identical with the secular administrative district controlled by the royal vill. Between the seventh and eleventh centuries many smaller churches with a single priest were founded by pious local landowners and were endowed with their own parishes, which were carved out from the original area of the minster *parochiae*. Displaced by Viking attacks and under pressure from changes brought about by the tenth-century Reformation, the minster churches were in decline by the Late Anglo-Saxon period. Their role had been substantially superseded by the local churches, which had created parishes for themselves within the area of the original *parochiae* and left to the minster an area often no bigger than the size of a large parish. By the Medieval period, then, there was often nothing to distinguish the minster church from an ordinary parish church, but its residual rights and physical structure.

The rights of minster churches over parish churches in the former area of their *parochia* in some cases survived for many years after their origin and purpose had been forgotten. Typical of these were the pensions that the former minster church at Bexhill in Sussex still received in the Medieval period from churches at Ninfield, Hoo, Bulverhythe and Hastings. These were payments once given to the minster in compensation for the loss of revenue when the parish churches had been founded with the Bexhill *parochia*. Studies of Anglo-Saxon charters, Medieval documents, Domesday Book and, for Kent, the Domesday Monachorum have enabled the pattern of minsters and their *parochiae* to be reconstructed. The arrangement is complex and the evidence difficult to interpret, because the pattern did not remain static throughout the Middle and Late Anglo-Saxon periods. The minster churches at Stoke-by-Guildford and Godstone in Surrey, and Teynham in Kent were very probably later foundations to fill gaps in the existing framework of *parochiae* or to replace minsters ravaged by the Vikings. Only rarely is there a specific statement recording a minster church and its subordinate churches, though the Domesday Monachorum does give such a list for eleventh-century Kent. More common are references which just hint at the former importance of some churches. A twelfth-century grant, for example, mentions the church at Petworth, which had a very large parish, 'with its appurtenances' of the church at Tillington and the chapels of River and Duncton in Sussex (Round 1899: 510).

The size and shape of the surviving fabric may also be a clue to the former importance of a church. Minsters were often larger than ordinary parish churches and built with especially long chancels to accommodate the number of priests who served them. The fragmentary Anglo-Saxon remains within Farnham and Godalming churches suggest that these were churches of considerable size, and at the latter, pre-Conquest sculptural pieces have been found implying an elaborately decorated building. The evidence of documents indicates that both were minsters. Minster-in-Sheppey church retains a north wall from the Anglo-Saxon minster and it shows that the original building was particularly tall, with high windows constructed with a surround of flat pieces of stone, apparently to resemble Roman brick. If the place-name did not suggest the particular importance of the church at Lyminster near Arundel in Sussex, then the capacious nave and very long, thin Anglo-Saxon walls would have indicated that this also was a minster church served by a community of priests.

Below the level of minsters were churches of lesser status, which had been founded by local landowners on their estates. These were the churches which, in the Medieval period became parish churches, though in Anglo-Saxon times a full parish system had yet to develop. The churches were the possession of the founder and a symbol of his or her status; they are often called *Eigenkirchen* or proprietorial churches. Some of the *Eigenkirchen* may have been founded as early as the eighth century, but the time of greatest expansion was the Late Anglo-Saxon period. By the time of Domesday Book it has been estimated that 60–70 per cent of those churches which, in the Medieval period, would have parochial status had already been established in Surrey and in Kent, where there are early lists of churches, the proportion is much higher. Domesday Book itself does not provide a complete record of the churches in existence in the later eleventh century, only of the more important ones. Nor can an examination of the fabric of the present church buildings always show if there was an Anglo-Saxon church on the site. Excavations beneath many churches have revealed the foundations of earlier buildings, which were subsequently either demolished or modified and concealed behind later alterations.

Most of the upstanding fabric of the church of St Thomas the Martyr at Pagham in West Sussex is from the thirteenth century, but before heating ducts were laid beneath the floor, it was possible to excavate the interior of the building. This uncovered evidence of a number of earlier phases including the foundations of the western end of a narrow, Late-Saxon church which was previously unknown. Re-used in the structure of a later grave was a fragment from a tenth- or eleventh-century cross head, probably from a memorial cross which had stood in the church ground (Freke 1980). More complete plans of 'lost' Anglo-Saxon churches have been found in other excavations in Sussex. Among the masonry of the foundations of St Nicholas, Angmering, which fell into disuse in the late sixteenth century were traces of two periods of pre-Conquest building. The second of the Anglo-Saxon churches on the site had a semi-circular apsidal chancel and it must have been of a similar plan to the slightly smaller chapel discovered through archaeological work at Chilgrove in West Dean. Both the Angmering and Chilgrove buildings probably began as simple one-room structures, onto which the apses were later added.

Even the upstanding Anglo-Saxon churches which are still surviving today may themselves not be the first buildings on the site. They may have replaced or partly replaced earlier structures which had become too small for a growing congregation and though no excavation in the South-East has yet found traces of any timber-built church, elsewhere in England these have been shown to have preceded the first masonry churches. Anglo-Saxon churches grew organically as new parts were added onto existing buildings and there was little consistency in the size and shape of the *Eigenkirchen* as they were the product of the wealth of the landowner, the number of the congregation and local practice. As a result there is a great diversity in plan and form of Anglo-Saxon churches.

By comparison with later Medieval churches, Anglo-Saxon churches often appear small and unornamented. The size of the building is frequently emphasized by a simple, long and narrow plan and a small chancel arch which effectively divides the nave and chancel into two separate cells. Porticus, though a feature of the early Kent group, were not widely copied in later churches, and where they occur, they do not have the effect of the transepts of Medieval churches, which were integrated into the body of the building and give a feeling of space and volume. The Anglo-Saxon porticus were isolated from the rest of the church and intended for private prayer. Beyond the chancel arch was the east end which was either square in plan or semi-circular. The rounded apsidal end is a feature of a number of standing churches in the South and East of England and, as the two excavations mentioned above and archaeological discoveries at Herne in Kent suggest, may have been even more common.

There are few sources of good building stone in the South-East and the Anglo-Saxon masons were forced to rely on the material which was to hand. A recent study of the tower at Sompting in Sussex showed that between the first- and second-floor levels a variety of types of stone were used, indicating either the re-use of salvaged materials or of stone fragments lying around the stonemason's yard. Above the second-floor level different types of building stone occurred in horizontal bands, reflecting the arrival of deliveries of stone while the masons were constructing the church (Aldsworth, pers. comm.). Local Roman sites often provided a convenient quarry for building material and many churches incorporate Roman brick in their foundations or walls. Only very rarely has it been shown that the brick was actually of Anglo-Saxon manufacture. The stone from Roman buildings was also pillaged and at Selham in Sussex, a Roman capital, perhaps brought from a local site, was reused on one side of the chancel arch and the impost above it is a Roman string-course on which Saxon masons carved a simple pattern of foliage. A number of churches in Kent were actually adapted from standing Roman structures or were built on top of Roman buildings. The abandoned church at Stone-by-Faversham, Saint Martins in Canterbury and perhaps Lydd church all incorporate Roman walls. A church at Lullingstone stands on top of a Romano-Celtic temple mausoleum, part of the large Roman villa there. Elsewhere in the villa there is evidence for later Roman Christian worship. There is no evidence for direct continuity of religious practice and the builders of the late Saxon church were probably unaware of the previous function of the building whose walls and foundations they used. The attraction of the site may more likely have been the abundant Roman brick.

From the diversity of Anglo-Saxon church plans it is possible to isolate a group of churches in South-West Surrey which were built to a common design and probably constructed within a short period of one another as the formerly remote Wealden areas became settled and it became necessary to increase the provision of churches. Hascombe, Godalming church, Alfold and perhaps Cranleigh are all two-cell churches with originally square east ends made to a common size in the Late-Anglo-Saxon period. It is possible that they are the work of a single gang of itinerant craftsmen, but equally they may have been constructed locally, according to a master plan current in the district (Blair forthcoming; Rodwell 1986). These Surrey churches, built late in the Anglo-Saxon period, suggest that this may have been a period of considerable activity. In Kent it is suggested that a number of the holders of land in 1066 were the same people who had recently founded churches. *Ælsiescirce*, listed in the eleventh century, for example, was probably the *Eigenkirche* of Ælsi who held land nearby at Eastbridge. Through the documentary record, an examination of standing fabric and archaeological excavation, it may be possible to gradually reconstruct the complex ecclesiastical history of the South-East.

Place-names

Place-names give an insight into the Anglo-Saxon landscape and settlement which the excavated evidence alone cannot do. They reflect the way in which the countryside was perceived and the manner in which it was used. Unfortunately though, the study of place-names is still at a very early stage. Only in the last twenty years has a rough chronology of the main elements used in English place-names been constructed, particularly through work done on names in the South-East. The main problem which has faced scholars is that it is very difficult to date the formation of a place-name, because its first record in a document may be many centuries after it was first used.

A number of methods have been employed to attempt to date the periods when certain types of place-name were formed. One approach has been to examine place-names in use at an early date. All the names known from English sources written before the year 731 were noted and of these, half the place-names were found to be those that refer to the topography of a place, its position in the landscape. These names, which simply describe a place in relationship to its surroundings, such as its location on a hill or island or by a stream, are likely to precede the next type of names which relate a place to a particular family or individual. Place-names were probably not given by the people who lived at that place; they did not need a name to refer to their home and land. The names were given by neighbours and officials, who needed to distinguish one place in the area from another. Names developed only gradually, as the property and people came to be identified with one another.

To study this type of place-name the distribution of certain name elements has been compared with the pattern of known archaeological sites so that it has been possible to isolate names which were contemporary with those sites. The results show that place names containing the Old English (OE) element *hām* meaning 'village' or 'estate' coincide fairly well with the areas of Early-Anglo-Saxon cemeteries and they are likely to have been among the names used for the adjoining settlements. Clapham in Sussex, for example, lies near a possible Anglo-Saxon barrow. More generally, *hām* names rarely occur north of the Downs in Sussex except for a few examples in the Hailsham area. In Kent the names are frequent in the eastern part of the county, where there was Early Anglo-Saxon settlement, in the west of Kent north of the Pilgrim's Way and along and parallel with the valleys of the rivers Darenth, Medway and Stour. In brief, they occur in all the areas of fertile soil which were occupied by the Germanic settlers. *Hām* names in Surrey are scattered throughout the county, except in the extreme south (Dodgson 1973). But not all names which end in -ham derive from the OE -*hām*, for there is another place-name element, *hamm*, which means 'land in a river bend' or 'dry ground in a marsh' and this was used throughout the Anglo-Saxon period. It is necessary to distinguish carefully between names from -*hām* and *hamm* before concluding that the place was in an area of early settlement.

Names containing the element -*ingas* are partly found in the areas of Early-Anglo-Saxon cemeteries, but they also extend into other regions. The most likely interpretation is that they were formed during a period of secondary colonization, when the Anglo-Saxon settlements expanded beyond the original area of occupation into new regions. In Kent names such as Brishing extend south beyond the area of the cemeteries and are found on the less attractive clay and poorer chalk soils, as if settlements so named were founded after the best land had been occupied. In Sussex -*ingas* names occur both on and also north of the Downs where the cemeteries mostly lie. The evidence suggests a sequence of place-names which begins with names of topographic type, and is succeeded by names with the elements -*hām* and then -*ingas*, with names such as Warlingham in Surrey which contains both elements coming somewhere in between the two (Dodgson 1966).

For the most part the Anglo-Saxons did not choose to use the existing names which had been given by the Celts and Romano-Britons, but extensively renamed the landscape. Only a few of the earlier names were taken over by the Germanic settlers, though in some cases they adopted elements from the earlier languages. The British name for Chichester, *Noviomagus*, was forgotten and the town was called by the Anglo-Saxons *Cisseceastre* which uses the Latin word *castrum* meaning 'a fortified town'. The same element appears on the Anglo-Saxon name for the Saxon Shore fort at Pevensey, *Andredesceaster* which was derived from the Romano-British name, *Anderitum*. Curiously, though a form of the traditional name was initially adopted by the Anglo-Saxons, it had been replaced by an entirely new name by the late eighth century and it is from this that the modern place name derives. The reason for the capricious rejection of the older name is not clear, nor is it apparent why groups of Celtic place names were perpetuated in a few areas. The Croydon area of Surrey and the north-west corner of Sussex, where there are the names Pen Hill in Elsted and Torberry in Harting, have concentrations of surviving Celtic names.

At no time have place-names remained fixed and unchanged. As settlements were abandoned or moved, old names could be lost and new names replace them. Many place-names derive from the name of the occupant or lord of a settlement and as they died or were superseded, so the name could vary. One of the best-documented examples of such changes is recorded in a ninth-century charter for an estate which lay in the area of Somerfield in Kent. The original charter granted a place called *Pleghelmestun* or 'the farm of Pleghelm'. Later endorsements show that it was subsequently called *aet Berwicum*, 'the outlying dependency' and later still *Wieghelmestun* which means 'the farm of Wighelm'. This last name stuck and there was a manor called Wilmington as late as the nineteenth century, though now this place name too has been forgotten. But a third addition to the charters suggests the same place was also briefly called Delham, after yet another tenant or lord (Ward 1936).

In a few cases the individuals after which a place has been named can actually be identified. The lord of Blackmanstone in Kent before the Norman Conquest was Blaecman and he was very probably also the founder of *Blacemannescirce* mentioned in the Domesday Monachorum. Bishopstone in Sussex was a property of the bishops of Chichester and it had been granted to them in about the 770s. The name means 'the farm of the bishop' and nearby are Norton, 'the north farm' and Sutton 'the south farm', both named from their position in relation to the central vill (Fig. 7.5a). The place names Ersham, Yeverington and Jevington which lie close to one another in eastern Sussex derive from the personal names Gifric, Gefhere and Gefa (the personal name Gifric is deduced but not attested in any extant Old English documents). These all contain the stem *Gef-* and it seems quite likely that these places were the names of settlements owned by members of a single family. The use of alliterative names was a not-uncommon custom among close relations.

For the archaeologist place-names are particularly valuable for the information they give about the condition of the land and its use. The heavily wooded character of the Weald is very clearly shown by the number of names connected with the clearance of trees which are found there. The element *leah*, for example, which has the primary meaning of a clearing in woodland, occurs in Sussex almost exclusively in this area, though in Surrey the distribution is more widespread. The element *ersc*, 'an enclosure' shows this Wealden distribution in both counties very strongly. In Surrey the element *falod*, meaning 'an animal fold', coincides closely with the *ersc* place names and marks an area which was first used for the seasonal grazing of stock driven from settlements beyond the Weald. On the other side of the county boundary, in Sussex, there are a corresponding number of *falod* names, but names of this type are very rare in the eastern part of the Weald where an equivalent term, the OE *denn*, indicating an animal pasture, was used instead (Darby 1963). This is one of the most common roots of place names in parts of Southern Kent and North-Eastern Sussex. Names of this sort may link the Wealden pasture lands with the parent settlements. Thus Tenterden was the *denn* of the people of Thanet, though this had replaced the earlier name of *Brentingsleag*. The extensive common pastures in the South-East gave rise to place names coming from the OE *gemaennes* meaning 'common property'. Stelling Minnis in Kent, Minnis Rock in Hastings and Manhood Hundred south of Chichester come from this word and it occurs in a number of places in North-West Sussex, in an area which had been common woodland pasture in the Weald (Gardiner 1984).

At the eastern end of the Weald *hamm* place names are particularly common, especially in the valleys of the rivers Rother and Lympne. The names here emphasize the importance to the Anglo-Saxon settlers of the rich pasture lands in the broad valley bottoms. By contrast, places on the high Wealden ridges, which are called 'downs' locally, are often given names which include the colours black and brown. Browndown and Blackhurst, both in Sussex, record the sombre colours of the infertile heathland or dense woodland which was the only vegetation growing on the poor soils. Another element of topography is recorded in *cumb* and *denu* names, which both mean 'valley'. The difference between these two words has been investigated in the South-East and it seems very probable that they were used not arbitrarily, but quite specifically. A *cumb* was a valley containing flowing water and a *denu* was without any stream or river (Coates 1981). Such nuances of place-name usage provide a direct insight into the precise way in which names were given and into the Anglo-Saxon perception of landscape.

Vikings

The Vikings first appeared on the South Coast sometime in the last decade or so of the eighth century. Landing at Portland they promptly killed the king's reeve, who had thought that they were traders and had ordered them to go to the royal vill at Dorchester. It was quickly appreciated that not only were the Vikings not interested in trade, but they were a very serious threat to the country. A charter of Offa of 792 makes provision for the defence in Kent against the 'pagan sailors' who may have already appeared in the county, and a few years later 6 acres of land inside the walls of Canterbury were given to the minster of Lyminge as a refuge against the Vikings. Raiding by the Vikings in the following few decades was sporadic, but after the sack of the Isle of Sheppey in 835 the attacks became more frequent and more serious. Kent, with its long coastline and considerable wealth, was particularly vulnerable and suffered badly. The Anglo-Saxon Chronicle records that great damage was done throughout Kent in 841, and in the following year the Vikings raided the town and trading centre of Rochester. In 850/1 for the first time they remained over the winter in England, on Thanet. Canterbury and London were sacked and the Mercian King and his army put to flight. The West Saxon king, Aethelwulf, however, was able to rout the Vikings at *Aclea*, an unidentified place in Surrey.

The battle was a significant turning point in the power struggle between the kingdoms for it established the pre-eminence of Wessex whose kings already controlled Kent, Surrey, Sussex and Essex, in Southern England. The victory at *Aclea* was of minor importance, though, in the war against the Vikings. In 865 a larger host of Vikings, the Great Army, landed in East Anglia and was augmented in 871 by a second army. The latter ravaged the Thames Valley and spent the winter of 871–2 in London, which they may have used as a base for raiding Kent in subsequent years. A hoard dating from this period was found in Croydon in 1862, where it had been buried by a member of a Viking band. It contained hack silver, pennies from Wessex, Mercia and East Anglia and coins from Carolingian France, the spoils of earlier raids on both sides of the Channel. It also included Kufic coins from Arab lands which had reached Scandinavia by way of Russia, reflecting the wide contacts of the Vikings. Croydon, as a large estate belonging to Christ Church, Canterbury was an attractive place for Viking treasure seekers and may have been a convenient point for collecting payments of food and money from surrounding lands (Brooks 1984: 152).

The turning point in the battle against the Danes came in the 880s when Alfred was able to rally the men of Wessex. The Vikings had occupied Northumbria, Mercia and East Anglia, and the South-East, though not conquered, remained subject to raiding. In order to protect the county, Alfred constructed a series of fortified centres or burhs to act as refuges for the population. The effectiveness of this policy was proven by the events of 884–5. The Vikings landed in two groups in Kent and while one half of the host harried the east of the county, the other besieged Rochester which had been fortified against them. The people in the city held out until Alfred arrived, took the Viking encampment and the Danes retreated to their boats in such haste that they left their horses behind.

A record of the fortifications built against the Vikings has survived in a text called the *Burghal Hidage*. The main part of the text may date from this period in the 880s, although later additions were made in the early tenth century. It lists the West Saxon burhs beginning in the South-East and proceeding in a clockwise direction through Southern England and ending with Southwark (Fig. 8.8). Kent is not included, although there undoubtedly were similar fortified positions in the county, including Rochester. To each of the burhs a value in hides is given according to the length of wall to be defended. Each hide or area of land produced one man, and every pole (5½ yards) of wall was manned by four men. The burhs fall into two groups, those with a large hidage which were intended to be permanent settlements and commercial centres, and those with a smaller assessment which served just as forts.

Eorpeburnan, the first burh listed in the Burghal Hidage, was alloted 324 hides and belongs to the second group. This place-name is not known, but the fort has been identified both with the earthworks at Castle Toll in Newenden, Kent or, less convincingly, with the town of Rye in Sussex (Kitchen 1984). The bank and ditch at Newenden cut off the end of a peninsula of dry land between the marshes of the River Rother and Hexden Channel. Excavations there found that built within the fort was a thirteenth-century castle, but across the neck of the peninsula was an undated ditch, possibly of Viking age. Initially the ditch was intended to be a massive 13 m broad, but this was not completed and a smaller ditch 9 m wide and 2 m deep was constructed. *Eorpeburnan* may have been the fort which was stormed by the Danes in 892 after they had rowed their ships up the River Lympne. That fort, when attacked was only half completed. This documentary record and the archaeological evidence point to the practical problems Alfred had actually to carry out his scheme of defence. His biographer, Asser, complains of burhs not begun or begun too late because of the slackness of the people (Davison 1972).

Hastings, Burpham near Arundel and Eashing near Guildford are the other *burhs* with a low valuation in hides and intended as temporary forts. The site of Hastings burh is not known and it may have been lost through coastal erosion or under the nineteenth- and twentieth-century development in the town. Burpham resembles *Eorpeburnan* for it too is on a peninsula surrounded on three sides by river marshes (Plate 8.3). These faces of the fort are defended by natural cliffs and on the fourth side is an impressive bank and ditch. The gateway through the bank and an area behind it were excavated and a series of superimposed buildings found. These suggest that Burpham was occupied over a considerable period and evidence of iron-working also argues that this was

Plate 8.3 (*a* and *b*) Burpham fort, near Arundel. The fort constructed as a defence against the Vikings occupied a natural tongue of land rising sharply above the river flood-plain which surrounds it on three sides (see (*a*) above). On the fourth side a high bank and ditch was thrown up to control access from the north (see (*b*) below). It is shown from the inside; the modern village lies outside the fort.

more than a temporary refuge in times of trouble. A permanent community was probably settled in the burh and this may have moved out beyond the confines of the defences to become the present village (Sutermeister 1976). The burh at Eashing has only recently been identified for it lacks any major earthworks and relies for its defence on steep valleys. Only on the south-east is it protected by a now rather poorly preserved bank (Aldsworth and Hill 1971). *Eorpeburnan*, Burpham and Eashing are situated close to rivers and part of their purpose was to control access from the sea up river.

Three burhs in the South-East were given large assessments in the Burghal Hidage and were intended to act as commercial as well as defensive centres. The burh at Chichester encompassed the area within the walls of the Roman town and that at Southwark occupied roughly the same land on which the Roman suburb had been built. The site of the burh at Lewes had never had any significant level of Roman occupation and the defences were constructed overlooking the River Ouse, either on what was a new site, or possibly in an existing royal centre. The bank and ditch of the burh cannot be traced now, but it is probable that they followed the line of the Medieval wall on the west side. These larger burhs were probably intended to serve as shire towns and both Lewes and Chichester have retained this function up to the present day. Southwark appears in the Burghal Hidage as *Suthringa geweorche* or 'defensive works of the men of Surrey', which identifies it with a broader area too. Excavations in all three towns have found Late Anglo-Saxon occupation. In the late ninth and early tenth centuries there was an upsurge in the urban activity which very likely was connected with the stimulus given to the growth of towns by the development of burhs by the West Saxon kings. As the Viking threat receded the level of commercial activity grew and, more importantly, laws were passed to concentrate trading in towns.

In the South-East there were almost a hundred years of comparative peace before the Vikings returned. In 980 the Viking raids resumed and the second wave of attacks followed much the same course as the first. It began with coastal raiding, with Kent again suffering incursions on Thanet and at Folkestone and Sandwich. A few peaceful years followed with no raids recorded, but in 994 there were more widespread attacks afflicting Essex, Kent, Sussex and Hampshire. They were carried out by the largest army seen in England for a half century with a fleet of 94 ships and a force of more than 2,000 warriors. In 997 an army landed in England and settled down and began to harry Southern England over a number of years. It established itself on the Isle of Wight and extorted supplies from the mainland opposite in Sussex and Hampshire. During 999 the Vikings sailed round the coast into the Medway, where they were opposed by Kentish levies at Rochester. The Danes beat them and, taking to horseback, laid waste a large part of the west of Kent. The year 1000 opened with the English armies faced by a better-organized and better-led Danish force.

The second wave of the Viking raids produced no great defensive works such as the burhs of Alfred, but stray finds, many of them discovered through dredging in rivers, can augment the historical record and show something of the equipment of the Danes. The raids of the late tenth and eleventh centuries were often conducted on horseback and the Vikings were the first to realize the advantage given by stirrups, which allowed a rider to fight more effectively. The distribution of Viking stirrup finds fits well with the movements of the Danish armies between 993 and 1017. In the South-East they have been found in the Thames valley, at Battersea for example, and one has been discovered near Canterbury. An attack on London about 1000 is the most likely context for the deposition of a hoard of Viking spears, axes and an anchor found near London Bridge. Another axe was found at Maidstone and a spearhead was discovered at Staines. The effect of a Viking attack is most graphically given by finds made in Canterbury over a number of years. So many pieces of tenth-century metalwork have been found that it has been suggested that the most likely context for their loss is the capture and sack of the city in 1011. The host that took Canterbury was particularly barbaric and kidnapped the archbishop only to kill him the following year by pelting him with bones after a drunken meal.

Anglo-Saxon Industry

The South-East is particularly well-endowed with the natural resources which were exploited by Anglo-Saxon industry. There are many sources of clay for the production of pottery, the long coastline of Kent and Sussex offers many suitable situations for salt working, and the Weald is one of the few areas of iron ore in Southern England; only outcrops of good building stone are lacking.

By the Late-Anglo-Saxon period it is possible to talk of a pottery industry as opposed to domestic manufacture, but the production of pottery in the South-East in no way compares with the superior products of Eastern England. There was no product which was being made in mass and traded over such a wide area as Thetford Ware, and no kiln was regularly producing glazed pottery such as Stamford or Winchester Wares. Small quantities of poorly made glazed pottery from the late ninth or early tenth century found in Canterbury were the results of an unsuccessful experiment to make a similar ware. By contrast with the Stamford and Thetford industries, pottery production in the South-East was small-scale and crude in method. Much, probably most of the pottery here, was not even wheel-thrown; it was coil- or slab-built and trued up on a *tournette* with features such as sharply everted rims, typical of Late-Anglo-Saxon wares from the Chichester region, often applied after-

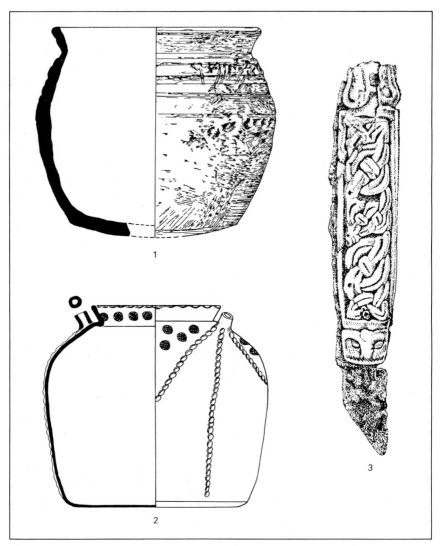

Figure 8.7 Late Anglo-Saxon artifacts. Stamp decoration is common on vessels of this period from the Chichester area (2), but occurs less frequently on pots from Canterbury (1). A bone knife, also from Canterbury, with Anglo-Saxon decoration reflects Viking influence (3) (scales: 1:¼; 2:⅛; 3:¹⁄₁).

wards by hand. The pots were then fired in clamp kilns, producing blotchy fabric with most of the surface oxidized, giving a red or orange colour, but with grey patches where it had been reduced. Such methods of manufacture were not suited for mass production because they were time-consuming. The six kilns producing wheel-thrown pottery found at Chapel Street in Chichester, which had a mean archaeomagnetic date of the mid-eleventh century, however, do suggest an industry of some scale or perhaps longevity.

The products of Late Anglo-Saxon kilns were mainly limited to cooking pots, which represent many of the vessels excavated, dishes, pitchers and large storage jars. The pottery found inside Chichester and in the surrounding areas is often ornamented with stamp impressions which appear to be in the tradition of pagan Anglo-Saxon pottery and even uses designs found on the earlier pots (Cunliffe 1974) (Fig. 8.7, cf. Fig. 8.3). A number of storage jars are decorated with elaborate patterns of raised bands. These may have had a functional purpose to strengthen these very large vessels or make them easier to handle, but there is a possibility that the decoration is skeuomorphic. It may recall leather containers or sacks made up of many pieces of hide stitched together or which had been similarly strengthened with leather bands. The published pottery from Canterbury, by contrast, is unornamented, though boss-decorated local wares were found in a Mid-to-Late-Anglo-Saxon pit in the outer court of St Augustine's Abbey.

Pottery produced in Hampshire was also traded in West Sussex. Portchester Ware, named after the place where it was first recognized, is a distinct wheel-turned product possibly made in the Wickham area. It is often rilled and occasionally rouletted. Pottery of this type has been found in Chichester and at Fishbourne. Its most easterly occurrence by far is at Lancing, Sussex, where it was discovered on a saltworking site and it may have reached there in exchange for salt which was traded to Hampshire.

The find of Portchester Ware is the sole piece of archaeological evidence for Anglo-Saxon salt manufacture in the South-East, but Domesday Book indicates that Sussex in particular, and Kent were the main centres in England for the production of salt from a marine source. In Sussex saltworking was mainly practised in the area of the Pevensey Marsh, the Adur Valley and the Rye area where a hundred salterns are recorded. The corresponding area of Kent, the Romney Marsh, was a similar centre of manufacture and there were also concentrations of salterns along the Wantsum and Swale channels. It is very probable that the same methods which were employed in the Medieval period had been used previously by the Anglo-Saxon industry. The English climate is unsuitable for the production of salt by the total evaporation of sea water and the methods used required the heating of brine to drive off the water. In 732 Æthelberht of Kent granted land at Sampton suitable for the roasting of salt and gave 120 wagon loads of wood for this process. (Sawyer 1968: no. 23). A similar grant was made in the same place a century later, which might argue that this was an early centre of salt manufacture. The brine used was not obtained directly from the sea, but was concentrated by washing water through salt-impregnated silt or sand. The used silt and sand accumulated in large mounds and, if the Anglo-Saxons followed the Medieval practice, these heaps were then used as convenient places of work, raised above the height of tidal flooding. Those mounds containing only small quantities of burnt clay distinguishing the Anglo-Saxon and Medieval salt works from the Roman and earlier salterns which mostly comprise burnt material giving the soil a red colour.

The only place at which the archaeological evidence for salt manufacture has been studied in detail is the Adur river valley in Sussex. The river is tidal for some distance from its mouth and, although more than a metre of alluvium has been laid down in some places since the late eleventh century, before recent agricultural work the mounds stood quite prominently above the flood plain. The saltern mounds occur in groups along the valley, reflecting contemporary or subsequent sites of production and the majority of these are no doubt post-Conquest, though Domesday Book records in the Adur Valley at least 58 of the 309 salterns listed in Sussex (Holden and Hudson 1981).

Both the archaeological and written evidence for iron manufacture is very sparse and the single excavated iron-smelting site gives a poor impression of Anglo-Saxon methods. Yet iron was used widely for agricultural tools as the *Gerefa*, an Old English text giving advice to the sagacious reeve, indicates. It catalogues a huge collection of tools that the well-equipped Anglo-Saxon estate should have: an axe, an adze, a bill, a saw, a sickle, a share and coulter for a plough to name but a few. Examples of iron tools including the shoe of a spade and a draw knife have been excavated at the Middle Anglo-Saxon site at Sampton. There must have been a high demand for iron. The ores of the Weald provided a suitable source for iron manufacture and fuel would have been readily available from the wooded countryside. An iron-smelting site of Middle Anglo-Saxon date was found in Ashdown Forest in the Weald during 1980 (Plate 8.4). The ore used would have first been roasted to drive off some of the impurities and the resulting ore 'fines' then placed in the smelting furnace with charcoal. The charcoal may have been prepared at the site in a small trench discovered near to the furnace. The smelting furnace was a crude structure, which used a primitive process. Only minimum smelting conditions were achieved and the slag was not tapped from the furnace. At the end of smelting, the iron bloom was removed and worked in one of the two forging hearths adjacent (Tebbutt 1982).

The compact arrangement on the Ashdown Forest site of nearly all the processes of iron manufacture within a small area argues that this was a very small-scale operation and the methods employed would have produced only limited quantities of iron. It is hard to understand how sites of this type could constitute an industry and satisfy the demand for iron from Southern England, but this single example may not be typical of iron production, particularly by the Late Anglo-Saxon period. Yet Domesday Book mentions for Sussex only

---

Plate 8.4   The primitive ninth-century iron furnace (background) at Millbrook, Ashdown Forest, East Sussex barely achieved minimum conditions for smelting. The hearth (foreground) was for forging the iron after it had been smelted. Scale 1 m. (Photograph by C. F. Tebbutt, with acknowledgements to the Sussex Archaeological Society.)

one *ferraria* or ironworks, which argues that they were of little financial worth.

Domesday Book does record a few quarries in the South-East, though there are not many areas of good-quality stone for building. The Lower Greensand formation was worked at Limpsfield in Surrey, where there were two quarries in 1086 and at Grittenham near Petworth, at Iping and Stedham, all in Sussex. At Bignor nearby, a quarry was operated specifically to make millstones. The same geology provided Kentish Rag, used for example in Lydd church and Bargate stone seen in the vertical pilasters and quoins on Sompting church tower. It was also utilized in carved stones in Jevington and Bexhill churches. Very often the less ambitious churches would exploit any local source of stone, even if not ideal for the purpose. Flint, which occurs in bands in the chalk, was employed widely as a building material in Saxon churches on the Downs, but it is not certain if the material used was quarried, or simply collected from the surface of fields. Calcareous tufa is found in the churches of Leeds and Northfleet in Kent. The church at Stoke d'Abernon, Surrey, includes large blocks of Upper Greensand, firestone, and Battle Abbey, to commemorate the Norman success at Hastings, was constructed of local stone found nearby. Since few buildings apart from churches were made of stone, local quarries may have been opened to supply the needs of specific buildings. Only the sources of better-quality stone may have been worked regularly, as the Domesday record implies. On the other hand, the Lower Greensand quarries in Domesday Book may have expanded only after the Conquest, when work began on the construction of many monasteries and churches under the Normans.

Stone of a higher quality had to be brought into the South-East, either from elsewhere in Southern England or, less commonly, from abroad. The cross head from Reculver and the pilasters in the lower part of the church tower at Sompting (Aldsworth, pers. comm.) are made from stone imported from Northern France, but the use of such stone is comparatively rare. Stone was more frequently moved within the country. Stone from the Bath and Box areas was transported as far as Godalming and Kingston in Surrey, which significantly are both on rivers, suggesting it may not have come overland all the way. The coast of Sussex as far east as Lewes was supplied by stone from Quarr on the Isle of Wight and the distribution again argues for the importance of water-borne transport. These 'foreign' stones were used sparingly in the construction of churches and employed particularly for architectural features, such as mouldings which required careful carving, windows and quoins which carried particular weight (Jope 1964).

What has been described here as industry barely conforms to a modern conception of industry. The production of materials by the Anglo-Saxons, like the industry of the Medieval period about which much more is known, was unlikely to have been a full-time profession. It was probably an adjunct to other work. Conversely though, all the industries mentioned required specialized knowledge to some degree. Iron, for example, was probably not smelted by individuals who required some metal to mend their ploughs. Production, even on a small scale was done by experienced craftsmen either to order or speculatively, for sale in the market place. The presence of industry within an economy implies the opportunity to exchange or trade the products and, where the industries are mostly making utilitarian goods in some quantity, it argues for a market economy.

The manufacture of pottery is the best-understood industry because of the abundant remains, but it is likely to reflect the production of other utilitarian goods for it was a cheap, ubiquitous product. The change in the scale of pottery production appears to take place during the tenth century in the major centres of Winchester, London and Canterbury. In Chichester, and in Lewes which has been suggested as a centre of manufacture, the shift to mass production must have come towards the end of that century or a little later. The growth of market places in towns made possible the emergence of full-scale production of pottery, but also, no doubt of salt and iron. These industries which have left a tangible trace must stand for those dealing in organic materials which have not survived. The Domesday rent of 16,000 herrings from Iford in Sussex suggests fishing carried out on a commercial scale and in that sense was an industry just as much as salt manufacture. The proximity of Iford to the town at Lewes, then, is surely not coincidental.

Late Anglo-Saxon Towns

As the threat of Viking raids receded from the South-East during the tenth century, some of the burhs set up as a defensive network against the Vikings developed into commercial and administrative centres. The Grately decrees, issued in 930, established the number of moneyers who could mint coins in each town. Already some of the burhs had emerged as more significant centres in a hierarchy of central places, which developed with competition between markets (Fig. 8.9). Canterbury came second only to London with seven moneyers, Rochester was a significant centre with three, and Lewes with two was established as a more important town than Chichester or Hastings which had only one moneyer apiece. These numbers can be taken as an expression of commercial activity within the towns and can be compared with the total number of moneyers known to have been operating at various centres throughout the whole of the Late Anglo-Saxon period. Using this measure, Canterbury was still predominant among the towns of the South-East, but was followed more closely by Southwark, Lewes and Dover. Hastings, Rochester, Chiches-

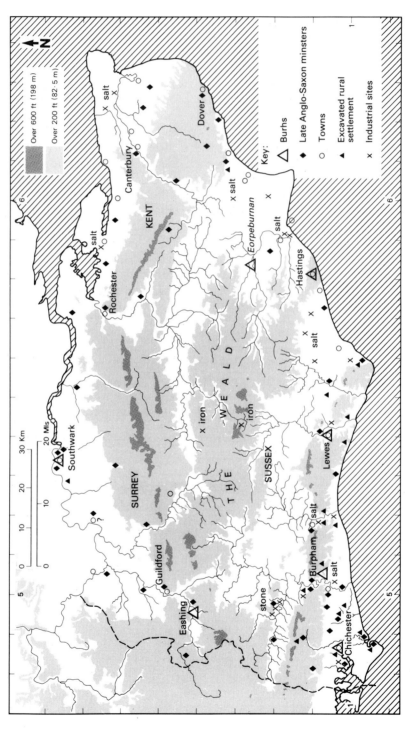

Figure 8.8 South-East England in the Late Anglo-Saxon Period. Kent is not covered by the Burghal Hidage List, though there must have been burhs in that county. The importance of trade with the Continent is suggested by the number of ports along the coasts of eastern Sussex and Kent. The Weald remained a relatively sparsely populated area.

ter and Guildford had lesser numbers of moneyers and there were other mints of decreasing significance (Hill 1981: 130) (Fig. 8.8).

From its early origins Canterbury had continued to grow in spite of Viking raids. By 932 it had a *hrypera ceap* or cattle market, a specialized place of trade indicating a high level of commerce. This was one of at least three extramural street markets. As in the earlier period, goods were still imported from abroad, probably coming through the harbour at Fordwich, lower down the Stour. Excavations in the town have discovered Badorf-type ware dated to 850–950, which arrived from the Rhineland and Pingsdorf ware, which is slightly later, showing that trade contacts continued throughout the Anglo-Saxon period. The results of the excavations indicate a developed town with rubbish pits, property boundaries, cellared buildings and timber halls recorded. The stratigraphic sequence in St George's Street shows how the town grew and urban authority took control. The road was first established according to documentary evidence in the tenth century and was gradually worn away by traffic into a hollow way depressed below the level of the adjoining land. As authority was asserted in the town, it was surfaced sometime during the Late Anglo-Saxon period by a layer of gravel and then continued to be maintained and repaired with subsequent layers. Within Canterbury, occupation deposits progressively accumulated, covering the Roman roads and foundations of buildings, though many upstanding walls would have continued to be visible. The amphitheatre was not demolished until the eleventh century, when robbing of the Roman masonry began, but this is likely to have taken place mostly after the Norman Conquest, when many stone buildings were erected.

The population of Canterbury at Domesday has been estimated at between 3,000 and 6,000; that of Lewes at the same date was 2,000. Excavations in Lewes have recovered Saxo-Norman pottery from six locations within the town, indicating certain occupation along the central ridge and the probable northern part of the burh around St John-sub-Castro. It has been suggested that the streets on the southern part of the town are 'remarkably equidistant' (Rudling 1983; 47) and may be the result of deliberate planning, but like all the evidence for Late-Saxon town planning, this requires critical examination.

Chichester had a population of between 1,200 and 1,500 in the late eleventh century, but the area enclosed by the walls is likely to have been a little larger than Lewes. It was therefore less densely settled and like Canterbury may have included farmland within the town. Excavations which have concentrated in the north-west quadrant of the town have shown that this area was heavily occupied during the Late-Anglo-Saxon period. The south-west quadrant, on the other hand, was sufficiently open for room to be found to accommodate the cathedral when it was moved from Selsey after the Conquest. Finds from the excavations have comprised mainly rubbish pits with the vestigial remains of a few structures The larger size and greater number of rubbish pits from the tenth and eleventh centuries by comparison with pits of an earlier date suggest that the population of the town increased rapidly. This argues that the numbers of inhabitants in the eighth and ninth centuries, when the town was re-occupied, may have been very low indeed.

Guildford, the last of the shire towns in the South-East had, on the basis of Domesday figures, a population of about 750. Surrey generally had a low level of urbanization, because it lacked direct access to the sea and therefore to foreign trade and also stood in the shadow of London. Guildford may have grown to replace the burh at Eashing, which lay in an unsuitable site for an urban centre. In default of much archaeological evidence, topographic analysis of the town has suggested that it developed from a nucleus around St Mary's church and expanded when a larger area was planned and laid out in the Late-Anglo-Saxon period (O'Connell and Poulton 1984). Like the other so-called planned towns, Chichester and Lewes, it is not evident that the town was laid out in a systematic way at one date. The central road, the intramural street and the rectilinear pattern of minor streets which are the suggested elements of many 'planned' towns may equally well have arisen through the constraints enforced by the town walls and organic growth.

Below the level of the shire towns were the secondary market centres (Fig. 8.9). The larger of these were bigger than the smaller shire towns. Sandwich, for example, may have had a population of about 2,000. These towns are a rather heterogeneous collection, but they may be considered in various groups according to their origins. Some of the towns had developed from Roman walled towns or forts, the defences of which served to give protection against the Vikings and the towns also had good communications along surviving Roman roads. In addition to Canterbury and Chichester, Rochester, Pevensey and Dover grew within surviving Roman defences and the early forms of the place-name for Hastings suggest it too might have grown from some Roman establishment. In spite of the activities of the Vikings, Rochester continued to prosper, though limited excavations in the town have revealed little of this period. In Rochester Castle a layer of gravel from the Late-Anglo-Saxon period was discovered in 1976 containing a coin of Alfred, a tenth-century axe and imported Pingsdorf pottery. The Medieval town of Pevensey stood outside the walls of the Saxon Shore fort and on the eastern side, but it has been suggested that the Anglo-Saxon town was probably within the walls, which is why excavations in the Medieval town found nothing earlier than the twelfth century (Taylor 1969). It may have moved its position either soon after the castle was fortified by the Normans, or more gradually in the post-Conquest period. The port dues paid in 1066 show that its position with access to the sea was one of the reasons for its growth. Dover is very inadequately covered by Domesday Book, yet it had an early mint and must have been a major port. It is hoped that the recent excavations will indicate its true importance.

A second group of towns are those which had begun as Middle-Anglo-Saxon trading settlements. Some of the *wic* ports failed to develop into towns. Woolwich, Greenwich and Selsey, if it was such a place, did not grow into urban settlements. Aldwych, Middle-Saxon London, may have moved into the protective enclosure of the Roman city wall, perhaps after 886 when Alfred took it from the Vikings. Sandwich and Fordwich prospered despite their vulnerability to sea-borne attack, and grew as the population figures for the former indicate. They both continued to serve as ports and in the early eleventh century were granted the profits of justice within their respective towns in return for providing the king with ships and seamen against the Vikings. This arrangement formed the basis of the Cinque Ports confederacy.

Romney and probably Hythe were also given this privilege. They emerged together with a number of other ports as towns towards the end of the Anglo-Saxon period. New Romney replaced the older town of Old Romney on a more convenient site nearer the sea. Westwards along the coast, situated on a shingle bank like New Romney, was the port of Old Winchelsea. The site of this is now totally lost for it was washed away during the late thirteenth-century and is now under the sea. The Abbey of Fecamp was granted the tolls of this developing port in the early eleventh century to augment their possession of the nearby manors of Brede and *Rameslie*. The latter included another port at Rye which was valuable as a channel of communication between the abbey in Normandy and its English possessions. The speed of the growth of Rye is implied by its Domesday description as a 'new borough'. Beyond Hastings, still further along the coast, was Bulverhythe. The place-name means 'the harbour of the citizens' and it is usually suggested that it was a subsidiary port for the people of Hastings. It is, however, equally possible that there was a small town here, lying to the east of Bexhill, for Domesday Book records twenty burgesses under the entry for Bullington, which lay very close by Bulverhythe. Thus along this short length of the south-eastern coast of Kent and Sussex was a group of ports which developed in the years around 1000 to serve the increased level of contact with France, and such was the scale of trade of the wealth of the hinterland that they were able to develop into towns. None of these towns, excepting Rye, has been subject to archaeological investigation and no finds datable to before the thirteenth century were discovered there.

In addition to these were two further Late Anglo-Saxon ports at Seasalter and Arundel. The town of Seasalter lay on the North Kent coast and was a probable trading centre for salt, which gave the place its name, and for fish. Seasalter may well have also participated in cross-Channel trade, for in the marshes not far away was found the tenth-century Graveney boat in which was a pot imported from Northern France or Belgium (Fenwick 1978). Arundel in Sussex is not situated on the coast but lies on a river estuary a few miles from the sea. Just as Guildford replaced the burh at Eashing, so Arundel may have grown as nearby Burpham, another burh fort, declined. No port is recorded here in 1066, though it may have been omitted by mistake, for twenty years later a harbour and borough are noted.

The final group of Late-Anglo-Saxon towns are those which developed from royal *tuns*. These were often the centres of hundreds and also the sites of

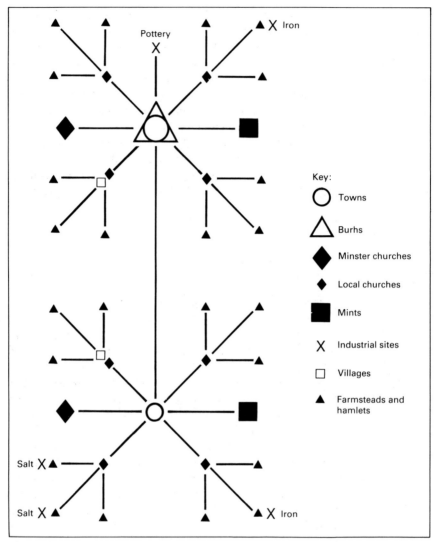

Figure 8.9 Late Anglo-Saxon society. In the Late Anglo-Saxon period the number of towns increased. Villages also grew up, often around local churches which were increasingly usurping the role of minster churches. Industry was gradually developing in the towns and countryside.

minster churches. They were therefore already places of religious importance and of administration and may have been developed as markets for royal officials to sell off the surplus food rents given by tributary lands, and not required for consumption by the king and his household (Neale 1979). Faversham and Milton Regis in Kent are recognizably royal centres from the sixth century and both have large surrounding hundreds, which may indicate the territory that they formerly administered. There was a market at Faversham and probably one at Milton according to Domesday Book. Kingston in Surrey has already been discussed. Its name indicates its ownership and there was there an important minster church. Guildford is similar in origin, for it was a royal property mentioned in King Alfred's Will and close by at Stoke there was a minster church. The town about which most is known is Steyning in Sussex, a Late Anglo-Saxon port and the burial place of King Æthulwulf, father of King Alfred. Excavations there have found imported French pottery, which was brought in through the historically documented Port of St Cuthman, and the evidence of an extensive Middle and Late-Anglo-Saxon settlement lying to the west and south of the minster church. Iron was worked and loomweights indicate textile production. Apart from the usual range of cattle, sheep and pig bones, the faunal remains show that deer were hunted and fish caught in the estuary of the Adur.

Late Anglo-Saxon Rural Settlement and Society

Though the search for the origin of towns has had some success in locating the period of growth and the course of urban expansion, the study of the origin of villages has been more problematic. Yet in the Late-Anglo-Saxon period the overwhelming majority of people continued to live in the countryside and the economy remained dominated by the products of agriculture. Locating their settlements has proved so difficult because in much of the South-East people lived not in nucleated villages, which might have left archaeological evidence over a reasonable area, but in dispersed farms which have left almost no trace. The tentative conclusion from field and documentary work is that the main period of village growth may no longer be placed in the period of the Germanic migrations, but must be considerably later. Stuart Rigold (1982) has commented that perhaps all the villages in Kent were late Medieval formations, while Blair (forthcoming) notes that there was a reorganization in Surrey in the eleventh, twelth and thirteenth centuries from dispersed farmsteads to nucleated settlements. In both counties the predominanat type of Late Anglo-Saxon rural settlement appears to have been the farm or hamlet and in Sussex the most thoroughly excavated village site, at Hangleton near Hove, revealed no evidence for occupation before the late twelfth century.

This view of the settlement development in the South-East is not contradicted by evidence from other parts of the country such as Norfolk. There the number of villages increased with the rapidly rising density of population in the tenth and eleventh centuries and the amalgamation of separate farms in a process which has been termed 'settlement balling'. In Hampshire the same date is given for formation of nucleated villages with their churches and manor houses, though it is stressed that there continued to be many dispersed farms and hamlets. The precise moment when the shift in settlement occurred to a centralized village, whether in the late Medieval period or somewhat earlier, appears to have been due to local factors. On the most fertile soils this happened at an earlier date than in the areas of woodland and infertile sands and clays. Indeed, in some parishes in the Weald the churches stood in isolation until small hamlets developed around them in the post-Medieval period. But on the richest soils of West Sussex, on the coastal Plain, Late-Anglo-Saxon finds have been made around the churches of Westbourne and Aldingbourne, the chapel of Bilsham and the hamlet of Fishbourne, suggesting that villages may have formed there before the Conquest. Further north in a similar band of light, fertile soils in the valley of the western Rother, the villages are also likely to have been early, and here Anglo-Saxon pottery has been identified from close to the church at Harting.

On the Weald Clay soils east of the Vale of Rother the picture is quite different. In the area of Kirdford the land was divided up into a number of woodland pastures which were common to settlements on the south coast, but in the clearings which had been created a series of isolated farms developed. The villages and hamlets of this region were created much later. Domesday Book captures some of the Wealden farms at a stage in the colonization of the woodland and is particularly informative about settlement in the Battle area of East Sussex. This was a particularly remote area of infertile soils on the sandstone ridges behind Hastings and the few farms here were enumerated individually or in small groups. Each farm was assessed at the rate of one virgate and to each was ascribed a single tenant (Searle 1963). There was no semblance of villages in the sparsely occupied landscape of dispersed farmsteads.

The changes in settlement patterns only make sense in the wider context of the changes which took place in Anglo-Saxon society in the centuries before the Conquest. During the Middle and Late Anglo-Saxon period, land and the concommitant powers over it were gradually being devolved from the king at the centre to the church and to lay lords. These were able to exercise at a local level closer and more effective control of their tenants. They were able to extend their power because, at the same time, the social structure of the family was becoming weakened. The bonds of kinship which tied together blood relations into a mutually supportive group were gradually being dissolved. Instead of the assistance of the king, the unity and strength this had provided was substituted by new relationships with the lords which provided the necessary security. The rather modest dues which had once been collected to sustain the king and his household were diverted to the benefit of private lords, and the size of the renders increased to sustain this new and growing level in the social hierarchy. The nature of the dues changed. From being collective tributary payments of food falling on a large group, they became rents extracted from individuals in money or through work services.

As land was granted out by the king to lords, large estates were created from parts of the areas which had once paid food rents to a royal *tun*. Some of the new estates covered many square kilometres, in area, such as the estate of South Malling stretching for 35 kms in a north-easterly direction from near Lewes in the south to the Kent–Sussex border. This had been carved out of a larger area based upon the royal settlement at Beddingham. The estate of South Malling is particularly well documented because it lasted through into the Medieval period. Though some estates may have been formed by the amalgamation of land, the overall movement in the Middle- and Late-Anglo-Saxon periods was towards the fission of the great units of land into smaller estates.

The motive force behind the division of land was the expansion of population. A reasonable estimate may be made of population density at Domesday, but there is no reliable means of calculating the degree by which it had increased in the preceding centuries. In the more populous areas there was necessarily a shift from a subsistence strategy of extensive exploitation to one of intensive, localized agriculture. The long-distance droving of animals to distant pastures in the Weald declined in scale, though it still persisted, for Domesday Book records that many of the vills beyond the Weald paid renders for the woodland animal pastures they used. In the Weald of Kent it has been possible to trace the division of commons into smaller portions and their allocation to specific manors (Witney 1976: 78 ff.). Control of resources became tighter, more localized and dependent on the controlling authority of the lord.

On the richer, more productive arable soils where the population was most dense and the land was exploited most intensely, strong seigneurial authority first developed. In such areas the opportunities for extracting a larger agricultural surplus from the peasants was so much greater and the lord had more of an interest in exercising stronger control over his tenants. By concentrating the population in a single place, a nucleated village, the peasantry could be more effectively managed. Conversely, in remote areas of poor land it was difficult to organize an efficient system for extracting the surplus product and it was less rewarding; here lordship was weakest and the family stayed a stronger force well into the Medieval period.

Abbreviations

Anglo-Saxon Engl. *Anglo-Saxon England*
Ant. J. *Antiquaries Journal*
Arch. *Archaeologia*
Arch. Cant. *Archaeologica Cantiana*
Arch. J. *Archaeological Journal*
Arch. Newsletter *Archaeological Newsletter*
BAR *British Archaeological Reports*, Oxford
Berkshire Arch. Journal *Berkshire Archaeological Journal*
Bull. Inst. Arch. *Bulletin of the Institute of Archaeology*, London
Bull. Surrey Arch. Soc. *Bulletin of the Surrey Archaeological Society*
CBA Council for British Archaeology
CUP Cambridge University Press
Current Arch. *Current Archaeology*
Econ. Hist. Rev. *Economic History Review*
Engl. Hist. Rev. *English Historical Review*
HMSO Her Majesty's Stationery Office
Inst. Brit. Geog. Conf. *Institute of British Geographers' Conference*
J. Arch. Sc. *Journal of Archaeological Science*
J. Brit. Arch. Ass. *Journal of the British Archaeological Association*
J. Hist. Geog. *Journal of Historical Geography*
J. Roy. Anthrop. Inst. *Journal of the Royal Anthropological Institute*
Kent Arch. Review *Kent Archaeological Review*
Med. Arch. *Medieval Archaeology*
Num. Chron. *The Numismatic Chronicle.*
OUP Oxford University Press
Oxford J. Arch. *Oxford Journal of Archaeology*
Phil. Trans. of the Roy. Soc. *Philosophical Transactions of the Royal Society*
Proc. Hants. Field Club and Arch. Soc. *Proceedings of the Hampshire Field Club and Archaeological Society.*
PPS *Proceedings of the Prehistoric Society*
PPS East Anglia *Proceedings of the Prehistoric Society of East Anglia*
P. Roy. Anthropol. Inst. *Proceedings of the Royal Anthropological Institute*
RIB *The Roman Inscriptions of Britain* by R. G. Collingwood and R. P. Wright, Oxford, 1965.

342

Surrey Arch. Coll.   Surrey Archaeological Collections
Surrey Arch. Soc.   Surrey Archaeological Society
Surrey Arch. Soc. Bulletin   Bulletin of the Surrey Archaeological Society
Sussex Arch. Coll.   Sussex Archaeological Collections
Sussex Arch. Soc. Newsletter   Sussex Archaeological Society Newsletter
Trans. London Middlesex Arch. Soc.   Transactions of the London and Middlesex
     Archaeological Society
Trans Roy. Hist. Soc.   Transactions of the Royal Historical Society
World Arch.   World Archaeology

Further Reading

Because of the exceptional length of the bibliography it was felt that the reader might appreciate having a brief list of significant works extracted from the bibliography and organized by chapter. As there are few general works, these include important excavation reports on key sites.

Chapter 1

Curwen, E. C. (1954) *The Archaeology of Sussex*, 2nd edn, London.

Dimbleby, G. W. (1962) *The Development of the British Heathlands and Their Soils*, Oxford Forestry Memoirs 23.

Drewett, P. L. (ed.) (1978) *Archaeology in Sussex to A.D. 1500*, CBA Research Report 29.

Gallois, R. G. (1965) *The Wealden District*, HMSO, London.

Kerney, M. P., Brown, E. H. and Chandler, T. J. (1964) *The Late Glacial and Post-Glacial History of the Chalk Escarpment near Brook, Kent*, Phil. Trans. R. Soc. London, B248, 135–204.

Leach, P. E. (ed.) (1982) *Archaeology in Kent to A.D. 1500*, CBA Research Report 48.

Rankine, W. F. (1956) *The Mesolithic Of Southern England*, Surrey Arch. Soc. Research Papers No. 4.

Waechter, J. d'A. (1969) 'Swanscombe, 1968', *Proc. Roy. Anthropol. Inst. 1969*, 53–61.

Chapter 2

Drewett, P. L. (1975*a*) 'The excavation of an oval burial mound of the third millennium B.C. at Alfriston, East Sussex, 1974', *PPS* 41, 119–52.

Drewett, P. L. (1977) 'The excavation of a Neolithic causewayed enclosure on Offham Hill, East Sussex, 1976', *PPS* 43, 201–41.

Holgate, R. (1981) 'The Medway Megaliths and Neolithic Kent', *Arch. Cant.* 97, 221–34.

Scaife, R. G. and Burrin, P. J. (1983) 'Floodplain development in the vegetational history of the Sussex High Weald and some archaeological implications', *Sussex Arch. Coll.* 121, 1–10.

Whittle, A. W. R. (1977) 'The Earlier Neolithic of S. England and its Continental Background', *BAR* Supplementary Series 35.

Chapter 3

Bradley, R. (1970) 'The excavation of a beaker settlement at Bell Tout, East Sussex, England', *PPS* 36, 312–79.

Drewett, P. L. (1976) 'The excavation of four round barrows of the second millennium B.C. at West Heath, Harting, 1973–75', *Sussex Arch. Coll.* 114, 126–50.

Drewett, P. L. (1982) *The Archaeology of Bullock Down, Eastbourne, East Sussex: the Development of a Landscape*, Sussex Arch. Soc. Monograph 1.

Ellison, A. B. (1980) 'The Bronze Age', *Sussex Arch. Coll.* 118, 31–42.

Chapter 4

Burstow, G. P. and Holleyman, G. A. (1957) 'Late Bronze Age settlement on Itford Hill, Sussex', *Sussex Arch. Coll.* 23, 167–212.

Champion, T, (1980) 'Settlement and environment in Later Bronze Age Kent', in Barrett, J. and Bradley, R. (eds) 'The British Later Bronze Age', *BAR* 83(i), 223–46.

Holden, E. W. (1972) 'A Bronze Age cemetery barrow at Itford Hill, Beddingham', *Sussex Arch. Coll.* 110, 70–117.

Longley, D. (1980) *Runnymede Bridge 1976: Excavations on the Site of a Late Bronze Age Settlement*, Surrey Arch. Soc. Research Vol. 6, Guildford.

Needham, S. and Burgess, C. (1980) 'The Later Bronze Age in the Lower Thames Valley: the metalwork evidence', in 'The British Later Bronze Age', *BAR* 83(ii), 437–470.

Chapter 5

Bird, J. and Bird, D. G. (eds) (1987) *The Archaeology of Surrey to 1540*. Dorking.

Cunliffe, B. W. (1978*a*) *Iron Age Communities in Britain*, 2nd edn, London.

Drewett, P. L. (ed.) (1978) *Archaeology in Sussex to A.D 1500*, CBA Research Report 29.

Leach, P. E. (ed.) (1982) *Archaeology in Kent to A.D. 1500*, CBA Research Report 48.

Chapter 6

Black, E. W. (1987) *The Roman Villas of South-East England*, *BAR* 171.

Cunliffe, B. W. (1973) *The Regni*, London.

Cunliffe, B. W. (1968) *Fifth Report on the Excavations of the Roman Fort, Richborough, Kent*, Society of Antiquaries Research Report No. 23.

Cunliffe, B. W. (1971) *Excavations at Fishbourne*, Society of Antiquaries Research Reports 26 and 27.

Detsicas, A. (1983) *The Cantiaci*, Gloucester.

Chapter 7

Bell, M. G. (1977) 'Excavations at Bishopstone', *Sussex Archaeol. Collect.* 115.

Hawkes, S. C. (1982) 'Anglo-Saxon Kent *c.* 425–725', in Leach, P. E. (ed.), *Archaeology in Kent to A.D. 1500*, CBA Research Report 48, Council for British Archaeology, London, pp. 64–78.

Welch, M. G. (1983) 'Early Anglo-Saxon Sussex', *BAR* British Ser. 112.

Yorke, B. A. E. (1983) 'Joint Kingship in Kent *c.* 560 to 785', *Arch. Cantiana* 48, 11–28.

Chapter 8

Blair, W. J. (forthcoming) *Landholding, Church and Settlement in Early Medieval Surrey*, Surrey Archaeological Society, Guildford.

Brandon, P. F. (ed.) (1978) *The South Saxons*, Phillimore, Chichester.

Haslam, J. (ed.) (1984) *Anglo-Saxon Towns in Southern England*, Phillimore, Chichester.

Hill, D. (1981) *An Atlas of Anglo-Saxon England*, Basil Blackwell, Oxford.

Hodges, R. (1982) *Dark Age Economics: the Origins of Towns and Trade A.D. 600–1000*, Duckworth, London.

Bibliography

Addyman, P. V. and Leigh, D. (1973) 'The Anglo-Saxon village at Chalton, Hampshire: second interim report', *Med. Arch.* **17**, 1–25.

Adkins, L. and Adkins, R. (1984) 'Two Roman coffins from near St. Mary's Church, Beddington', *Surrey Arch. Coll.* **75**, 281–4.

Adkins, L. and Adkins, R. (1986) *Under the Sludge: Beddington Roman Villa: Excavations at Beddington Sewage Works 1981–1983.* Beddington, Carshalton and Wallington Arch. Soc.

Adkins, L. and Adkins, R. (forthcoming) *Excavations at Beddington: Prehistoric Settlement and Roman Villa.* London and Middlesex Arch. Soc. and Surrey Arch. Soc.

Adkins, L., Adkins, R. A. and Perry, J. G. (1968) 'Excavations at Prehistoric and Roman Beddington, 1984–85', *London Archaeologist* Vol. 5, No. 6, 152–6.

Ager, B. M. (1985) 'The smaller variants of the Anglo-Saxon Quoit Brooch', *Anglo-Saxon Studies in Arch. and Hist.* **4**, 1–58.

Aldsworth, F. G. (1979) ' "The Mound" at Church Norton, Selsey, and the site of St. Wilfrid's Church', *Sussex Arch. Coll.* **117**, 103–7.

Aldsworth, F. G. (1983) 'A Bronze Age hoard and settlement at Yapton', *Sussex Arch. Coll.* **121**, 196–8.

Aldsworth, F. G. (1986) 'Bignor Roman Villa – rediscovered', *Popular Arch.* Vol. 7, No. 4, 2–13.

Aldsworth, F. G. and Hill, D. (1971) 'The Burghal Hidage – Eashing', *Surrey Arch. Coll.* **68**, 198–201.

Alexander, J. (1961) 'Excavations at the Chestnuts Megalithic Tomb, Addington, Kent', *Arch. Cant.* **76**, 1.

Allen, D. F. (1961) 'The origins of coinage in Britain: a reappraisal', pp. 97–308 in Frere, S. S. (ed.), *Problems of the Iron Age in Southern Britain.* London.

Allen, M. J. (1982) 'Results of environmental work at Norton Hill (TQ 466 017)', *Lewes Arch. Group Newsletter* **60**, 5–6.

Allen, M. J. (1984) *Ashcombe Bottom Excavation.* Lewes Arch. Group Report, Lewes.

Applebaum, S. (1966) 'Peasant economy and types of agriculture', pp. 99–107 in Thomas, C (ed.), *Rural Settlement in Roman Britain.* CBA, London.

Applebaum, S. (1975) 'Some observations on the economy of the Roman Villa at Bignor, Sussex', *Britannia,* **6**, 118–32.

Arnold, C. (1980) 'Wealth and social structure: a matter of life and death', pp. 81–152 in Rahtz, P. *et al.* (eds), *Anglo-Saxon Cemeteries.* BAR British Ser. 82.

Ashbee, P. (1970) *The Earthen Long Barrow in Britain*. Dent.

Ashbee, P. and Dunning, G. C. (1960) 'The Round Barrows of East Kent', *Arch. Cant.* 74, 48.

Ashbee, P., Smith, I. F. and Evans, J. G. (1979) 'Excavations of three Long Barrows near Avebury, Wiltshire', *PPS* 45, 207–300.

Baker, C. A. *et al.* (1978) 'Woodland continuity and change in Epping Forest', *Field Studies* 4, 645–69.

Barker, G. and Webley, D. (1978) 'Causewayed Camps and Early Neolithic economies in Central Southern England', *PPS* 44, 161–86.

Barrett, A. A. (1979) 'The career of Tiberius Claudius Cogidubnus', *Britannia*, X, 227–42.

Barrett, J. C. (1980) 'The pottery of the later Bronze Age in lowland England', *PPS* 46, 297–319.

Bartholomew, P. (1982) 'Fifth-century facts', *Britannia*, 13,. 261–70.

Beckensall, S. G. (1967) 'The excavation of Money Mound', *Sussex Arch. Coll.* 105, 13–30.

Bedwin, O. R. (1978*a*) 'Iron Age Sussex – the Downs and Coastal Plain', pp. 41–51 in Drewett, P. L. (ed.), *Archaeology in Sussex to A.D. 1500*, CBA Research Report 29.

Bedwin, O. R. (1978*b*) 'Excavations inside Harting Beacon Hillfort, West Sussex, 1976', *Sussex Arch. Coll.* 116, 225–240.

Bedwin, O. R. (1978*c*) 'The excavation of a Romano-British site at Ranscombe Hill, South Malling, East Sussex, 1976', *Sussex Arch. Coll.*, 116, 241–55.

Bedwin, O. R. (1979*a*) 'Excavations at Harting Beacon, West Sussex; Second season, 1977', *Sussex Arch. Coll.* 117, 21–135.

Bedwin, O. R. (1979*b*) 'Report on excavations carried out adjacent to the cemetery at Saxonbury, 1975', *Sussex Arch. Coll.* 117, 101–2.

Bedwin, O. R. (1979*c*) 'Bronze Age Pottery from Cross Lane, Findon, West Sussex', *Sussex Arch. Coll.* 117, 254–5.

Bedwin, O. R. (1980*a*) 'Neolithic and Iron Age material from a coastal site at Chidham, West Sussex, 1978', *Sussex Arch. Coll.* 118, 163–70.

Bedwin, O. R. (1980*b*) 'Excavations at Chanctonbury Ring, Wiston, West Sussex, 1977', *Britannia* 11, 173–222.

Bedwin, O. R. (1981*a*) 'An excavation at the Trundle 1980', *Sussex Arch. Coll.* 119, 208–14.

Bedwin, O. R. (1981*b*) 'Excavations at the Neolithic Enclosure on Bury Hill, Houghton, W. Sussex 1979', *PPS* 47, 69–86.

Bedwin, O. R, (1981*c*) 'Excavations at Lancing Down, West Sussex, 1980', *Sussex Archeol. Coll.* 119, 37–56.

Bedwin, O. R. (1982*a*) 'The Pre-Roman Iron Age on Bullock Down', pp. 73–96 in Drewett, P. L. *The Archaeology of Bullock Down, Eastbourne, East Sussex: The development of a landscape*, Sussex Archaeological Society Monograph 1.

Bedwin, O. R. (1982*b*) 'Excavations at Halnaker Hill, Boxgrove, West Sussex', *Bulletin, Institute of Arch.* 19, 92–5.

Bedwin, O. R. (1983) 'The development of prehistoric settlement on the West Sussex Coastal Plain', *Sussex Arch. Coll.* 121, 31–44.

Bedwin, O. R. (1984*a*) 'Aspects of Iron Age settlement in Sussex', pp. 46–51 in Cunliffe

B. and Miles, D. (eds) *Aspects of the Iron Age in Central Southern Britain*, University of Oxford, Committee for Archaeology Monograph 2.

Bedwin, O. R. (1984*b*) 'The excavation of a small hilltop enclosure on Court Hill, Singleton, West Sussex, 1982', *Sussex Arch. Coll.* **122**, 13–22.

Bedwin, O. R. (1986) 'Excavations at Seaford Head, East Sussex 1983', *Sussex Arch. Coll.* **124**, 25–33.

Bedwin, O. R. and Holgate, R. (1985) 'Excavations at Copse Farm, Oving, West Sussex', *PPS* 51, 215–45.

Bedwin, O. R. and Orton, C. (1984) 'The excavation of the eastern terminal of The Devil's Ditch (Chichester Dykes), Boxgrove, West Sussex, 1982', *Sussex Arch. Coll.* **122**, 63–74.

Bedwin, O. R. and Pitts, M. W. (1978) 'The excavation of an Iron Age settlement at North Bersted, Bognor Regis, West Sussex, 1975–76', *Sussex Arch. Coll.* **116**, 293–346.

Bell, M. G. (1975) 'A field survey of the Parish of Elsted and adjacent areas, West Sussex', *Bull. Inst. Arch.* **12**, 58–61.

Bell, M. G. (1976) 'The excavation of an early Romano-British site and Pleistocene landforms at Newhaven, Sussex', *Sussex Arch. Coll.* **114**, 218–305.

Bell, M. G. (1977) 'Excavations at Bishopstone', *Sussex Arch. Coll.* **115**, 1–299.

Bell, M. G. (1981) 'Valley Sediments as Evidence of Prehistoric Land-use: a study based on dry valleys in South East England', PhD Thesis, University of London (unpublished).

Bennett, F. J. (1913) 'Excavations at Coldrum, Kent', *J. Roy. Anthrop, Inst.* 43, 79.

Bennett, P. (1980) '68–69A Stour Street', *Arch. Cant.* 96, 406–410.

Bennett, P. (1981) '68–69A Stour Street', *Arch. Cant.* 96, 279–81.

Bennett, P. (1984) 'The topography of Roman Canterbury. A brief re-assessment', *Arch. Cant.* 100, 47–56.

Bird, D. G. (1986) 'Wanborough', *Bull. Surrey Arch. Soc.* 209, 4–5.

Bird, D. G. (1987) 'The Romano-British period in Surrey', in Bird, J. and Bird, D. G. (eds) *The Archaeology of Surrey to A.D 1540*.

Bird, J. and Bird, D. G. (eds) (1987) *The Archaeology of Surrey to 1540*. Dorking.

Bishop, M. W. (1971) 'The non-Belgic Iron Age in Surrey', *Surrey Arch. Coll.* 68, 1–30.

Black, E. W. (1983) 'The Roman Villa at Bignor in the Fourth Century', *Oxford J. Arch.* 2, 93–107.

Black, E. W. (1985) 'The dating of relief-patterned flue-tiles', *Oxford J. Arch.* 4, 353–76.

Black, E. W. (1986) 'Romano-British burial customs and religious beliefs in South-East England', *Arch. J.*, 143, 201–39.

Black, E. W. (1987) 'The Roman Villas of South-East England'. *BAR* 171.

Blagg, T. F. C. (1981) 'Some Roman architectural traditions in early Saxon churches of Kent', pp. 50–5 in Detsicas, A. (ed.) *Collectanea Historica: essays in memory of Stuart Rigold*, Kent Archaeological Society, Maidstone.

Blagg, T. F. C. (1982) 'Roman Kent', pp. 51–60 in Leach, P. (ed.) *Archaeology in Kent to A.D. 1500*, CBA Research Report 48.

Blair, W. J. (forthcoming) *Landholding, Church and Settlement in Early Medieval Surrey*, Surrey Archaeological Society, Guildford.

Bland, R. F. (1979) 'The 1973 Beachy Head Treasure Trove of third century Antoniniani', *Num. Chron.* 7th Series, XIX, 61–107.

Blockley, K, and **Day, M.** (1979) 'Marlowe Car Park excavations', *Arch. Cant.* **95,** 267–70.

Bogaers, J. E. (1979) 'King Cogidubnus in Chichester: another reading of *RIB 91'*, *Britannia*, **10,** 243–54.

Bohannan, P. (1965) 'The Tiv of Nigeria', in J. L. Gibbs (ed.) *Peoples of Africa*, Holt, Rinehart and Winston, New York, 551–646.

Boon, G. C. (1969) 'Belgic and Roman Silchester: the excavations of 1954–8', *Arch.* **102,** 1–81.

Bourdillon, J. and **Coy, J.** (1980) 'The animal bones', pp, 79–121 in Holdsworth, P. (ed.) *Excavations at Melbourne Street, Southampton, 1971–76*, CBA Research Report 33.

Boyd-Dawkins, W. (1864) 'On a Romano-British cemetery and a Roman camp at Hardham in West Sussex', *Sussex Arch. Coll.* **16,** 52–64.

Bradley, R. (1970) 'The excavation of a beaker settlement at Belle Tout, East Sussex, England', PPS **36,** 312–79.

Bradley, R. (1971*a*) 'Stock raising and the origins of the hillfort on the South Downs', *Ant. J.* **51,** 8–29.

Bradley, R. (1971*b*) 'A field survey of the Chichester entrenchments', pp. 17–36 in Cunliffe, B. W. (ed.) *Excavations at Fishbourne*, Society of Antiquaries Research Reports 26 and 27.

Bradley, R., Lobb, S., Richards, J. and **Robinson, M.** (1980) 'Two Late Bronze Age settlements on the Kennet Gravels: excavations at Aldermaston Wharf and Knights Farm, Burghfield, Berkshire', PPS **46,** 217–95.

Brandon, P. F. (1978) 'Medieval Sussex', pp. 84–6 in Drewett, P. L. (ed.), *Archaeology in Sussex to A. D. 1500*, CBA Research Report 29.

Brodribb, G. (1981) 'Beauport Park', *Current Arch.* **7,** 177–81.

Brooks, N. P. (1984) *The Early History of the Church of Canterbury: Christ Church from 597 to 1066*, Leicester University Press, Leicester.

Brothwell, D. (1972) 'Palaeodemography and earlier British populations', *World Arch.* **4,** 75–87.

Brown, P. D. C. (1971) 'The church at Richborough', *Britannia*, **2,** 225–31.

Burchell, J. P. T. (1928) 'Lower Halstow', *PPS East Anglia* **5,** part 3, 289.

Burchell, J. P. T. and **Piggott, S.** (1939) 'Decorated prehistoric pottery from the bed of the Ebbsfleet, Northfleet, Kent', *Ant. J.* **19,** 405.

Burgess, C. (1980) *The Age of Stonehenge*, Dent, London.

Burstow, G. P. (1958) 'A Late Bronze Age urnfield on Steyning Round Hill, Sussex', *PPS* **24,** 158.

Burstow, G. P. and **Holleyman, G. A.** (1957) 'Late Bronze Age settlement on Itford Hill, Sussex', *PPS* **23,** 167–212.

Bushe-Fox, J. P. 1925. *Excavation of the late-Celtic urnfield at Swarling, Kent.*

Caesar (100–44 BC) *Gallic War* (De Bello Gallico), Trans. S. A. Handford, *Caesar: the conquest of Gaul.* Penguin Classics, 1951.

Calkin, J. B. (1934) 'Implements from the higher raised beaches of Sussex', *PPS East Anglia* **7,** 333–47.

Cam, H. M. (1932) '*Manerium Cum hundredo*: the hundred and hundredal manor', *Engl. Hist. Rev.* **47,** 353–71.

Canham, R. (1979) 'Excavations at Shepperton Green 1967 and 1973', *Trans. London Middlesex Arch. Soc.* **30,** 97–124.

Carter, H. H. (1976) 'Fauna of an area of Mesolithyic occupation in the Kennet Valley considered in relation to contemporary eating habits', *Berkshire Arch. Journ.* **68**, 1–3.

Case, H. (1977) 'The beaker cultures in Britain and Ireland', in R. Mercer (ed.) 'Beakers in Britain and Europe', *BAR* Supplementary Series **26**, 71–101.

Champion, T. (1980*a*) 'Settlement and environment in Later Bronze Age Kent', in Barrett, J. and Bradley, R. (eds) 'The British Later Bronze Age', *BAR* 83(i), 223–46.

Champion, T. (1980*b*) 'Pottery in the first millennium B.C.', *Sussex Arch. Coll.* **118**, 43–52.

Christie, P. M. (1960) 'Crig-a-Mennis: a Bronze Age barrow at Liskey, Perranzabuloe, Cornwall', PPS **26**, 76–97.

Clark, A. J. (1960) 'A cross-valley dyke on the Surrey-Kent border', *Surrey Arch. Coll.* **57**, 72–4.

Clark, A. J. (1977) 'Geophysical and chemical assessment of air photograph sites', in Hampton, J. N. and Palmer, R. (eds) 'Implications of aerial photography in archaeology', *Arch. J.* **134**, 157–93.

Clark, J. G. D. (1932) *The Mesolithic Age in Britain*, CUP.

Clark, J. G. D. (1934) 'A Late Mesolithic site at Selmeston, Sussex', *Ant. J.* **14**, 134–58.

Clark, J. G. D, and Rankine, W. F, (1939) 'Excavations at Farnham, Surrey (1937–38): the Horsham Culture and the Question of Mesolithic Dwellings', PPS **5**, 61–118.

Clark, J. G. D., Higgs, E. S. and Longworth, I. H. (1960) 'Excavations at the Neolithic site at Hurst Fen, Mildenhall, Suffolk, 1954–58', PPS **27**, 202–45.

Clarke, D. L. (1970) *Beaker Pottery of Great Britain and Ireland*, CUP.

Clarke, G. (1979) *The Roman Cemetery at Lankhills*, Winchester Studies **3**.

Cleal, R. M. J. (1982) 'A re-analysis of the ring ditch site at Playden, E. Sussex', *Sussex Arch. Coll.* **120**, 1–17.

Cleere, H. (1976) 'Some operating parameters for Roman ironworks', *Bull. Inst. Arch.* **13**, 233–46.

Cleere, H. (1977) 'The Classis Britannica', pp. 16–19 in Johnston, D. E. (ed.) *The Saxon Shore*, CBA Research Report 18.

Cleere, H. and Crossley, D. (1985) *The Iron Industry of the Weald*, Leicester.

Coates, R. (1981) 'On *cumb* and *denu* in the place-names of the English south-east', *Nomina* 5, 29–38.

Collins, D. and Collins, A. (1970) 'Cultural evidence from Oldbury', *Bull. Inst. Arch.* 8–9 (1968–9), 151–76, London.

Collis, J. R. (1974) 'A functionalist approach to pre-Roman coinage', pp. 1–11 in Casey, J. and Reece, R. (eds), 'Coins and the Archaeologist', *BAR* **4**.

Collis, J. R. (1976) 'Town and market in Iron Age Europe', pp. 3–23 in Cunliffe, B. W. and Rowley, T. (eds) 'Oppida in Barbarian Europe', *BAR* Supplementary Series 11.

Cook, N. (1936) 'The Neolithic', in 'Archaeology in Kent, 1936', *Arch. Cant.* 48, 234–5.

Cooper, T. S. (1984). 'The Roman Villa at Whitebeech, Chiddingfold: excavations in 1888 and subsequently', *Surrey Arch. Coll.* **75**, 57–83.

Corcoran, J. X. P. W. (1963) 'Excavations at the bell-barrow in Deerlemp Wood, Wooton', *Surrey Arch. Coll.* **60**, 1–18.

Cowen, J. D. (1967) 'The Hallstatt sword of bronze on the Continent and in Britain', *PPS* 33, 377–444.

Crouch, K. (1978) 'New thoughts on Roman Staines', *London Archaeologist*, 3, 180–86.

Crow, D. A. (1930) 'Excavations at Ditchling Beacon', *Sussex Arch. Coll.* 71, 259–61.

Cunliffe, B. W. (1968) *Fifth Report on the Excavations of the Roman Fort, Richborough, Kent*, Society of Antiquaries Research Report No. 23.

Cunliffe, B. W. (1971) *Excavations at Fishbourne*, Society of Antiquaries Research Reports 26 and 27.

Cunliffe, B. W. (1973) *The Regni*, London.

Cunliffe, B. W. (1974) 'Some late Saxon stamped pottery from southern England', pp. 127–36 in Evison, V. I. *et al.* (eds) *Medieval Pottery from Excavations*, John Baker, London.

Cunliffe, B. W. (1975) *Excavations at Porchester Castle: Volume I: Roman*, Society of Antiquaries Research Report 32.

Cunliffe, B. W. (1976*a*) 'The origins of urbanisation in Britain', pp. 135–161 in Cunliffe, B. W. and Rowley, T. (eds) '*Oppida in Barbarian Europe*', *BAR*, Supplementary Series 11.

Cunliffe, B. W. (1976*b*) *Iron Age Sites in Central Southern England*, CBA Research Report 16.

Cunliffe, B. W. (1978*a*) *Iron Age Communities in Britain*, 2nd edn, London.

Cunliffe, B. W. (1978*b*) 'Settlement and population in the British Iron Age: some facts, figures and fantasies', pp. 3–24 in Cunliffe, B. W. and Rowley, T. (eds) *Lowland Iron Age Communities in Europe*, *BAR* Supplementary Series 48.

Cunliffe B. W. (1980) 'Excavations at the Roman fort at Lympne, Kent, 1976–78', *Britannia*, XI, 227–88.

Cunliffe, B. W. (1981) 'Money and society in pre-Roman Britain', pp. 29–39 in Cunliffe, B. (ed.), *Coinage and Society in Britain and Gaul*, CBA Research Report 38.

Cunliffe, B. W. (1982) 'Social and economic development in Kent in the pre-Roman Iron Age', pp. 40–50 in Leach, P. E. (ed.), *Archaeology in Kent to A.D. 1500*, CBA Research Report 48.

Cunliffe, B. W. (1984) *Danebury: an Iron Age hillfort in Hampshire*, CBA Research Report 52.

Cunliffe, B. W. and Rowley, T. (eds) (1976) *Oppida in Barbarian Europe*, *BAR* Supplementary Series 11.

Cunliffe, B. W. and Rowley, T. (eds) (1978) *Lowland Iron Age Communities in Europe*, *BAR* Supplementary Series 48.

Curwen, E. (1931) 'Prehistoric remains from Kingston Buci', *Sussex Arch. Coll.* 72, 185–217.

Curwen, E. (1936) 'On Sussex flint arrowheads', *Sussex Arch. Coll.* 77, 15–26.

Curwen, E. and Curwen, E. C. (1922) 'Two unrecorded long barrows', *Sussex Arch. Coll.* 67, 103–38.

Curwen, E. and Curwen, E. C. (1926) 'Harrow Hill flint mine excavation 1924–5', *Sussex Arch. Coll.* 67, 103–38.

Curwen, E. and Curwen, E. C. (1927) 'Excavations in the Caburn, near Lewes', *Sussex Arch. Coll.* 68, 1–56.

Curwen, E. and Curwen, E. C. (1938) 'Late Bronze Age ditches at Selmeston', *Sussex Arch. Coll.* **79**, 195–8.

Curwen, E. C. (1925) 'Palaeoliths from a raised beach in Sussex', *Ant. J.* **5**, 72–3.

Curwen, E. C. (1928) 'The antiquities on Windover Hill', *Sussex Arch. Coll.* **69**, 94–101.

Curwen, E. C. (1929) 'Excavations in the Trundle, Goodwood, 1928', *Sussex Arch. Coll.* **70**, 33–85.

Curwen, E. C. (1930) 'Wolstonbury', *Sussex Arch. Coll.* **71**, 237–45.

Curwen, E. C. (1931) 'Excavations in the Trundle, Second Season, 1930', *Sussex Arch. Coll.* **72**, 100–50.

Curwen, E. C. (1932) 'Excavations at Hollingbury Camp, Sussex', *Ant. J.* **12**, 1–16.

Curwen, E. C. (1933) 'Excavations on Thundersbarrow Hill', Sussex', *Ant. J.* **13**, 109–33.

Curwen, E. C. (1934*a*) 'Excavations at Whitehawk Neolithic Camp, Brighton, 1932–3', *Ant. J.* **14** (2), 99–133.

Curwen, E. C. (1934*b*) 'A Late Bronze Age farm and a Neolithic pit-dwelling on New Barn Down, Clapham, Near Worthing', *Sussex Arch. Coll.* **74**, 153–7.

Curwen, E. C. (1936) 'Excavations in Whitehawk Camp, Brighton, Third Season, 1935' *Sussex Arch. Coll.* **77**, 60–92.

Curwen, E. C. (1943) 'Roman lead cistern from Pulborough, Sussex', *Ant. J.* **23**, 155–7.

Curwen, E. C. (1948) 'A bronze cauldron from Sompting, Sussex', *Ant. J.* **28**, 157–63.

Curwen, E. C. (1949) 'A flint dagger factory near Pulborough, Sussex', *Ant. J.* **29**, 192.

Curwen, E. C. (1954) *The Archaeology of Sussex*, 2nd edn, London.

Darby, H. C. (1963) 'Place-names and the geography of the past', pp. 6–18 in Brown, A. and Foote, P. (eds), *Early English and Norse Studies Presented to Hugh Smith in Honour of his Sixtieth Birthday*, London.

Detsicas, A. P. (1975) 'Excavations at Eccles, 1974. Thirteenth Interim Report', *Arch. Cant.* **91**, 41–5.

Detsicas, A. P. (1976) 'Excavations at Eccles, 1975. Fourteenth Interim Report', *Arch. Cant.* **92**, 157–63.

Detsicas, A. P. (1977) 'Excavations at Eccles, 1976. Final Interim Report', *Arch. Cant.* **93**, 55–9.

Detsicas, A. P. (1983) *The Cantiaci*, Gloucester.

Detsicas, A. P. (1985) 'A salt panning site at Funton Creek', *Arch. Cant.* **101**, 165–8.

Dimbleby, G. W. (1962) *The Development of the British Heathlands and their Soils*, Oxford Forestry Memoirs 23.

Dimbleby, G. W. and Bradley, R. J. (1975) 'Evidence of pedogenesis from a Neolithic site at Rackham, Sussex', *J. Arch. Sc.* **2**, 179–86.

Dodgson, J. McN. (1966) 'The significance of the distribution of the English place-name in *-ingas*, *-inga-* in south-east England', *Med. Arch.* **10**, 1–29.

Dodgson, J. McN. (1973) 'Place-names from *ham* distinguished from *hamm* names in relation to the settlement of Kent, Sussex and Surrey', *Anglo-Saxon Engl.* **2**, 1–50.

Down, A. (1974) *Chichester Excavations* 2, Phillimore, Chichester.

Down, A. (1978*a*) *Chichester Excavations* 3, Phillimore, Chichester.

Down, A. (1978*b*) 'Roman Sussex – Chichester and the Chilgrove Valley', pp. 52–8 in Drewett, P. L. (ed.), *Archaeology in Sussex to A.D. 1500*, CBA Research Report 29.

Down, A. (1979) *Chichester Excavations* 4, Phillimore, Chichester.

Down, A. (1981) *Chichester Excavations* 5, Phillimore, Chichester.

Down, A. (1982) 'Cattlemarket, Phases 1–3', *Report for 1982, The Chichester Excavations Committee*, 3–5.

Down, A. (1986) 'Theological College, Westgate', *The Archaeology of Chichester and District 1985*, The Chichester Excavations Committee, 11–14.

Down, A. and **Rule, M.** (1971) *Chichester Excavations* 1, Phillimore, Chichester.

Drew, C. D. and **Piggott, S,** (1936) 'The excavation of Long Barrow 163a on Thickthorn Down, Dorset', *PPS* 2, 77–96.

Drewett, P. L. (1970*a*) 'The excavation of two Round Barrows and associated fieldwork on Ashey Down, Isle of Wight, 1969', *Proc. Hampshire Field Club Arch. Soc.* 27, 35–56.

Drewett, P. L. (1970*b*) 'The excavation of a turf-walled structure and other fieldwork on Croham Hurst, Croydon, 1968–69', *Surrey Arch. Coll.* 67, 1–19.

Drewett, P. L. (1975*a*) 'The excavation of an oval burial mound of the third millennium B.C. at Alfriston, East Sussex, 1974', *PPS* 41, 119–52.

Drewett, P. L. (1975*b*) 'The excavation of a turf barrow at Minsted, West Sussex, 1973', *Sussex Arch. Coll.* 113, 54–65.

Drewett, P. L. (1975*c*) 'A Neolithic pot from Selmeston, East Sussex', *Sussex Arch. Coll.* 113, 193–4.

Drewett, P. L. (1976) 'The excavation of four round barrows of the second millennium B.C. at West Heath, Harting, 1973–75', *Sussex Arch. Coll.* 114, 126–50.

Drewett, P. L. (1977) 'The excavation of a Neolithic Causewayed Enclosure on Offham Hill, East Sussex, 1976', *PPS* 43, 201–41.

Drewett, P. L. (ed.) (1978) *Archaeology in Sussex to A.D. 1500*, CBA Research Report 29.

Drewett, P. L. (1981) 'Rescue Archaeology in Sussex, 1980', *Bull. Inst. Arch.* 18, 21–47.

Drewett, P. L. (1982) *The Archaeology of Bullock Down, Eastbourne, East Sussex: the development of a landscape*, Sussex Archaeological Society Monograph1.

Drewett, P. L. (1983) 'A Peterborough Ware Sherd from the Long Down Flint Mines', Shorter Note in *Sussex Arch. Coll.* 121, 95.

Drewett, P. L. (1985) 'Settlement, economy, ceremony and territorial organization in Sussex, 4th–2nd Millennium B.C.', PhD thesis, University of London (unpublished).

Drewett, P. L. (1986) 'The excavation of a Neolithic Oval Barrow at North Marden, West Sussex, 1982', *PPS* 52.

Dudley, D. R. and **Webster, G.** (1965) *The Roman Conquest of Britain, A.D. 43–57*, London.

Dunning, G. C. (1966) 'Neolithic occupation sites in East Kent', *Ant. J.* 46, pt. 1, 1–25.

Ellaby, R. L. (1977) 'A Mesolithic site at Wonham', *Surrey Arch. Coll.* 71, 7–12.

Ellison, A. B. (1975) 'Pottery and settlement of the Later Bronze Age in Southern England', PhD thesis, University of Cambridge.

Ellison, A. B. (1978) 'The Bronze Age of Sussex', in Drewett, P. L. (ed.), *Archaeology in Sussex to A.D. 1500*, CBA Research Report 29.

Ellison, A. B. (1980) 'The Bronze Age', *Sussex Arch. Coll.* 118, 31–42.

Ellison, A. B. (1981) 'Towards a socioeconomic model for the Middle Bronze Age in Southern England' in Hodder, I., Isaac, G. and Hammond, N. (eds) *Pattern of the Past: Studies in honour of David Clarke*, CUP, Cambridge.

Ellison, A. B. and Drewett, P. L. (1971) 'Pits and post-holes in the British Early Iron Age: some alternative explanations', *PPS* 37, 183–94.

English, J. and Gower, J. L. (1985) 'Alfoldean Roman Posting-Station (TQ 118330), Interim Report', *Sussex Arch. Soc. Newsletter* 47, 456–7.

Evans, A. J. (1890) 'On a Late-Celtic Urnfield at Aylesford, Kent', *Arch*, 52, 315–88.

Evans, J. G. (1972) *Land Snails in Archaeology*, London.

Evans, J. G. (1978) Comment on Barker, G. and Webley, D., 1978, *PPS* 44, 185–6.

Evans, J. H. (1953) 'Archaeological horizons in the North Kent Marshes', *Arch. Cant.* 66, 128.

Evans, K. J. (1974) 'Excavations on a Romano-British site, Wiggonholt, 1964', *Sussex Arch. Coll.* 112, 97–151.

Evans-Pritchard, E. (1940) *The Nuer*, Oxford.

Everitt, A. (1977) 'River and Wold: reflections on the historical origin of regions and pays', *J. Hist. Geog.* 3, 1–19.

Fell, C. E. (1984) *Women in Anglo-Saxon England*, Colonade Books, London.

Fenwick, V. (1978) 'The Graveney boat: a tenth century find', *BAR*, British Series 53.

Ferguson, J. (1980) 'Application of data coding to the differentiation of British flint mine sites', *J. Arch. Sc.* 7, 277–86.

Field, D. (1985) 'Felday Enclosure, Holmbury St. Mary (TQ 108 447)', *Surrey Arch. Soc. Bulletin* 206, 2.

Flight, C. and Harrison, A. C. (1978) 'Rochester Castle 1976', *Arch. Cant.* 94, 27–60.

Fowler, J. (1929) 'Palaeoliths found at Slindon', *Sussex Arch. Coll.* 70, 197–200.

Fox, C. F. and Wolseley, G. R. (1928) 'The Early Iron Age site at Findon Park, Findon, Sussex', *Ant. J.* 8, 449–60.

Fox, C. (1959) *Life and Death in the Bronze Age*, Routledge and Kegan Paul, London.

Freke, D. J. (1980) 'Excavations in the parish church of St. Thomas the Martyr, Pagham, 1976', *Sussex Arch. Coll.* 118, 245–56.

Frere, S. (1967) *Britannia*, London.

Frere, S. (1982) 'The Bignor Villa', *Britannia*, 13, 135–95.

Fulford, M. (1973) 'A fourth-century colour-coated fabric and its types in South-East England', *Sussex Arch. Coll.* 111, 41–4.

Gallois, R. G. (1965) *The Wealden District*, HMSO, London.

Gardiner, M. F. (1984) 'Saxon settlement and land division in the western weald', *Sussex Arch. Coll.* 122, 75–83.

Garton, D. (1981) 'An Early Mesolithic site at Rackham, West Sussex', *Sussex Arch. Coll.* 118, 145–52.

Garwood, P. (1984) 'The Cuckmere Valley Project fieldwalking programme, 1982–83', *Bull. Inst. Arch.* 21, 49–68.

Godwin, H. (1962) 'Vegetational history of the Kentish chalk downs as seen at Wingham and Frogholt', *Veroff. Geobot. Inst. Zurich* 37, 83–99.

Godwin, H. (1975) *A History of the British Flora*, 2nd edn, Cambridge.

Goodchild, R. G. (1938) 'Martin Tupper and Farley Heath', *Surrey Arch. Coll.* **46**, 10–25.

Goodchild, R. G, (1949) 'The Celtic Gods of Farley Heath', *Surrey Arch. Coll.* **50**, 150–1.

Goodman, C. H. (1924) 'Blackpatch flint mine excavation, 1922', *Sussex Arch. Coll.* **65**, 69–111.

Green, C. (1980) 'Handmade pottery and society in Late Iron Age and Roman East Sussex', *Sussex Arch. Coll.* **118**, 69–86.

Green, M. G. (1976) 'A Corpus of religious material from the civilian areas of Roman Britain', *BAR* **48**.

Green, T. K. (1970) 'Roman tileworks at Itchingfield', *Sussex Arch. Coll.* **108**, 23–38.

Green, T. K. (1979) 'Techniques for studying comb signature distributions', pp. 363–73 in McWhirr, A. (ed.) 'Roman brick and tile', *BAR*, International Series 68.

Grierson, P. (1959) 'Commerce in the Dark Ages: a critique of the evidence', *Trans. Roy. Hist. Soc.* 5th Ser., 9, 123–40.

Grinsell, L. V. (1931) 'Sussex in the Bronze Age', *Sussex Arch. Coll.* **72**, 30–68.

Grinsell, L. V. (1934) 'Sussex barrows', *Sussex Arch. Coll.* **75**, 220.

Grinsell, L. V. (1940) 'Sussex Barrows: supplementary paper', *Sussex Arch. Coll.* **81**, 214.

Gulliver, P. (1965) 'The Jie of Uganda', in Gibbs, J. L. (ed.) *Peoples of Africa*, Holt, Rinehart and Winston, New York.

Hamilton, B. C. (1933) 'Suspected flint mines on Bow Hill', *Sussex Notes and Queries* 4 (8), 246–7.

Hamilton, S. (1984) 'Earlier First Millennium pottery from the excavations at Hollingbury Camp, Sussex, 1976–9', *Sussex Arch. Coll.* **122**, 55–61.

Hampton, J. (1977) 'Roman Ashtead', in A. A. Jackson (ed.), *Ashtead, a Village Transformed*, 26–34.

Hannah, J. (1932) 'Philpots Camp, West Hoathly', *Sussex Arch. Coll.* **73**, 156–67.

Hanworth, R. (1968) 'The Roman Villa at Rapsley, Ewhurst', *Surrey Arch. Coll.* **65**, 1–70.

Hanworth, R. (1987) 'The Iron Age in Surrey', in Bird, J. and Bird, D. G. (eds), *The Archaeology of Surrey to A.D. 1540*.

Hanworth, R. and Tomalin, D. J. (1977) *Brooklands, Weybridge: the excavation of an Iron Age and Medieval Site*, Surrey Arch. Soc. Research Vol. 4.

Harding, D. W. (1974) *The Iron Age in Lowland Britain*, London.

Hartridge, R. (1978) 'Excavations at the Prehistoric and Romano-British site on Slonk Hill, Shoreham, Sussex', *Sussex Arch. Coll.* **116**, 69–141.

Hassall, M. W. C. (1977) 'The historical background and military units of the Saxon Shore', pp. 7–10 in Johnston, D. E. (ed.) *The Saxon Shore*, CBA Research Report 18.

Hassall, M. W. C. and Tomlin, R. S. D, (1977) 'Inscriptions', *Britannia* 8, 426–49.

Hastings, F. A. (1965) 'Excavation of an Iron Age farmstead at Hawk's Hill, Leatherhead', *Surrey Arch. Coll.* **62**, 1–43.

Hawkes, C. F. C. (1931) 'Hillforts', *Antiquity* 5, 60–97.

Hawkes, S. C. (1958) 'The Anglo-Saxon cemetery at Finglesham, Kent: a reconsideration', *Med. Arch.* 2, 1–71.

Hawkes, S. C. (1973) 'The dating and social significance of burials in the Polhill cemetery', pp. 186–201 in Philp, B., *Excavations in West Kent 1960–1970*, Kent Archaeological Rescue Unit, Dover.

Hawkes, S. C. (1982*a*) 'Anglo-Saxon Kent *c*. 425–725', pp. 64–78 in Leach, P. E. (ed.), *Archaeology in Kent to A.D. 1500*, CBA Research Report 48.

Hawkes, S. C. (1982*b*) 'Finglesham. A cemetery in east Kent', pp. 24–5 in Campbell, J. (ed.), *The Anglo-Saxons*, Phaidon Press, London.

Hawkes, S. C. and Pollard, M. (1981) 'The gold bracteates from sixth century Anglo-Saxon graves in Kent, in light of a new find from Finglesham', *Frühmittelalterliche Studien* 13, 382–92.

Hedges, J. and Buckley, D. G. (1978) 'Excavations at a Neolithic Causewayed Enclosure, Orsett, Essex, 1975', *PPS* 44, 219–308.

Helbaek, H. (1952) 'Early crops in Southern England', *PPS* 18 (2), 194–233.

Hill, D. (1981) *An Atlas of Anglo-Saxon England*, Basil Blackwell, Oxford.

Hodges, R. (1982) *Dark Age Economics: the origins of towns and trade A.D. 600–1000*, Duckworth, London.

Hodson, F. R. (1960) 'Reflections on the ABC of the British Iron Age', *Antiquity* 34, 318–19.

Hodson, F. R. (1962) 'Some pottery from Eastbourne, the "Marnians" and the pre-Roman Iron Age in southern England', *PPS* 28, 140–55.

Hodson, F. R. (1964) 'Cultural groupings within the British pre-Roman Iron Age', *PPS* 30, 99–110.

Hogarth, A. C. (1973) 'Structural features in Anglo-Saxon graves', *Arch. J.* 130, 104–19.

Hogg, A. H. A. (1934) 'Dyke near Bexley, Kent', *Antiquity* 8, 218–22.

Holdon, E. W. (1972) 'A Bronze Age cemetery barrow at Itford Hill, Beddingham', *Sussex Arch. Coll.* 110, 70–117.

Holden, E. H. (1974) 'Flint mines on Windover Hill, Wilmington', *Sussex Arch. Coll.* 112, 154.

Holden, E. W. (1979) 'A Bronze Age loom weight from Cross-in-Hand, Sussex', *Sussex Arch. Coll.* 117, 227–8.

Holden, E. W. and Bradley, R. (1975) 'A Late Neolithic site at Rackham', *Sussex Arch. Coll.* 113, 83–103.

Holden, E. W. and Hudson, T. P. (1981) 'Salt-making in the Adur Valley, Sussex', *Sussex Arch. Coll.* 119, 117–48.

Holdsworth, P. (ed.), *Excavations at Melbourne Street, Southampton, 1971–76*, CBA Research Report 33.

Holgate, R. (1981) 'The Medway Megaliths and Neolithic Kent', *Arch. Cant.* 97, 221–34.

Holgate, R. (1986) 'Excavations at the Late Prehistoric and Romano-British enclosure complex at Carne's Seat, Goodwood, West Sussex, 1984', *Sussex Arch. Coll.* 12, 35–50.

Holleyman, G. A. (1935) 'The Celtic field-system in South Britain', *Antiquity* 9, 443–54.

Holleyman, G. (1937) 'Harrow Hill excavations, 1936', *Sussex Arch. Coll.* 78, 230–51.

Holleyman, G. A. and Curwen, E. C. (1935) 'Late Bronze Age lynchet-settlements on Plumpton Plain, Sussex', *PPS* 1, 16–38.

Holmes, J. (1984) 'Excavations at Hollingbury Camp, Sussex, 1967–9', *Sussex Arch. Coll.* **122**, 29–53.

Horsfield, T. W. (1824) *The History and Antiquities of Lewes*, privately printed.

Hubbard, R. (1980) 'The Environmental evidence from Swanscombe and its implications for Paleolithic Archaeology' in Leach, P. (ed.), *Archaeology of Kent to A.D. 1500*, CBA Research Report No. 48.

Hutchinson, J. N., Poole, C., Lambert, N. and Bromhead, E. N. (1985) 'Combined archaeological and geotechnical investigations of the Roman fort at Lympne, Kent', *Britannia* **16**, 209–36.

Jacobi, R. (1978) 'The Mesolithic of Sussex', in P. L. Drewett (ed.), *Archaeology of Sussex to A.D. 1500*, CBA Research Report No. 29.

Jacobi, R. (1980) 'Mesolithic Kent', in Leach, P. (ed.), *Archaeology in Kent to A.D. 1500*, CBA Research Report No. 48.

Jacobi, R. and Tebbutt, C. F. (1981) 'The excavation of a Mesolithic rock shelter at Hermitage Rocks', *Sussex Arch. Coll.* **119**, 1–36.

James, F. (1899) 'Bronze Age Burials at Aylesford', *Proc. Soc. Antiq.* **17**, 373–7.

James, S., Marshall, A. and Millett, M. (1984) 'An early Medieval building tradition', *Arch. J.* **141**, 182–215.

Jenkins, F. (1957) 'The cult of the *Dea Nutrix* in Kent', *Arch. Cant.* **71**, 38–46.

Jenkins, F. (1958) 'The cult of the "pseudo-Venus" in Kent', *Arch. Cant.* **72**, 60–76.

Jessup, R. F. (1955) 'Excavation of a Roman barrow at Holborough, Snodland', *Arch. Cant.* **68**, 1–61.

Jessup, R. F. (1959) 'Barrows and walled cemeteries in Roman Britain', *J. Brit. Arch. Ass.*, 3rd series, **22**, 1–32.

Jessup, R. F. (1970) *South-East England*, Thames and Hudson.

Jessup, R. F. and Cook, N. C. (1936) 'Excavations at Bigberry Camp, Harbledown', *Arch. Cant.* **48**, 151–68.

Johnson, B. (1975) *Archaeology and the M.25*, Surrey Archaeological Society, Guildford.

Johnson, S. (1976) *The Roman Forts of the Saxon Shore*, London.

Johnston, D. E. (ed.) (1977) *The Saxon Shore*, CBA Research Report 18.

Johnston, D. and Williams, D. (1979) 'Relief patterned tiles – a re-appraisal', pp. 375–393 in McWhirr, A. (ed.), 'Roman brick and tile', *BAR* International Series 68.

Jolliffe, J. E. A. (1933) *Pre-Feudal England: the Jutes*, OUP.

Jones, M. U. and Bond, D. (1980) 'Later Bronze Age settlement at Mucking, Essex', in Barrett, J. and Bradley, R. (eds) 'The Later British Bronze Age', *BAR* 83(i), 471–82.

Jones, P. (1982) 'Saxon and Medieval Staines', *Trans. London Middlesex Arch. Soc.* **33**, 186–213.

Jope, E. M. (1964) 'The Saxon building-stone industry in southern and Midland England', *Med. Arch.* **8**, 91–118.

Keef, P. A. M., Wymer, J. J. and Dimbleby, G. W. (1965) 'A Mesolithic site on Iping Common, Sussex, England', *PPS* **31**, 85–92.

Keiller, A. and Piggott, S. (1939) 'The Badshot Long Barrow', in Oakley, K. P. (ed.) *A Survey of the Prehistory of the Farnham District*, Surrey Arch. Soc.

Kellaway, G. A., Redding, J. H., Shephard-Thorn, E. R. and Destombes, J.-P. (1975)

'The Quaternary history of the English Channel', *Phil. Trans. of the Roy. Soc.* A279, 189–218.

Kelly, D. B. (1971) 'Quarry Wood Camp, Loose: a Belgic oppidum', *Arch. Cant.* 86, 55–84.

Kenny, J. A. (1985) 'Excavations at Rummages Barn, Binderton, West Sussex, 1983', *Sussex Arch. Coll.* 123, 61–72.

Kent, J. P. C. (1978) 'The origins and development of Celtic gold coinage in Britain', *Actes du Congres International d'Archeologie: Rouen, 3, 4, 5, juillet, 1975*, 313–24.

Kent, J. P. C. (1981) 'The origins of coinage in Britain', pp. 40–2 in Cunliffe, B. W. (ed.) *Coinage and Society in Britain and Gaul*, CBA Research Report 36.

Kent. J. P. C. *et al.* (1974) 'A Visigothic gold tremissis and a fifth century firesteel from the Marlowe Theatre site, Canterbury', *Ant. J.* 63, 371–3.

Kerney, M. P., Brown, E. H. and Chandler, T. J. (1964) 'The Late Glacial and Post-Glacial history of the chalk escarpment near Brook, Kent', *Phil. Trans. Roy. Soc.* B248, 135–204.

Kinnes, I. (1979) *Round Barrows and Ring Ditches of the British Neolithic*, British Museum Occasional Paper, No. 7.

Kirby, D. P. (1978) 'The church in Saxon Sussex', pp. 160–73 in Brandon, P. F. (ed.), *The South Saxons*, Phillimore, Chichester.

Kitchen, F. (1984) '*The Burghal Hidage*: towards the identification of *Eorpeburnan*', *Med. Arch.* 28, 175–8.

Klein, W. G. (1928) 'Roman temple at Worth, Kent', *Ant. J.* 8, 76–86.

Lacaille, A. D. (1966) 'Mesolithic Facies in the Transpontine Fringes', *Surrey Arch. Coll.* 63, 1–43.

Lane-Fox, A. H. (1869) 'Further remarks on the hill forts of Sussex: being an account of excavations at Cissbury and Highdown', *Arch.* 42, 53–76.

Leach, P. E. (ed.) (1982) *Archaeology in Kent to A.D. 1500*, CBA Research Report 48.

Leach, P. E. (1983) 'Excavations at Barkhale', *Sussex Arch. Coll.* 121, 11–30.

Leakey, L. S. B. (1951) *Preliminary Excavations of a Mesolithic Site at Abinger Common, Surrey*, Surrey Arch. Soc. Research Paper No. 3.

Little, R. I. (1961) 'The excavation of a Romano-British settlement in Kings Wood, Sanderstead', *Surrey Arch. Coll.* 58 35–46.

Longley, D. (1976) *The Archaeological Implications of Gravel Extraction in North-west Surrey*, Surrey Arch. Soc. Research Volume No. 3, 1–36.

Longley, D. (1980) *Runnymede Bridge 1976: Excavations on the Site of a Later Bronze Age Settlement*, Surrey Arch. Soc. Research Volume No. 6, Guildford.

Longworth, I. H. (1961) 'The origins and development of the primary series in the collared urn tradition in England and Wales', *PPS* XXVII, 263–306.

Longworth, I. H. (1970) 'The secondary series in the collared urn tradition in England and Wales', in Filip, J. (ed.) *Actes du VIIe Congres International des Sciences Préhistoriques et Protohistoriques: Prague, 1966*, Prague.

Lowther, A. W. G. (1946) 'Report on excavations at the site of the Early Iron Age camp in the grounds of Queen Mary's Hospital Carshalton, Surrey', *Surrey Arch. Coll.* 49, 56–74.

Lowther, A. W. G. (1947) 'Excavations at Purberry Shot, Ewell, Surrey', *Surrey Arch. Coll.* 50, 9–46.

Lowther, A. W. F. (1948) *A Study of the Patterns on Roman Flue-tiles and their Distribution*, Surrey Arch. Soc. Research Paper No. 1

Lyne, M. A. B. and **Jefferies, R. S.** (1979) *The Alice Holt/Farnham Roman Pottery Industry*, CBA Research Report 30.

Lysons, S. (1817*a*) *Reliquae Britannico-Romanae* Vol. 3 *Remains of a Roman Villa Discovered at Bignor in Sussex*, drawings, not text.

Lysons, S. (1817*b*) 'An Account of the Remains of a Roman Villa, discovered at Bignor, in Sussex', *Arch.* **18**, 203–21.

Lysons, S. (1821) 'An account of further discoveries of the remains of a Roman Villa at Bignor in Sussex', *Arch.* **19**, 176–7.

Mabey, R. (1975) *Food for Free*, Fontana, London.

Margary, I. D. (1964) 'Dry Hill Camp, Lingfield, Surrey', *Surrey Arch. Coll.* **61**, 100.

Margary, I. D. (1965) *Roman Ways in the Weald*, 3rd edn. Phoenix House, London.

Margary, I. D. (1967) *Roman Roads in Britain*, 2nd edn. London.

McCrerie, A. (1956) 'Kits Coty House, Smythe's Megalith and the General's Tomb', *Arch. Cant.* **70**, 251.

McWhirr, A. (1979) 'Tile-kilns in Roman Britain', pp. 97–189, in McWhirr, A. (ed.), *Roman Brick and Tile*, *BAR* International Series 68.

Meaney, A. L. (1981) *Anglo-Saxon amulets and curing stones*, *BAR* British Series 96.

Meats, G. W. (1979) *The Lullingstone Roman Villa*, 1, Kent Archaeological Society.

Megaw, J. V. S. and **Simpson, D. D. A,** (1979) *Introduction to British Prehistory*, Leicester.

Mellars, P. (1976) 'Fire ecology, animal populations and man: a study of some ecological relationships in Prehistory', *PPS* **42**, 15–46.

Merrifield, R. (1983) *London, City of the Romans*, London.

Metcalf, D. M. (1984) 'Monetary circulation in southern England in the first half of the eighth century', pp. 27–70 in Hill, D. and Metcalf, D. M. (eds), *Sceattas in England and on the Continent*, *BAR* British Series 128.

Miller, M. (1978) 'The last British entry in the "Gallic Chronicles"', *Britannia* **9**, 315–18.

Millett, M. (1980) 'Aspects of Romano-British pottery in West Sussex', *Sussex Arch. Coll.* **118**, 57–68.

Monaghan, J. (1983) 'An investigation of the Romano-British pottery industry on the Upchurch marshes', *Arch. Cant.* **98**, 27–50.

Monaghan, J. (1987) *Upchurch and Thameside Roman Pottery*, *BAR* 173.

Money, J. H. (1960) 'Excavations at High Rocks, Tunbridge Wells, 1954–56', *Sussex Arch. Coll.* **98**, 173–221.

Money, J. H. (1962) 'Excavations at High Rocks, Tunbridge Wells, 1954–56', *Sussex Arch. Coll.* **100**, 149–51.

Money, J. H. (1968) 'Excavations in the Iron Age hillfort at High Rocks, near Tunbridge Wells, 1957–61', *Sussex Arch. Coll.* **106**, 158–205.

Money, J. H. (1976) 'Excavations in the two Iron Age hillforts on Castle Hill, Capel, near Tonbridge, 1965 and 1969–71', *Arch. Cant.* **91**, 61–85.

Money, J. H. (1977) 'The Iron Age hillfort and Romano-British ironworking settlement at Garden Hill, Sussex: interim report on excavations, 1968–76', *Britannia*, **8**, 339–50.

Money, J. H. (1978) 'Aspects of the Iron Age in the Weald', in Drewett, P. L. (ed), *Archaeology in Sussex to A.D. 1500*, CBA Research Report 29.

Money, J. H. (1979) 'Iron Age and Romano-British settlement in Eridge Park', *Sussex Arch. Coll.* 117, 258.

Monk, M. A. and Fasham, P. J. (1980) 'Carbonised plant remains from two Iron Age sites in Central Hampshire', *PPS* 46, 321–44.

Morrison, A. (1980) *Early Man in Britain and Ireland*, Croom Helm, London.

Muckelroy, K. (1981) 'Middle Bronze Age trade between Britain and Europe: a maritime perspective', *PPS* 47, 275–98.

Musson, C. (1970) 'House-plans and Prehistory', *Current Arch.* 2, 267–75.

Musson, R. C. (1950) 'An excavation at Combe Hill Camp near Eastbourne', *Sussex Arch. Coll.* 89, 105–16.

Musson, R. C. (1954) 'An illustrated catalogue of Sussex Beaker and Bronze Age pottery', *Sussex Arch. Coll.* 92, 106–24.

Myres, J. N. L. (1978) *A corpus of Anglo-Saxon pottery*, CUP.

Nail, D. (1965) 'The meeting-place of Copthorne Hundred', *Surrey Arch. Coll.* 62, 44–53.

Neale, F. (1979) 'The relevance of the Axbridge Chronicle', pp. 10–12 in Rahz, P., *The Saxon and Medieval Palaces at Cheddar: excavations 1960–62 BAR* British Series 65.

Neale, K. (1973) 'Stane Street (Chichester-London): the third mansio', *Surrey Arch. Coll.*, 69, 207–10.

Needham, S. and Burgess, C. (1980) 'The Later Bronze Age in the Lower Thames Valley: the metalwork evidence', in 'The British Later Bronze Age', *BAR* 83(ii), 437–70.

Needham, S. and Longley, D. (1980) 'Runnymede Bridge, Egham: a Late Bronze Age riverside settlement, in 'The British Later Bronze Age', BAR 83(ii), 397–436.

Nightingale, M. D. (1952) 'A Roman land settlement near Rochester', *Arch. Cant.* 55, 150–9.

Norris, N. E. S. and Burstow, G. P. (1948) 'A Prehistoric and Romano-British site at West Blatchington, Hove', *Sussex Arch. Coll.* 89, 1–54.

Oakley, K. P., Rankine, W. F. and Lowther, A. W. G. (1939) *A Survey of the Prehistory of the Farnham District*, Surrey Arch. Soc., Guildford.

O'Connell, M. and Poulton, R. (1984) 'The towns of Surrey', pp. 37–51 in Haslam, J. (ed.), *Anglo-Saxon Towns in Southern Britain*, Phillimore, Chichester.

Orme, B. (1981) *Anthropology for Archaeologists*, Duckworth, London.

Palmer, S. (1984) *Excavations of the Roman and Saxon site at Orpington*, London Borough of Bromley, Bromley.

Parfitt, K. (1986) 'The Deal Man', *Current Arch.* 101, 167–8.

Payne, G. (1880) 'Celtic remains discovered at Grovehurst, Milton', *Arch. Cant.* 13, 122.

Peacock, D. P. S. (1977) 'Bricks and tiles of the Classis Britannica: petrology and origin', *Britannia*, 8, 235–48.

Penn, W. S. (1965) 'Springhead-map of discoveries', *Arch. Cant.* 80, 107–17.

Philp, B. (1969) *The Roman Fort at Reculver*, Dover.

Philp, B. (1973) *Excavations in West Kent, 1960–1970*, Dover.

Philp, B. (1981) *The Excavation of the Roman Forts of the Classis Britannica at Dover, 1970–1977*, Dover.

Philp, B. (1984) *Excavations in the Darenth Valley, Kent*, Dover.

Philp, B. (1985) 'The excavation of a Roman ritual shaft at Keston', *Kent Arch. Review* **82**, 35–8.

Piercy-Fox, N. (1969) 'Caesar's Camp, Keston', *Arch. Cant.* **84**, 185–99.

Piggott, S. (1962) *The West Kennet Long Barrow*, HMSO, London.

Pitt-Rivers, A. H. L. F. (1877) 'Excavations in the Camp and Tumulus at Seaford, Sussex', *J. Roy, Anthrop. Inst.* **6**, 187–99.

Pitt-Rivers, A. H. L. F. (1881) 'Excavations at Mount Caburn Camp near Lewes', *Arch.* **46**, 423–95.

Pitts, M. W. (1979) 'A Gazetteer of Roman sites and finds on the West Sussex Coastal Plain', *Sussex Arch. Coll.* **117**, 63–83.

Pitts, M. W. (1980) 'A Gazetteer of Mesolithic finds on the West Sussex coastal plain,' *Sussex Arch. Coll.* **118**, 153–62.

Pollard, R. J. (1982) 'Roman pottery in Kent: a summary of production and market trends', pp. 61–3 in Leach, P. E. (ed.) *Archaeology in Kent to A.D. 1500*, CBA Research Report 48.

Potter, T. W. and Johns, C. M. (1983) 'New light on the Canterbury Late Roman Treasure', *Arch. Cant.* **99**, 283–6.

Pull, J. H. (1932) *The Flint Mines of Black Patch*, Williams and Norgate, London.

Radcliffe-Brown, A. R. (1952) *Structure and Function in Primitive Society*, Cohen and West, London.

Rahtz, P. A. and ApSimon, A. M. (1962) 'Excavations at Shearplace Hill, Sydling St. Nicholas, Dorset, England', *PPS* **28**, 289–328.

Rankine, W. F. (1956) *The Mesolithic of Southern England*, Surrey Arch. Soc. Research Paper No. 4.

Ratcliffe-Densham, H. B. A. (1968) 'A woman of Wessex Culture', *Sussex Arch. Coll.* **106**, 38–48.

Ratcliffe-Densham, H. B. A. and M. M. (1953) 'A Celtic farm on Blackpatch', *Sussex Arch. Coll.* **91**, 69–83.

Ratcliffe-Densham, H. B. A. and M. M. (1961) 'An anomalous earthwork of the Late Bronze Age, on Cock Hill, Sussex', *Sussex Arch. Coll.* **99**, 78–101.

Ratcliffe-Densham, H. B. A. and M. M. (1966) 'Amberley Mount; its agricultural story from the Late Bronze Age', *Sussex Arch. Coll.* **104**, 6–25.

Reece, R. (1980) 'Town and country: the end of Roman Britain', *World Arch.* **12**, 77–92.

Reynolds, P. J. and Langley, J. K. (1979) 'Romano-British corndrying oven: an experiment', *Arch. J.* **136**, 27–42.

Rigold, S. E. (1968) 'The "double minsters" of Kent and their analogies', *J. Brit. Arch. Ass.* 3rd Series, **31**, 27–37.

Rigold, S. E. (1977) '*Litus Romanum* – the Shore Forts as mission stations', pp. 70–5 in Johnston, D. E. (ed.), *The Saxon Shore*, CBA Research Report 18, Council for British Archaeology, London.

Rigold, S. E. (1982) 'Medieval archaeology in Kent', pp. 84–6 in Leach, P. E. (ed.), *Archaeology in Kent to A.D. 1500*, CBA Research Report 48, Council for British Archaeology, London.

Rivet, A. L. F. (1964) *Town and Country in Roman Britain*, 2nd edn, London.

Roberts, M. B., Bates, M. R., Macphail, R. J. and Current, A. P. (1986) 'Excavations of the Lower Palaeolithic site at Amey's Eartham Pit, Boxgrove, West Sussex', *PPS* **52**, 215–46.

Robertson-Mackay, R. (1962) 'The excavation of the causewayed camp at Staines', Middlesex, *Arch. Newsletter* 7, 131–4.

Rodwell, W. (1976) 'Coinage, oppida and the rise of Belgic power in South-Eastern Britain', pp. 181–366 in Cunliffe, B. W. and Rowley, T. (eds) *Oppida in Barbarian Europe*, BAR Supplementary Series 11.

Rodwell, W. (1978) 'Buildings and settlements in South-East Britain in the Late Iron Age', pp. 25–41 in Cunliffe, B. W. and Rowley, T. (eds) *Lowland Iron Age Communities in Europe*, BAR Supplementary Series 48.

Rodwell, W. (1986) Anglo-Saxon church building: aspects of design and construction, pp. 156–75 in Butler, L. A. S. and Morris, R. K. (eds), *The Anglo-Saxon Church*, CBA Research Report 60, Council for British Archaeology, London.

Roe, D. (1968) *A Gazetteer of British Lower and Middle Palaeolithic Sites*, CBA Research Report, No. 8, London.

Roe, D. (1975) 'Some Hampshire and Dorset hand-axes and the question of "Early Acheulian" in Britain', *PPS* 41, 1–9.

Ross, A. (1967) *Pagan Celtic Britain*, London.

Ross, A. (1968) 'Shafts, pits, wells – sanctuaries of the Belgic Britains?', pp. 255–86 in Coles, J. M. and Simpson, D. D. A. (eds) *Studies in Ancient Europe: essays presented to Stuart Piggott*, Leicester.

Round, J. H. (1899) *Calendar of Documents Preserved in France*, 1, HMSO, London.

Rudkin, D. J. (1986) 'The excavation of a Romano-British site by Chichester Harbour', *Sussex Arch. Coll.* **124**, 51–77.

Rudling, D. R. (1979) 'Invasion and response: Downland settlement in East Sussex', pp. 339–56 in Burnham, B. C. and Johnson, H. B. (eds) *Invasion and Response, BAR* 73, 339–56.

Rudling, D. R. (1982*a*) 'Rural settlement in Late Iron Age and Roman Sussex', pp. 269–88 in Miles, D. (ed.), 'The Romano-British countryside, studies in rural settlement and economy', *BAR* 103, 269–88.

Rudling, D. R. (1982*b*) 'The Romano-British farm on Bullock Down', pp. 97–142, in Drewett, P. L. (ed.), *The Archaeology of Bullock Down, Eastbourne, East Sussex: the development of a landscape*, Sussex Archaeological Society Monograph 1.

Rudling, D. R. (1983) 'The archaeology of Lewes: some recent research', *Sussex Arch. Coll.* **121**, 45–77.

Rudling, D. R. (1985*a*) 'Recent archaeological research at Selmeston, East Sussex', *Sussex Arch. Coll.* **123**, 1–26.

Rudling, D. R. (1985*b*) 'Trial excavations at Ditchling Beacon, East Sussex, 1983', *Sussex Arch. Coll.* **123**, 251–4.

Rudling, D. R. (1985*c*) 'Excavations on the site of the Southwick Roman Villa, 1965 and 1981', *Sussex Arch. Coll.* **123**, 73–84.

Rudling, D. R. (1986) 'The excavation of a Roman Tilery on Great Cansiron Farm, Hartfield, East Sussex', *Britannia*, 17, 191–230.

Rudling, D. R. (1987*a*) 'Excavations at Yapton, West Sussex', *Sussex Arch. Coll.* **125**.

Rudling, D. R. (1987*b*) 'The investigation of a Roman tilery at Dell Quay, West Sussex', *Sussex Arch. Coll.* **125**.

Rudling, D. R. (1987*c*) 'The Romano-British farm on Bullock Down', *Sussex Arch. Coll.* **125**.

Rudling, D. R. and **Aldsworth, F.** (1986) 'Excavations at Bignor Roman Villa, 1985', *Sussex Arch. Soc. Newsletter* **48**, 484–5.

Rowlands, M. J. (1976) 'The organisation of Middle Bronze Age metalworking' *BAR* **31**.

Salisbury, E. F. (1961) 'Prehistoric flint mines on Long Down, Eartham, 1955–1958', *Sussex Arch. Coll.* **99**, 66–73.

Salway, P. (1981) *Roman Britain*, OUP.

Sawyer, P. H. (1968) *Anglo-Saxon Charters: an annotated list and bibliography*, Royal Historical Society, London.

Scaife, R. G. (1982) 'Late Devensian and early Flandrian vegetation changes in southern England', pp. 57–74 in Bell, M. G. and Limbrey, S. (eds), *Archaeological Aspects of Woodland Ecology, BAR* International Series 146.

Scaife, R. G. and **Burrin, P. J.** (1983) 'Floodplain development in the vegetational history of the Sussex High Weald and some archaeological implications', *Sussex Arch. Coll.* **121**, 1–10.

Scaife, R. G. and **Burrin, P. J.** (1985) 'The environmental impact of prehistoric man as recorded in the Upper Cuckmere Valley at Stream Farm, Chiddingly', *Sussex Arch. Coll.* **123**, 27–34.

Searle, E. (1963) 'Hides, virgates and tenant settlement at Battle Abbey', *Econ. Hist. Rev.* 2nd Series, **16**, 290–300.

Sheldon, H. (1978) *Southwark Excavations 1972–4*, 2 vols, Joint Publication No. 1 of the London and Middlesex Archaeological Society and the Surrey Archaeological Society.

Sheldon, J. (1978) 'The environmental background', in Drewett, P. L. (ed.) *Archaeology in Sussex to A.D. 1500*, CBA, London.

Shepherd, J. F. (1979) 'The social identity of individuals in isolated barrows and barrow cemeteries in Anglo-Saxon England', pp. 47–79 in Burnham, B. C. and Kingsbury, J. (eds), *Space, Hierarchy and Society, BAR* International Series 59, British Archaeological Reports, Oxford.

Sieveking, G. de G., **Craddock, P. T., Hughes, M. J., Bush, P.** and **Ferguson, G.** (1970) 'The characterization of prehistoric flint mine products', *Nature* **228**, 15–76.

Simmons, I. and **Tooley, M.** (1981) *The Environment in British Prehistory*, Duckworth, London.

Sims-Williams, P. (1983*a*) 'Gildas and the Anglo-Saxons', *Cambridge Medieval Celtic Studies* **6**, 1–30.

Sims-Williams, P. (1983*b*) 'The settlement of England in Bede and the Chronicle', *Anglo-Saxon Engl.* **12**, 1–41.

Smith, D. J. (1969) 'The mosaic pavements', pp. 71–125 in Rivet, A. L. F. (ed.), *The Roman Villa in Britain*, London.

Smith, I. F. (1956) 'The decorative art of Neolithic ceramics in South-East England and its relations', PhD thesis, University of London (unpublished).

Smith, I. F. (1965) *Windmill Hill and Avebury, excavations by Alexander Keiller, 1925–1939*, OUP.

Smith, J. T. (1978) 'Villas as a key to social structure', pp. 149–85 in Todd, M. (ed.) *Studies in the Romano-British Villa*, Leicester.

Smith K. (1977) 'The excavations of Winklebury Camp, Basingstoke, Hampshire', *PPS*, **43**, 31–129.

Smith, R. A. (1911) 'A Palaeolithic industry at Northfleet, Kent', *Arch.* **62**, 515–32.

Spain, R. J. (1984) 'Romano-British Watermills', *Arch. Cant.* **100**, 101–28.

Stead, I. M. (1984) 'Some notes on imported metalwork in Iron Age Britain', pp. 43–66 in Macready, S. and Thompson, F. H. (eds), *Cross-Channel Trade between Gaul and Britain in the pre-Roman Iron Age*, Soc. Ant. London Occasional Paper 4.

Stebbing, W. P. D. (1934) 'An Early Iron Age site at Deal'. *Arch. Cant.* **46**, 207–9.

Stjernquist, B. (1967) 'Ciste a Cordoni (Rippenzisten): Produktion – funktion – diffusion', *Acta Archae Lundensia*, Series in 4°, 6.Bonn/Lund.

Strabo, *Geography*, trans. H. L. Jones, Heinemann, London, 1927.

Strong, D. (1968) 'The monument', pp. 40–73 in Cunliffe, B. W., *Fifth Report on the Excavations of the Roman Fort, Richborough, Kent*, Society of Antiquaries Research Report No. 23.

Sutcliffe, A. J. and Kowalski, K. (1976) 'Pleistocene rodents of the British Isles', *Bulletin of the British Museum (Natural History)* **27**(2), 1–147.

Sutermeister, H. (1976) 'Burpham: a settlement site within the Saxon defences'. *Sussex Arch. Coll.* **114**, 194–206.

Tatton-Brown, T. W. T. (1977) 'Excavations in 1977 by the Canterbury Archaeological Trust', *Arch. Cant.* **93**, 212–18.

Tatton-Brown, T. W. T. (1978) 'Interim report on excavations in 1978 by the Canterbury Archaeological Trust', *Arch. Cant.* **94**, 270–8.

Taylor, A. J. (1969) 'Evidence for a pre-Conquest origin for the chapels in Hastings and Pevensey castles', *Chateau Gaillard* **3**, 144–51.

Taylor, J. J. (1980) *Bronze Age Goldwork of the British Isles*, CUP.

Taylor, M. V. (1944) 'A clay figurine from Chichester', *Ant. J.* **24**, 152–4.

Tebbutt, C. F. (1970) 'Dry Hill Camp, Lingfield', *Surrey Arch. Coll.* **67**, 119–20.

Tebbutt, C. F. (1974) 'The Prehistoric occupation of the Ashdown Forest area of the Weald', *Sussex Arch. Coll.* **112**, 34–43.

Tebbutt, C. F. (1979) 'Prehistoric finds from Possingworth Park, Framfield', *Sussex Arch. Coll.* **117**, 230–1.

Tebbutt, C. F. (1982) 'A Middle-Saxon iron smelting site at Millbrook, Ashdown Forest, Sussex', *Sussex Arch. Coll.* **120**, 19–35.

Tester, P. J. (1963) 'A decapitated burial at Custon', *Arch. Cant.* **78**, 181–2.

Thompson, F. H. (1979) 'Three Surrey hillforts: excavations at Anstiebury, Holmbury and Hascombe, 1972–1979', *Ant. J.* **79**, 245–318.

Thompson, F. H. (1983) 'Excavations at Bigberry, near Canterbury, 1978–80', *Ant. J.* **63**, 237–78.

Thompson, F. H. (1984) 'Oldbury Hillfort', *Kent Arch. Review* **76**, 140–4.

Thompson, F. H. (1985) 'Excavations at Oldbury 1984', *Kent Arch. Review* **80**, 239–44.

Thompson, I. (1982) *Grog-tempered 'Belgic' Pottery of South-Eastern England*, BAR 108.

Thorley, A. (1971) 'Vegetational history of the Vale of the Brooks', *Inst. Brit. Geog. Conf.* Part 5, 47–50.

Toms, H. S. (1912) 'Excavations at the Beltout Valley entrenchments', *Sussex Arch. Coll.* **55**, 41–55.

Tooley, M. J. (1978) *Sea-level Changes in North-West England during the Flandrian Stage*, OUP.

Vince, A. G. (1984) 'The Aldwych: Mid-Saxon London discovered', *Current Arch.* 93, 310–12.

Wade, A. G. (1924) 'Ancient flint mines at Stoke Down, Sussex', *PPS East Anglia* 4, 82–91.

Waechter, J. d'A. (1969) 'Swanscombe, 1968', *P. Roy. Anthropol. Inst.* 1969, 53–61.

Wainwright, G. J. (1970) 'The excavations of Balksbury Camp, Andover, Hants.', *Proc. Hants. Field Club and Arch. Soc.* 26, 21–55.

Wainwright, G. J. (1979) *Mount Pleasant, Dorset: Excavations, 1970–1971*, Society of Antiquaries Research Report 37, London.

Wainwright, G. J. and Longworth, I. H. (1971) *Durrington Walls: Excavations 1966–1968*, Society of Antiquaries Research Report 29, London.

Wainwright, G. J. and Spratling, M. (1973) 'The Iron Age settlement of Gussage All Saints', *Antiquity* 47, 109–30.

Ward-Perkins, J. B. (1944) 'Excavations on the Iron Age hillfort of Oldbury, near Ightham, Kent', *Arch.* 90, 127–76.

Ward, G. (1936) 'The Wilmington Charter of A.D. 700', *Arch. Cant.* 48, 11–28.

Welch, M. G. (1971) 'Late Romans and Saxons in Sussex', *Britannia* 2, 232–7.

Welch, M. G. (1983) *Early Anglo-Saxon Sussex*, BAR British Series 112.

Whimster, R. (1981) *Burial practices in Iron Age Britain*, BAR 90.

White, G. M. (1936) 'The Chichester amphitheatre: preliminary excavations', *Ant. J.* 16, 149–59.

Whittle, A. W. R. (1977) 'The earlier Neolithic of S. England and its Continental background', *BAR* Supplementary Series 35.

Wickenden, N. (1986) 'Excavations at Chelwood Gate: interim report', *Sussex Arch. Soc. Newsletter* 48, 467.

Williams, J. H. (1971) 'Roman building-materials in South-East England', *Britannia*, 2, 166–85.

Williamson, R. P. R. (1930) 'Excavations in Whitehawk Neolithic Camp, near Brighton', *Sussex Arch. Coll.* 71, 57–96.

Wilson, A. E. (1939) 'Excavations at the Caburn, 1938', *Sussex Arch. Coll.* 80, 193–213.

Wilson, A. E. (1940) 'Report on the excavations at Highdown Hill, Sussex, August 1939', *Sussex Arch. Coll.* 81, 173–204.

Wilson, A. E. (1950) 'Excavations on Highdown Hill, 1947', *Sussex Arch. Coll.* 89, 163–78.

Wilson, D. M. and Hurst, J. G. (1958) 'Medieval Britain in 1957', *Med. Arch.* 2, 183–213.

Wilson, D. R. (1968) 'Sites explored', *The Journal of Roman Studies* 58, 176–206.

Winbolt, S. E. (1923) 'Alfoldean Roman station', *Sussex Arch. Coll.* 64, 81–104.

Winbolt, S. E. (1924) 'Alfoldean Roman station: second report', *Sussex Arch. Coll.* 65, 112–57.

Winbolt, S. E. (1927) 'Excavations at Hardham Camp, Pulborough, April, 1926', *Sussex Arch. Coll.* 68, 89–123.

Winbolt, S. E. (1930) 'Excavations at Saxonbury Camp', *Sussex Arch. Coll.* 71, 222–36.

Winbolt, S. E. (1936) *With a Spade on Stane Street*, London.

Winbolt, S. E. and Margary, I. D. (1933) 'Dry Hill Camp, Lingfield', *Surrey Arch. Coll.* 41, 79–92.

Wing, A. S. (1980) 'An analysis of the pollen fallout at Wellingham Peat Bog, Nr. Lewes, Sussex and a consideration of some of its climatic and historical implications', University of Sussex typescript in Barbican House Library, Lewes.

Witney, K. P. (1976) *The Jutish Forest: a study of the Weald of Kent from 450 to 1380 A.D.*, Athlone Press, London.

Wolseley, G. R. and Smith, R. A. (1924) 'Discoveries near Cissbury', *Ant. J.* 4, 347–59.

Wolseley, G. R. and Smith, R. A. (1927) 'Prehistoric and Roman settlements on Park Brow', *Arch.* 76, 1–40.

Wolseley, G. R., Smith, R. A. and Hawley, W. (1927) 'Prehistoric and Roman settlements on Park Brow', *Arch.* 76, 1–40.

Wood, E. S. and Thompson, N. P. (1966) 'A Food Vessel from Abinger Hammer, Surrey', *Surrey Arch. Coll.* 63, 44.

Wood, I. N. (1983) *The Merovingian North Sea* (Occasional papers on Medieval topics 1), Viktoria Bokforlag, Alingas, Sweden.

Wood, I. N. (1984) 'The end of Roman Britain: Continental evidence and parallels', pp. 1–25 in Lapidge, M. and Dumville, D. (eds), *Gildas: new approaches*, Boydell Press, Woodbridge.

Woodcock, A. G. (1978) 'The Palaeolithic in Sussex', in Drewett, P. L. (ed.) *Archaeology in Sussex to A.D. 1500*, CBA Research Report No. 29, 8–14.

Woodcock, A. G., Kelly, D. B. and Woolley, A. R. (undated) *The Petrological Identifications of Stone Implements from South-East England*, East Sussex County Council, Lewes.

Woodruff, C. H. (1904) 'Further discoveries of Late Celtic and Romano-British interments at Walmer', *Arch. Cant.* 26, 9–23.

Worsfold, F. H. (1943) 'Late Bronze Age site at Minnis Bay, Birchington, Kent, 1938–40', *PPS* 9, 28.

Wymer, J. J. (1968) *Lower Palaeolithic Archaeology in Britain as Represented by the Thames Valley*, London.

Wymer, J. J. (1980) 'Palaeolithic Kent', in Leach, P. (ed.), *Archaeology of Kent to A.D. 1500*, CBA Research Report No. 48.

Wymer, J. J. and Bonsall, C. J. (1977) *Gazetteer of Mesolithic sites in England and Wales with a gazetteer of Upper Palaeolithic sites in England and Wales*, CBA Research Report No. 20.

Yorke, B. A. E. (1983) 'Joint kingship in Kent *c.* 560 to 785', *Arch. Cant.* 99, 1–19.

Yorke, B. A. E. (1985) 'The kingdom of the East Saxons', *Anglo-Saxon Engl.* 14, 1–36.

Young, C. (1981) 'The Late Roman mill at Ickham and the Saxon Shore', pp. 32–40 in Detsicas, A. (ed.), *Collectanea Historica* (Maidstone).

Yule, B. (1982) 'A third century well group and later Roman settlement in Southwark', *London Archaeologist* 4, 243–49.

Index

(Numbers in italic refer to plates or figures)